M000236816

NFL DRAFT
2014 PREVIEW

NOLAN NAWROCKI

This book is available in quantity at special discounts
for your group or organization.
For further information, contact:

Triumph Books LLC
814 North Franklin Street
Chicago, Illinois 60610

Phone: (312) 337-0747
www.triumphbooks.com

Printed in U.S.A.
ISBN: 978-1-62937-023-1

Design and production: Mark Schoeck
Scouting and research: Matt Feminis
Research and editing: Chuck Wasserstrom, Michelle Wasserstrom
Network administrator: Bob Boklewski

PHOTOS COURTESY

AP Images
Alabama Athletics
Auburn Athletics
Clemson Athletic Communications
Jeffrey A. Camarati
Michigan State Athletics
Notre Dame Athletics
Ohio State Athletics
Oklahoma State Athletics

Oregon Athletics
Paul Hokanson
Pittsburgh Athletics
Texas A&M Athletics
UCF Athletic Communications
UNC Athletic Communications
University of Louisville
University of Michigan
USC Athletic Communications

CONTENTS

Almost every player included in this book was an exceptional college football player or athlete and stands among the best in the country. NFL standards are the most stringent in the world, and it requires immense grit to rigorously compete against the world's most nuanced pros. All players graded were measured against these most demanding measures.

Included with many player profiles is a "Scout's Take," actual feedback reflecting unique and consensus opinions from NFL evaluators, stemming anywhere from veteran area scouts blanketing a region of the country to the savvy GMs going over the top of it when they can fit it into their ever-busy schedules. Much of the information was gathered through the course of the fall, up until the day of publishing this book, and reflects hundreds of conversations aimed at pinpointing the measurables, critical traits, football instincts, work ethic, toughness, competitiveness, leadership, intelligence, temperament, character, scheme fit and league value of the nation's top talent.

Some information and grades might have changed by the time the book is being read, as more workouts and interviews take place following the March 17th press date and verified measurements and character research is ascertained. The most up-to-date information can be found at NFL.com.

Much gratitude is owed to everyone who helped contribute to the production of this book in some way, from college coaches and sports information directors to all the NFL executives, scouts and coaches with whom I have had the pleasure to talk football. It takes a community to raise a scout, and I'm very appreciative for all you continue to teach me.

A special thank-you belongs to Andy Fenelon and the NFL Media team for green-lighting the project, Noah Amstadter and the Triumph Books team for seeing it through, Ron Pollack for his insight and guidance and to Matt Feminis, Mark Schoeck and Chuck and Michelle Wasserstrom for their diligence making it come to life. Not to be forgotten is the late Joel Buchsbaum and the PFW family that helped found independent draft analysis. I'm most thankful for the understanding and fortitude of my inspiration, Christie and the A-team.

—*Nolan Nawrocki*

DRAFT OUTLOOK

This year's draft could go down in history as the one that changed the way it exists. With more than 100 players deciding to enter early for the first time, it has the potential to be one of the richest in talent, yet also one of the most immature and could bring about changes to the rules regarding underclassmen and the ability to scout them earlier.

Three underclassmen — Auburn OLT **Greg Robinson**, Clemson WR **Sammy Watkins** and South Carolina DE **Jadeveon Clowney** — stand at the top of the draft dripping with potential and have the chance to become NFL franchise building blocks. The senior class is not without star talent, as Buffalo disruptive LB **Khalil Mack** and Texas A&M rock-solid OL **Jake Matthews** grade highly enough to warrant consideration with the top overall pick.

This year's quarterback class is deeper than usual, but lacks a surefire, can't-miss star. Three underclassmen — Texas A&M's **Johnny Manziel**, Louisville's **Teddy Bridgewater** and UCF's **Blake Bortles** — have generated the most draft discussion. Manziel is the most fearless playmaker, Bridgewater the most polished, NFL-ready passer and Bortles features the most upside. Collectively, the class is solid, with the potential for as many as seven eventual starters from a group that includes the pedigreed **Derek Carr** (Fresno State), quick-triggered **Jimmy Garoppolo** (EIU), ultra-competitive **AJ McCarron** (Alabama) and the fireballers **Zach Mettenberger** (LSU) and **Logan Thomas** (Virginia Tech).

Ohio State workhorse **Carlos Hyde** heads a quality crop of instinctive runners also featuring Arizona's highly productive **Ka'Deem Carey**, Florida State's decisive **Devonta Freeman** and Washington's competitive **Bishop Sankey**. LSU's thundering **Jeremy Hill**, Auburn's versatile **Tre Mason**, Boston College grinder **Andre Williams** and Towson's do-it-all **Terrance West** all stand a chance to contribute heavily.

The deepest and most talented position group of the class comes at receiver, which could easily feature six to eight first-rounders this year in a star-studded, young crop of playmakers. Watkins is an explosive playmaker, and USC's

Marqise Lee is very skillfully nuanced. Size is a unique theme of the class, with Texas A&M's big-play weapon **Mike Evans**, Florida State's imposing **Kelvin Benjamin** and Mississippi's soft-handed **Donte Moncrief** all offering wide catching radiuses. LSU features a pair of circus-catchers in **Odell Beckham** and **Jarvis Landry**, and Fresno State's sure-handed **Davante Adams** and Oregon State's dynamic **Brandin Cooks** are capable of creating big plays.

The TE crop also received a big boost from juniors, featuring North Carolina playmaker **Eric Ebron**, Notre Dame's versatile **Troy Niklas** and a talented cast with blemishes that includes Oregon's **Colt Lyerla**, Washington's **Austin Seferian-Jenkins** and Texas Tech's **Jace Amaro**. The underclassmen took the TE class from marginal to respectable.

This year's tackle class is both rich and voluminous in talent. Robinson is the most dominating run blocker; Matthews the most safe and versatile; Michigan's **Taylor Lewan** the most explosive and Notre Dame's **Zack Martin** the most dependable, though he projects best inside along with UCLA's light-footed **Xavier Su'a-Filo**. Mississippi's road-grader **Gabe Jackson** headlines a gritty guard class. No upper-echelon center exists in this year's crop, but there is some unique mass in the group, including USC's **Marcus Martin**, and enough functional performers to earn starter jobs.

Defensively, more talent exists on the edges than on the interior. Clowney is a rare physical specimen who looked destined for the top overall pick the first day he stepped on campus. Notre Dame's **Stephon Tuitt** and Missouri's **Kony Ealy** are capable of fitting inside or outside in multiple fronts. Pittsburgh's **Aaron Donald** and Minnesota's **Ra'Shede Hageman** offer disruptive inside rush potential. The Irish's **Louis Nix**, Florida State's **Timmy Jernigan** and Tennessee's **Daniel McCullers** can all stack the point effectively.

The top of the linebacker class is as rich as it has been since 2009 and may carry more potential impact. Mack can play any linebacker position. Alabama's **C.J. Mosley** is a tackling machine. UCLA's **Anthony Barr** brings a dangerous first-step as the draft's most explosive edge rusher. Ohio State's **Ryan Shazier** is the draft's fastest and rangiest linebacker.

The secondary crop is stronger on the edges than down the middle and features quality depth at cornerback. Oklahoma State CB **Justin Gilbert** is the draft's most talented man-cover corner along with Ohio State's explosive **Bradley Roby**. Michigan State CB **Darqueze Dennard** is the top press cover man. TCU's **Jason Verrett** is the draft's most feisty cornerback, and Virginia Tech's **Kyle Fuller** has the best pure cover skills. Two junior safeties — Louisville anvil **Calvin Pryor** and Alabama's solid **Ha Ha Clinton-Dix** — could fit into the first round in a safety crop lacking depth.

The overwhelming number of underclassmen truly distinguishes this draft and invites discussion on rule changes or a new structure that encourages prospects to pursue their degrees and avoid rash decisions that many could come to regret.

QUARTERBACKS

CENTRAL FLORIDA QB
BLAKE BORTLES

NAWROCKI'S TOP 10

10	TOM SAVAGE
9	TAJH BOYD
8	ZACH METTENBERGER
7	LOGAN THOMAS
6	AJ McCARRON
5	JIMMY GAROPPOLO
4	JOHNNY MANZIEL
3	DEREK CARR
2	TEDDY BRIDGEWATER
1	

EDITOR'S NOTE:

e — Measurement is estimated.

#00 — Player's jersey number.

GRADE — Player's grade reflects consensus league value where player should expect to be drafted.

On all positions, 40-yard-dash times are taken from the Combine when available and are curved to account for conditions (turf, wind, track shoes).

QB BLAKE BORTLES, #5 (JUNIOR)
CENTRAL FLORIDA ▶ GRADE: 6.32
Ht: 6-5 | Wt: 232 | Sp: 4.89 | Arm: 32 7/8 | Hand: 9 3/8

History: Operated a wing-T offense in high school. The Florida prep redshirted in 2010. Saw action in 10 games in '11 and completed 75-of-110 (68.2 percent) for 958 yards, six touchdowns and three interceptions. In '12, made all 14 starts and threw for 251-399-3,059-25-7 (62.9). Was MVP of the Beef 'O' Brady Bowl after throwing for three scores and rushing for another. Earned American Athletic Conference Offensive Player of the Year in '13 after tossing 259-382-3,581-25-9 (67.8) in 13 starts. Threw for 301 yards (three TDs) and rushed for 93 yards (one score) to earn Tostitos Fiesta Bowl MVP honors. One of only two UCF quarterbacks to pass for more than 3,000 yards in multiple seasons (Daunte Culpepper). Had 195 career rushing attempts for 561 yards (2.9-yard average) and 15 touchdowns. Was 22-5 in 27 career starts for head coach George O'Leary's pro-style offense featuring option elements.

Strengths: Possesses prototype size and outstanding stature in the pocket to brush off the rush and keep plays alive. Stands tall and delivers the ball in the face of heavy pressure. Keeps his eyes downfield while climbing the pocket, can avoid the first wave and make plays with his feet (deceptively quick and plays faster than timed speed). Good field vision and release point. Is efficient throwing on the run and excels on bootlegs and play-action passing. Good zip and accuracy on short-to-intermediate throws — can fit the ball into tight windows. Fine touch to drop the ball in the bucket — delivers a catchable ball with good anticipation. Senses pressure and evades the rush. Doesn't take many unnecessary sacks. Can extend plays when the pocket folds. Carries a sense of calm in critical situations. Engineered comeback victories, beat Penn State and Louisville on the road and took a mid-major program to a BCS bowl. Recorded a 32 1/2-inch vertical jump, 9-foot-7 broad jump (third-best among QBs) and displayed fine touch, timing, accuracy and anticipation in Combine passing drills. Ripped the ball a solid 56 miles per hour.

Weaknesses: Winds to uncork it deep and generate slightly above-average arm strength. Operated in an offense where he made a lot of one-look reads and short lateral tosses. Does not spin spirals consistently — too many throws come out with loose wobble and could struggle to cut the wind and handle the elements of cold-winter climates. Tends to throw off his back foot when pressured, negating his accuracy. Works heavily out of the gun — will have to adapt to snaps under center and deep drops. Operates an offense predicated on the short passing game that inflates his completion percentage. Ball handling/security could stand to improve (fumbled nine times as a junior). Struggled to throw receivers open vs. better competition (see Ohio State in 2012 and South Carolina in '13) and will require time to adjust to the closing speed of NFL defensive backs. Footwork could use some polishing — deteriorates under duress and does not look natural on deep drops. Is only two-year starter, can improve his overall understanding of the game and become more consistent with his mechanics.

Future: Possesses ideal size, athletic ability, intangibles and enough arm strength to develop into an upper-echelon quarterback. Is not yet a franchise quarterback, but has all the physical ingredients to become an outstanding NFL starter and his arrow is very clearly ascending. Warrants top-10 consideration.

Draft projection: First-round pick.

Scout's take: "I'll be honest — I was a little disappointed watching Bortles. The first game I charted, most of his passes were screens and quick tosses to backs or receivers. I thought I was going to see lasers down the field, and it was not that way. All indications are that he is a top-5 pick. I am not grading him there. I had him in the third round after watching the first game. After seeing four more, I am giving him a first-round grade. He grows on you. I like the size, ability to scan the entire field and have seen him make a variety of throws. I would like to see a tighter ball and a more fluid release. He is a trifecta of three prime quarterbacks — he has the flutterball of (Peyton) Manning, he is big and strong like (Ben) Roethlisberger and he stands tall and straight-legged in the pocket like Andrew Luck. He might not be as good as any of them, but he has characteristics of all three. He is very intriguing."

QB TAJH BOYD, #10

CLEMSON ▶ GRADE: 5.22
Ht: 6-0 5/8 | Wt: 222 | Sp: 4.86 | Arm: 30 3/4 | Hand: 9 5/8

History: Led his Virginia prep team to a 43-2 record and two state titles. Played his senior season with a torn ACL in his left knee. Redshirted in 2009. Made seven appearances in '10, completing 33-of-63 passes for 329 yards (52.7 percent), four touchdowns and three interceptions and rushing 23 times for 33 yards (1.4-yard average) and one touchdown. Started all 14 contests in '11 and threw for 298-499-3,828-33-12 (59.7) while rushing 142-218-5 (1.5). The ACC Player of the Year made all 13 starts in '12, tossing 287-427-3,896-36-13 (67.2) and running 186-514-10 (2.8). Was a finalist for the Johnny Unitas and Manning Awards in '13 after posting 283-413-3,851-34-11 (68.5) through the air and 154-400-10 (2.6) on the ground in 13 starts. Became the first QB in ACC history with 30-plus TD passes in three seasons and set the conference mark with 107 career TD passes. Team captain. Graduated in December. Had a 32-8 mark in 40 career starts for head coach Dabo Swinney's up-tempo, spread offense.

Strengths: Quick set-up. Can sling it when he's in rhythm and has a clean pocket. Good zip short-to-intermediate. Can launch deep throws with ease and flashes touch to drop it in the bucket. Shows composure in the face of a blitz and is willing to take a hit to make a play. Makes plays with his feet, be it rolling the pocket, extending plays or throwing on the move (left or right). Slippery and elusive to escape the rush and is a threat to tuck and run. Functional straight-line speed and run strength for a quarterback (will lower his shoulder on defenders). Experienced, three-year starter. Terrific football character. Has a likeable personality.

Weaknesses: Lacks ideal height and weight has tended to fluctuate, pushing to nearly 240 the second half of 2011 season. Sails downfield throws and can improve his accuracy. Inconsistent decision-making. Did not take snaps under center in a pistol, read-option offense and production was inflated by an NFL-caliber supporting cast of skill talent. Will require patience adapting to pro-style passing. Needs to quicken his eyes and improve his field vision. Does not always see the deep safety or short-hole defender. Impatient making reads before fleeing the pocket. Durability could be a concern given his style — needs to learn to slide.

Future: A short, stocky, fairly nifty, strong-armed quarterback most ideally suited for a vertical-power system, Boyd projects best as a career backup or No. 3 quarterback in the pros and compares very favorably to Ravens 2007 fifth-rounder Troy Smith.

Draft projection: Fifth- to sixth-round pick.

Scout's take: "I like Boyd, and I don't like him. He is short, but stout and can win with his feet. His lower body is built sturdy like Russell Wilson. He has a talented arm and spins it pretty good. He got exposed in the Florida State game. They have to keep it simple for him. That's what concerns me the most."

QB TEDDY BRIDGEWATER, #5 (JUNIOR)

LOUISVILLE   ▶ GRADE: 6.24
Ht: 6-2 1/8 | Wt: 214 | Sp: 4.80e | Arm: 33 | Hand: 9 1/4

History: The dual-threat QB was a three-year starter for Miami (Fla.) powerhouse Northwestern High School. Named Big East Freshman of the Year in 2011 after completing 191-of-296 passes for 2,195 yards (64.5 percent) with 14 touchdowns and 12 interceptions in 13 games (started final 10 games). Became the first true freshman to start at QB for Louisville since Stu Stram in 1976. Threw for 287-419-3,718-27-8 (68.5) while playing in all 13 games (12 starts) in '12 to earn conference's Offensive Player of the Year Award. Only non-start was due to a fractured left wrist and a sprained right ankle suffered against UConn in which he returned to the field in a triple-overtime loss and nearly rallied a victory, as he did vs. Rutgers the following week to claim a BCS bid. Produced another stellar campaign in '13, tossing 303-427-3,970-31-4 (71.0) in 13 starts. Earned his sports administration degree in only three years and graduated in December. Scored six career rushing touchdowns and had a 27-8 record in 35 games as a starter in offensive coordinator Shawn Watson's college-tailored, pro-style, West Coast offense.

Strengths: Terrific competitor. Extremely driven to succeed. Well-prepared and confident in his approach. Operated a progression-read offense where he is asked to scan the whole field and help steer protections. Footwork is very clean and in rhythm — throws on balance with sound mechanics, a fluid delivery and smooth stroke. Very good timing, touch and anticipation — throws receivers open. Is patient working through his reads and will step up in the pocket. Sells play-action hard and takes what the defense gives him. Poised in the face of the blitz and often anticipates it coming. Is very mentally and physically tough — played through a broken left wrist with a sprained ankle in what was essentially the 2012 Big East championship game, coming off the bench to captain the Cardinals to a come-from-behind victory. Is a student of the game with a very good understanding of football concepts. Plays like a coach on the field, knows the responsibilities of everyone on the field and can get teammates lined up correctly. Makes few mental errors. Consistently moves the chains and comes through in the clutch. Is given a lot of autonomy to make pre-snap reads and adjustments at the line of scrimmage and understands how to exploit defenses. Meticulous in his preparation. Identifies with the game and really works at his craft. Smart, determined and focused. Showed gradual improvement every season. Is only 21 years old — very mature for his age and can see the big picture. Football is extremely important to him. Highly respected, unselfish team leader. Rises to the occasion on big stages.

Weaknesses: Has a very lean, narrow frame with limited bulk (playing weight hovered around 200 pounds) and small hands. Does not drive the ball with velocity down the field and can be affected by blustery field conditions (see Cincinnati, 2013). Can improve placement and touch on the deep ball. Adequate athlete. Is not an overly elusive scrambler — struggles escaping the rush and buying a second chance with his feet vs. pressure. Passing stats are padded from operating a passing game that relies heavily on short, lateral tosses. Long-term durability could become a concern without continued strength and weight gains.

Future: A calculated, football-smart, precision-matchup rhythm passer, Bridgewater would be best suited entering a warm-weather or dome environment such as those most common in the South divisions. Would stand to benefit heavily from operating a short, dink-and-dunk rhythm passing game. Compensates for a lack of elite arm talent and prototype measureables with the intangibles and football intelligence that could elevate the other 52 players around him. Instinctive passer with the laser-beam determination to become a Pro Bowl-caliber passer in the right system.

Draft projection: First-round pick.

Scout's take: "Bridgewater may not be as athletic as some of the others when it comes to beating you with his feet, but he is a better passer with a stronger arm. It's easy to say he didn't play anyone, but we're grading his skill set. Who did Aaron Rodgers play when he was at Cal? Even Alex Smith at Utah? They both got a lot of national attention against soft schedules."

QB DEREK CARR, #4

FRESNO STATE   ▶ GRADE: 6.10
Ht: 6-2 3/8 | Wt: 214 | Sp: 4.69 | Arm: 31 1/2 | Hand: 9 1/8

History: Married. His brother, quarterback David Carr, was the No. 1 overall pick by the Houston Texans in 2002. Finished his prep career in California after spending two years in

Texas. Joined Fresno State in the spring of 2009 and saw limited action in five contests in the fall, completing 10-of-14 passes for 112 yards with zero touchdowns and zero interceptions. Redshirted in '10. Led the WAC in passing yards after tossing 279-446-3,544-26-9 (62.6) in 13 starts in '11. Threw for 344-511-4,104-37-7 (67.3) in '12 while making all 13 starts. Was named Mountain West Offensive Player of the Year for a second straight season in '13 after a monster year, throwing 453-659-5,082-50-8 (68.7) in 13 starts. Became the fourth QB in FBS history to throw for more than 5,000 yards and 50 touchdowns and the first QB in Fresno State history with more than 3,000 yards three times. Three-time team captain with a 24-15 career record in 39 games as a starter.

Strengths: Athletic with very good feet — can roll the pocket, evade the rush or escape when pocket crumbles. Terrific arm talent — releases quickly and can make all the throws. Quick-armed with wrist snap. Can alter his platform and throw on the move or off his back foot. Throws come out on time and accurately. Drills short-to-intermediate throws and flashes touch. Likes to play and it shows. Sells out to make a play. Record-breaking production. Adapted to coaching/system change and receiver turnover. Improved ball security — fumbled only once as a senior compared to 12 times the previous two seasons. Fine intangibles for the position — advanced maturity, leadership and intelligence. Shows poise and moxie. On-field general who commands the huddle. Passionate about the game and works at his craft. Three-time captain.

Weaknesses: Lacks ideal height and has relatively small hands. Bulk is just adequate. Could stand to improve as a deep passer. At times tries to do too much and forces some throws. Occasionally throws off balance unnecessarily and sails some throws. Operated out of the shotgun and pistol and made a lot of short/lateral throws and half-field reads. Production is inflated by spread offense and porous Mountain West Conference defenses — nine 2013 opponents (excluding an FCS opponent) ranked between 81st and 125th nationally in scoring defense and/or passing defense. Had his worst game in the Las Vegas Bowl against USC.

Future: Athletic, tough, instinctive, strong-armed, highly competitive quarterback who will impress in workouts, interviews and on the board and improved his draft standing with those skills in the postseason. Elevated the Fresno State program and profiles like a gunslinger, though he'd be better served in the long run honing his game-management skills. Will be a starter sooner rather than later and the degree to which he's able to make those around

him better will determine his ceiling.

Draft projection: Top-50 pick.

Scout's take: "After the Senior Bowl, Carr is going to get in the first round. He came in there cold turkey and was the best quarterback there. He knew the offense. He made the adjustments. He was the most accurate passer there. Think of all the quarterbacks who went to the Senior Bowl and struggled with timing and new receivers. So many teams need quarterbacks — he is going to go."

QB DAVID FALES, #10

SAN JOSE STATE ▶ GRADE: 5.18

Ht: 6-1 5/8 | Wt: 212 | Sp: 5.01 | Arm: 31 3/4 | Hand: 9 1/4

History: His brother, Austen, is a quarterback at San Jose State. Also lettered in basketball as a California prep. Began his collegiate career at Nevada where he redshirted behind Colin Kaepernick. Transferred to Monterey (Calif.) Peninsula College for the next two seasons, where he threw for 4,635 yards and 37 touchdowns. Moved on to San Jose State for the '12 campaign and completed 327-of-451 passes for 4,193 yards (72.5 percent) with 33 touchdowns and nine interceptions in 13 starts and was the FBS most accurate passer. Named MVP of the Military Bowl after recording 395 yards and two touchdowns. Threw for 312-487-4,189-33-13 (64.1) in 12 starts in '13. Was one of only two QBs, joining Fresno State's Derek Carr, with 4,000-plus yards in both '12 and '13. Had a 17-8 career record in 25 starts. Team captain

Strengths: Well built (works hard in the weight room). Sets up cleanly and with balance. Nice play fake. Compact, three-quarters release with clean, quick arm action. Throws a clean spiral with good short-to-intermediate accuracy. Flashes touch. Confident and competitive. Tough and durable. Sparkling intangibles — outstanding personal and football character. Leads vocally and by example and is universally respected. Intelligent, passionate, motivated football junkie who takes pride in his craft and puts the time in to improve.

Weaknesses: Lacks ideal height and has relatively small hands. Average foot athlete and escapability. Can improve maneuverability in the pocket. Not yet sophisticated with his eyes. Tends to stare down his primary. Arm strength is just functional — struggles to drill velocity throws on a line and is not a natural deep thrower. Accuracy wanes downfield. Needs to improve against the blitz. Just a two-year starter.

Future: Burst onto the scene as a junior-college transfer in 2012 when he led the nation in completion percentage (72.5), executing a quarterback-friendly system and putting himself on the NFL radar. Concerns about his

QUARTERBACKS

height and arm strength will limit his appeal, but at worst should be a quality backup in a precision-matchup system.

Draft projection: Late draftable pick.

Scout's take: "I like the kid and his makeup and character, but he's an undersized guy with average arm strength at best."

QB JIMMY GAROPPOLO, #10

EASTERN ILLINOIS   ▶GRADE: 5.75
Ht: 6-2 1/4 | Wt: 226| Sp: 4.97 | Arm: 31 | Hand: 9 1/4

History: Last name is pronounced "gah-ropp-ah-low." The Illinois prep started the final eight games of his true freshman season in 2010, completing 124-of-211 passes for 1,639 yards (58.8 percent) with 14 touchdowns and 13 interceptions. Made all 11 starts in '11 and tossed 217-349-2,644-20-14. Threw for 331-540-3,823-31-15 (61.3) in 12 starts in '12. Named the Walter Payton Award winner, given to top player in FCS, in '13 after recording a monster 375-568-5,050-53-9 (66.0) in 14 contests. Threw for 450 yards and six touchdowns in the Panthers only regular season loss to Northern Illinois. Is one of only two quarterbacks to throw for more than 5,000 yards in a season (Taylor Heinicke, 2012) in FCS history. Was named the Offensive MVP of the East-West Shrine Game. Had eight career rushing touchdowns and a 23-22 record in 45 starts.

Strengths: Has a very quick trigger and good wrist snap that translates to a smooth throwing motion and clean, compact delivery (no windup). Lightning release quickness. Urgent decision maker. Sells play-action. Athletic enough to slide in the pocket and buy time with his feet while keeping his eyes downfield. Good anticipation — throws his receivers open. Can change ball speeds and drop it in a bucket. Does not take unnecessary sacks and will dump the ball. Will deliver the ball looking down the barrel of a gun. Tough-minded and poised in the pocket — can withstand a hit and pop back up. Highly competitive. Smart, respected, vocal team leader. Very durable, experienced, four-year starter. Good football intelligence.

Weaknesses: Is a tad undersized with small hands and short arms. Uses a three-quarters delivery that could lead to batted balls. Works heavily out of the shotgun in a spread offense and footwork could require adjustment to working from under center. Does not always feel pressure in the pocket. Does not rip the deep out or drive the ball with high RPMs. Undershoots and often hangs the deep ball. Makes receivers work for the ball downfield and deep accuracy could stand to improve. Makes a lot of simple, one-look reads and was not heavily challenged

by consistent pressure or complex looks in the Ohio Valley Conference.

Future: A highly decorated FCS passer, Garoppolo could excite quarterback coaches with his quick delivery, mental make-up and work habits, yet he still needs to prove he can fit the ball into tight windows and do more than carve up soft shells the way he regularly did on his way to a record-breaking performance in college. Possesses the physical tools to eventually earn an NFL starting job in a rhythm passing game with continued refinement, but is more of a caretaker than a game changer and will require some patience adapting to the NFL game.

Draft projection: Top-50 pick.

Scout's take: "He's the fast riser in the group. I had him parked in the fourth (round) heading into the postseason. He acquitted himself very nicely in the all-star games. He's sound mechanically. Everyone keeps talking about the other three big-name quarterbacks. I'm not sure this kid won't be better than all of them in three years. I wouldn't be surprised if he creeped into the back of the first — I wouldn't."

QB-RB-SS JORDAN LYNCH, #6

NORTHERN ILLINOIS   ▶GRADE: 5.05
Ht: 6-0 1/8 | Wt: 217 | Sp: 4.74 | Arm: 29 3/4 | Hand: 8 7/8

History: Also played safety as an Illinois prep at Chicago-area Mount Carmel. Redshirted in 2009. Saw action in nine games in '10 as a backup to Colts 2012 seventh-rounder Chandler Harnish, completing 4-of-6 passes for 13 yards (66.7 percent) with one touchdown and zero interceptions while rushing 31 times for 362 yards (11.7-yard average) and three touchdowns. Spent '11 campaign as Harnish's backup, appearing in 13 games and posting 15-20-166-1-0 (75.0) and rushing 45-246-3 (5.5). Had a breakout season in '12, throwing for 237-394-3,138-25-6 (60.2) while scampering for 294-1,815-19 (6.2) on the ground in 14 starts and finished seventh in the Heisman balloting. Became the first player in FBS history to rush for more than 1,500 yards and throw for 3,000 yards in the same season. Was a Heisman Trophy finalist and named the MAC Offensive Player of the Year in '13 after tossing 253-404-2,892-24-8 (62.6) and rushing 292-1,920-23 (6.6) in 14 games. Rushed for 316 yards at Central Michigan and an FBS record by a QB 321 yards vs. Western Michigan. Had a 24-4 career record in 28 starts.

Strengths: Exceptional competitor. Tough, physical runner — drops his shoulder and barrels through contact with determination. Very good competitive speed. Rare agility and change of direction — recorded a Combine-best

6.55-second 3-cone shuttle time and showed outstanding agility in RB drills at his pro day. Exceptional overall production. Outstanding work habits. Carried the offense and willed the team to victory.

Weaknesses: Is short and operates heavily in the gun in an offense that features rolling pockets that allow him to see the field more clearly. Many of his throws involve simplified, one-look reads to stationary targets. Tends to bird-dog his primary target. Is jittery and quick to tuck and run in the pocket. Accuracy is sporadic at each layer, short to deep. Must improve timing and anticipation. Recorded a 29 1/2-inch vertical jump.

Future: A gritty competitor, Lynch ran to set up the pass and was feared more as an option runner than as a pocket-moving passer. Could contend for a job as a No. 3 quarterback if he learns to refine his passing instincts. Developmental project with immediate value as a practice-squad, read-option quarterback. Toughness and competitiveness could translate well as a box safety or hybrid running back, though odds could be long unless he fully embraces a position change.

Draft projection: Late draftable pick.

Scout's take: "He's just a guy. He's probably going to land in the fifth round. He's an undersized, run-around West Coast quarterback. That's what he is. If he's starting for you, you're in trouble."

QB JOHNNY MANZIEL, #2 (SOPH-3)

TEXAS A&M　　　▶ GRADE: 5.90

Ht: 5-11 3/4 | Wt: 207 | Sp: 4.66 | Arm: 31 3/8 | Hand: 9 7/8

History: The Texas prep was named a Parade All-American after throwing 45 touchdown passes and rushing for 30 more as a senior. Redshirted in 2011. Was arrested in June '12 for three misdemeanors after breaking up a fight with a friend and pled guilty to failure to identify with other two charges dropped. Burst onto the scene in the fall, becoming the first freshman to win the Heisman Trophy, the Davey O'Brien Award and the Manning Award after completing 295-of-434 passes for 3,706 yards (68.0 percent) with 26 touchdowns and nine interceptions in 13 starts. Also rushed 201 times for 1,410 yards (7.0-yard average) and 21 touchdowns. Became the only player in NCAA history to have 5,000 total yards and 1,000 rushing yards in a single season and set the SEC record with 5,116 yards of total offense. Was scheduled to be a counselor at the Manning Passing Academy in July '13 but was dismissed after oversleeping and missing meetings. Missed the first half of the season opener against Rice after being suspended for an "inadvertent violation" of NCAA rules pertaining to if he accepted money for autographs. Had a stellar sophomore season in '13, throwing for 300-429-4,114-37-13 (70.0) and rushing 144-759-9 (5.3) in 13 games (12 starts). Set at least 35 NCAA, SEC or school records in his brief two year career. Had a 19-6 career record in 25 starts.

Strengths: Has big hands and grips the ball well on the move. Dynamic athlete. Exceptional game-day competitor — rises to the occasion. Has a passion for the game. Played on the biggest of stages and revels in having his back against the wall. Stepped up against a national championship Alabama defense in 2012 and has proven he can command come-from-behind victories, as he capped his career in the Chick-fil-A bowl vs. Duke by overcoming a 21-point halftime deficit. Sufficient timing, ball placement and accuracy (68.9 percent career passing percentage). Terrific scrambling ability. Reverse spins and buys time in the pocket while continuing to scan the field — can still set his feet, alter his throwing motion and manipulate his arm and throwing platform. Houdini-like escapability (uses subtle, nifty sidestep moves) and improvisational ability in the pocket to pull a rabbit out of his hat and create magic. Has peripheral, wide-eyed running vision (sometimes appears to have eyes in back of his head) and a very good feel for spacing. Carries the ball with a fearless confidence that he will find a way to create and usually gains positive yardage on broken plays when he appears trapped. Is mentally and physically tough — will pop back up from hard collisions and respond to a challenge. Record-setting and award-winning two-year production. Has a knack for sustaining drives and possesses playmaking ability to create on third downs and in critical situations to keep the sticks moving.

Weaknesses: Has an unorthodox body type with marginal height, rounded shoulders and an underdeveloped body. Will need to learn to do a better job protecting his body and sliding. Feels pocket ghosts and often takes off running at the first flash of coverage. Undisciplined — plays his own offense and presses to make plays. Cannot see over the pocket easily and almost never steps up into it, creating extra difficulties for OL coaches to coordinate blocking schemes and for offensive linemen to anticipate where the pocket will be. Dances around the pocket too much and creates needless sacks rolling into protection when the pocket is clean. Struggled vs. LSU and Missouri when he was forced to stay inside the pocket. Has not worked from under center, and footwork and set-up will require refinement. Often throws the ball up in the air and relies on big receivers to adjust to it and make plays, highly benefiting from the playmaking ability of a talented supporting cast featuring Mike Evans and an offensive line stocked with first-round talent. Tends to overshoot the deep ball and throw off his back foot, leading to some underthrows (too many dirtballs on the move) and diminished accuracy. Needlessly pats the ball when he scans the field. Could stand to do a better job carrying out play-action fakes. Has not developed a reputation as a worker or for doing the extras. Suspect intangibles — not a leader by example or known to inspire by his words. Carries a sense of entitlement and prima-donna arrogance seeking out the bright lights of Hollywood. Is known to party too much and is drawn to all the trappings of the game. Lacks ideal starting experience (only two years), operated a non-traditional offense and has a lot to learn.

Future: A once-in-a-generation, run-around, ad-lib, sandlot-style quarterback who consistently won games playing a brand of fast-paced, jailbreak football that often goes off script and can be difficult both to game plan with and against. Is most comfortable on the move outside the pocket where he can find open throwing lanes and see the field and will command mush rush and extra spy defenders. Has defied the odds and proven to be a great college-

system quarterback, but still must prove he is willing to work to be great, adjust his hard-partying, Hollywood lifestyle and be able to inspire his teammates by more than his playmaking ability. Overall character, leadership ability and work habits will define his NFL career. Rare competitiveness and third-down efficiency could carry him a long way, yet he could be challenged to avoid a Ryan Leaf-like, crash-and-burn scenario if he does not settle down and mature. A high-risk, high-reward pick, Manziel stands to benefit from entering the NFL at a time when moving pockets are trending.

Draft projection: Top-50 pick.

Scout's take: "Manziel is the master of improvise. His mechanics are horrible. He is chaos in the pocket. There is is no pressure and he does a reverse pivot and starts running and throws on the run. You see little jump passes. I would not build my franchise around him. I put him in the third round for the league, but I wouldn't want him. There is nothing traditional or orthodox about him. ... Michael Vick was the same way — running, scrambling, moving around — they don't like the pocket. ...There are some (scouts) in our building that put huge grades on him. Someone is going to get enamored with him. The key is — you better know how to manage him."

QB JEFF MATHEWS, #9

CORNELL ▶ GRADE: 5.20

Ht: 6-3 3/4 | Wt: 223 | Sp: 5.23 | Arm: 32 1/8 | Hand: 10 1/8

History: Admires his sister, Katie, who is a quadriplegic after a 2006 auto accident. The California prep also played basketball and was not offered an FBS scholarship. Named Ivy League Rookie of the Year in 2010 after completing 172-of-314 passes for 1,723 yards (54.8 percent) with seven touchdowns and seven interceptions in 10 games (nine starts). Became the first Big Red freshman to earn a varsity start. Won the Bushnell Cup (Ivy League Player of the Year) in '11 after tossing 250-368-3,412-25-11 (70.0) in 10 starts and setting the league record for passing yards. Threw for 251-405-3,196-18-11 (62.0) in nine starts to lead the conference in attempts, completions and passing yards in '12. Missed the Monmouth game with a neck injury and dealt with a right knee injury during second half of season. Recorded 228-360-2,953-22-13 (63.3) in nine starts in '13, missing only the Columbia game with a concussion. Three-time team captain (first in Cornell history). Finished his career with 47 school records, 18 Ivy League records, nine rushing touchdowns and a 12-25 record in 37 starts.

Strengths: Experienced, four-year starter. Very good arm strength. Good decision maker — works through progressions. Fine accuracy and placement — places the ball well. Highly intelligent, extremely determined, vocal team leader with an intricate command of the offense. Is given a lot of pre-snap responsibility to read defenses and audible into the right play. Outstanding football intelligence. Fiery on-field temperament. Challenges his teammates. Good eyes, anticipation and awarenesss. Coach on the field. Is very tough and battles through injuries. Outstanding production — re-wrote the school's record books.

Weaknesses: Marginal athlete. Limited mobility to avoid the rush and buy time with his feet. Can do a better job sensing pressure and hastening his release. Relies too much on his arm. Accuracy diminishes on the move. Struggles to manipulate his arm and release the ball from multiple angles. Average setup and release quickness.

Future: Very driven, Ivy-League pocket passer with physical limitations that could relegate him to a backup role in the pros. Is the type who can be trusted to step in with limited practice reps and finish a game. Might have the most long-term potential as a coach, yet has the intangible qualities that could allow him to stick in the league for 10-plus years. Has traits to surprise as a spot-starter once he acclimates to the pro game.

Draft projection: Late draftable pick.

QB AJ McCARRON, #12

ALABAMA ▶ GRADE: 5.65

Ht: 6-3 1/4 | Wt: 220 | Sp: 4.94 | Arm: 31 1/2 | Hand: 10

History: Given name is Raymond. His younger brother, Corey, is a tight end for the Crimson Tide. The Alabama prep threw for 66 touchdowns and nine interceptions as a three-year starter. Redshirted in 2009. Saw action in all 13 games in '10, including eight as a reserve quarterback, and completed 30-of-48 passes for 389 yards (62.5 percent) with three touchdowns and zero interceptions. Was primarily the holder for field goals and extra points. Became the starter in '11 and led Alabama to a National Championship after tossing 219-328-2,634-16-5 (66.8) in 13 games. Led the nation with a 175.28 passer efficiency in '12 and the Crimson Tide to back-to-back National Championships after posting 211-314-2,933-30-3 (67.2). The 30 TD passes set the school record while playing through shoulder and knee injuries. Had a standout senior campaign in '13, winning the Maxwell Award (college football Player of the Year), the Johnny Unitas Golden Arm Award and finishing second in the Heisman Trophy voting. Set the Alabama record for passing yards after tossing 226-336-3,063-28-7 (67.3) in 13 starts. Had a 36-4 record in 40 career starts with all four losses coming to opponents ranked in the Top 15. Team captain.

Strengths: Well-versed operating a pro-style offense and makes NFL-style progression reads. Is comfortable working from under center and in the gun. Mobile enough to sidestep the first wave. Good field vision, timing and anticipation. Very good short-to-intermediate accuracy (evidenced by a 66.9 percent career completion rate). Throws with accuracy on the move — good wrist snap. Delivers the ball under duress. Has enough arm strength to fit the ball into spots. Consistent throwing mechanics — has a smooth stroke. Good caretaker and decision-maker. Mature leader. Smart and articulate. Highly competitive team leader — holds teammates accountable. Very well-prepared. Directed back-to-back national championship offenses.

Weaknesses: Surrounded by an NFL-caliber supporting cast with a very good offensive line that provides a lot of time to dissect the field. Does not have a big-time, vertical arm. Average athlete. Makes occasional bone-headed decisions. Heaves the deep ball and forces receivers to make adjustments. Does not drive the deep out.

Future: An efficient game-managing quarterback who has shown he can carry an offense at times throughout his career, but more often is dependent on a terrific supporting cast. Grades out most highly for his intangibles and decision-making, knowing when and where to go with the ball, and could earn an NFL starting job.

Draft projection: Second- to third-round pick.

Scout's take: "I'm bending on McCarron. Does he have enough arm talent when protection breaks down? Nothing breaks down for him in college. ...As much as I like him, he always had a ton of weapons. I don't get wowed by his game. He's good, not great. I thought he really struggled to rally the team and make plays and be productive vs. Colorado State. I put him in the second. I couldn't put him in the first. With quarterbacks — sometimes it shocks you where they go. You think, 'That guy went there?!' He is as prepared as any of the others. He is big, athletic enough and runs a pro-style offense. There are qualities about him to like."

QB ZACH METTENBERGER, #8

LSU ▶ GRADE: 5.27

Ht: 6-4 7/8 | Wt: 224 | Sp: 5.20e | Arm: 32 3/8 | Hand: 9 3/4

History: The Georgia prep graduated early and enrolled at the University of Georgia in January 2009 and redshirted in the fall. Was arrested in March '10 and pleaded guilty to two counts of misdemeanor sexual battery and was dismissed from the Bulldogs. Spent the '10 campaign leading Butler County CC (Kan.) to an 11-1 record and the JUCO National Championship game after completing 176-of-299 passes for 2,678 yards (58.9 percent) with 32 touchdowns and four interceptions. Transferred to LSU in '11, seeing limited action in five games and posted 8-11-92-1-0 (72.7). Made all 13 starts in '12 and threw for 207-352-2,609-12-7 (58.8). In '13, logged 192-296-3,082-22-8 (64.9) in 12 starts. Did not play in the Outback Bowl against Iowa after suffering a torn ACL in his left knee against Arkansas in the regular-season finale. Is the only LSU quarterback to throw for 2,500 or more yards in back-to-back seasons. Two-time team captain and had a 19-6 record in 25 starts at LSU and 30-7 as a collegiate QB. Did not work out at the Combine because of knee injury.

Strengths: Exceptional size. Outstanding arm strength — spins it with velocity and can make all the throws. Can drill the deep out and fit it into a tight window across the field throwing to his left. Ran an NFL-style offense under coordinator Cam Cameron and learned how to become more of a leader as a senior.

Weaknesses: Heavy-footed with a long delivery, which translates to the pocket closing on him quickly when he moves and is forced off a spot. Takes unnecessary sacks and is rattled easily under duress. Really labors to hasten his release and get rid of the ball quickly when needed. Has tunnel vision and arms the ball too much. Tends to trigger late and frequently underthrows the deep ball. Does not throw

receivers open and forces them to adjust. Can learn to take pace off the ball and throw with more touch, better timing and anticipation. Had a very strong supporting cast with NFL-caliber receivers and a stout offensive line. Weight fluctuated early in his career and arrived at LSU pushing 260 pounds. Is coming off an ACL injury and will require some rehabilitation time. Character will require closer scrutiny.

Future: Pure dropback, strong-armed thrower who will require patient, confidence-building play-calling and a clean pocket to function at a high level in the NFL. Has starter talent in a vertical, downfield passing attack if he can learn to take command of a huddle and continue progressing as a decision-maker. How he interviews with teams could go a long way toward determining his draft status.

Draft projection: Fourth- to fifth-round pick.

Scout's take: "He was immature when he first got to college, but he has settled down. We interviewed him. He's a little aloof. He has not had a strong father figure in his life. He is smart enough to figure it out if he is in the right system. He improved this year. What you have to figure out is how much the ACL (injury) is going to hurt him. I think it'll drop him a couple rounds, and I didn't have him graded highly to begin with. I think those receivers made him. Look how often they have to adjust to the ball."

QB STEPHEN MORRIS, #17

MIAMI (FLA.) ▶ GRADE: 5.20

Ht: 6-1 7/8 | Wt: 213 | Sp: 4.63 | Arm: 32 3/4 | Hand: 10 1/4

History: The Miami native stayed home for college and saw action in six games, starting the final four contests, as a true freshman in 2010. Completed 82-of-153 passes for 1,240 yards (53.6 percent) with seven touchdowns and nine interceptions. Played in five games (started against Maryland) and threw for 26-37-283-0-2 (70.3) in '11. Had back surgery after the season and missed '12 spring practice. Earned the starting job in the fall and posted 245-421-3,345-21-7 (58.2) in 12 starts. Set the school's single-season total offense record with 3,415 yards, breaking Bernie Kosar's 1984 record (3,412). Set the ACC record with 566 passing yards against NC State. Started all 13 contests in '13, throwing for 198-344-3,028-21-12 (57.6). Became only the second QB in school history with multiple 3,000-yard seasons (Gino Torretta). Two-time team captain. Finished 17-13 in 30 career starts under three offensive coordinators — Mark Whipple (2010), Jedd Fisch (2011-12) and James Coley (2013).

Strengths: Very good arm strength and athletic ability. Can move around the pocket and buy extra time. Throws with velocity and can rifle the ball into tight spots. Can drill back-shoulder throws. Can adapt his arm and throwing platform and release it from a variety of angles under duress with ease. Has natural leadership traits.

Weaknesses: Average overall size with a relatively thin build. Sporadic accuracy. Sprays the ball and struggles to hit receivers in stride (best with stationary targets). Does not throw his receivers open. Marginal timing, anticipation and rhythm. Struggles to handle pressure and presses to create plays — eyes drop to the rush very quickly and vacates the pocket prematurely. Makes too many head-scratching decisions. Birddogs his primary target and will force the ball. Career 57.7 completion percentage is indicative of inaccuracy at all layers even with a clean pocket. Makes his receivers consistently work for the ball.

Future: Was forced to cycle through three offenses in four years at the helm and never grew comfortable as a passer. Teases evaluators with his arm and athletic talent, but must prove he can hone his accuracy and decision-making. Has moldable talent for a backup role and enough raw tools to pique the interest of a patient, quarterbacks coach. Will require a strong offensive line and a full supporting cast of weapons to function. Developmental talent.

Draft projection: Fifth- to sixth-round pick.

Scout's take: "He has the best arm talent of anyone in the Southeast. He has starter arm-strength. His accuracy is bad. He won't come into a game and win for you because of his accuracy issues. He has developmental possibilities. If you take him too high, he will disappoint you. The bottom of (the) fourth round) is the right resting spot for me for what we are looking for. I know other teams have him as a free agent. I just think he has some talent to work with. Instead of letting the game flow, he presses and tries to create too much and it forces him into a lot of bad decisions and leads to critical interceptions."

QB AARON MURRAY, #11

GEORGIA   ▶ GRADE: 5.17

Ht: 6-0 1/2 | Wt: 207 | Sp: 4.85e | Arm: 30 5/8 | Hand: 9 1/8

History: The Florida prep was a Parade and U.S. Army All-American in addition to being named Mr. Football as a junior. Suffered a broken left fibula early in his senior season but returned to lead the team to a 4A state championship. Enrolled at Georgia in the spring of 2009 and redshirted in the fall. Named team's Most Valuable Offensive Player in '10 after completing 209-of-342 passes for 3,049 yards (61.1 percent) with 24 touchdowns and eight interceptions in 13 starts. Made all 14 starts in '11 and recorded 238-403-3,149-35-14 (59.1). Graduated in May '12. Had a record-setting fall by recording school marks for passing yards and touchdown passes with 249-386-3,893-36-10 (64.5) in 14 starts. Finished his stellar four-year career by tossing 225-347-3,075-26-9 (64.8) in 11 starts before suffering a torn ACL in his left knee against Kentucky. Is the only QB in SEC history to throw for more 3,000 yards in all four seasons and is the conference's career record holder in touchdowns (121) and passing yards (13,166). Was a two-time Academic All-American and named the SEC Scholar Athlete of the Year. Two-time team captain. Had 16 career rushing touchdowns and went 35-17 in 52 starts. Did not perform at the Combine because of knee injury.

Strengths: Has a quick release and is light enough on his feet to escape the first wave and make some plays on the move. Solid decision-maker — takes what the defense gives him. Fine short-to-intermediate accuracy. Good intangibles. Encouraging team leader with a likeable personality. Leads by example. Serves well as the face of the program. Outstanding work ethic. Is very intelligent and football smart. Experienced, four-year starter in the SEC.

Weaknesses: Short and short-armed with a low release point that leads to batted balls. Very small-framed with a thin waist and a body that is not built to withstand the punishment that comes in the pocket. Average arm talent. Has to set his feet and everything needs to be perfect to function well. Could stand to improve his footwork. Marginal deep-ball accuracy — tends to overstride and forces receivers to adjust. Many passes are pre-determined and often throws to spots. Loses poise under duress and can be rattled easily by pressure. Gets too jittery and anxious (overanalyzes) in big games and has a very low winning percentage vs. top-10 teams. Long-term durability is concerning.

Future: Smallish, game-managing pocket passer still recovering from a torn ACL. Would benefit from a moving pocket that can create open throwing lanes, yet does not have the foot quickness desired for a rollout passing game. Possesses a skill set most ideally suited for a backup or No. 3 role in a dink-and-dunk offense. Intelligence, intangibles and experience are all pluses.

Draft projection: Late draftable pick.

Scout's take: "Aaron Murray to me fits right in there with the Graham Harrell's of the world. He's a third quarterback because he is smart. He has all the records at Georgia because he started there as a freshman. This kid is everything you want intangibly. He's a good college quarterback."

QB BRYN RENNER, #2

NORTH CAROLINA   ▶ GRADE: 5.10

Ht: 6-3 1/4 | Wt: 228 | Sp: 4.87 | Arm: 30 3/8 | Hand: 9 1/8

History: His father, Bill, is a former punter for the Green Bay Packers (1986-87) and his sister, Summer, is a Rockette at Radio City Music Hall. The Virginia prep was one of the top ranked quarterbacks in country while also playing basketball and baseball. Redshirted in 2009. Played in 15 games for the Tar Heels baseball team in the Spring '10 before deciding to focus on football. Saw limited action in three games in the fall, completing 1-of-2 passes for 14 yards (50 percent) with zero touchdowns and zero interceptions as the backup to Texans 2011 fifth-rounder T.J. Yates. Took over as the starter in '11 and threw for 239-350-3,086-26-13 (68.3) in 13 games. Left the NC State game with concussion-like symptoms. Broke his own school record for touchdown passes in '12 after tossing 276-422-3,356-28-7 (65.4) in 12 starts. Was the first Tar Heel QB to reach 3,000 yards passing twice in a career. Had an injury-plagued senior campaign in '13, posting 152-231-1,765-10-5 (65.8) in only seven starts. Missed the Virginia Tech game with a left foot injury. Left the NC State game with a left (non-throwing) shoulder injury and missed the final five games. Had surgery on Nov. 6 to repair a torn labrum and a fractured scapula. Had an 18-14 record in 32 career games.

Strengths: Sets up with balance. Clean three-quarters release. Can throw with timing and anticipation short-to-intermediate. Understands ball placement — tries to put throws where only his receivers can make a play. Flashes touch. Tough and competitive. Commands the huddle and shows good on-field demeanor. Three-year starter.

Weaknesses: Lacks ideal height. Arm strength is just functional — struggles to drive velocity throws on a line. Does not push the ball downfield often, and accuracy wanes when he does. Needs a clean pocket to have success — flustered when his rhythm is broken. Could stand to quicken his eyes. Tends to lock on and force throws into traffic. Slow-footed (not a scramble threat). Lacks ideal intangibles — judgment, intelligence and preparation should be checked out.

Future: Renner waited his turn behind Texans 2011 fifth-round pick T.J. Yates, but did not show drastic improvement over the course of his career, which ended with season-ending left (non-throwing) shoulder surgery in early November. Renner, whose arm strength limits his ceiling, lacks exceptional physical traits and will have to compete for a job as a pocket-passing, short-to-intermediate clipboard holder.

Draft projection: Late draftable pick.

QB TOM SAVAGE, #7

PITTSBURGH   ▶ GRADE: 5.21

Ht: 6-3 7/8 | Wt: 228 | Sp: 4.97 | Arm: 31 5/8 | Hand: 9 5/8

History: His brother, Bryan, was a quarterback for Wisconsin (2004-05) and Hofstra (2007-08). The Pennsylvania prep was a three-year starter at QB and a U.S. Army All-America selection. Had a foot injury as a junior that ended his season. Began his college career at Rutgers in 2009, where he earned Freshman All-America honors as a true freshman by completing 149-of-285 passes for 2,211 yards (52 percent) with 14 touchdowns and seven interceptions in 12 games (11 starts). Threw for 43-83-521-2-3 (51.8) in six games in '10, started the first four games before injuring his right hand and losing his starting job. Transferred to Arizona to play for Head Coach Mike Stoops but had to sit out the '11 season due to NCAA transfer rules. After Stoops was fired and Rich Rodriguez hired, he decided to transfer again to an offense that suited him better. Tried to go back to Rutgers but hardship waiver was denied by the NCAA so he enrolled at Pittsburgh. Had to sit out the '12 season as a transfer. Finally returned to the field in '13 and started all 13 games for Pitt, throwing for 238-389-2,958-21-9 (61.2). Suffered a concussion against Virginia and bruised ribs in the Little Caesars Bowl vs. Bowling Green. Had a 17-11 record in 28 career starts. Team captain.

Strengths: Terrific size. Sets with balance. Easy, compact, high three-quarters release. Spins a catchable ball. Excellent arm strength to complete NFL throws — capable of sticking outs from the deep hash or launching balls 60 yards on the money. Experience in pro-style offense. Smart and hardworking. Solid personal and football character. Has tools to work with. Team captain.

Weaknesses: Needs to speed up his clock and show better awareness in the pocket. Needs to quicken his eyes, expand his field vision and learn to manipulate safeties. Tends to stare down his target. Forces some throws into traffic. Erratic accuracy. Slow of foot — not a scramble threat. Can improve play-action fake. Had some duds — struggled against Florida State, Virginia and Virginia Tech. Mental toughness needs to be looked into.

Future: Big, inconsistent pocket passer who took a circuitous route to Pittsburgh, where he played a full season for the first time since 2009. Is inconsistent and in need of more reps, but has ample arm talent to warrant developmental consideration if teams deem his intangibles worthy of an investment.

Draft projection: Fifth- to sixth-round pick.

Scout's take: "Savage was rusty. He was out a couple of years, but he might have a chance to be pretty good once he knocks all the rust off. He got it rolling pretty good once he got his rhythm down. He is smart. I could see him developing into a player down the road."

QB CONNOR SHAW, #14

SOUTH CAROLINA   ▶ GRADE: 5.10

Ht: 6-0 3/8 | Wt: 206 | Sp: 4.66 | Arm: 30 | Hand: 9 1/4

History: Comes from an athletic family as

his father played football at Western Carolina, his mom played basketball at North Georgia and his brother, Jaybo, was a quarterback at Georgia Southern. Threw for 30 touchdowns and ran for 17 more his senior year as a Georgia prep. Graduated early to participate in 2010 spring practice and saw action in nine games as a true freshman in the fall, completing 23-of-33 passes for 223 yards (70 percent) with one touchdown and two interceptions. Also rushed 32 times for 165 yards (5.2-yard average) with zero touchdowns. Threw for 123-188-1,448-14-6 (65.4) and ran for 135-525-8 (3.9) in '11 in 10 games. Started the season opener against East Carolina and then took over the job after for an ineffective Stephen Garcia and made the final eight starts. In '12, started all 11 games he played and tossed 154-228-1,956-17-7 (school record 67.5) while rushing 131-435-3 (3.3). Didn't play against East Carolina and missed most of UAB contest with a right shoulder injury. Missed the Clemson game with a sprained left foot, which required surgery in January '13 and missed spring practice. Saved the best for his senior year, setting career highs with 180-284-2,447-24-1 (63.4) passing and 154-558-6 (3.6) rushing in 13 games (12 starts). Only non-start was Missouri (left knee, sprained MCL and LCL) but came off the bench to lead the Gamecocks to a come-from-behind win in double OT. Holds the South Carolina record for wins as a starting QB after going 27-5 in 32 career starts, including 17-0 at home.

Strengths: Fine touch and accuracy. Very good mobility and movement in the pocket. Tough and gritty competitor. Produced a rare 24-1 TD-INT ratio as a senior and cut down on mental mistakes that characterized his play earlier in his career. Workaholic, gym rat. Extremely determined. Vocal presence. Smart and instinctive — is the son of a coach and understands football concepts. Plays through pain. Has a 27-5 career starting record, has rallied his team to victory off the bench and carries a calm, confident, poised field presence. Mentally and physically tough. Three-year starter in the SEC.

Weaknesses: Is undersized and injury-prone with multiple foot and shoulder injuries. Played in a non-traditional, gimmicky offense featuring many simple reads and has a tendency to birddog his primary target. Operated heavily out of the shotgun, and mechanics will require seasoning. Average arm strength — does not generate velocity on the move and comes up short on the deep ball. Can be too jittery vs. pressure and quick to tuck and run.

Future: Lacks prototype measurements and arm talent and played in a high-percentage, dink-and-dunk passing game that has not translated well to the pros, yet possesses the intangibles, toughness, football intelligence and escapability to warrant developing. Is the type of player scouts root for. A Jeff Garcia, make-it type quarterback likely to will his way into a job.

Draft projection: Late draftable pick.

QB LOGAN THOMAS, #3

VIRGINIA TECH ▶ GRADE: 5.42

Ht: 6-6 1/8 | Wt: 248 | Sp: 4.59 | Arm: 34 1/4 | Hand: 10 7/8

History: The Virginia prep participated in the U.S. Army Bowl and was the top-ranked tight end prospect in the country. Redshirted in 2009. Saw action in seven games in '10 as a quarterback and wide receiver, completed 12-of-26 passes for 107 yards (84.6 percent) with zero touchdowns and zero interceptions. Ran the ball six times for 22 yards (3.7-yard average) and zero touchdowns, in addition to catching a 2-yard touchdown pass vs. Wake Forest. Started all 14 games at quarterback in '11 and threw for 234-391-3,013-19-10 (60.0) while rushing 153-469-11 (3.1). Set the school record for rushing touchdowns by a QB. Led the Hokies in rushing in '12 with 174-524-9 (3.0) and throwing 220-429-2,976-18-16 (51.3) in 13 starts. Made every start for the Hokies for a third straight season, tossing 227-402-2,907-16-13 (56.5) and rushing 162-344-4 (2.1) in 13 games. Was knocked out of the Sun Bowl early with a head injury. Team captain. Finished his career with 9,103 yards and 53 touchdowns, both school records. Had a 26-14 record in 40 career starts.

Strengths: Outstanding size, stature and strength — towers over the line, has natural throwing lanes from the pocket and is able to make plays in the grasp. Athletic — can climb the pocket, escape and run for the sticks. Load to bring down. Generates easy velocity with a quick, compact release and can make all the throws. Is very competitive and will sell out to make a play. Has upside. Tough and durable — started 40 consecutive games. Vocal leader.

Weaknesses: Plateaued as a sophomore. Uneven performance. Inconsistent footwork and mechanics. Shoddy ball placement. Still developing touch and deep-ball accuracy. Needs to quicken his eyes and expand his field vision. Needs to learn to protect himself — is not elusive and represents a big target to defenders. Struggled in big games, including a nightmare performance against Alabama. Too careless with the football — 39 INTs and 23 fumbles as a starter. Career 50-percent passer on third down.

Future: Unrefined, strong-armed, sturdy pocket passer who looks the part and has intriguing, raw arm talent, though he is a converted tight end whose inexperience showed throughout a yo-yo career in Blacksburg. Has definite developmental value given his starter-caliber skill set and intangible makeup. Would benefit from coaching continuity, more specifically a QB coach capable of refining his crude talent.

Draft projection: Third- to fourth-round pick.

Scout's take: "He is as raw as they come. I did not like him last year. He did not have much help around him — no receivers or running backs like they used to have. Everything about him is raw."

QB DUSTIN VAUGHAN, #10
WEST TEXAS A&M   ▶ GRADE: 4.85
Ht: 6-4 7/8 | Wt: 235 | Sp: 4.96 | Arm: 33 | Hand: 8 7/8

History: The Texas native played basketball and baseball in addition to being a punter. Redshirted in 2009. Saw limited action in four games in '10 as the third-string QB, completing 7-of-12 passes for 96 yards (58.3 percent) with zero touchdowns and zero interceptions. Threw for 227-382-3,316-25-6 (59.4) in 11 games (10 starts) in '11 after taking over as the starter in Week 2. His first career start was at Cowboys Stadium vs. Texas A&M-Kingsville. Was named the Lone Star Conference Offensive Player of the Year in '12 after posting 359-555-4,712-45-13 (64.7) in 15 starts. Also earned Capital One/CoSIDA Academic Player of the Year for Division II. Had an unbelievable senior season in '13, leading the NCAA (all divisions) in passing yards after racking up 447-675-5,401-53-10 (66.2) in 14 starts. Was the only QB in the NCAA to top 5,000 yards, was the runner-up for the Harlon Hill Award (best player in Division II) and set the all-time Division II record for passing yards. Made 39 career starts and had a 31-8 record. Team captain.

Strengths: Excellent size. Good short-to-intermediate accuracy when he has time to set his feet and step into throws. Very intelligent. Superb leadership qualities and intangibles. Highly respected, vocal team leader. Very competitive. Urgent, demanding, on-field presence. Outstanding production. Tough and durable.

Weaknesses: Has small hands. Most balls are flat with little arc and not easily catchable. Plays in a spread-pistol offense operating exclusively out of the gun and featuring a lot of simple, one-look reads. Very average mobility to escape the rush and create plays in the pocket with his feet. Will force the ball under duress and needs to hone his decision-making. Is late to trigger and takes unnecessary sacks. Has not faced top competition and windows will tighten in the pros.

Future: A developmental, dink-and-dunk pocket passer with intriguing intangibles and leadership qualities sought for a supportive backup or No. 3 role. Will require time to acclimate to the speed of the NFL game.

Draft projection: Priority free agent.

QB KEITH WENNING, #10
BALL STATE   ▶ GRADE: 5.00
Ht: 6-2 5/8 | Wt: 218 | Sp: 5.01 | Arm: 31 1/4 | Hand: 10

History: The Ohio prep had a 49-4 record as a starter and lettered in basketball and baseball. Saw action in all 12 games as a true freshman in 2010, starting the final 10, and completed 128-of-235 passes for 1,373 yards (54.5 percent) with 14 touchdowns and 14 interceptions. Made all 12 starts in '11, tossing 287-449-2,786-19-11 (63.9). In '12, started 12 games and posted 301-460-3,095-24-10. Caught a 12-yard touchdown pass against Indiana. Missed the regular season finale against Miami (OH) with a fractured right ankle but returned to start the Beef 'O' Brady Bowl. Became the first Ball State QB to throw for more than 4,000 yards in a season in '13 after tallying 319-498-4,148-35-7 (64.1) in 13 starts. Set the school's career records for completions (1,035), attempts (1,642), passing yards (11,402) and touchdowns (92). Had 13 career rushing touchdowns and a 27-20 mark in 47 starts. Two-time team captain.

Strengths: Experienced, four-year starter with a solid build. Very smart and understands the offense. Outstanding football character and personal character — works at his craft, is driven to succeed and will represent a franchise well. Respected leader. Football is very important to him. Very tough and highly competitive. Has directed 10 fourth-quarter comebacks in his career. Consistent in his approach.

Weaknesses: Average arm strength, athletic ability and pocket mobility to avoid the first wave and make throws off-balance and under duress. Carries a heaviness in his body and lacks twitch. Works almost exclusively out of the gun and will need to adapt to working from under center. Cannot easily manipulate his arm and throwing platform. Does not drive the deep out, and accuracy and placement diminishes downfield. Production is inflated from regularly facing inferior MAC competition.

Future: Heavy-bodied, dink-and-dunk, rhythm passer who could be challenged to fit the ball into tight NFL windows. Has the makeup desired in a No. 3 QB and could develop into a functional backup in a West Coast passing game.

Draft projection: Priority free agent.

RUNNING BACKS

NAWROCKI'S TOP 10

Player	Rank
DE'ANTHONY THOMAS	10
JERICK McKINNON	9
TERRANCE WEST	8
KA'DEEM CAREY	7
BISHOP SANKEY	6
DEVONTA FREEMAN	5
ANDRE WILLIAMS	4
JEREMY HILL	3
TRE MASON	2
OHIO STATE RB **CARLOS HYDE**	1

RB-KR ANTONIO ANDREWS, #5

WESTERN KENTUCKY ▶ GRADE: 5.20
Ht: 5-10 1/8 | Wt: 225 | Sp: 4.72 | Arm: 31 1/4 | Hand: 9 1/2

History: High school quarterback who led his team to a 29-0 record and two state championships while totaling 6,733 yards (passing and rushing) and 106 touchdowns, earning Kentucky's Gatorade Player of the Year award as a senior. Originally attended Air Force prep school before transferring to WKU in 2010 when he played eight games (one start) and rushed 32 times for 174 yards (5.4-yard average) and two touchdowns with five receptions for 37 yards (7.4) and zero touchdowns. Backed up Buccaneers RB Bobby Rainey in '11 when he played eight games and carried 15-42-0 (2.8) and caught 2-16-0 (8.0). Missed two games while nursing a high left ankle sprain, and was suspended for two games following a Twitter rant criticizing WKU fans. Broke out in '12, piling up 304-1,728-11 (5.7) on the ground and 37-432-3 (11.7) receiving in 13 games (12 starts). Was second on the depth chart to open the season, but started as an injury replacement in Week Two and never relinquished the job. Led the nation in all-purpose yards for the second consecutive season in '13, amassing 267-1,730-16 rushing and 41-478-0 (11.7) receiving while starting all 12 games. For his career, also returned 42 kickoffs for 1,780 yards (20.9) and 42 punts for 382 yards (9.1), including one touchdown. Concluded his career with the NCAA record for most all-purpose yards over a two-year span (5,770).

Strengths: Good size. Nice vision to pick and slide. Shows instinctive jump-cut ability. Lowers his pads and finishes runs with forward lean. Picks up yards after contact. Effective short-to-intermediate receiver — has body control to adjust to throws. Can handle a heavy workload. Record-breaking two-year production — was the nation's leading all-purpose gainer 2012-13. Has punt- and kickoff-return experience. Scheme versatile. Showed more burst as a senior.

Weaknesses: Must learn to better protect the ball — fumbling has been an issue. Average initial quickness, explosiveness and elusiveness. Monotone short stepper. Dull burst through the hole. Does not have an extra gear to pull away — gets tracked down from behind. Inconsistent pad level and leg drive — limited power. Occasional concentration drop. Struggles in pass protection. Clocked a pedestrian 40-time as high as 4.84 seconds at the Combine, a RB-low 1.81-second, 10-yards split and recorded a 29 1/2-inch vertical jump.

Future: Compact, well-built, mid-major workhorse with a blend of one-cut and downhill elements. Generally gains what is blocked for him and has enough power to earn a job as a No. 2 tandem back in a man- or zone-blocking scheme. However, he is not a talented enough runner to overlook or tolerate his fumbles and deficient pass protection, and he will have to earn trust before he earns carries.

Draft projection: Fourth- to fifth-round pick.

Scout's take: "A lot of teams are sleeping on him. He does it all. He blocks. He catches. He is good in pass pro. He can make NFL runs through trash. He's not a burner — he's quicker than fast. Whoever coached him at the Senior Bowl is going to try to sneak him late. I'd take him in the third round and think he could be a starter. I'd love to get him in the fourth."

RB-KR GEORGE ATKINSON III, #4 (JUNIOR)

NOTRE DAME   ▶ GRADE: 5.11
Ht: 6-1 3/8 | Wt: 218 | Sp: 4.43 | Arm: 33 1/4 | Hand: 9 3/8

History: Father, George, was a two-time all-pro defensive back in the NFL from 1968-1979 for Oakland and Denver. His twin brother, Josh, is a cornerback for Notre Dame. The California prep rushed 172 times for 1,669 yards and 17 touchdowns as a senior in 2010, seeing action at running back, wide receiver and defensive back. Also was a track standout, finishing third in the state in the 100-meter finals in '09 (10.66). Saw action in all 13 games for Notre Dame as a freshman in '11, returning 35 kickoffs for a school-record 915 yards and two touchdowns (26.1-yard average) while rushing nine times for 27 yards (3.0) and two touchdowns. In the spring of '12, he ran indoor and outdoor track, placing third in the 200-meter finals at the Big East Indoor Championships (21.47). Also ran 10.36 in a qualifying round 100-meter dash, the second-fastest clocking ever for a Notre Dame track runner (Raghib "Rocket" Ismail, 10.34 in 1991). In the fall, he played in 12 games for the Irish (four starts) and rushed 51-

361-5 (7.1) and had kickoff returns of 22-441-0 (20.0). Missed the Oklahoma game with flu-like symptoms. Appeared in 12 games (four starts) in '13, carrying 93-555-3 (6.0) with kickoff returns of 31-780-0 (25.2). Had an 80-yard touchdown run September 28 against Oklahoma, the longest run from scrimmage for a Notre Dame player since 2000. Was suspended from the Pinstripe Bowl against Rutgers for violating team rules (he claimed via Twitter that he was caught texting during a team meal, but no official reason was given; he subsequently deleted that tweet). Concluded his Notre Dame career as the school's all-time leader in kickoff returns (88) and kickoff return yards (2,136).

Strengths: Outstanding timed speed — has been clocked below 10.4 seconds in the 100 meters. Has kickoff-return experience and returned two for scores as a freshman. Can take it the distance when he gets in the clear. Has plenty of tread on his tires having carried just 153 times at Notre Dame. Has NFL bloodlines.

Weaknesses: Has an upright, linear running style — exposes himself to some violent hits. Does not convert speed to power. Gears down to cut. Struggles to create on his own. Limited elusiveness and tackle-breaking ability — too often grounded by the first tackler or ankle tackles. Crude eyes and instincts. Head-scratching career production. Has underachiever traits. Competitiveness and coachability need to be examined.

Future: A pedigreed, height-weight-speed prospect who slipped down the depth chart as a junior, Atkinson made a premature jump to the NFL knowing he likely would have been behind underclassmen had he returned as a senior. Is not a natural running back, but has raw tools to warrant consideration as a developmental, one-cut slasher. Better tester than football player. Solid Combine numbers.

Draft projection: Late draftable pick.

RB ZACH BAUMAN, #34

NORTHERN ARIZONA   ▶ GRADE: 5.00
Ht: 5-8 1/2 | Wt: 194 | Sp: 4.65e | Arm: 29 1/2 | Hand: 8 3/4

History: Two of his cousins played in the NFL — Rashad Bauman, a cornerback with Washington and Cincinnati from 2002-2005, and five-time Pro Bowl running back Greg Pruitt, who played for Cleveland and the Los Angeles Raiders from 1973-1984. Helped lead his high school team to back-to-back Arizona state championships while also lettering in basketball and track. Started as a true freshman for NAU in 2010 and made an immediate impact, rushing for 167 yards and four touchdowns in his collegiate debut against Western New Mexico. Went on to lead the Big Sky with 16 touchdowns, starting all 11 games and rushing 237 times for 1,059 yards (4.5-yard average) and 14 touchdowns with 28 catches for 308 yards (11.0) and two touchdowns. Started all 11 games in '11 and carried 271-1,435-15 (5.3) and caught 29-352-1 (12.1). Became the first player in school history to surpass the 1,000-yards mark in his first three seasons in '12, amassing 225-1,182-8 (5.3) rushing and 34-216-1 (6.4) receiving in 11 starts. After the season, he had his right knee scoped to repair a torn meniscus. In '13, became the ninth player in FCS history to record four 1,000-yard seasons, rushing for 270-1,456-9 (5.4) and catching 44-305-1 (6.9) in 12 starts. Closed his collegiate career with his 25th 100-yard rushing game in a playoff loss to South Dakota State. The three-time first-team All-Big Sky selection finished his career with 5,132 career rushing yards — third-best in conference history. Left NAU as the school's all-time leader in rushing yards, all-purpose yards (6,316) and points scored (306). Played in the East-West Shrine Game and led all running backs with 47 yards on the ground. Team captain.

Strengths: Very good balance and run skills. Churns through contact and is surprisingly nifty — sets up his runs. Extremely tough competitor. Outstanding work ethic. Excellent character. Good ball security. Experienced four-year starter.

Weaknesses: Very average size. Marginal acceleration, long speed and elusiveness. Only shows one gear. Limited bulk to square up in pass protection. Lacks upper-body strength.

Future: A short, thickly built, bowling bowl running with the balance, vision, work ethic and intangibles to earn a roster spot and overachieve in the pros.

Draft projection: Priority free agent.

RB KAPRI BIBBS, #5 (JUNIOR)

COLORADO STATE ▶ GRADE: 5.05
Ht: 5-9 3/8 | Wt: 212 | Sp: 4.76 | Arm: 31 3/8 | Hand: 8 1/2

History: First name is pronounced "kuh-PREE." Was a Chicago-area prep running back, running his way into the Illinois football record book in 2010 after recording a 520-yard, seven-touchdown game. As a junior and senior, he combined to rush for 61 touchdowns and 4,210 yards. Also lettered in bowling and

track. Initially was a member of Colorado State's 2011 recruiting class, but failed to qualify academically. Spent the '11 season at Snow CC (Ephraim, UT), where he played in 11 games and rushed 74 times for 415 yards (5.6-yard average) and six touchdowns with one reception for 7 yards. Did not play in '12, attending classes at Front Range CC in Colorado before enrolling at Colorado State. In '13 in his only FBS season, he amassed 281-1,741-31 (6.2) on the ground and 8-59-0 (7.4) receiving despite starting only seven of CSU's 14 games. His 31 rushing touchdowns tied for the most in FBS. On November 9 vs. Nevada, he set a Rams single-game rushing record with 312 yards (on 30 carries). The following week, he tied a Mountain West record by scoring six touchdowns during a 291-yard performance at New Mexico. Scored at least three rushing touchdowns in eight games, tying Barry Sanders' single-season mark (Oklahoma State, 1988). Did not run any shuttles at the Combine because of a turf toe injury.

Strengths: Good initial quickness. Nice vision and balance. Has one-cut ability — shows burst when he sticks his foot in the ground and gets upfield. Runs hard. Will be a 21-year-old rookie and has tread on his tires.

Weaknesses: Average power and tackle-breaking ability. Lacks extra gear to pull away. Questionable third-down ability — minimal production/exposure as a receiver and pass protection needs work. Does not adjust to throws or catch naturally. Carries the ball loosely. One-year wonder. Showed he could be contained (Alabama, Boise St., Utah St.). Recorded a 29-inch vertical jump and timed

Future: Compactly built, productive, monotone runner lacking exceptional traits to distinguish himself from other recyclable backs. Would have been better served returning to school, if for no other reason than to improve in pass protection. Workout numbers could dictate draft value.

Draft projection: Priority free agent.

RB ALFRED BLUE, #4 (JUNIOR)

LSU ▶ GRADE: 5.25
Ht: 6-2 3/8 | Wt: 223 | Sp: 4.63 | Arm: 32 3/8 | Hand: 9 7/8

History: Baton Rouge-area native who earned all-state honors after rushing for 1,695 yards and 25 touchdowns as a high school senior. Played in 11 games (one start) as a true freshman for LSU in 2010, rushing 20 times for 101 yards (5.1-yard average) and one touchdown. Missed two games with a foot injury. Appeared in 13 games in '11 (one start) and carried 78-539-7 (6.9). Missed one game with an ankle injury and overcame the loss of his family's home in a September fire. Was off to a great start in '12 before tearing the ACL in his left knee in Week 3, which necessitated season-ending surgery. Started the first three games, including back-to-back 100-yard contests, and carried 40-270-2 (6.8) and caught 7-45-0 (6.4). Returned in '13 and played in all 13 games (two starts), amassing 71-343-1 (4.8) rushing and 5-62-0 (12.4) receiving. Was awarded a fifth season of eligibility by the NCAA due to the hardship rule, but decided to decline to pursue a pro career. Despite making only seven collegiate starts, he finished his LSU career with 209-1,253-11 (6.0) rushing and 16-105-0 (6.6) receiving.

Strengths: Terrific size and musculature. Inside-outside ability. Nice vision, instincts and patience. Has good speed for a back his size — opens up his stride in the clear. Strong runner — heavy on contact. Powers through arm tackles and runs with forward lean. Wields an effective stiff-arm. Looks to have good hands in limited exposure. Flashes playmaking ability. Has tread on his tires — averaged just 52 carries per season at LSU. Has experience in a pro-style offense and on special teams. Clear upside.

Weaknesses: Average initial quickness and lateral agility. Smoother than he is explosive. Can run with more consistent intensity and pad level on a carry-by-carry basis — does not always run angry or lower his pads. Shows some stiffness as a route runner. Weak in pass protection — needs to improve willingness, awareness, technique and physicality. Was never the feature back at LSU (seven career starts). Suffered a torn ACL in 2012. Made controversial, homophobic remarks and maturity should be looked into. Recorded a 4.56-second, 20-yard shuttle time, the second-slowest of any back at the Combine.

Future: A physically gifted runner who would have been the No. 1 back at most schools given his combination of size, speed, power and competitiveness. Is a second-round talent on talent alone, but injuries and a stacked stable of LSU runners limited Blue's opportunity to shine. Scheme-versatile runner who is a prime candidate to elevate his stock prior to the draft and be a far more productive pro than college player if he proves he can stay healthy.

Draft projection: Fourth- to fifth-round pick.

Scout's take: "When you see him in person, he looks like the spitting image of (Vikings RB) Adrian Peterson athletically and the way that he is built. (Blue) is big, strong and athletic with soft hands. He has good strength, balance and burst. He pushes the line of scrimmage. Take away the injury factor, and I don't know what there is not to like if you're grading him on his traits. What's crazy there is they live by a running back-by-committee approach — 1-2-3. They have four guys in rotation and all of them are talented. That's why you see guys like Stevan Ridley and Joseph Addai coming out of there with little production and still having success in the pros."

RB KA'DEEM CAREY, #25 (JUNIOR)

ARIZONA ▶ GRADE: 5.42

Ht: 5-9 3/8 | Wt: 207 | Sp: 4.69 | Arm: 31 3/4 | Hand: 9 1/2

History: Had a storied Arizona prep career, rushing for nearly 4,500 yards and 71 touchdowns during his final two high school seasons. Played in 11 games for Arizona as a true freshman in 2011 and rushed 91 times for 425 yards (4.7-yard average) and six touchdowns with 15 receptions for 203 yards (13.5) and two touchdowns. Also returned 26 kickoffs for 549 yards (21.1). Missed the season finale against Louisiana-Lafayette after suffering a concussion during practice. Moved into the starting lineup in '12 and led FBS in rushing yards (1,929) and rushing yards per game (148.4), amassing 303-1,929-23 (6.4) on the ground and 36-303-1 (8.4) receiving. Started all 13 games, setting a school single-season rushing mark. In a five-touchdown performance November 10 against Colorado, he rushed for 366 yards to set the Pac-12 and UA single-game rushing records. Had a pair of run-ins with the law following the season. In December, he was charged with misdemeanor assault and disorderly conduct stemming from a domestic violence incident with his then-pregnant ex-girlfriend (the charges were later dropped). In January '13, he was kicked out of a UCLA-UA basketball game at McKale Center following an altercation with a campus security officer. As a result, he was suspended for the '13 season-opener and did not start the second game. Once he returned to the playing field, he appeared in 12 games (11 starts) and piled up 349-1,885-19 (5.4) rushing and 26-173-1 (6.7) receiving. Surpassed the 100-yards rushing mark in all 12 contests, extending his overall streak to 16 games — the longest streak in Pac-12 history. Had a pair of four-touchdown games, including a 48-206-4 effort vs. Oregon. Was a consensus All-America selection for the second straight year and concluded his Arizona career as the school's all-time leader in rushing yards (4,239), rushing touchdowns (48) and all-purpose yards (5,483).

Strengths: Outstanding two-year production — piled up 3,814 yards and 42 touchdowns on the ground from 2012-13, ranking among the nation's most prolific. Terrific compete level and determination — runs with energy, doesn't go down easily and punctuates runs. Tries to punish tacklers and keeps his legs pumping — grinds out yards after contact. Good feet, acceleration and lateral agility. Spins off contact. Reliable dump-off option. Gets upfield with urgency after the catch and has enough shiftiness to create. Willing to throw a shoulder blow into rushers. Can handle a heavy workload — averaged 26 carries per game the last two seasons.

Weaknesses: Lacks ideal size and has a narrow, high-cut build with a lean lower body. Upright running style exposes his body to some direct hits and durability could be an issue. Does not string moves together and does not have elite breakaway speed. Average wiggle and elusiveness (cuts off his heels). Faced light boxes in a spread, zone-read offense. Had nearly 850 touches in college and body has already endured a lot of punishment. Has been removed from some team boards for off-the-field transgressions/suspensions. Must prove commited.

Future: Highly productive, hard-charging slasher who runs more competitively than he does powerfully and picks up yardage in chunks. Has some first-round traits and is one of the most instinctive runners in this year's draft class, though his stock could be affected by off-the-field troubles and an average Combine showing.

Draft projection: Second- to third-round pick.

Scout's take: "(Carey) does not have home run speed — I only saw one big run this year for 30 yards when he reversed field and scored. He is very good in the hole and has great agility and balance. It's why he is getting all those yards. I think he is talented enough to sneak into the first if you're just grading the talent. …He showed up at his pro day and looked like he hadn't worked out in two months. He looked very heavy and slow. He will be a steal if he ever gets his life in order. He could drop like a rock after the way he worked out."

FB J.C. COPELAND #44

LSU ▶ GRADE: 5.09
Ht: 5-11 1/8 | Wt: 271 | Sp: 4.97 | Arm: 32 | Hand: 10

History: Full name is Javoddron Reon Holloway Copeland. Was a highly recruited defensive tackle as a Georgia prep, recording 27 sacks in his senior year and signing with LSU after initially committing to Tennessee. Moved in as a surrogate with his high school football coach, Bubba Jeter, in order to lessen the burden on his mother — who was struggling to find work and care for his three sisters. Arrived on the LSU campus in 2010 and was converted to fullback in fall camp. Appeared in four games as a true freshman, but did not have any stats. Saw action in all 14 games in '11, including four late-season starts, and carried the ball twice for zero yards. Was LSU's primary fullback in '12, playing in 13 games (12 starts) and rushing 21 times for 67 yards (3.2-yard average) and four touchdowns with three receptions for 54 yards (18.0) and zero touchdowns. Had some on-field issues, committing three personal fouls over a four-game span. Played in 11 games (six starts) in '13, rushing 13-25-3 (1.9) and receiving 4-31-0 (7.8). Missed two games after suffering a concussion when he slipped leaving the team shower room and landed on the back of his head. Returned to the field for the Alabama game and had a costly fumble — his only lost fumble as a collegian. Did not touch the ball again during LSU's final three-plus games. Was invited to the NFLPA Collegiate Bowl and earned game MVP honors after scoring on a pair of 1-yard runs — his first-ever multiple-touchdown game.

Strengths: Exceptional bulk. Good upper-body strength to lock on and torque defenders. Can move the pile with sheer mass in short-yardage/goal-line situations.

Weaknesses: Could improve sustain on the move (slips off some blocks). Gets hung up in traffic. Average athletic ability, leg drive and contact balance. Does not consistently generate movement as much as he should. Can improve ball security (see Alabama on goal line). Runs upright — struggles to sink and unlock his hips. Limited route runner. Recorded a 4.63-second 20-yard shuttle time.

Future: Split time as a senior and did not

look as powerful as he did as a junior in an isolation-lead blocking role. Could benefit from slimming down and gaining some agility to connect better with moving targets.

Draft projection: Priority free agent.

Scout's take: "He's strong, but he's too heavy and can't redirect. He's too much of a hit-and-whiff blocker for my liking. He is a dinosaur in today's game."

RB TIM CORNETT, #35

UNLV   ▶ GRADE: 5.02

Ht: 6-0 1/4 | Wt: 209 | Sp: 4.48 | Arm: 31 | Hand: 9 1/4

History: The Houston-area prep turned in a huge senior year in his only year of varsity football, rushing 152 times for 1,569 yards — an average of 10.3 yards per carry. Also lettered in track. Played in all 13 games (six starts) for UNLV in 2010 and became the first freshman to lead the Rebels in rushing, carrying the ball 144 times for 546 yards (3.8-yard average) and six touchdowns with 13 receptions for 98 yards (7.5) and two touchdowns. Also returned 14 kickoffs for 333 yards (23.8). Saw action in 11 games (six starts) in '11 and had 119-671-7 (5.6) on the ground, 10-54-0 (5.4) receiving and 6-202-1 (33.7) in kickoff returns. Was suspended for one game for a violation of team rules. In '12, he piled up 242-1,232-7 (5.1) on the ground and 14-108-0 (7.7) receiving in 13 starts. Tore the labrum in his left shoulder in fall practice and played all year with it before undergoing post-season surgery. In '13, he became just the second UNLV player to have multiple 1,000-yard campaigns, amassing 264-1,284-15 (4.9) rushing and 30-164-0 (5.5) receiving. Had a career-best 220-yard performance November 21 at Air Force, scoring four touchdowns. After entering the year with only one collegiate fumble, he had two fumbles as a senior — including his only career turnover September 28 in his 589th Rebel rushing attempt. Became the first player to lead UNLV in rushing four times, finishing his college career with 3,733 rushing yards.

Strengths: Thick, muscular build. Outstanding timed speed. Is tough and will play through injuries (battled through a torn left labrum as a junior). Very good weight-room worker. Terrific production — UNLV's all-time leading rusher. Has kickoff-return experience.

Weaknesses: Tight-hipped and straight-linish. Marginal power and tackle-breaking strength — limited yards after contact.

Minimal creativity to set up runs — takes little more than the defense gives him. Runs tall and is easily turned on contact. Struggles to take the corner. Average balance and body control. Struggles negotiating through traffic. Does not play to his timed speed. Passive blocker.

Future: A one-cut zone runner lacking ideal balance and competitiveness desired on the front lines and the temperament for special teams. More of a workout warrior than football player at this stage of his development and will be challenged to produce against better competition.

Draft projection: Priority free agent.

RB ISAIAH CROWELL, #1 (JUNIOR)

ALABAMA STATE   ▶ GRADE: 5.10

Ht: 5-11 | Wt: 224 | Sp: 4.57 | Arm: 31 3/8 | Hand: 9 1/4

History: The highly coveted Georgia prep began his college career at Georgia. The five-star recruit, a four-year letterwinner in football and track, rushed for nearly 4,900 yards and 61 touchdowns during his prep career. Was the SEC Freshman of the Year in 2011, playing in 12 games (seven starts) and rushing 185 times for a team-high 850 yards (4.6-yard average) and five touchdowns with eight receptions for 59 yards (7.4) and one touchdown. Missed one game with a sprained left ankle and was suspended one game after failing a UGA-administered drug test. His Georgia career came to a swift end in June 2012 when he was arrested for three weapons charges, including two felonies (the charges were later dropped). A week after being dismissed from the team, he transferred to Alabama State — an FCS school — in order to avoid redshirting. Was the SWAC Newcomer of the Year in '12, recording 159-843-15 (5.3) on the ground and 11-95-0 (8.6) receiving in 11 starts. Despite battling a nagging ankle injury for much of '13, he amassed 170-1,121-15 (6.6) rushing and 7-27-0 (3.9) in 12 games (11 starts).

Strengths: Good vision and run strength — runs hard and has a knack for finding seams. Presses the line of scrimmage and shows nice short-area burst to attack the outside.

Weaknesses: Average balance and tackle-breaking power. Cannot make his own holes and goes down too easy on contact, especially inside. Minimal receiving production. Soft, disinterested pass protector. Lacks top finishing speed. Effort waned late in games. Beats to the tune of his own drummer. Extremely immature and has a history of off-field issues. Can be difficult to coach.

Future: An adequate-sized back with the run instincts and perimeter running skills to compete for a job in a situational role if he learns to commit himself to the process and figures out what it means to be a pro.

Draft projection: Late draftable pick.

Scout's take: "Crowell tapped out of a game in the first quarter last year. He only wants to do what he wants to do. He doesn't like the process. It's all about him. There are more issues than the gun incident. He's immature. ...He runs hard, but he only runs hard when he has a seam. He's not a fit-and-drive a hole-type where he will run you over."

RB TIMOTHY FLANDERS, #20

SAM HOUSTON STATE   ▶ GRADE: 4.85

Ht: 5-8 5/8 | Wt: 207 | Sp: 4.74 | Arm: 30 1/4 | Hand: 9 1/4

History: His younger brother, James, is a running back for Tulsa. His older brother, John, was a defensive back and four-year letterman for Tulsa. Oklahoma prep who rushed for 2,134 yards and 34 touchdowns as a senior. Initially went to Kansas State in 2009, but transferred after one redshirt year in order to see more playing time. Walked on at Sam Houston State during the summer of 2010 and soon became the team's starter. Went on to lead the Southland Conference in rushing as a freshman, starting 10 games and rushing 172 times for 948 yards (5.5-yard average) and 13 touchdowns with 11 receptions for 24 yards (2.2) and zero touchdowns. Missed one game with an undisclosed injury. Broke out in '11, racking up 298-1,644-22 (5.5) on the ground and 34-414-2 (12.2) receiving in 15 starts. Had 2,058 all-purpose yards in earning conference Player of the Year honors. Rushed for 287 yards against Montana in the FCS semifinal game. Repeated as Southland Player of the Year in '12, piling up 288-1,642-17 (5.7) rushing and 13-128-1 (9.8) receiving in 15 starts. Despite battling a nagging foot injury in '13, he played in 14 games (13 starts) and ran for 241-1,430-14 (5.9) while catching 6-63-1 (10.5). Had a 280-yard performance against Eastern Washington and a 170-yard/two-touchdown game against Texas A&M. The three-time Walter Payton Award finalist became the first Sam Houston player to earn first-team all-league honors four times. Was the first Southland Conference running back to gain more than 5,000 yards and score more than 400 points, concluding his college career as his school's recordholder in rushing yards (5,664), carries (999), all-purpose yards (6,293), touchdowns (70) and 100-yard games (30). Finished his career in the FCS all-time Top 10 in rushing yards, rushing touchdowns and scoring.

Strengths: Thickly built with a low center of gravity. Good run vision and patience allowing holes to develop. Drives his legs on contact. Rose to the occasion vs. better competition (see Texas A&M). Very durable. Dedicated gym rat. Very gregarious, well-respected personality.

Weaknesses: Has very small hands. Had 999 college carries and took a lot of hits. Average creativity — not dynamic and does not string moves together. Lacks top-end speed to pull away from the pack. Not a powerful tackle-breaker and often goes down on initial contact (average yards after contact). Does not create his own hole. Will need work in pass protection.

Future: Tough, competitive, hard-nosed runner with the eyes, instincts and intangibles to earn a role. Has make-it qualities that could endear him to a coaching staff and add life to a locker room.

Draft projection: Priority free agent.

RB DAVID FLUELLEN, #22

TOLEDO   ▶ GRADE: 5.22

Ht: 5-11 1/8 | Wt: 224 | Sp: 4.67 | Arm: 33 3/8 | Hand: 9 1/8

History: His last name is pronounced "flu-ELL-in." His brother, Jhamal, played running back at Syracuse and Maine and went to training camp with the CFL's Hamilton Tiger-Cats. The New York prep originally committed to Buffalo before opting to sign with Toledo. Was a finalist for New York State High School Player of the Year honors after rushing for 1,638 yards and 19 touchdowns as a senior. Appeared in nine games as a true freshman for Toledo in 2010 and rushed 38 times for 224 yards (5.9-yard average) and one touchdown with five receptions for 39 yards (7.8) and zero touchdowns. Missed four games with a sprained MCL in his left knee. Spent much of '11 as a backup before starting three late-season contests. In 13 games, he carried 97-493-4 (5.1) and caught 16-155-2 (9.7). Had his best collegiate season in '12, playing in 12 games (11 starts) and recording 259-1,498-13 (5.8) rushing and 32-246-0 (7.7) receiving. Surpassed the 100-yards mark in six straight games — including a trio of 200-plus affairs. Missed one game with a right ankle injury and parts of two games with a head injury. In '13, despite playing in only nine games, he amassed

167-1,121-10 (6.7) on the ground and 27-222-0 (8.2) receiving. Became the first Toledo running back to record 100 yards both rushing and receiving in one game, accomplishing the feat against Missouri (17 rushes for 111 yards, 10 catches for 100 yards). Had six consecutive 100-yard games before injuring his left ankle October 26. Missed three of Toledo's final four games with the ankle injury, which turned out to be a small fracture that wasn't discovered until a late November MRI. Over his final two college seasons, he missed a full contest or significant time in a game nine times due to injury. Concluded his Toledo career with 3,336 rushing yards and 4,082 all-purpose yards.

Strengths: Excellent size. Runs hard downhill and can pick and slide and find creases. Good vision, leg churn and contact balance to finish runs. Tough and physical — squares his shoulders to the line and will seek to deliver punishment. Nice balance and agility. Can power through arm tackles. Good production. Has a strong support structure and strong character.

Weaknesses: Average speed. Tends to run a bit upright. Can do a better job of securing the ball tightly — will flag it. Limited make-you-miss. Lacks home-run speed to pull away from the pack. Is not a nuanced pass protector — developing eyes and awareness. Could improve sustain. Inconsistent catcher. Has missed games in three of the last four seasons with knee, ankle and back injuries and will struggle to make it through a season healthy.

Future: A competitive, inside power runner with a hard, upright running style that could lend itself to injuries in the pros. Could carve a role as a solid backup and function well between the tackles in a rotation.

Draft projection: Fifth- to sixth-round pick.

Scout's take: "He had a strong showing at the Senior Bowl. I like his eyes and patience. He's a chunk runner. You're not going to see him break away, but he is what plays in the league. He has make-it qualities."

RB DEVONTA FREEMAN, #8 (JUNIOR)

FLORIDA STATE   ▶ GRADE: 5.57

Ht: 5-8 1/4 | Wt: 206 | Sp: 4.58 | Arm: 29 3/8 | Hand: 9 5/8

History: Miami-area prep who rushed for 308 yards in the 2010 Class 6A state championship game in his only year as a starter. Rushed for 2,208 yards and 26 touchdowns as a senior before enrolling early at Florida State in January 2011. Began his freshman year fourth on the Seminoles' depth chart, but rose to the starting tailback role in the second half of the season due to injuries. Played in 12 games (seven starts) and rushed 120 times for 579 yards (4.8-yard average) and eight touchdowns with 15 receptions for 111 yards (7.4) and zero touchdowns. Recorded the fifth-most rushing yards for a true freshman in FSU history. Was hampered late in the year after aggravating a previous back injury. Began '12 as the backup tailback and took over the starting job down the stretch, appearing in 14 games (five starts) and tallying 111-660-8 (5.9) on the ground and 10-86-0 (8.6) receiving. Broke out in '13, earning All-ACC honors after becoming the first FSU player to reach the 1,000-yards mark since Warrick Dunn in 1996. Started all 14 games for the national champions, amassing 173-1,016-14 (5.9) rushing and 22-278-1 (12.6) receiving. Scored at least one touchdown in each of his last 10 games, including a three-yard score against Auburn in the BCS National Championship.

Strengths: Well-built with a compact frame. Very good eyes and lateral agility in the hole — shimmies through small spaces and can create yardage where there is none. Squares his shoulders to the line and runs efficiently. Good lower-body strength, surprising power and superb balance. Tough and runs hard. Catches outside his frame and can make the difficult catch. Strong and nifty after the catch. Reliable in pass protection. Terrific competitor. Extremely durable and never missed a game. Works at his craft and is a student of the game.

Weaknesses: Lacks ideal size and power for a bellcow back and does not run heavily between the tackles. Does not possess home-run speed. Ran behind one of the most talented offensive lines in college football in an offense stacked with talent. Has been nagged by back injuries.

Future: Compactly built, downhill slasher with the agility and balanced skill set to emerge as a workhorse back. Earned the top assignment in a very talented backfield and carries a similar build, running style and all-around utility as San Francisco 49ers 2005 third-round pick Frank Gore. Has innate run skills and a nose for finding the end zone. Could prove to be a better pro than college player.

Draft projection: Second- to third-round pick.

Scout's take: "No. 8 is short, but he is really

talented. He's too small to be a bellcow. He played around 205, but he can be at least 215. He has a nice bubble (butt) on him and his lower body is solid. There's no dancing with him — he just hits it hard. I like his running style. It will play well at our level."

RB TYLER GAFFNEY, #25

STANFORD ▶ GRADE: 5.23
Ht: 5-11 1/2 | Wt: 220 | Sp: 4.49 | Arm: 30 1/4 | Hand: 9

History: His father, Gene, was a pitcher for the University of San Diego in the early 1980s. Was a four-sport athlete as a prep in San Diego, participating in football, baseball, basketball and track. On the gridiron, he had 5,547 rushing yards and 99 touchdowns during his high school career. Moved on to Stanford, where he double-majored in sociology and psychology while playing both football and baseball. Saw action in 12 games as a true freshman for the Cardinal in 2009 and rushed 22 times for 87 yards (4.0-yard average) and one touchdown with two receptions for 39 yards (19.5) and no touchdowns. Backed up current Arizona Cardinals RB Stepfan Taylor in '10 and played in 10 games, carrying 60-255-4 (4.3) and catching 3-60-2 (20.0). Missed three games due to an ankle injury. Again backed up Taylor in '11 and tallied 74-449-7 (6.1) on the ground and 12-79-1 (6.6) receiving. Meanwhile, he was a three-year starting outfielder for Stanford's nationally ranked baseball team, batting .301 with a .406 on-base percentage. Was selected by the Pittsburgh Pirates in the 24th round of the '12 draft and elected to pursue a professional baseball career. Spent that summer with the Class-A State College Spikes in the New York-Penn League and hit .297 in 38 games. After the one-year hiatus from football, he returned in '13 for both his senior season and to complete his degree — and was a starting running back for the first time. Amassed 330-1,709-21 (5.2) on the ground and 15-86-1 (5.7) receiving in 14 starts. Rushed a school-record 45 times vs. Oregon.

Strengths: Excellent size. Effective inside runner. Nice vision and patience. Runs behind his pads — churns his legs through contact and fights for extra yards. Good hands as a receiver out of the backfield. Highly competitive. Tough and durable. Well-conditioned athlete — showed he could handle a heavy workload after a year away from the gridiron (averaged 24 carries per game). Very solid in pass protection. Recorded a 6.78-second 3-cone

time at the Combine, finishing second among backs.

Weaknesses: Tight-hipped and straight-linish. Limited twitch and wiggle. Gears down to cut. Average quickness to and through the hole. Runs duck-footed and lacks breakaway speed — tracked down from behind. Has split his time and training between two sports.

Future: Gaffney, who doubles as a baseball player, rejoined the Cardinal football team after a one-year stint in Class A. Did not skip a beat, shouldering the load as a feature back and putting himself back on the NFL radar by showing inside running skills as a big, athletic, downhill back willing to grind out the tough yards. Has the determination and competitiveness to earn a backup role for a power-running team.

Draft projection: Fourth- to fifth-round pick.

RB MARION GRICE, #1

ARIZONA STATE ▶ GRADE: 5.14
Ht: 6-0 | Wt: 208 | Sp: 4.60e | Arm: 32 | Hand: 9 1/4

History: The Houston-area prep wanted to go to Texas A&M, but an unfulfilled academic requirement left him without a four-year option. Accepted an offer to play from Blinn Junior College (Texas). While in high school in 2008, he picked up misdemeanor assault and criminal mischief charges when he was part of a group that fired paintball guns at bystanders from a moving truck. Appeared in 10 games for Blinn in 2010 and ran 160 times for 1,169 yards (7.3-yard average) and 17 touchdowns with eight receptions for 90 yards (11.3) and zero touchdowns. Was a second-team NJCAA All-America selection in '11 after carrying 174-1,052-16 (6.0) and catching 14-171-2 (12.2) — earning him an invitation from Arizona State. Despite not starting any games for ASU in '12, he crossed the goal line 19 times (11 rushing, eight receiving) — leading FBS running backs in receiving touchdowns. Rushed 103-679-11 (6.6) and caught 41-425-8 (10.4). In late December, his close friend, Joshua Woods, was murdered over a new pair of Air Jordans; eight days later, he returned to the Sun Devils for their Kraft Fight Hunger Bowl appearance against Navy and was named the game's MVP, rushing 14-159-2. Was a Hornung Award Finalist in '13, amassing 191-996-14 (5.2) on the ground, 50-438-6 (8.8) receiving and 21-507-0 (24.1) returning kickoffs. Was the only player in the country to surpass the 400-yards mark in each of those categories. Averaged 176.5 all-purpose yards per game, ranking third in FBS. Missed the final three games with a left leg injury. Had 39 touchdowns in his 24-game ASU career and did not lose a fumble in 406 touches.

Strengths: Good balance and body control. Has loose ankles and very good lateral agility. Explosive one-cut ability. Displays vision and elusiveness in the open field. Sees the cutback and weaves in and out of traffic. Has some wiggle to shake tacklers in space. Good receiver — bursts into routes, adjusts to passes and has soft hands. Fumbled only once the last two seasons. Blue-collar work ethic. Solid character.

Weaknesses: Has a lean, narrow frame. Needs to bulk up and get stronger. Not equipped to pound between the tackles — gets tall inside and doesn't push the pile (soft on contact). Weak tackle-breaker who cannot be counted on for yards after contact. Can become a more disciplined route runner. Questionable awareness in pass protection. Statistical production belies inconsistency.

Future: Fluid perimeter runner/receiver with playmaking ability, though his game is rough around the edges, requiring more polish and attention to detail. Profiles as a third-down/change-of-pace back, but his football intelligence has to catch up with his physical gifts in order to earn trust he can handle the role.

Draft projection: Fifth- to sixth-round pick.

Scout's take: "I don't know what you do with him. He has good hands, but not great speed or make-you-miss. He's a one-cut runner with average run strength. I worry how much he'll be able to retain. He's not a blocker. He's going to get overdrafted. People might get enamored with his stats. I think it's inflated from the competition. I kept watching more and more trying to see it. I couldn't get excited about him."

FB-H-BACK RYAN HEWITT, #85

STANFORD   ▶ GRADE: 5.05

Ht: 6-4 1/8 | Wt: 246 | Sp: 4.91 | Arm: 32 | Hand: 9 1/4

History: His last name is pronounced "HUE-it." The Colorado prep was coached by nine-year NFL WR Dave Logan, who played for Cleveland and Denver. Was a three-year letterwinner at tight end and also lettered in basketball. Was recruited by Stanford as a tight end, but mainly lined up at fullback during his collegiate career. After a redshirt year in 2009, he appeared in 13 games in '10; had

two receptions for 16 yards (8.0-yard average) and zero touchdowns and did not have any rushing attempts. Was the primary blocking fullback for Stepfan Taylor in '11, rushing 10-35-0 (3.5) and catching 34-282-5 (8.3) in 13 games (11 starts). Finished third on the team in receptions as a top target for Andrew Luck. Of his 44 offensive touches, 30 either resulted in a first down or touchdown. Appeared in 12 games (7 starts) in '12 and carried 13-32-1 (2.5) and caught 14-129-1 (9.2), again serving as Taylor's primary fullback. Missed the first two games of the season with an ankle injury. Was the primary blocking back for Tyler Gaffney in '13, rushing 5-8-0 (1.6) and receiving 9-46-0 (5.1) in 13 games (11 starts). Missed an early season game with a bruised knee.

Strengths: Fairly quick out of his stance. Attacks with urgency. Understands angles and positioning. Can block on the move. Good hands — catches away from his body and had 34 receptions as a sophomore. Lined up in multiple spots and has special-teams experience. Cares about the game and puts the work in. Clean character.

Weaknesses: Needs to bulk up and get stronger. Athletic ability and speed are just adequate. Marginal value as a runner. Fairly straight-linish. Limited explosion and body power as a lead blocker. Tweener traits.

Future: Smart, jack of all trades, master of none with a tweener skill set. Will go as far as his versatility, blocking, hands and special-teams utility carry him and could be best in a "move" blocking role.

Draft projection: Priority free agent.

RB JEREMY HILL, #33 (SOPH-3)

LSU   ▶ GRADE: 5.65

Ht: 6-0 5/8 | Wt: 233 | Sp: 4.66 | Arm: 32 5/8 | Hand: 10 3/8

History: Was a top Louisiana prep running back in 2010, rushing 302 times for 2,260 yards (7.5-yard average) and 36 touchdowns en route to being named to the Parade All-America team. Before graduating high school, though, he was arrested on sexual assault charges. Sat out the 2011 season and enrolled at Louisiana State early the following year, participating in spring drills. Made his collegiate debut in the fall of '12 and played in 11 games (five starts), rushing 142-755-12 (5.3) and catching 8-73-0 (9.1). Did not play in LSU's first two games and carried the ball just 13 times through six weeks, but went on to lead the Tigers in rushing. Started the

final five games; in his first college start, he became the first true LSU freshman to rush for 100 yards against Alabama (29-107-1). Ran afoul of the law again in April '13, as he was arrested and charged with simple battery after being caught on video punching a man outside a bar near campus. After pleading guilty to a predatory attack for the second time in 15 months, he was given a six-month suspended jail sentence and two years of probation; as a result, he is on probation until July 12, 2015. Was suspended by coach Les Miles for the '13 opener and for the first quarter of LSU's ensuing game. Once he returned to the field, he registered one of the top seasons in school history, rushing 203-1,401-16 (6.9) and catching 18-181-0 (10.1) in 12 games (11 starts). His rushing total was the second-best single-season mark in school history, while his average yards per carry established a SEC record (eclipsing Garrison Hearst's 6.8 in 1992). Tied a school mark with seven 100-yard games, including a 28-216-2 performance in the Outback Bowl. Concluded his two-year college career with 2,410 all-purpose yards and no fumbles lost.

Strengths: Outstanding size. Good initial quickness — gets rolling downhill in a hurry. Quick feet for a bigger back. Slashes through holes. Spins off tackles and picks up yards after contact. Shows good hands in limited exposure — effective short receiver. Productive in a pro-style power offense — averaged nearly 7 yards per carry as a sophomore.

Weaknesses: Shows some hip tightness and does not string moves together. Can do a better job running behind his pads between the tackles — enters the hole upright, negating his ability to move the pile. Developing vision. Gears down to cut laterally and slide to another hole. Average second-level burst. Lacks elite top-end speed to pull away from the pack and can be tracked down before reaching the edge. Was not used extensively as a receiver and did not run a variety of routes. Was contained by Alabama. Has a 29-inch vertical jump. Character, maturity and stability must be investigated thoroughly.

Future: Big, thickly built, athletic slasher with an overinflated sense of his abilities and character red flags, which could cause some teams to shy away. Fits best in a downhill scheme and has potential to be a 20-carry back in the NFL, but must run to his size more consistently and prove his unstable behavior is behind him.

Draft projection: Second- to third-round pick.

Scout's take: "If you can get him in the third round, you'd be happy. It's hard to make it when you don't have the speed. Green Bay would like Hill a lot. That is their kind of guy. He's a little bit like the big kid the Steelers took from Michigan State (Le'Veon Bell) in the second (round) last year. Bell was a better kid and more well-rounded, I thought."

RB CARLOS HYDE, #34

OHIO STATE   ▶ GRADE: 6.25
Ht: 5-11 7/8 | Wt: 230 | Sp: 4.55e | Arm: 32 | Hand: 9 5/8

History: Grew up in Cincinnati before moving to Florida after his freshman year of high school. Participated in football, basketball and track as a prep — rushing for 1,653 yards and 16 touchdowns as a senior. Committed to Ohio State, but didn't qualify academically, so he spent the 2009 fall semester at Fork Union Military Academy (Virginia) in order to raise his ACT score. Followed in the footsteps of Eddie George, who also started at Fork Union before heading to Ohio State. Arrived in Columbus in 2010 and played in seven games as a true freshman, rushing 24 times for 141 yards (5.9-yard average) and zero touchdowns. Started the first three games of the '11 season due to a teammate's suspension; played in 13 games overall and carried 106-566-6 (5.3) and caught 10-73-0 (7.3). Played in 10 games (eight starts) in '12 and piled up 185-970-16 (5.2) on the ground and 8-51-1 (6.4) receiving. Missed two games with a sprained MCL in his right knee. Was involved in an assault investigation during the summer of '13; was a "person of interest" after an altercation with a woman at a bar. Charges were dismissed, but he was suspended for OSU's first three games for conduct not representative of the football program. Was a force upon returning to the gridiron, amassing 208-1,521-15 (7.3) rushing and 16-147-3 (9.2) receiving in 11 games (nine starts). Averaged 156.1 rushing yards per game in conference play and ended his career with nine consecutive 100-yard games. Became the first 1,000-yard running back during Urban Meyer's tenure as a head coach. Did not start against Illinois due to an academics issue, but came off the bench to put on a 24-246-4 performance out of the backfield — along with a touchdown catch. Also had a 226-yard game against Michigan, the most ever for an OSU runner in that storied rivalry. Named the Big Ten's Running Back of the Year.

Strengths: Very well built — looks every bit the part. Outstanding size, explosive power and run strength — can be his own blocker and create his own holes. Punishes linebackers running downhill and almost always falls forward. Superb contact balance and finishing strength — does not go down easily and can barrel through arm tackles. Extremely powerful short-yardage/goal-line runner. Gets better with a lather as the game progresses. Took over the game in the fourth quarter vs. Northwestern (2013) and willed team to victory. Surprisingly quick in short spaces and can plant hard and go. Is solid in pass protection and can stonewall blitzers in their tracks. Good awareness and anticipation to react to stunts and adjust to movement. Soft hands-catcher. Plucked the ball very naturally at his pro day workout.

Weaknesses: Lacks elite breakaway speed. Average elusiveness and make-you-miss. Is still learning what it means to really work and be a pro — entered program with some underachiever traits early in career. Weight fluctuated earlier in his career and needs to pay more attention to nutrition. Has missed at least two games in three seasons.

Future: A big, strong, powerful, NFL-caliber back who carried the Buckeyes' offense as a senior and proved he can be a workhorse. Solid all-around, chunk runner well-built for the physicality of the AFC North.

Draft projection: Top-50 pick.

Scout's take: "The top back for me is at Ohio State. He is an NFL feature back. He has it all. His only negative is that he does not have top, finishing speed, but (heck), he is making chunks all the time. That is all you get in the league — tight quarters, put your shoulder down and plow. He has better run skills that Trent Richardson coming out. I thought Richardson was limited with his vision. Hyde is a power guy. He was softened up by the two-back attack they used a lot his sophomore year. When they went to more of a pure power run game his junior year, there wasn't anyone who could stop him. He is a gamer."

RB STORM JOHNSON, #8 (JUNIOR)

CENTRAL FLORIDA   ▶ GRADE: 5.34
Ht: 5-11 5/8 | Wt: 209 | Sp: 4.59 | Arm: 32 | Hand: 9 1/2

History: Full name is Westleigh Storm Johnson. The Atlanta-area prep earned all-state honors in 2009 after rushing for 1,937 yards and 31 touchdowns. Originally committed to LSU before signing with Miami. The Hurricanes planned to redshirt him in 2010, but then-coach Randy Shannon wound up using him in 10 games as a true freshman. Rushed nine times for 119 yards (13.2-yard average) and one touchdown with nine kickoff returns for 194 yards (21.6) and zero touchdowns. Had the team's longest run of the year, a 71-yard touchdown scamper against South Florida. Did not play in three games due to coach's decisions. In April '11, he was one of several Miami players involved in an incident at a UM residential hall that resulted in police being called. He was reportedly going to be suspended by new coach Al Golden for the season opener before electing to transfer to Central Florida. After sitting out the '11 season due to transfer rules, he returned to the field in '12 and carried 113-507-4 (4.5) and caught 10-20-0 (2.0). Appeared in 13 games, starting five of UCF's first six games. Had only 21 carries the rest of the year, missing one game and not touching the ball in two others. Broke out in '13, tallying 213-1,139-14 (5.3) on the ground and 30-260-3 (8.7) receiving in 13 starts. Had five 100-yard games, including a 20-124-3 performance against Baylor in the Tostitos Fiesta Bowl.

Strengths: Excellent size and strength to run between the tackles. Has quick feet, gets out of the blocks well and shows some giddyup for a bigger back. Nice leg drive and forward lean. Surprisingly slippery. Good open-field ability — displays nice peripheral vision and elusiveness to run to daylight. Creates after the catch — can turn a screen or dump-off into a long gain. Scheme-versatile.

Weaknesses: Has tight hips and struggles to string moves together. Lacks elite top-end speed — cannot gain the edge or pull away from the pack. Gears down and chops his steps to cut. Too often tripped up by ankle tackles. Pass protection needs work. Shaky ball security — eight fumbles in 366 carries 2012-13 (always totes in right hand). Only one year as a feature back.

Future: A Miami transfer, Johnson is a big, nifty-footed runner with enough run strength and burst to be productive in a downhill power scheme or as a one-cut zone runner. However, he will have to take better care of the football and make strides in pass protection to earn carries.

Draft projection: Fourth- to fifth-round pick.

Scout's take: "I was not as wowed by him as I thought I would be. I thought he was an effective, middle-round type. He's big, but he should play stronger. He has some physicality to his play. He's an upright, high pad-level runner between the tackles. He's not really strong inside. When he is on the move, he is a physical runner."

RB HENRY JOSEY, #20 (JUNIOR)

MISSOURI ▶ GRADE: 5.08
Ht: 5-8 1/8 | Wt: 194 | Sp: 4.43 | Arm: 30 1/4 | Hand: 9 1/2

History: Has a 2-year-old son, Henry Jr. Was a two-way player as a Texas prep at running back and defensive back. Over his final two high school seasons, he ran for 2,636 yards and 35 touchdowns. Saw action in all 13 games (one start) for Missouri as a true freshman in 2010, rushing 76 times for 437 yards (5.8-yard average) and five touchdowns with four receptions for 19 yards (4.8) and zero touchdowns. Entered the '11 season third on the depth chart, but moved into the starting lineup in Week Three and went on a tear. In that contest against Western Illinois, he played just one half — and put on a 14-263-3 performance. Was fifth in the nation in rushing when he suffered a horrific left knee injury against Texas November 12, tearing his patellar tendon, ACL, MCL and both the lateral and medial menisci — requiring three operations. For the season, he amassed 145-1,168-9 (8.1) on the ground, 10-91-0 (9.1) receiving and 6-149-0 (24.8) returning kickoffs in 10 games (eight starts). The 8.1-yards per carry set a school record. Had follow-up surgeries in March and May of '12 and spent that season rehabilitating the knee. After missing nearly 22 months of action, he returned to the gridiron in '13 and picked up where he left off — starting 14 games and piling up 174-1,166-16 (6.7) on the ground and 10-65-1 (6.5) receiving. Became just the second tailback in Mizzou history to record two 1,000-yard campaigns. Had five rushes of 50-plus yards, including a 68-yard TD sprint against Murray State in his first game back and an 86-yard run vs. Kentucky.

Strengths: Quick-footed and agile — smooth handling. Nice one-cut ability and burst through the hole. Good long speed. Averaged 7.4 yards per carry his last two seasons. Did not fumble as a junior. Well-liked and highly respected by teammates and coaches. Exhibited mental toughness persevering through injury.

Weaknesses: Durability is a concern — is small-framed and not built to withstand the constant pounding of the pro game. Limited run strength (not a pile mover). Exposes himself to some violent hits. Was used sparingly as a receiver and returner. Benefited from wide splits and light boxes.

Future: Short, darting, change-of-pace zone runner who will have to carve a niche as a third-down back. With a son to support and the memory of a gruesomely severe knee injury in 2011 (torn ACL, MCL, meniscus and patellar tendon), departed school early despite tepid draft projections. Is the type you root for, but will have to prove his chops as a receiver and pass protector to stick.

Draft projection: Late draftable pick.

RB-KR TRE MASON, #21 (JUNIOR)

AUBURN ▶ GRADE: 5.80
Ht: 5-8 1/2 | Wt: 207 | Sp: 4.49 | Arm: 30 | Hand: 9

History: His father, Vincent "DJ Maseo" Mason, is a member of the Grammy Award-winning hip hop group De La Soul. Was a top Florida prep running back, rushing for 1,643 yards and 24 touchdowns as a senior in 2010. Played in 12 games as a true freshman for Auburn in '11, rushing 28 times for 166 yards (5.9-yard average) and one touchdown while returning 24 kickoffs for 633 yards (26.4) and one touchdown. Led the SEC in kickoff return average. Won the kickoff return job in camp and scored on a 97-yard scamper in his collegiate debut. After seeing limited action down the stretch, including losing his job as the kick returner, he was forced into a prominent role in the Chick-fil-A Bowl after starter Michael Dyer was suspended — and responded with a 9-64-1 performance against Virginia. Did not play in one game (coach's decision). Had a much larger role in '12, splitting time at running back and rushing 171-1,002-8 (5.9) and catching 7-86-0 (12.3) in 12 games (five starts). Was the first non-QB to lead Auburn in total offense since Bo Jackson in 1985. Had a breakout campaign in '13, piling up 317-1,816-23 (5.7) on the ground, 12-163-1 (13.6) receiving and 15-395-1 (26.3) returning kickoffs in 14 games (12 starts). Was a Heisman Trophy finalist, breaking Bo Jackson's single-season school mark with his SEC-high rushing yardage total. Also set school single-year records for all-purpose yards (2,374) and rushing touchdowns in winning SEC Offensive Player of the Year honors. Over Auburn's final three games against Alabama, Missouri and Florida State, he racked up 663 yards on the ground — including a memorable 46-304-4 affair against Mizzou in the SEC Championship Game. Followed up that performance with 195 rushing yards vs. Florida State, the most ever for a running back in a BCS Championship game.

Strengths: Low center of gravity and pad level. Quick out of the blocks. Good vision to pick and slide. Can jump-cut abruptly and change the angle of pursuit. Darts through holes — excellent stop-and-start quickness. Spins off contact. Forward lean. Runs bigger than his size and finishes runs. Flashes good hands and creativity as a short receiver in limited exposure. Trustworthy in pass protection — faces up rushers. Has kickoff-return experience and has shown he can take it the distance. Proved capable of handling a heavy workload and played big in big games against top competition. Has a 38 1/2-inch vertical jump.

Weaknesses: Lacks ideal size and could stand to bulk up to withstand a pounding. At times dances more than he should instead of taking what the defense gives. Seldom used as a receiver out of the backfield and could sharpen his route running. Can take better care of the football — eight fumbles the last two seasons. Durability could be an issue given his running style. Played in an up-tempo, power-spread system and benefited from light boxes, fatigued defenses and a strong offensive line.

Future: The SEC Player of the Year, Mason is a compactly built, nifty-footed runner with a balanced skill set to merit 20 touches per game at the next level. Fits in multiple schemes and has the chops to make an impact as a rookie.

Draft projection: Second- to third-round pick.

Scout's take: "I like that little back. I put him at the bottom of 2. He was the most complete back that I came across. He has return ability. I think he is a good inside runner. He's not a big dude, but he runs hard, has quick feet and good pad level. I'm not sure he has elite long speed. He catches the ball well and blocks pretty good. I never saw the guy make that many mistakes — that is what I liked. He showed consistency and versatility — he never has to come out of a game."

RB-CB-RS JERICK McKINNON, #1

GEORGIA SOUTHERN ▶ GRADE: 5.37
Ht: 5-8 7/8 | Wt: 209 | Sp: 4.39 | Arm: 30 1/4 | Hand: 8 5/8

History: His brother, Lester Norwood, won four letters as a free safety at Florida. Was an all-state quarterback as an Atlanta-area prep, lettering in both football and track. As a senior, he passed for over 1,500 yards and ran for more than 1,300. As a true freshman

for Georgia Southern in 2010, he played in 10 games (including one start at quarterback) and rushed 109 times for 495 yards (4.5-yard average) and three touchdowns and completed 3-of-9 pass attempts (33.3 percent) for 24 yards with zero touchdowns and one interception. Did not play in five games. In '11, he saw action in 13 games (starting six times out of the A-back position and once at tailback) and scored touchdowns running, throwing and receiving. Carried 80-537-7 (6.7), passed 3-6-37-1-0 (50.0) and caught 6-127-1 (21.2). Also had two interceptions and a 41-yard kickoff return in an FCS playoff game against Maine. Was utilized on defense in GSU's three playoff games, recording four tackles at cornerback. Did not play in one game due to an undisclosed injury. Broke out in '12, starting 14 games — two at tailback, one at A-back, one at B-back and the final 10 at quarterback. Amassed 269-1,817-20 (6.8) on the ground, 20-49-597-7-3 (40.8) through the air and 1-15-0 receiving. Rushed for 316 yards against Central Arkansas, the second-highest single-game total in school history (Adrian Peterson, 333 in 1999). Appeared in 10 games (nine starts) in '13, recording 161-1,050-12 (6.5) rushing, 8-17-171-4-1 (47.1) passing, 3-23-0 (7.7) receiving and 3-33-0 (11.0) returning kickoffs. Started five games at quarterback, two at the A-back position and two at the B-back spot. In GSU's first-ever victory over a BCS school, he ran for 9-125-1 against Florida. Missed a late-season game with an ankle injury. Concluded his college career with 3,899 rushing yards, the third-highest total in school annals.
Strengths: Very good athlete. Outstanding weight-room strength — bench-presses twice his weight and squats three times it. Tough runner — slams hard inside and usually falls forward. Good versatility. Superb worker. Efficient cut blocker. Led all backs at the Combine with 32 bench-press reps. Has a 40 1/2-inch vertical jump.
Weaknesses: On the short side. Runs a bit upright and hesitant. Average burst to the perimeter. Not a creative, make-you-miss runner. Very limited career receiving production (10 career catches). Not stout in pass protection.
Future: Adjusted from a triple-option quarterbacking role as a junior to a tailback role as a senior and possesses the athletic ability to warrant a chance as a change-of-pace back in the pros. Could even be tried

as a return man and cornerback, where he began his college career. Would benefit from focusing on one position and will require some time to develop. Displays some similarties to Chicago Bears 1999 fifth-round pick Jerry Azumah.
Draft projection: Fourth- to fifth-round pick.
Scout's take: "That was my sleeper. He was an unknown. He woke everyone up at the Combine. I still think he's raw, but he's got too much talent to work with. He's a hard worker. It's important to him. He's a guy, when it gets closer, that I'd really like to figure out where he's going to land."

FB TREY MILLARD #33

OKLAHOMA   ▶ GRADE: 5.12
Ht: 6-2 3/8 | Wt: 247 | Sp: 4.75e | Arm: 31 | Hand: 9 1/8

History: Last name is pronounced "MILL-ard." Was OU's primary fullback as a true freshman in '10, rushing 24 times for 74 yards (3.1-yard average) and three touchdowns with 16 receptions for 135 yards (8.4) and one touchdown in 14 games (two starts). Earned all-Big 12 honors in '11 after recording 24-169-2 (7.0) rushing and 13-127-1 (9.8) receiving in 13 games (three starts). The fullback had a career-long 61-yard touchdown run at Kansas State. Had 63 touches in '12, tallying 33-198-0 (6.0) on the ground and 30-337-4 (11.2) receiving in 13 games (eight starts). Had a career-best receiving day against Texas, catching 5-119-1 — including a 73-yard reception. Was in the midst of a solid '13 campaign when he tore his left ACL October 26, necessitating season-ending surgery. It marked the first time he missed collegiate action. In OU's first eight games (five starts), he had rushed 17-97-1 (5.7) and caught 11-78-1 (7.1). Earned all-conference honors for the third straight year. Concluded his career with 32 special teams tackles. Ran for the first time since knee surgery in February '14. Team captain.
Strengths: Outstanding size. Hits with some thump and is an efficient lead blocker. Nice run skills — shows vision, patience and subtle moves to avoid direct contact. Soft hands. Adjusts well to the ball and possesses better body control and agility than a traditional iso-lead blocking fullback. Blue-collar worker. Leads by example. Quietly competitive. Determined short-yardage runner capable of finding a crease and slamming through the line. Has a special-

teams temperament (has delivered knockout shots). Solid all-around production. Versatile, lines up all over the field (fullback, tailback, in the slot) and does everything well (can run, block, catch and cover kicks). Very intelligent and football smart.

Weaknesses: Limited burst, change of direction and short-area explosion — one-speed runner with no gear change. Average power and tackle-breaking ability. Shows some tightness as a route runner. Not a true hammer as a lead blocker and does not jolt defenders on contact. Might not be 100 percent as a rookie following ACL surgery.

Future: A versatile jack-of-all-trades, Milllard brings the most value as a core special-teams contributor. Is best suited for a role as a fullback in a matchup-based offense where he could fill a variety of roles. Has been very reliable and durable throughout his career, but late October ACL injury could still require some rehabilitation as a rookie and could affect his draft standing.

Draft projection: Priority free agent.

Scout's take: "The highest graded player (Oklahoma has) is the fullback this year. He's a starter in the league. He's okay. He has nice hands. He's a good enough athlete and tough and all that. Fullbacks just don't get drafted highly any more. They go 5 to 7 if they are any good. It's become an obsolete position in the league."

RB ADAM MUEMA, #4 (JUNIOR)

SAN DIEGO STATE   ▶ GRADE: 5.09

Ht: 5-9 5/8 | Wt: 202 | Sp: 4.55e | Arm: 29 7/8 | Hand: 9 3/4

History: Last name is pronounced "MOO-eh-ma." Suffered a horrific injury at a high school graduation party in May 2010 while defending a friend's parent, as an assailant struck him in the face with a bat. His injuries required 36 stitches, his orbital bone was fractured, and when the vision in his left eye began to deteriorate it was discovered he had a macular hole in the retina of the eye. Doctors performed surgery to place a gas bubble behind his eye, allowing the hole to heal. Went to San Diego State and redshirted in '10. Backed up current Denver RB Ronnie Hillman in '11, playing in six games (one start) and rushing 42 times for 253 yards (6.0-yard average) and three touchdowns with two receptions for three yards (1.5) and one touchdown. Did not play in the season's first seven games. Was pressed into service as a starter late in the year against Boise

State and responded with a 13-119-2 effort in his first college start. Moved into the starting lineup in '12 and tallied 237-1,458-16 (6.2) on the ground and 9-147-1 (16.3) receiving in 13 games. Despite being limited by hamstring and ankle injuries in '13, he became the fourth Aztec running back to put up consecutive 1,000-yard seasons, amassing 256-1,244-15 (4.9) rushing and 18-98-0 (5.4) receiving in 13 games. Concluded his SDSU career with 13 100-yard games in 27 starts, including four 200-yard efforts — a figure surpassed in school history only by Marshall Faulk. Went to the Combine and left early, saying he believed that God said the Seattle Seahawks would select him in May's draft. After leaving, he wasn't heard from for a few days until he showed up at the Florida facility where he had been preparing for Indy. He was reportedly still dressed in his combine gear and had been at the Fort Lauderdale airport for three straight days. He has since been dropped by his agent and returned to California.

Strengths: Has a strong, compact build. Good vision, quickness, agility and short-area burst — makes subtle moves and can sort his way through tight spaces, find small creases and make the first tackler miss. Sets up runs and has good lower-body power to kick through arm tackles. Runs hard with a low center of gravity and does not go down easy. Good receiving skills and open-field running vision to create after the catch. Outstanding production.

Weaknesses: Average size. Lacks bellcow power and run strength ideally suited to carry a full workload. Likes to bounce a lot and press the edges. Will need more technique work in pass protection. Did not regularly face top competition and will be more challenged by the speed of the NFL game.

Future: A herky-jerky, off-tackle/perimeter runner most ideally suited for a zone ground game such as the Eagles, Seahawks or Packers, Muema could earn a complementary role as a change-of-pace back. Could be a surprise, late-round find if he can find more stability .

Draft projection: Priority free agent.

Scout's take: "That was one of the wilder situations I have encountered at the Combine. They said he was meditating on his bed. He wants to be a free agent and play for the Seahawks. That is the story. I think he was scared to run his 40. He is quicker than fast. He's probably a 4.7 guy."

RB-KR **LADARIUS PERKINS**, #27

MISSISSIPPI STATE ▶ GRADE: 5.23

Ht: 5-7 3/8 | Wt: 195 | Sp: 4.46 | Arm: 31 | Hand: 9 5/8

History: The Mississippi prep played both running back and defensive back. Rushed for 1,915 yards and 29 touchdowns as a senior. Also was a track standout, earning state titles in both the 100 and 200 meters. Originally committed to Auburn before staying home to play for Mississippi State. After sitting out in 2009 as a redshirt, he played in 13 games for the Bulldogs in '10 and rushed 101 times for 566 yards (5.6-yard average) and three touchdowns with nine receptions for 247 yards (27.4) and three touchdowns. Also was used on special teams, recording 14-281-0 (20.0) on kickoffs and 1-16-0 on punts. Backed up Colts RB Vick Ballard in '11 when he played in 13 games and carried 87-422-2 (4.9) and caught 13-59-2 (4.5) to go with 16-363-0 (22.7) on kickoff returns. Moved into the starting lineup in '12 and tallied 205-1,024-8 (5.0) on the ground, 19-160-2 (8.4) receiving and 16-325-0 (20.3) on kickoff returns in 12 starts. Crossed the goal line in each of his first seven starts and had four 100-yard efforts. His 1,509 all-purpose yards were the fifth-highest total in school history. Missed one game with an injured left quad. Sprained an ankle in the '13 season opener and was hobbled by the injury all year, totaling 137-542-2 (4.0) on the ground and 27-248-3 (9.2) receiving in 12 starts. Missed one game due to the ankle injury. Concluded his college career ranking second in school history in all-purpose yards (4,253) and fifth in rushing (2,554). Team captain.

Strengths: Compact and muscular. Strong hips. Quick-footed and shifty. Good acceleration from static start. Short-area burst is best asset. Stops and starts quickly. Darts through holes. Hits another gear when he gets into the second level. Competitive speed. Willing blocker. Led team in all-purpose yards as redshirt freshman. Well-respected with outstanding football and personal character.

Weaknesses: Lacks ideal bulk to handle a heavy workload week to week. Has some hip tightness. Average eyes and instincts. Not a pile mover. Tends to pitter patter instead of pressing the hole. Gears down to cut. Did not put the ball on the ground often, but carries loosely and at times in the wrong hand.

Future: Undersized, competitive, change-of-pace back who was bothered by an ankle injury as a senior, but offers enough of a balanced skill set, including good acceleration, to be a better pro than college player. Showed well at the Combine and evaluators would benefit to revisit junior tape for a better indication of his ability.

Draft projection: Fifth- to sixth-round pick.

FB **JAY PROSCH**, #35

AUBURN ▶ GRADE: 5.10

Ht: 6-0 3/4 | Wt: 256 | Sp: 4.65e | Arm: 30 1/8 | Hand: 10

History: His last name rhymes with "posh." Alabama prep who earned all-state honors at linebacker as a senior and as an offensive lineman as a junior. Played in the Alabama/Mississippi All-Star Game in 2009. Recorded a 440-pound bench press and 590-pound squat in high school. Began his college career at Illinois, where he made the transition to fullback by upping his weight from 245 to 255 while dropping his body fat from 11 percent to nine percent. Played in 13 games (seven starts) for the Illini as a true freshman in 2010, including a start in the season opener. Only touched the ball one time all year — a one-yard reception. Was the primary fullback and a key special teams player in '11, appearing in 12 games (five starts) and rushing twice for nine yards (4.5-yard average) and zero touchdowns while recording 11 special-teams tackles. Did not play in the Kraft Hunger Bowl due to a staph infection in his left knee. After the season, he obtained an NCAA waiver to transfer to Auburn in order to be close to home; his mother, Iris, had been diagnosed with a terminal form of brain cancer (she passed away in September '12). Was Auburn's main fullback in '12, appearing in all 12 games (seven starts) and carrying 12-38-2 (3.2) while catching 5-19-0 (3.8). Played in 14 games in '13, including 11 starts at H-back, but did not have any rushing attempts. Caught 5-95-1 (19.0), including a 56-yard reception vs. Texas A&M. Was a starter on three special teams units despite breaking a thumb during the season.

Strengths: Exceptional weight-room strength. Outstanding peripheral blocking vision — scans wide and locates. Generates power through his lower body and drives defenders out of the hole. Very good hip roll and explosion. Runs his feet on contact. Intense, determined competitor. Good finisher. Is fairly light on his feet for as big and strong as he is. Can create a surge in short-yardage situations and power through the line. Catches the ball easily. Core special teams performer. Outstanding personal and football character — highly respected, team leader. Versatility is a big plus. Very durable.

Weaknesses: Robotic, overly muscled, tightly wound mover. Has very short arms and struggles to lock on and sustain on the move. Marginal elusiveness — gears down to cut. Unsudden route-runner. Limited receiving production / touches.

Future: An old-school, throwback fullback with explosive power to pave the way as an iso-lead blocker and enough speed and athletic ability to carve a niche as a core special teams performer. Valuable pass protector with good hands and short-yardage running power to contribute when needed.

Draft projection: Late draftable pick.

Scout's take: "How many fullbacks get drafted every year? You know exactly what he is. He's stiff. What you see is what you get. ...I am not a fan. There's a chance he gets drafted late. He is a big, good-looking, robotic dude. He stops his feet on blocks and tends to get overextended and doesn't play with a lot of leverage and power. There's not a low of 'wow' to him."

RB SILAS REDD, #25

USC   ▶ GRADE: 5.05

Ht: 5-9 3/4 | Wt: 212 | Sp: 4.69 | Arm: 30 3/4 | Hand: 9

History: The Connecticut prep rushed for 1,924 yards and 25 touchdowns as a senior in 2009. Also participated in basketball and lacrosse. Enrolled at Penn State in January 2010 after graduating a semester early from high school. As a true freshman, he played in 12 games and rushed 77 times for 437 yards (5.7) and two touchdowns, caught four passes for 27 yards (6.8) and zero touchdowns and returned seven kickoffs for 147 yards (21.0) and zero touchdowns. Missed one game due to an undisclosed injury. Late in the campaign, he was cited for disorderly conduct after being caught relieving himself in public at 4:13 a.m. Had a breakout campaign in '11, amassing 244-1,241-7 (5.1) on the ground and 9-40-0 (4.4) receiving in 13 games (11 starts). Had six 100-yard games — including five in succession. An injury to his collarbone and sternum slowed him late in the year. Following the Jerry Sandusky scandal, he was granted immediate eligibility

by the NCAA to transfer to USC without being forced to sit out a season. Arrived on the Southern Cal campus and moved into a co-starter role in '12, appearing in 12 games (six starts) at tailback and tallying 167-905-9 (5.4) rushing and 9-113-1 (12.6) receiving. Was sidelined for one game with a sprained right ankle. Was limited to just six games (four starts) in '13 due to injuries, recording 81-376-1 (4.6) rushing and 10-45-1 (4.5) receiving. Missed most of spring practice after tearing cartilage in his left knee, necessitating arthroscopic surgery. Was on the shelf for the first five games recuperating. After returning to action, he injured his right knee November 9 and missed three of USC's final four games. Between Penn State and USC, he combined for 2,959 rushing yards and 12 career 100-yard games.

Strengths: Good eyes and cutback ability. Is well-built with a yoked-up musculature and very good thickness. Is subtly shifty and nimble enough to sidestep the first tackler and avoid direct hits. Good leg drive — keeps churning on contact and is surprisingly strong for a smallish back. Tough, willing blocker — shows good eyes and awareness in pass protection and seeks to finish.

Weaknesses: Has very small hands and is not a crafty route runner. Lacks burst to take the corner and the breakaway speed to pull away. Bulked up as a senior following left-knee surgery in the spring and lost a half-step. Limited knee extension (does not open his stride). Split time in a rotation and was not a full-time starter at USC.

Future: A one-cut, inside zone runner, Redd is a solid, all-around performer with a No. 2 skill set. Can pick up yardage in chunks and would most ideally be suited for a ground game such as the Seahawks, Eagles or Packers.

Draft projection: Priority free agent.

Scout's take: "Redd is just a guy. He is well put-together. He is a thick dude. He was the highest rated guy I had on the (spring) list going in. He's not a full-time starter there. He plays in a rotation. He's quicker than fast and has balance and enough speed."

RB BISHOP SANKEY, #25 (JUNIOR)

WASHINGTON   ▶ GRADE: 5.55

Ht: 5-9 1/2 | Wt: 209 | Sp: 4.49 | Arm: 31 | Hand: 10

History: The blue-chip prospect from Spokane rushed for 4,355 yards as a prep.

Saw action in 12 games in 2011 as a reserve tailback and special teams player, rushing 28 times for 187 yards (6.7-yard average) and one touchdown. Grabbed six passes for 14 yards (2.3) and zero touchdowns while returning seven kickoffs for 134 yards (19.1). Started 12-of-13 games (all but season opener) in which he played in '12 and produced 289-1,439-16 (5.0), which is the third-highest rushing total in UW history. Hauled in 33-249-0 (7.5) and was the MVP of the MAACO Las Vegas Bowl after setting the school's bowl record with 205 yards rushing and 74 yards receiving. Had a record-breaking '13 season, setting UW single-season mark for rushing yards with 1,870 breaking Corey Dillon's 1996 mark (1,695 yards) and had 37 career rushing touchdowns (Napoleon Kaufman, 34). The Doak Walker Award finalist amassed 327-1,870-20 (5.7) on the ground and scored a rushing touchdown in each game while averaging 143.8 rushing yards per game and hauling in 28-304-1 (10.9) receiving. Team captain.

Strengths: Solid, compact built with good thickness through his lower body. Good vision and balance to pick and slide. Subtle lateral agility to pick, slide and accelerate. Reads his blocks and instinctively runs to daylight. Fluid gate and efficient movement. Runs competitively. Good hands to pull in throws off his body. Was productive with a heavy workload in a pro-style offense. Benchpressed 225 pounds 26 times and blazed a 4.0-second 20-yard shuttle time and 6.75-second 3-cone time.

Weaknesses: Shows some hip tightness. Average explosion, finishing speed and elusiveness. Has shown he can be contained by good defenses. Needs to become a more dependable, physical, fundamentally sound pass protector. Can be tracked from behind and too often is grounded by single-tacklers or tripped up by the ankles. Is not a robust tackle-breaker.

Future: The Pac-12's leading rusher, Sankey is an instinctive, competitive and shifty, low-to-the-ground hard runner. Can be effective as a complementary zone runner capable of moving the chains and picking up chunk yards.

Draft projection: Third- to fourth-round pick.

Scout's take: "I've gotten into some arguments about this one. I think Sankey is legit. My first impression was kind of vanilla. The more you start studying the kinetics and bend and run strength. He has some toughness in him. He is a compact, short, poor man's Maurice Jones-Drew. He's the same kind of back."

RB LACHE SEASTRUNK, #25 (JUNIOR)
BAYLOR ▶ GRADE: 5.28
Ht: 5-9 1/2 | Wt: 201 | 40: 4.51 | Arm: 30 | Hand: 9 1/4

History: First name is pronounced "Lake." Ranked as a Top 5 overall prospect as a Texas prep after rushing for 4,217 yards and scoring 52 total touchdowns. Was also an accomplished track athlete, competing in the 100 meters (personal best 10.33 seconds) and the long jump (21-8). Began his career at Oregon in 2010, where he traveled but did not play and redshirted. It was later discovered that his advisor, Willie Lyles, accepted a $25,000 payment from Oregon after he signed his letter of intent. Oregon was placed on three years probation and lost some scholarships as a result of the NCAA investigation. Decided to transfer because he thought "something was about to go down" at Oregon and because of his grandparents bad health ended up at Baylor. Had to sit out the '11 season due to NCAA transfer rules and lost a year of eligibility. Played in a game for the first time in three years in '12 and was named the Big 12 Offensive Newcomer of the Year. Carried the ball 131 times for 1,012 yards (7.7-yard average) and seven touchdowns in 13 games (six starts) after starting slowly — had only 181 yards after seven contest but amassed 831 yards in his final six contests. Grabbed nine passes for 107 yards (11.9) and one touchdown. Led the Big 12 with 107.0 yards per game in '13 after recording 158-1,177-11 (7.4) on the ground in 11 games (eight starts). Suffered a groin injury against Oklahoma and missed the next two games (Texas Tech, Oklahoma State). Is the first player in Baylor history to top 1,000 yards rushing in multiple seasons. Five of his 19 touchdowns came on plays of longer than 68 yards.

Strengths: Quick-footed and nifty with very good competitive speed to pull away in the open field. Deceptively fast. Keeps his feet churning on contact and can elude the first tackler and power through arm tackles. Runs low to the ground with good lower-body strength. Weaves through traffic and has a knack for hitting cutback lanes. Very good run balance to stop and start. Had the best vertical jump (41½ inches) and broad jump (11'2') of any back at the Combine.

Weaknesses: Does not run big or keep his shoulders squared to the line. Will press and try to do too much — can improve patience and do a better job of letting his blocks develop. Very limited career receiving production. Played in an offense that featured big running lanes and helped inflate his production. Can be tracked down from behind. Beats to the tune of his own drum and can be susceptible to hanger-ons.

Future: Good-sized, productive, zone runner with enough physical traits to warrant consideration as a complementary back. Benefited from an offense featuring a lot of fly sweeps and lateral runs that have not translated well to the NFL game. Overall character will require closer evaluation and can determine draft status.

Draft projection: Fourth- to fifth-round pick.

Scout's take: "He has the speed, but I don't know how tough he is. I don't know how explosive his speed is. He does not play big. I don't think the offense translates well to the NFL game. Do you remember all the yards (Jets 2012 sixth-rounder) Terrance Ganaway had a few years ago? He's out of the league now. The Lyles guy that got him in trouble at Oregon is still with him and is his manager. That scares me."

RB CHARLES SIMS, #5

WEST VIRGINIA   ▶ GRADE: 5.35

Ht: 6-0 | Wt: 214 | Sp: 4.48 | Arm: 31 | Hand: 8 1/4

History: Was a three-star recruit from Houston, who stayed home to play for the Cougars. The true freshman earned the Conference USA Freshman of the Year Award after rushing 132 times for 698 yards (5.3-yard average) and nine touchdowns to lead the squad in yards and touchdowns. Played in all 14 games (nine starts) and caught 70 passes for 759 yards (10.8) and one touchdown — fourth-leading receiver in Cougars high octane offense. Sat out the '10 after being ruled ineligible by the NCAA but was allowed to redshirt. Returned to lead the team in rushing in '11, producing 110-821-9 (7.5) on the ground and contributing 51-575-4 (11.3) as a receiver in 13 games (nine starts). Did not play against North Texas. Was named the team MVP in '12 after tallying a team-high 142-851-11 (6.0) rushing and 37-373-3 (10.1) receiving in only nine starts. Dealt with leg injuries all year, missing the Tulsa and Tulane games (sprained right ankle) and UCLA (groin) in addition to sitting out the second half of three games. Graduated in May of '13 with a health education degree and asked to be released from his scholarship but UH put a number of restrictions on his transfer — no Texas schools, no American Athletic Conference teams (former Big East) and no one on their '13 schedule. Chose West Virginia over California and was named the Big 12 Newcomer of the Year after racking up a team-high 208-1095-11 (5.7) on the ground and tied for team lead in receptions with 45-401-3 (8.9) in 12 starts. Ranked second in the conference with 1,549 all-purpose yards.

Strengths: Quick-footed with first-step suddenness and short-area burst. Fluid and fast — accelerates in a hurry and shows speed to the edge. Explosive one-cut ability — understands how to get downhill. Loose lower body with nice ankle flexion to cut sharply. Flashes ability to spin off contact. Soft hands — catches easily away from his body (had 70 catches as a freshman and averaged more than 10 yards per catch for his career). Creates after the catch. Hardworking and leads by example.

Weaknesses: Does not have an ideal build for the position and durability is a concern — is narrow with a relatively thin lower body. Needs to bulk up. Relatively tall running style. Can do a better job running behind his pads and converting speed to power. Shows some hip tightness. Average tackle breaker (too often grounded by single tacklers). Ran exclusively out of the pistol/shotgun formation. Has very tiny hands and carries loosely at times. Lacks elite, top-end "wow" speed. Blocking is a question mark. Will be a 24-year-old rookie.

Future: Athletic, competitive, tough, upright slasher who is an asset as a receiver — hands rate among the best on a RB in recent years. Cannot project as a bellcow, but offers playmaking ability as part of a tandem in a zone scheme. Speed and durability could determine ultimate draft value.

Draft projection: Third- to fourth-round pick.

Scout's take: "He'll go in the fourth

round probably. The only guys that push themselves up at the Combine with speed are the receivers and cornerbacks. Sims runs tall. He's not a real good blocker. I'm not sure how good his hands are. He's an adequate blocker. He doesn't catch the ball very well. He is a no. 2 back. Those guys are a dime a dozen. Think of all the no. 2's who were free agents or late-round picks. You can find them later in the draft."

RB-FB JEROME SMITH, #45 (JUNIOR)
SYRACUSE ▶ GRADE: 5.05
Ht: 5-11 1/8 | Wt: 220 | Sp: 4.84 | Arm: 30 7/8 | Hand: 9 3/4

History: The Delaware prep saw action in two games in 2010 before surgery on his left shoulder (torn labrum) and receiving a medical redshirt. Returned in '11 and saw action in all 12 games, carrying the ball 37 times for 134 yards (3.6) and one touchdown. Became the starter in '12 and led the team in rushing yards after tallying 227-1,171-3 (5.2) in 13 games (12 starts) — only non-start was Stony Brook when the Orange went with three wide receivers. Set career highs in the Pinstripe Bowl vs. West Virginia with 152 yards on 29 carries. Made all 13 starts in '13 and again led the team in rushing with 200-914-12 (4.6). Caught 17 career passes for 161 yards (9.5) and one touchdowns. Team captain and graduated in December.

Strengths: Compact, muscular build. Functional vision and strength to pound between the tackles. Runs hard and finishes runs. Nice short-area burst. Enough lateral agility to slide away from penetration and bounce. Good leaping ability. Solid personal and football character. Tough and hardworking.

Weaknesses: Average initial quickness. Pedestrian foot speed — pounds the ground and gets tracked down from behind. Tight hips. Gears down to cut. Limited elusiveness. Cannot create his own yardage. Used sparingly as a receiver — just 17 career receptions. Pass-protection technique needs work. Contained by average defenses.

Future: Good-sized, downhill, monotone runner who left school with a year of eligibility remaining despite lacking exceptional athletic traits. Will have to earn his keep as an inside runner, though he faces an uphill battle to earn a spot as a reserve.

Draft projection: Priority free agent.

RB LORENZO TALIAFERRO, #15
COASTAL CAROLINA ▶ GRADE: 5.18
Ht: 6-0 1/4 | Wt: 229 | Sp: 4.58 | Arm: 32 | Hand: 8 3/8

History: The Virginia prep rushed for 1,678 yards and 21 touchdowns as a senior. Spent two seasons at Lackawanna College (Scranton, Pa.), recording 19 carries for 96 yards (5.1-yard average) and one score and nine receptions for 68 yards (7.6) and one touchdown in 10 games in 2010; and 76-431-3 (5.7) rushing, 12-193-4 (16.1) receiving and 22-579-1 (26.3) as a kick returner in 10 contests in '11. Moved to Coastal Carolina for the '12 season and saw action in 12 games (three starts), logging 80-357-4 (4.5) on the ground and 4-38-0 (9.5) through the air. Missed the season opener against North Carolina A&T with an undisclosed injury. Had a monster '13 campaign, earning Big South Offensive Player of the Year honors after leading the conference in rushing and rushing touchdowns with 276-1,729-27 (6.3) while adding 23-153-2 (6.7) as a receiver in 15 starts. The Walter Payton Award finalist set 11 school records and five conference rushing marks. Team captain.

Strengths: Outstanding size. Very good production. Is patient and follows his blocks. Finds creases and is adept navigating through traffic without losing speed — good eyes. Nice spin move. Competes hard. Strong short-yardage producer. Runs hard and usually falls forward. Catches outside his frame. Helps chip in pass protection and is alert to see the blitz. Good football intelligence and awareness.

Weaknesses: Has very small hands. Limited speed and burst to the perimeter. Monotone runner who takes time to get rolling downhill. Much of his production is blocked for him. Plays in a spread offense where he is usually moving laterally at the snap and not stepping downhill. Stiff route runner. Regularly matched up against lesser competition.

Future: A big, small-school producer with a solid all-around skill set to compete for a job as a role player in a zone scheme. Will need to contribute on special teams to earn a spot.

Draft projection: Late draftable pick.

Scout's take: "I didn't know a lot about him before the Senior Bowl. He showed me something. He got out there and competed. He's well-built. I saw some toughness. You saw improvement as the week went along. He's got a chance."

RB-RS DE'ANTHONY THOMAS, #6 (JUNIOR)

OREGON   ▶ GRADE: 5.36

Ht: 5-8 5/8 | Wt: 174 | Sp: 4.44 | Arm: 29 7/8 | Hand: 8 1/8

History: The five-star recruit out of Los Angeles was rated as the top athlete in the county as a prep. Rushed for 1,299 yards on only 114 carries (11.4-yard average) as a senior. Also starred in track, running the fastest 200 meters (20.61 seconds) in the country in the Spring of 2010. Burst onto the collegiate scene in '11, earning Pac-12 Co-Offensive Freshman of the Year and was a first-team Pac-12 kick returner. Saw action in all 14 games (six starts, including the last five), rushing 55 times for 595 yards (10.8-yard average) and seven scores while grabbing 46 passes for 605 yards (13.2) and nine touchdowns. Had a huge impact as a returner with 36 kick returns for 983 yards (27.3) including a 96-yard score against USC and a 93-yard touchdown vs. Washington State. Had only three punt returns for 52 yards (17.3). Was the only player in the nation with 400 or more yards as a rusher, receiver and kick returner. Continued his versatility in '12, becoming the first Oregon player in 47 years to score a touchdown rushing, receiving, returning a punt and a kickoff in the same season in 13 games (nine starts). Was the team's reception leader with 45-445-5 (9.0) while rushing 92-701-11 (7.6) and returning punts 13-222-1 (17.1) and kickoffs 16-389-1 (24.3), including a 94-yard KR touchdown in the Tostitos Fiesta Bowl against Kansas State and a 73-yard PR against Colorado. Also anchored the 4x100-meter relay that advanced to the NCAA Championships for the Ducks track team. Began the '13 campaign as the starting running back before injuring his left ankle on the opening kickoff against California and missing the next three games. Rushed 96-594-8 (6.2), grabbed 22-246-1 (11.2) while leading the team in kickoff returns with 21-513-1 (24.4) and an 86-yard touchdown against Utah in 10 games (five starts). Holds Oregon career records for kickoff return yards (1,885) and punt return average (17.1) .

Strengths: Has legit big-time sprinter's speed with very quick turnover (and is field-fast). Cat-quick to the corner, accelerates very quickly and can easily take the perimeter. Good vision and cutback ability — is patient and follows his blocks. Can tightrope-walk the sideline. Very quick to and through the hole once he sees a crease and can stick his foot in the dirt and go. Catches in stride with ease and can make difficult one-handed snags (see Arizona). Has home-run speed in the return game, with 3 career return TDs. Exceptional pro day performance.

Weaknesses: Very small. Does not play in a conventional-style offense and takes most carries moving laterally. Goes down too easily and looks for a soft landing spot. Lacks the size, strength and toughness to be an every-down back. Alligator-arms the ball in the middle of the field and does not consistently show timed speed. Needs to learn to appreciate the preparation process and would benefit from working more at his craft.

Future: A deluxe, specialty back and potential slot receiver with game-breaking return ability, Thomas can be an explosive mismatch weapon in multiple facets of the game. Diminutive stature will decrease the odds he'll be able to stay healthy in the pros, and his commitment to the game will dictate his future success. Rare speed creates a higher commodity on Draft Day.

Draft projection: Fourth- to fifth-round pick.

Scout's take: "The 'Black Mamba' is like Chris Rainey and Jeff Demps. He is legit fast. He's one of the fastest players I have graded on tape. I still don't know what you do with him. He is fast, but he's small and they don't run a conventional offense. Do you take him as a change-of-pace back? What change-of-pace backs have gone early like that and had any kind of production in the league. There are not many. You better have a plan for him."

RB TERRANCE WEST, #28 (JUNIOR)

TOWSON   ▶ GRADE: 5.37

Ht: 5-9 1/4 | Wt: 225 | Sp: 4.54 | Arm: 31 | Hand: 9 1/8

History: The Baltimore prep was a multi-sport athlete, participating in basketball, baseball and track in addition to football. Spent the 2010 season at Fork Union Military Academy (Virginia) after difficulty qualifying due to his SAT score. Burst onto the collegiate scene in '11 by winning the Jerry Rice Award (top freshman in FCS) and ECAC Offensive Rookie of the Year after rushing 194 times for 1,294 yards (6.7-yard average) and an FCS-leading 29 touchdowns in 11 games (one start). Had five catches for 25 yards (5.0) and did not play in the season opener against Morgan State. Led the Colonial Athletic Association in rushing yards per game (104.6) and scoring (90) in '12 after logging 195-1,046-14 (5.4) while grabbing 5-102-1 (20.4) in 10 games (six starts). Missed the Old Dominion game due to a death in the family. Set the NCAA FCS single season rushing mark and led all of college football in '13 with 413-2,519-41 (6.1) and grabbed 26-258-1 (9.9) in 16 games. Was the CAA Offensive Player of the Year, a finalist for the Walter Payton Award, led the Tigers to the FCS Championship game and set the FCS record for touchdowns in a season with 42. Had 354 yards and five touchdowns against Eastern Illinois in the playoffs. His 84 career rushing touchdowns tied the FCS record, set by Adrian Peterson (Georgia Southern 1998-2001) in only three seasons.

Strengths: Equipped to run between the tackles and withstand a pounding. Good vision — reads and cuts off blocks. Runs with attitude and power — stays behind his pads, churns out yards after contact and finishes runs. Opens up his stride in space and has competitive speed to break long runs. Rare production. Bore a heavy workload and thrived with a lather. Has a nose for the goal line — 83 rushing TDs in three seasons.

Weaknesses: Lacks elite timed speed. Average initial quickness and elusiveness. Tight hips. Can be more cognizant of ball security — tends to swing the ball away from his body and fumbled five times as a junior. Needs to polish his third-down skills, including route running and pass-protection awareness. Running style and college workload do not lend to longevity — tread is worn down from 780 carries in three seasons.

Future: Good-sized, compactly built, highly productive, physical workhorse and program-changer who took Towson to new heights while dominating inferior competition. Has the chops to factor prominently in a power-running scheme, showing the ability to slash and cut, run over defenders and contribute as a receiver.

Draft projection: Fourth-round pick.

Scout's take: "(West) doesn't have a lot of juice in his legs, and he's not proven. He has not had to face Southeastern Conference stacked boxes week in and week out. I do like the way he runs and plays the game. I would take him in the third (round)."

RB JAMES WHITE, #20

WISCONSIN ▶ GRADE: 5.01

Ht: 5-9 1/8 | Wt: 204 | Sp: 4.57 | Arm: 29 1/4 | Hand: 8 1/4

History: Distant cousin of NFL players Santana and Sinorice Moss. The Florida prep also played baseball. Named Big Ten Freshman of the Year in 2010 after leading the team in rushing with 156 carries for 1,052 yards (6.7-yard average) and 14 touchdowns while grabbing 11 passes for 88 yards (8.0) in 12 games. Did not play at Purdue with a left knee injury (sprained MCL). In '11, he saw action in all 14 games and logged 141-713-6 (5.1) on the ground and 15-150-0 (10.0) in the air. Missed most of '12 spring practice with left knee (tear in meniscus) injury. Spent the fall as a backup to Broncos 2013 second-rounder Montee Ball and was the second leading rusher with 125-806-12 (6.4) while grabbing 8-132-1 (16.5) in 14 games. Had 119 rushing yards, four rushing touchdowns and threw a 3-yard touchdown pass in the Big Ten Championship game against Nebraska. Was the Badgers second-leading rusher in '13 after amassing 221-1,444-13 (6.5) in 13 games, including the first 12 starts of his career (only non-start was Ohio State). Also hauled in 39-300-2 (7.7). Helped set the FBS single-season record with 3,052 rushing yards by teammates (Melvin Gordon 1,609). Had 670 career receiving yards, which set the school record for a running back. Had 39 career kickoff returns for 765 yards (19.6-yard average).

Strengths: Controlled mover with a low center of gravity. Good vision, balance and short-area burst. Shifty runner — cuts efficiently and jukes tacklers. Shows competitive speed. Finishes runs. Willing blocker in pass protection. Takes care of the football — fumbled just twice in 754 career touches. Has kickoff-return experience. Tough and competitive. Good football aptitude. Highly respected by teammates and coaches.

Weaknesses: Played in an offense that helped inflate his production. Undersized with exceptionally short arms and small hands. Run strength is just adequate. Limited power to move the pile or bust through tackles. Lacks bulk strength to stymie blitzers. Was never a feature back, splitting carries with Broncos 2013 second-rounder Montee Ball as a junior and Melvin Gordon as a senior.

Future: White had a very productive career despite splitting carries for four years, and offers a balanced enough skill set to factor as a recyclable, complementary, change-of-pace back in the pros.

Draft projection: Priority free agent.

RB JAMES WILDER, #32 (JUNIOR)

FLORIDA STATE   ▶ GRADE: 5.12
Ht: 6-2 5/8 | Wt: 232| Sp: 4.86 | Arm: 32 | Hand: 9 3/4

History: Has a daughter. Is the son of former NFL running back James Wilder, who had a 10-year career with Tampa Bay, Detroit and Washington. Was a five-star prospect and considered the best overall athlete in the country after playing running back and linebacker as a Tampa-area prep. Saw action in 12 games as a true freshman in 2011 as a reserve running back and special teams player, rushing 35 times for 160 yards (4.6-yard average) and one touchdown. Arrested in February of '12 on felony charges of obstructing a law enforcement officer without violence and battery on a law enforcement officer. Pleaded no contest to a misdemeanor charge of resisting arrest without violence in April and was placed on probation and ordered to anger management classes. Spent a week in jail in May after violating his probation. Was part of a running back trio in the fall, logging 110-640-11 (5.8) on the ground in 14 games (started against Duke). FSU had three backs with over 600 yards rushing for the first time since 1984. Was in trouble again in January of '13 after being charged with failure to appear in court because of a suspended license. Totaled 81-563-8 (7.0) in 13 games (one start vs. Maryland) in '13. Missed the NC State game with a concussion. Caught 24 career passes for 182 yards (7.6-yard average) and two touchdowns.

Strengths: Looks the part — built like a cut-up strong safety with tight skin and layered muscle. Equipped to withstand the pounding of inside running. Effective in short-yardage situations. Good balance. Runs behind his pads. Robust tackle-breaker — churns out yards after contact and carries defenders. Brandishes a stiff-arm. Explosive, well-conditioned athlete with very low body fat. Enters the league relatively fresh, having carried just 226 times in three seasons.

Averaged 7 yards per carry in 2013 and averaged a TD every 10 carries from 2012-13. Clear upside. Has NFL bloodlines. Recorded a 6.92-second 3-cone time.

Weaknesses: Has a long torso, runs upright and exposes his frame to hits. Lacks ideal foot speed — gets tracked down from behind. Tight-hipped with limited wiggle. Gears down to cut and does not string moves together. Lets throws into his body. Could stand to improve as a blocker. Was not a feature back in college. Durability has been an issue — hurt his shoulder and sustained a concussion in 2013. Has multiple arrests in his past — character and maturity need to be investigated. Marginal timed speed at the Combine.

Future: Physically gifted, energetic, pedigreed runner with potential to develop into a productive sledgehammer and be a better pro than college player if he embraces a violent running style, remains healthy and keeps his stays focused.

Draft projection: Late draftable pick.

Scout's take: "Wilder is good looking on the hoof. He is a bigger back that does not drive the pile. I wish he were more of that. I love the size and look of him. I just don't think he is an instinctive runner or quick-footed. He's going to really struggle at the next level, I think — he does not have the twitch. He's just a guy for me."

RB ANDRE WILLIAMS, #44

BOSTON COLLEGE   ▶ GRADE: 5.62
Ht: 5-11 3/8 | Wt: 230 | Sp: 4.56 | Arm: 33 1/2 | Hand: 9

History: The Pennsylvania prep rushed for 1,913 yards and 33 touchdowns as a senior. Lived in Georgia for his first two seasons of high school. Appeared in all 13 contests as a true freshman in 2010, starting the final two, and rushed 95 times for 461 yards (4.6-yard average) and two touchdowns. Led the team in rushing touchdowns in '11, posting 124-517-4 (4.2) in 10 games (seven starts). Missed two games due to injuries Clemson (ankle) and Florida State (abdominal). Did not participate in '12 spring practice after surgery to repair a torn labrum in his left shoulder. Was the team's leading rusher in the fall despite only playing in nine games (eight starts) and logging 130-584-4 (4.5). Missed the final three games with a torn abdominal muscle (left side) suffered against Wake Forest. Had a stellar senior campaign in '13, leading the nation in rushing yards (2,177), being a finalist for the Heisman Trophy and winning the Doak Walker (nation's premier running back) in addition to being a consensus All-America selection. Ran for 335-2,177-18 (6.5) in 13 starts and became the 16th player in FBS history to top the 2,000-yard mark. Rushed for over 200 yards in a game five times, including an Atlantic Coast Conference and school record 339 yards (42 attempts) against NC State. Averaged 167.5 yards per game on the ground to lead all Division I players. Was not used much as a receiver in his career, catching 10 passes for 60 yards (6.0-yard average) in four years. Graduated in December.

Strengths: Has very long arms with good overall musculature, wide shoulders and a thick, power base. Good vision to find creases. Runs with urgency and steps downhill fast. Shows an extra gear to kick it into overdrive and outrace defenders to the end zone. Good finishing speed — did not see him get tracked down from behind. Can power through arm tackles, brush off contact and clear his feet through traffic — very good contact balance. Solid anchor in pass protection. Keen blitz recognition. Smart and competitive.

Weaknesses: Much of his production is blocked for him — produced many runs of 20-plus yards untouched. Is not dynamic or creative and makes few tacklers miss. Can do a better job selling routes and settling into soft spots in zones. Very minimal receiving production — 10 career catches.

Future: Very strong, stocky, powerful runner with the instincts, contact balance and toughness to carry a heavy workload. Really emerged as a senior, when he led the nation in rushing, and proved worthy of a starting role. Limitations in the receiving game could diminish his value.

Draft projection: Second- to third-round pick.

Scout's take: "He might sneak into 2. He runs hard. He has good vision. He reminds me a little bit of 'Cadillac', 'Crazy Legs' (Carnell Williams). There are not a lot of backs that can be featured guys."

RB DAMIEN WILLIAMS, #26

OKLAHOMA ▶ GRADE: 5.05

Ht: 5-11 1/4 | Wt: 222 | Sp: 4.46 | Arm: 30 5/8 | Hand: 9 1/8

History: The San Diego area prep rushed for 2,287 yards and 24 touchdowns as senior.

Began his college career at Arizona Western College (Yuma, Ariz.) in 2010, where he rushed 95 times for 723 yards (7.6-yard average) and 10 touchdowns. Also caught seven passes for 183 yards (18.3) and two scores while returning nine kickoffs for 323 yards (35.9) and one touchdown. Was a first-team NJCAA All-America selection in '11 after rushing 259-1931-26 (7.5) and catching 20-317-4 (15.9) in 12 games. Moved to Oklahoma for the '12 campaign and led the Sooners in rushing with 176-946-11 (5.4) while grabbing 34-320-1 (9.4) in 13 games (nine starts). Was limited by an ankle injury against Iowa State. Recorded 114-553-7 (4.9) on the ground and 9-90-0 (9.0) as a receiver in nine games (one start against Texas Tech) in '13 before being dismissed from the team in November. Served two suspensions during the season for violating team rules — September 14 vs. Tulsa and November 23 at Kansas State.

Strengths: Layered with muscle and looks the part. Is quick-footed — can sidestep the first tackler and run through some arm tackles. Very good hands. Fine balance and body control. Catches the ball cleanly outside his frame and is nifty-footed to juke linebackers in the open field after the catch, displaying some creativity.

Weaknesses: Very average vision and feel to anticipate creases. Runs with blinders and misses holes. Not explosive to and through the hole. Lacks strength, power and drive to run inside and grind out tough yardage. Overwhelmed in pass protection — needs to learn how to sit to anchor and use his hands. Still has some JUCO habits and could learn to compete more consistently.

Future: Split time in a three-man backfield until being dismissed from the team for his multiple violations of team rules. Must prove he can stay disciplined and learn what it means to be a pro to make it. Is best running outside in a spread offense that features wide running lanes and could bring the most value to a team as a pass catcher in a change-of-pace role.

Draft projection: Priority free agent.

Scout's take: "No. 26 looks the part and is all muscled up and has a lot of speed. He just likes to bounce it outside all the time. His run instincts are average."

WIDE RECEIVERS

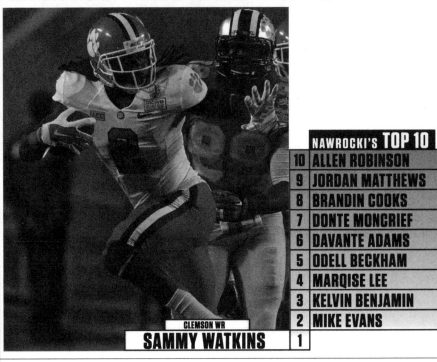

	NAWROCKI'S **TOP 10**
10	**ALLEN ROBINSON**
9	**JORDAN MATTHEWS**
8	**BRANDIN COOKS**
7	**DONTE MONCRIEF**
6	**DAVANTE ADAMS**
5	**ODELL BECKHAM**
4	**MARQISE LEE**
3	**KELVIN BENJAMIN**
2	**MIKE EVANS**
1	

CLEMSON WR
SAMMY WATKINS

EDITOR'S NOTE:
Z — Strong, physical flanker
X — Speedy, vertical split end
F — Quick, shifty slot receiver

WR [F]-RS JARED ABBREDERIS, #4

WISCONSIN ▶ GRADE: 5.27
Ht: 6-1 | Wt: 195 | Sp: 4.53 | Arm: 31 3/8 | Hand: 9 5/8

History: Married. Last name is pronounced "ab-bruh-DAIR-is." Was a high school quarterback and defensive back in Wisconsin, where he won a state championship, wrestled and was the Gatorade track athlete of the year. Walked on and redshirted in 2009, working as a scout team spread quarterback. Earned a scholarship in '10 before playing all 13 games (two starts) and recording 20 receptions for 289 yards (14.4-yard average) and three touchdowns. Started all 14 games in '11 and posted 55-933-8 (17.0). Broke a bone in his left foot against South Dakota in Week Four — was not diagnosed until after the season and he sat out '12 spring practice. In the fall, started 12-of-13 games and caught 49-837-5 (17.1). Sustained a concussion against Oregon State and did not play against Utah State. Also sustained a concussion against Penn State. Started 12-of-13 games in '13, totaling 78-1,081-7 (13.9) with six rushes for 119 yards (19.8) and two touchdowns. Did not start against Indiana (ribs). Did not play in the Senior Bowl (hamstring). Also returned 55 career punts for 587 yards (10.7), including a score, and 31 career kickoffs for 800 yards (25.8). Burlsworth Trophy winner as nation's best player to begin his career as a walk-on.

Strengths: Uses his hands well to swat away press. Stems his routes. Sells his patterns. Nice hands. Good field and boundary awareness. Gives effort to engage and shield cornerbacks as a blocker. Outstanding football intelligence — like a quarterback on the outside. Productive three-year starter. Mature and humble. Hardworking and coachable. Carved up Ohio State CB Bradley Roby to the tune of 10-207-1.

Weaknesses: Has a slender build and needs to bulk up and get stronger. Ordinary pop off the line. Builds to average speed. Could struggle to separate vs. quick-twitch covermen.

Lets throws into his body and breaks stride to catch. Not an jumpball player (30 1/2-inch vertical jump). Straightlinish after the catch — pedestrian agility and elusiveness. Has a history of concussions. Benchpressed 225 pounds only four times, lowest of all Combine participants.

Future: A former walk-on, Abbrederis went from afterthought to scholarship player to No. 1 receiver. While the blue-collar overachiever lacks exceptional athletic traits for the NFL, he's a steady "X" receiver whose hands and smarts could enable him to work his way into a No. 3 or No. 4 receiver role.

Draft projection: Fourth- to fifth-round pick.

Scout's take: "I'll tell you what's going to make him at the next level. He played in three different offenses in three years, and he got better and better. He's a very grounded kid. The game is important to him. He's not an assassin as a blocker, but he works at it. He's going to strengthen the locker room. He's one of those guys that just gets it."

WR LZ, FL DAVANTE ADAMS, #15 (JUNIOR)
FRESNO STATE ▶ GRADE: 5.96
Ht: 6-0 7/8 | Wt: 212 | Sp: 4.58 | Arm: 32 5/8 | Hand: 9

History: Also starred in basketball as a California prep. Redshirted in 2011, earning offensive scout team player of the year recognition. Was Mountain West Conference Freshman of the Year in '12 when he amassed 102 receptions for 1,312 yards (12.9-yard average) and 14 touchdowns in 13 starts, setting conference freshman records for catches and yards. Led the nation in receptions and receiving touchdowns and set a single-season school record for receiving yards in '13 when he started 12-of-13 contests and piled up 131-1,718-24 (13.1). Owns MWC records for single-season and career touchdown catches (38) as well as the school mark for career receptions (233).

Strengths: Has a rangy build with good body length and secure hands to palm the ball and make difficult one-handed grabs. Tracks and adjusts to the ball very well downfield. Extends outside his frame and plucks the ball out of the air. Natural hands-catcher. Terrific athlete with good leaping ability and anticipation to properly time jumps and highpoint the ball. Wins jumpballs in the red zone and shows very good hand-eye coordination to take the ball away from defenders. Exceptional production. Has a 391/2-inch vertical jump

Weaknesses: Lacks ideal functional playing strength to consistently beat the jam and can get hung up at the line. Long strider and is

not sudden out of his breaks. Production was inflated from a quick-hitting, lateral passing game.

Future: A rangy, sure-handed possession receiver with starter-caliber, positional traits. Lacks top-end speed and strength. As a 21-year-old, third-year sophomore entering the draft early, is still growing into his body and developing core strength. Comparing favorably to a poor man's Michael Crabtree, Adams possesses very intriguing upside to be groomed.

Draft projection: Top 50 pick.

Scout's take: "(Adams) has some size, but he's a possession receiver that can't run. He is a No. 2 receiver in the league. I'd love to have him as a No. 3."

WR [F]-RB-RS DRI ARCHER, #1
KENT STATE ▶ GRADE: 5.45
Ht: 5-7 3/4 | Wt:173 | Sp: 4.26 | Arm: 31 | Hand: 8 7/8

History: First name is pronounced "DREE". The Florida prep averaged 10.2 yards per carry as a senior, finished second in the 100-meter final of the state high school track meet (ahead of third-place Denard Robinson) and also lettered in baseball. Played in 11 games as a true freshman in 2009, rushing 58 times for 246 yards (4.2-yard average) and one touchdown with 19 receptions for 231 yards (12.2) and three touchdowns. Missed one game due to coach's choice. Appeared in all 12 games (one start at RB) in '10 and carried 40-140-1 (3.5) and caught 16-75-1 (4.7). Was academically ineligible in '11, missing the entire season. Returned to the field in '12 and had a breakout year, setting a Kent State single-season record with 23 touchdowns. Ran for 159-1,429-16 (9.0) and caught 39-561-4 (15.6) in 14 games (11 starts at slot receiver). Returned three kickoffs for touchdowns and averaged 36.9 yards on 16 kickoff returns. Was a finalist for the Paul Hornung Award, honoring the nation's most versatile player. Was the MAC's Special Teams Player of the Year and first-team all-MAC at both running back and kick returner. Injured his left ankle during the first series of the '13 season and was hampered for much of September, missing early season games against Bowling Green and Penn State and seeing limited action against LSU. Played in 10 games (nine starts at slot receiver) and carried 68-527-6 (7.8) and caught 25-327-4 (13.1). Had a 100-yard kickoff return touchdown against Northern Illinois. Despite making only 21 collegiate starts, he finished his Kent State career ranking among the school's all-time leaders with 4,980 all-purpose yards and 40 touchdowns (24 rushing, 12 receiving, four kickoff returns).

Strengths: Rare burst, acceleration and top-end speed to take the corner and create big plays. Can fly by MAC competition with top gear. Very good agility, balance, vision and creativity. Weaves through a crowd and can find daylight. Soft-handed and plucks the ball with ease. Extremely strong pound-for-pound. Very good career all-purpose yardage. Good versatility — contributes as a runner, slot receiver and return man. Four career kickoff-return TDs (and was kicked away from). Clocked a 4.16-second 40-yard dash in 18 steps on one official handheld Combine watch, tying Calvin Johnson's NFL Combine record for fewest steps. Has a 38-inch vertical jump.

Weaknesses: Very short and rail thin with limited strength or running power. Not a tackle-breaker and goes down easy on contact. Limited inside runner. Can be knocked off routes easily and struggles catching on contact. Not a nuanced route runner. Very marginal, underpowered blocker. Could stand to do a better job securing the ball in traffic. Is not ideally built to withstand a full NFL season.

Future:: An injury-riddled senior season cannot eclipse what an explosive playmaker Archer demonstrated he can be when healthy. Was slowed by an ankle injury early and did not return to junior form until late in senior season. Can make an immediate impact in the return game and add value as a multipurpose threat. Long-term durability is greatest concern given tiny frame.

Draft projection: Second- to third-round pick.

Scout's take: "I got him in the low 4.2's on my watch (at the Combine). He's the fastest player I've ever timed in 20-some years doing this. He beat Chris Johnson. He was flying. I'm not sure what you do with him with how small he is. Guys like him just don't last at our level. Name one of them who has. Tavon Austin stayed healthy in college, but look what happen when he got to our level. He was hurt before he played his first game. I think (Archer) has to be a slot receiver."

WR IX, ZI-PR ODELL BECKHAM, #3 (JUNIOR)
LSU   ▶ GRADE: 6.00
Ht: 5-11 1/4 | Wt: 198 | Sp: 4.41 | Arm: 32 3/4 | Hand: 10

History: Father, Odell Sr., was a running back for the Tigers (1989-92) and mother, Heather Van Norman, was an LSU All-American and national champion in track (1991-93). Odell Jr. was an all-purpose standout as a Louisiana

prep. As a true freshman in 2011 (wore jersey No. 33), played all 14 games (11 starts at "Z" receiver) and recorded 41 receptions for 475 yards (11.6-yard average) and two touchdowns. Started 12-of-13 games at the "Z" in '12 (team opened with extra tight end against Arkansas), tallying 43-713-2 (16.6). Was the Paul Hornung Award winner as the nation's most versatile player in '13 when he broke the LSU single-season all-purpose yards record (2,315) and snagged 59-1,152-8 (19.5) in 13 starts at "X" receiver. Also returned 68 career punts for 557 yards (8.2), including two scores, and 42 kickoffs for 1,044 yards (24.9).

Strengths: Quick hands and feet to slip the jam. Fluid and fast. Good balance. Sinks his hips and changes gears to create separation. Quick hands to pluck off his frame. Terrific leaping ability — climbs the ladder to snatch throws. Creates after the catch — shows burst and shiftiness as a runner. Has playmaking ability. Confident and competitive. Has kickoff- and punt-return experience. Productive three-year starter.

Weaknesses: Adequate height. Could stand to polish the finer points of his route running. Inconsistent making contested grabs — can be out-muscled in a crowd. Has some concentration drops. Can improve as a blocker. Was not an impactful punt returner. Was held in check by Florida and Alabama.

Future: Talented, competitive, productive, inconsistent college split end who projects as a big-play receiver in the pros. Offers versatility to toggle between "X," "Z" and slot given his ability to stretch the field and run after the catch. Brings added value as a kick returner.

Draft projection: First-round pick.

Scout's take: "Odell Beckham is a damn good player. I put him in the middle of the first (round). He is a little bit of a knucklehead, but he can play. The school has two video tapes of him and Landry making a bunch of ridiculous one-handed grabs, in practice and in games. It looked like some YouTube collaboration. It is crazy. You have to see it."

WR IZ, X, FI KELVIN BENJAMIN, #1 (JUNIOR)
FLORIDA STATE   ▶ GRADE: 6.30
Ht: 6-5 | Wt: 240 | Sp: 4.62 | Arm: 34 7/8 | Hand: 10 1/4

History: Highly recruited out of Florida prep power Glades Central, where he also played basketball. Played through a partially torn right knee ligament as a junior in 2009. Redshirted in '11. Played all 14 games in '12 and had 30 catches for 495 yards (16.5-yard average) and four touchdowns. Started all 14 games for the national champions in '13 when he led the Atlantic Coast Conference in touchdown receptions (including the game winner in the BCS Championship) by hauling in 54-1,011-15 (18.7).

Strengths: Possesses rare size with an 83-inch wingspan. Is a physical mismatch vs. defensive backs and linebackers. Eats cushion and separates with long strides. Strong approach to the ball — is not easily knocked off course and will enter the middle on crossers. Outstanding jumpball catcher — climbs the ladder, plucks the ball at its highest point and regularly snatches it out of the air with superb body control and the grace of a ballerina. Creates separation with his body. Adjusts surprisingly well for the low ball and tracks it well over his shoulder. Energetic football demeanor. Confident and competitive. Strong-handed. Uses his body well to shield the defender from the ball and can beat double coverage. Good run strength after the catch (see three tackles broken on TD run vs. Florida) and does not go down easy. Strong enough to handle defensive ends when motioned inside to chip and delivered some head-snapping, crackback blocks (see North Carolina St.). Emerged as a clutch, go-to, big-play receiver — caught the game-winning TD in the national championship game vs. Auburn and consistently was targeted in critical situations and in the red zone. Scorched Florida CB Loucheiz Purifoy and created mismatch problems from the slot.

Weaknesses: Lacks elite, top-end speed and many catches are contested. Hand use could improve releasing vs. tight, press coverage. Overly grabby. Is not yet a nuanced route runner and does not sink his hips and pop in and out of his breaks. Does not shake many defenders after the catch. Will make the easy concentration drop and focus could stand to improve at the break point (three drops vs. Florida). Seeks to run before securing the ball and double-catches more than he should. Blocking effort/sustainability has room to improve on the move. Has a 32 1/2-inch vertical jump and recorded the slowest 60-yard shuttle time (12.10 seconds) of any receiver at the Combine.

Future: A tight end-sized, intimidating, big-play receiver with a rare wingspan, Benjamin has the overall strength, length and wide catching radius that will demand extra coverage be rolled his way. Showed continual improvement, is still growing into the position,

and possesses the traits to become a legitimate No. 1 receiver. A very intriguing mismatch weapon with ascending talent.

Draft projection: Top-20 pick.

Scout's take: "The league is going back to big receivers now. (Benjamin) is in vogue. doesn't have elite speed — you don't see him get on top of (defensive backs) — but he's field fast. My problem is — I don't think he is a good route runner. He's a third-year junior with only two years of experience. If you lined him up in the slot, he could almost be like Jimmy Graham. ...He's a big red-zone (target). He's not always a natural catcher and not dynamic with the ball in his hands. He will jump and catch in traffic."

WR [Z] CHRIS BOYD, #80 (JUNIOR)

VANDERBILT   ▶ GRADE: 5.15

Ht: 6-4 | Wt: 206 | Sp: 4.72* | Arm: 32 5/8 | Hand: 9 5/8

*Strained his right quad while running 40.

History: Also played basketball as a Georgia prep. Redshirted in 2010. Started 7-of-13 games in '11 and caught 31 balls for 473 yards (15.3-yard average) and eight touchdowns. Started all 13 games opposite Jordan Matthews in 2012, recording 50-774-5 (15.5). Did not play in 2013 — was dismissed from the team in September after he entered a conditional guilty plea for his role in attempting to cover up the rape of an unconscious student (four other Vanderbilt players were charged with rape and aggravated sexual battery charges). According to an account by the Deputy Attorney General, Boyd was sent a picture of the aggravated rape, which he deleted. Additionally, Boyd was said to have abandoned the unconscious victim. Ultimately received an 11-month, 29-day suspended sentence for misdemeanor criminal attempt to commit accessory after the fact, and will have his record cleared if and when he completes unsupervised probation. Did not participate fully in the Combine because of a quad injury suffered running the 40, but continued to participate in most of skill drills.

Strengths: Excellent frame. Chews up ground with long strides. Controls his body and uses size to his advantage. Good hands — extends to catch off his body. Adjusts to throws. Good potential as a blocker — can engage and stalk. Good work ethic.

Weaknesses: Average burst off the line. Lacks elite top-end speed to separate vertically. Not strong to beat the jam. Shows some hip stiffness and is fairly straight-linish. Has to be hit in stride to pick up chunk yards after the catch.

Future: Tall, slender, short-to-intermediate possession receiver who could compete for a job as a No. 4 or No. 5 in a West Coast offense. After having sat the year out, Boyd's Combine performance was unspectacular and how he fares in the pro day process will affect his standing.

Draft projection: Priority free agent.

WR [X]-PR COREY "PHILLY" BROWN, #10
OHIO STATE   ▶ GRADE: 5.00
Ht: 5-11 3/8 | Wt: 178 | Sp: 4.47 | Arm: 31 3/4 | Hand: 9 3/8

History: Prepped in Pennsylvania, where he was a running back and track standout. Suffered an MCL tear as a junior. Appeared in all 13 games (one start) in 2010, tallying eight receptions for 105 yards (13.1-yard average) and a touchdown. Started all nine games played in '11, managing 14-205-1 (14.6). Missed four games (ankle). Started 11-of-12 games in '12 and caught 60-669-3 (11.1). Started all 14 games in '13, tallying 63-771-10 (11.9). Also returned 41 career punts for 400 yards (9.8), including two scores. Team captain. Did not lift at the Combine because of a right shoulder (A/C Joint) injury.

Strengths: Works himself open short-to-intermediate. Adjusts to throws. Quick enough to elude the initial tackler and pick up yards after the catch. Functional blocker. Lined up inside and outside and has punt-return experience.

Weaknesses: Has a lean build and relatively small hands. Needs to get stronger in order to combat the jam. Not an explosive athlete. Average initial quickness into routes. Lacks elite top-end speed to beat defenses vertically. Bland, unrefined route runner. Lets throws into his body. Inconsistent traffic player. Average production and playmaking.

Future: Adequate-sized, monotone, fairly nondescript receiver lacking exceptional athletic traits for the pro game and will need to prove himself in the return game to stick.

Draft projection: Priority free agent.

WR [X, F] -RS JOHN BROWN, #5
PITTSBURGH STATE (KANSAS) ▶ GRADE: 5.24
Ht: 5-10 | Wt: 179 | Sp: 4.37 | Arm: 30 1/2 | Hand: 8 1/2

History: Has a daughter. From Miami-Dade County, Florida. Began his college career at Mars Hill in 2008, when he played all 11 games (two starts) and caught 27 balls for 619 yards (22.9-yard average) and seven touchdowns. Added 29 kickoff returns for 718 yards (24.8), including an 87-yard score, and 15 punt returns for 117 yards (7.8). Did not play in '09 (academics). Redshirted at Coffeyville

(KS) Community College in '10. Signed with Division II Pitt State for '11 — started 12-of-14 games and hauled in 61-1,216-12 (19.9). Also had 24-616-1, including a 100-yard score, on kickoff returns and 27-369 (13.7), including two scores, on punts. Started all 10 games in '12, catching 63-973-8 (15.4) and returning punts 28-430-1 (15.4) and kickoffs 16-395 (24.7). Started all 12 games in '13 and posted 61-1,198-14 (19.6) receiving, 12-389-1 (32.4) on kickoffs and 23-264 (11.5) on punts. Was PSU's leading receiver three-straight years. Three-time captain. Did not lift at the Combine because of a left A/C joint injury.

Strengths: Athletic and flexible. Accelerates off the line. Field fast. Stretches the field and tracks deep throws. Gets in and out of breaks quickly. Good hands. Playmaking ability as a receiver and return man. Has worked as a gunner. Well respected, coachable team captain. Led all receivers at the Combine with a 2.46-second time in the 20-yard split.

Weaknesses: Lacks ideal size. Has very short arms and small hands. Limited functional strength. Can be jammed and rerouted. Can be outmuscled for contested catches. Cannot bust through tackles. Poor blocker. Will be a 24-year-old rookie.

Future: Lean, fluid, speedy Division II standout with a playmaker's resume. Will have to overcome size and strength limitations, but his burst and hands give him the opportunity to earn a role as a slot receiver and return man.

Draft projection: Late draftable pick.

WR [X] MARTAVIS BRYANT, #1 (JUNIOR)
CLEMSON   ▶ GRADE: 5.34
Ht: 6-3 3/4 | Wt: 211 | Sp: 4.46 | Arm: 32 5/8 | Hand: 9 1/2

History: Was a non-qualifier as a South Carolina prep and spent 2010 at Hargrave Military Academy (Va.). Joined Clemson in '11 when he played all 14 games (two starts) and tallied nine receptions for 221 yards (24.6-yard average) and two touchdowns. Appeared in 10 games in '12, managing 10-305-4 (30.1). Did not play against Boston College or Georgia Tech (groin), and was academically ineligible for the Chick-fil-A Bowl. Started 11-of-13 games in '13, totaling 42-828-7 (19.7). Did not start against Wake Forest as punishment for a throat slash gesture, and gave way to a fullback and tight end against Maryland. Also returned 14 career kickoffs for 291 yards (20.8).

Strengths: Superb body length with a long, rangy frame. Very good straight-line separation speed. Can drop his hips surprisingly well for as tall as he is and is fairly shifty after the catch. Good red-zone target — effective making back-shoulder catches. Flashes the ability to climb the ladder and highpoint the ball. Has return experience.

Weaknesses: Shaky hands — tends to double-clutch the ball and makes too many easy drops. Is not a polished route runner — is stiff in and out of his breaks. Lacks toughness desired to work the middle of the field. Must prove that he is willing to work to assimilate a playbook and learn the finer points of the game.

Future: A lean, long-limbed, rangy, outside-the-numbers, big-play receiver, Bryant declared for the draft early with underclassmen nipping at his playing time late in the season. Will require additional seasoning to make a mark in the pro game. A better tester than football player at this stage of his development, he has tools to be molded if he learns to hone his focus.

Draft projection: Fourth- to fifth-round pick.

Scout's take: "His demeanor, work ethic and motor are what trouble me. He has bad hands. The league is all about potential, and you look at his numbers on paper, he has a lot of it. This is just deep enough of a WR draft where you don't have to reach on a roll-of-the-dice receiver."

WR [F]-RS ISAIAH BURSE, #1

FRESNO STATE   ▶ GRADE: 5.20
Ht: 5-10 3/8 | Wt: 188 | Sp: 4.59 | Arm: 30 1/4 | Hand: 8 3/8

History: Played quarterback and safety as a California prep, leading his team to a small school state championship. Appeared in all 13 games as a true freshman in 2010 and caught 13 balls for 190 yards (14.6-yard average) and two touchdowns. Played all 13 games (one start) in '11, snagging 40-436-1 (10.9) while setting a single-season FBS record for kickoff returns and yards with 75-1,606 (21.4). Started 11-of-13 games in '12 and produced 57-851-6 (14.9). Started all 13 games in '13, racking up 100-1,026-6 (10.3). For his career, returned 126 kickoffs for 2,835 yards (22.5) and 29 punts for 344 yards (11.9). Also rushed 32 times for 191 yards (6.3) and completed a 43-yard touchdown pass as a freshman. Team captain.

Strengths: Good athlete. Shows some suddenness as a route runner to climb defensive backs and can create separation when he needs to with short-area burst and speed cuts. Keeps working zones to come free and has a knack for finding soft spots in coverage. Scrappy competitor. Carries a swagger. Strong-handed.

Field-fast. Catches on contact and fearlessly crosses the middle. Sifts through traffic and fights for extra yardage. Good vision, elusiveness and cutback ability in the return game. Football smart. Respected team leader.

Weaknesses: Has a small frame with short arms and tiny hands. Does not track the ball very well over his shoulder and makes some easy drops. Lacks run-after-the-catch strength and does not power through tackles. Average long speed — lacks top gear to kick it into overdrive and pull away from the pack. Could improve as a blocker

Future: Quicker-than-fast, short-striding slot receiver and sudden punt returner with the competitiveness and swagger desired to earn a role in multiple phases. Is crafty, fiery and tough enough to make it. Has similarities to Jaguars 2013 fourth-round pick Ace Sanders, though not as explosive.

Draft projection: Late draftable pick.

Scout's take: "He is a backup slot receiver because of limited run strength. I don't know if he's tough enough to be a punt returner at our level. That's what we need to find out."

WR [F] MIKE CAMPANARO, #3

WAKE FOREST   ▶ GRADE: 5.09
Ht: 5-9 3/8 | Wt: 192 | Sp: 4.49 | Arm: 30 | Hand: 9 3/4

History: Prepped in Maryland, where he was a standout running back, kick returner and safety — won a pair of state championships, amassed more than 6,500 yards and 90 touchdowns and notched eight kick return scores. Redshirted in 2009. Played all 12 games (one start) in '10 and caught 10 balls for 107 yards (1.7-yard average) and zero touchdowns. Started 10-of-12 games played in '11, snagging 73-833-2 (11.4). Injured his right hamstring against North Carolina State and sat out against Gardner-Webb. Started 9-of-10 games played at flanker in '12, managing 79-763-6 (9.7). Broke his right hand against Duke, missed two games and was restricted by a splint in others. Sat out '13 spring practice while recovering from left ankle surgery. At flanker in the fall, started all eight games played and paced Demon Deacon receivers for the second straight year with 67-803-6 (12.0). Was held out of the season opener against Presbyterian (tight hamstring) and missed the final three games because of a broken collarbone suffered against Syracuse. Owns the school record for career receptions (229).

Strengths: Has short-area quickness to separate short-to-intermediate. Good balance and hip flex. Adjusts to throws. Finds soft spots in zone coverage. Effective running drags and crossers. Tough, confident and competitive. Three-year starter. Solid character.

Weaknesses: Lacks ideal height and length — has extremely short arms and can be hemmed at the line. Limited functional strength. Small catch radius. Lacks elite top-end speed to take the top off. Spotty concentration — makes some focused grabs and drops others he shouldn't. Marginal blocker. Durability is an issue — has a small build, has been dinged up and could struggle to stay healthy. Has the smallest wingspan (701/2 inches) of any receiver at the Combine.

Future: Undersized, slippery, competitive inside receiver who brings a possession element to the slot. Lacks ideal explosiveness and will have to prove himself on special teams to earn an extended look.

Draft projection: Priority free agent.

Scout's take: "I saw him when he was really hot. I liked the kid. I liked his hands, but he had occasional drops."

WR [Z] BRANDON COLEMAN, #17 (JUNIOR)
RUTGERS   ▶ GRADE: 5.42
Ht: 6-6 | Wt: 225 | Sp: 4.56 | Arm: 34 | Hand: 9 1/4

History: Receiver-safety who also played basketball as a Maryland prep. Redshirted in 2010. Played all 13 games in each of his three seasons — started five in '11 and recorded 17 receptions for 552 yards (32.5-yard average) and six touchdowns. Started nine in '12 and posted 43-718-10 (16.7). Had off-season surgery on his right knee that kept him out of '13 spring practice and reportedly affected his play as a junior. In the fall, started all 13 contests and produced 34-538-4 (15.8). Team captain.

Strengths: Outstanding size and body length — presents a big target. Long arms enable him to slap away and swim off the jam. Covers ground with long strides. Tracks over his shoulder. Can post up smaller defensive backs. Has playmaking ability — averaged nearly 22 yards per catch and scored on one out of every five catches over three seasons. Has sheer size to shield as a blocker. Team captain.

Weaknesses: Not an elite athlete. Has some buildup — does not accelerate off the jam. Lacks big-time, explosive speed to blow by cornerbacks. Route running needs refinement. Not a confident hands catcher — lets throws into his body and drops balls he shouldn't. Shows some stiffness through his torso and is linear after the catch — gears down to cut and elusiveness is limited, as verified with a 4.56-second 20-yard shuttle time and a 7.36-second 3-cone time, both the slowest of any receiver at the Combine. Marginal special-teams utility.

Future: Big, tall, talented, West Coast receiver whose sheer size enables him to be effective outside the numbers, on slant routes and in the red zone, though inconsistency has prevented him from reaching his potential. Has the look of a No. 2 receiver, but his production fell off as a junior (played through a knee injury). He could have used another season to polish his skills.

Draft projection: Third- to fourth-round pick.

Scout's take: "I thought he played a lot better last year. You could see the knee (injury) was slowing him down. You have to go back to 2012 if you want a more pure evaluation. The doctors are going to have to sign off on him."

WR [F]-RS KAIN COLTER, #2
NORTHWESTERN   ▶ GRADE: 5.28
Ht: 5-10 1/2 | Wt: 198 | Sp: 4.50e | Arm: 31 | Hand: 10

History: Full name is Theodis Kain Colter. Father, Spencer, played on the 1990 Colorado national championship team. Prepped in Colorado where also played basketball and competed in track and field (long jump/triple jump). Originally committed to Stanford and then-head coach Jim Harbaugh, but signed with NU when an injury — tore the labrum and biceps tendon in his right (throwing) arm in the first game of his senior season and missed eight games — cooled Stanford's interest. Served as a backup quarterback in 2010 when he saw limited action in three games, completing 3-of-9 pass attempts (33.3 percent) for 38 yards with zero touchdowns and an interception. Played all 13 games in '11 —started the first three at quarterback in place of injured started Dan Persa and three more at receiver — and tossed 55-82-673-6-1 (67.1) whiling totaling 43 receptions for 466 yards (10.8-yard average) and three touchdowns. Was the quarterback in '12 when he started all 13 games (lined up at receiver to open the game against Indiana) and passed 101-149-872-8-4 (67.8) with 16-169-0 (10.6) receiving. Started all 11 games played in '13, throwing 63-80-577-4-3 (78.7) and catching 3-16-1 (5.3). Did not play against Minnesota or Michigan State (ankle). For his career, rushed 449 times for 2,180 yards (4.9) and 28 touchdowns. Had his ankle surgically repaired following the season and withdrew from the Senior Bowl. Two-time captain. Participates in the National College Players Association, a nonprofit player advocate group, and at the conclusion of his playing career, spearheaded and was a mouthpiece for a group of student-athletes attempting to unionize.

Strengths: Well-defined body with big, soft hands. Good short-area burst, quickness, agility and balance. Can work his way through zones and uncover underneath. Can stop on a dime and string some moves together. Good run vision and creativity to navigate through traffic. Extremely competitive. Highly intelligent and football smart. Articulate communicator. Adds intriguing versatility as a triggerman. Good pedigree — coach's son.

Weaknesses: Has short arms. Adequate run strength — does not power through tackles. Can improve using his hands to beat the jam. Lacks elite top-end speed to separate vertically. Has a lot of room to improve as a perimeter blocker.

Future: An athletic, undersized, multi-threat, option college quarterback who shared time in the slot, Colter displayed the playmaking ability, short-area burst, creativity and hands to become a Danny Amendola-type slot receiver and should be able to factor readily in the pros once he commits full-time to the position. Offers situational Wildcat quarterbacking capability and return ability with traits that project very well as a punt returner. Postseason ankle surgery will limit his spring workouts and could dip his draft standing.

Draft projection: Fourth- to fifth-round pick.

Scout's take: "He'll be ready to work out in April. He's close to being recovered. ... He is an impressive, all-around kid. He's a natural leader."

WR IF, XI BRANDIN COOKS, #7 (JUNIOR)

OREGON STATE ▶ GRADE: 5.85
Ht: 5-9 3/4 | Wt: 189 | Sp: 4.33 | Arm: 30 3/4 | Hand: 9 5/8

History: Also competed in the Junior Olympics (sprinter) and played basketball as a California prep. Played all 38 games of his career. Started three games at flanker as an injury replacement for James Rodgers in 2011 — caught 31 balls for 391 yards (12.6-yard average) and three touchdowns. Added eight kickoff returns for 179 yards (22.4). In '12, started all 13 games at flanker opposite Steelers '13 third-rounder Markus Wheaton, and produced 67-1,151-5 (17.2). Hurt his ankle against Oregon and missed most of the Nicholls State contest. Won the Biletnikoff Award as the nation's top receiver in '13 when he established Pac-12 single-season records for receptions and receiving yards (led FBS)— racked up 128-1,730-16 (13.5) with 12 punt returns for 72 yards (6.0) in 13 starts at flanker. Also had

61 career rushes for 340 yards (5.6) and two touchdowns. Owns OSU record for career touchdown catches (24). Team captain.

Strengths: Light on his feet with terrific balance. Sinks his hips with ease and pops out of breaks to separate. Tracks and adjusts. Quick hands. Good concentration, body control and boundary awareness. Can turn a short throw into a long gain. Shows elusiveness, creativity and vision after the catch. Unafraid to play in the tall trees. Highly productive — totaled 195 receptions for 2,881 yards (15.4-yard average) and 21 TDs in last two seasons. Confident and competitive. Has been exceptionally durable dating back to high school. Produced the best 20-yard shuttle time (3.81 seconds) and 60-yard shuttle time (10.72 seconds) of any Combine participant. Team captain. Will be a 21-year-old rookie.

Weaknesses: Size is just adequate — is small-framed with short arms and lacks ideal length and bulk. Vulnerable to the jam and reroute. Relatively small catch radius. Has small hands and double-catches some throws. Does not sky for the ball. Was not an impactful punt returner. Limited run strength. Poor blocker.

Future: Short, speedy, nifty-footed receiver who was unaffected by the departure of Steelers 2013 third-rounder Markus Wheaton, establishing himself as a playmaker in his own right by leading the nation with 133 yards per contest as a junior. Projects as a useful slot receiver with run-after-catch ability and some utility as an outside receiver.

Draft projection: Top 50 pick.

Scout's take: "He reminds me of T.Y. Hilton. Their playing styles are very similar. They need a little bit of space to get open. They'll struggle in traffic and get boxed out on contact. They don't always play big after contact. ...The other that he compares to is the kid in Pittsburgh from CMU (Antonio Brown). He's built like that but is faster as far as burst and speed. He's not a big-framed guy so he will go where Wheaton did. He might sneak into the second. He's a slot. That's what he is."

WR [X] DAMIAN COPELAND, #7

LOUISVILLE ▶ GRADE: 5.10
Ht: 5-11 | Wt: 184 | Sp: 4.51 | Arm: 31 3/8 | Hand: 9

History: Florida prep. Redshirted in 2009 when he suffered a broken foot. In '10, caught eight balls for 113 yards (14.1-yard average) and zero touchdowns, but was limited to eight games (torn meniscus). Lost his 2011 season while nursing a hamstring injury. Started 25-of-26 games the next two seasons and was the Cardinals' leading receiver both years — produced 50-628-2 (12.6) in '12 and 58-780-5 (13.4) in '13. Did not start against Miami in Russell Athletic Bowl when he gave way to a two-tight end formation. Graduated and was granted a sixth year of eligibility but elected to leave school. Injured his left thumb during Combine drills.

Strengths: Makes good adjustments to the ball and has a fairly wide catching radius. Runs with urgency after the catch and carries a swagger. Solid production — two-time team-leading receiver. Has a 40-inch vertical jump and recorded the best 3-cone time (6.53 seconds) of any receiver at the Combine.

Weaknesses: Limited functional strength to escape tight press coverage. Lacks a feel for coverage to beat zones. Can be fazed by traffic — will alter his routes and make some concentration drops. Not a nuanced route runner and creates little separation with savvy — gears down out of his breaks and gives up break points. Struggles to escape man coverage. Not creative after the catch. Soft blocker — does not finish. Durability was a considerable issue early in his college career (missed 17 games with knee, foot and hamstring injuries).

Future: Runs a lot of simple digs, slants and bubble screens and is effective as a short-area, stationary target when he has free releases. Could compete for a job in the slot.

Draft projection: Priority free agent.

WR [X] MIKE DAVIS, #1

TEXAS   ▶ GRADE: 5.24

Ht: 6-0 | Wt: 197 | Sp: 4.55e | Arm: 32 3/4 | Hand: 10

History: Highly recruited out of Dallas Skyline, where he also played basketball. As a true freshman in 2010, started 5-of-11 games played (three at split end, two at flanker) and recorded 47 receptions with 478 yards (10.2-yard average) and two touchdowns. Did not play against Oklahoma (knee). Played all 13 games in '11, starting the first 11 at split end, and led Longhorn receivers with 45-609-1 (13.5). Started 11-of-13 games at flanker in '12, catching 57-939-7 (16.5). Gave way to extra tight ends in non-starts. In '13, started 11-of-12 games played at the "X" receiver and snagged 51-727-8 (14.3). Did not play against Kansas State and did not start against Iowa State (ankle). Did not work out at the Combine because of a right foot injury (medical exclusion).

Strengths: Good size and athletic ability — looks the part. Makes the hard catch look easy and can make the acrobatic, in-air catch extending high outside the numbers. Is capable of stretching a defense and creating chunk plays in the passing game. Good field awareness working along the sideline.

Weaknesses: Very stiff. Average play speed. Is easily rerouted and fazed by traffic. Not strong after the catch and makes few big plays. Has a case of the drops — inconsistent hands. Lackadaisical route-runner and blocker. Inadequate on-field body language and temperament — is usually at the back of the line in practice drills and does not exhibit urgency in his play or leadership traits in the locker room. Reprimanded by the Big 12 for a late hit on a defender's knees after the whistle vs. Iowa State.

Future: A big, long, athletic receiver with inconsistent hands and questionable toughness and effort. Displays starter-caliber physical traits, yet his playing demeanor and approach turn off many evaluators and could force his draft status to sink. Is at his best outside the numbers as an "X" receiver.

Draft projection: Late draftable pick.

Scout's take: "He is very tight-hipped and I didn't like the way he ran routes. He is a fourth receiver in the league, maybe a fifth. He doesn't make a good team. I wouldn't draft him. If you draft him, you draft him late. He doesn't make plays. If the ball is placed in the right spot, he doesn't make any adjustments. He does not make tough catches in traffic."

WR [FI-RS] BRUCE ELLINGTON, #23 (JUNIOR)

SOUTH CAROLINA   ▶ GRADE: 5.39

Ht: 5-9 3/8 | Wt: 197 | Sp: 4.52 | Arm: 31 | Hand: 9 5/8

History: Cousin, Andre Ellington, starred as a running back for Clemson and plays for the Arizona Cardinals. South Carolina native was a highly recruited two-sport star who won a state championship as a quarterback and lettered four times in basketball. Did not play football in 2010. Played all 13 games in '11, starting two, and caught 17 balls for 211 yards (12.4-yard average) and a touchdown with 20 kickoff returns for 463 yards (23.1). Started all 13 games in '12, producing 40-600-7 (15.0) receiving with 18-406 (22.6) on kickoff returns. Started 11-of-13 games in '13 when he led Gamecock receivers with 49-775-8 (15.8). Added 5-108 (21.6) on kickoffs and 3-16 (5.3) on punts. For his career, carried 25 times for 148 yards (5.9) and one touchdown. Also was the starting point guard on the basketball team for three seasons. Graduated.

Strengths: Bursts off the line — eliminates cushion and threatens vertically. Field-fast — accelerates in a hurry and turns over a fluid stride. Highly athletic. Excellent balance and agility. Gets in and out of cuts quickly. Good hands. Can turn a short throw into a long gain. Is not afraid to work the middle and take a hit to make a play. Tough and competitive. Has traits to be considered as a kick returner. Highly respected with special intangibles — leads by example and is smart, determined and hardworking.

Weaknesses: Is short and small-framed — durability could be an issue. Could stand to become a more nuanced route runner. Can be outmuscled in a crowd — not a go-up-and-get-it guy. Limited run strength. Underpowered blocker. Too often was a non-factor — was held to one catch or less in five games as a junior. Was not a home-run hitter in the return game. Split his time with basketball.

Future: A two-sport athlete who has already graduated, Ellington opted to forgo basketball and his senior football season to enter the draft. While he lacks desirable height and might not be an elite tester, Ellington brings explosiveness, hands and playmaking ability to the slot. Arrow is pointing up, and his desirable intangibles inspire confidence he'll reach his potential, especially now that he's able to focus solely on football.

Draft projection: Third- to fourth-round pick.

Scout's take: "I think he'll bring more value in the return game initially than he does as a receiver. I wasn't real excited about him."

WR [Z, X] QUINCY ENUNWA, #18

NEBRASKA   ▶ GRADE: 4.80

Ht: 6-2 | Wt: 225 | Sp: 4.46 | Arm: 32 5/8 | Hand: 9 1/2

History: Prepped in California, where he also competed in the high jump. Saw very limited action in 10 games as a true freshman in 2010 and had one catch for 10 yards (10-yard average) and zero touchdowns. Started 7-of-13 games in '10, catching 21-293-2 (14.0). Started all 27 games 2012-13 — produced 42-470-1 (11.2) in '12 (14 games) and 51-753-12 (14.8) in '13 (13 games). Team captain.

Strengths: Looks the part with terrific size, long arms and an NFL musculature. Can elevate and snatch throws above his head. Strong after the catch. Sheer size and brawn to block out corners outside. Has hustle traits. Knows where the sticks are and is very football smart. Excellent intangibles — team captain with a professional approach and leadership traits. Was a 21-year-old senior.

Weaknesses: Lacks elite top-end speed to separate vertically. Shows some hip tightness. Is not fluid or sudden out of breaks (wastes

steps). Not a natural catcher — lets throws into his body, double catches some and drops catchable throws.

Future: Big, tough, athletic, West Coast receiver who broke out as a senior. Has a mixture of "Z" and "X" traits and could even be viewed as a developmental H-back prospect.

Draft projection: Priority free agent.

WR [Z, F] SHAQ EVANS, #1

UCLA   ▶ GRADE: 5.42

Ht: 6-1 1/4 | Wt: 213 | Sp: 4.46 | Arm: 32 | Hand: 9 3/8

History: Highly recruited California prep. Began his college career at Notre Dame in 2009 when he saw action in six games and caught seven balls for 61 yards (8.7-yard average) and zero touchdowns. Transferred to UCLA and sat out '10 per NCAA rules. Played 13 games in '11, starting five at flanker, and tallied 19-309-2 (16.3) with 17 punt returns for 115 yards (6.8). Served a one-game suspension against California for his role in a fight against Arizona. Started all 14 games at the "Z" receiver in '12, snagging 60-877-3 (14.6) with 8-85 (10.6) on punt returns. Was the Bruins' leading receiver for the second straight season in '13 when he started 12-of-13 games at the "Z" and totaled 47-709-9 (15.1). Non-start was against New Mexico State when the Bruins had 10 players on the field for the first play from scrimmage.

Strengths: Good size. Good enough hands — catches balls that he should and makes hard catches look easy, yet drops easy catches. Extends outside his frame for the ball and can pluck it. Competes in a crowd and can make contested catches. Tied for the fastest 10-yard split (1.47 seconds) of any Combine participant.

Weaknesses: Average production. Lacks top-end burst, acceleration and long speed. Does not threaten the field vertically. Soft-tempered blocker. Displays little creativity after the catch. Struggles to shake tight man coverage and create separation.

Future: Good-sized, sure-handed possession receiver with the toughness to work through the middle and catch in a crowd. Can make a living as a zone-beating, move-the-chains target.

Draft projection: Third- to fourth-round pick.

Scout's take: "I would like to have Shaq Evans. He is a good athlete. He is big and pretty. His M.O. is that he doesn't play hard. The staff is disappointed they could not get more out of him. His production is not great. I gave him a late third-round grade. The consensus is in the fourth-fifth. He is not a blatant soft guy. On height-weight-speed alone, he should get in the fourth (round), I would think."

WR [Z, X] MIKE EVANS, #13 (SOPH-3)

TEXAS A&M   ▶ GRADE: 6.35

Ht: 6-4 3/4 | Wt: 231 | Sp: 4.53 | Arm: 35 1/8 | Hand: 9 5/8

History: Father, Mickey, was murdered when Mike was nine. Native Texan who only played one season of varsity football — averaged 18 points, eight rebounds and five assists on the hardwood and was considered a Division I basketball recruit. Redshirted in 2011. Started all 26 games 2012-13 and was the Aggies' leading receiver both seasons — catching passes from quarterback Johnny Manziel, racked up 69 receptions for 1,1394 yards (20.2-yard average) and 12 touchdowns in '12 and 82-1,105-5 (13.5) in '13.

Strengths: Outstanding size and length. Functionally strong to power through the jam. Boxes out defenders and is a big red-zone target. Hardwood background is evident — outstanding leaper with "above-the-rim" skills to go over top of smaller DBs and highpoint throws. Creates late, subtle separation. Tracks and adjusts. Makes contested grabs — attacks throws and outmuscles defenders in a crowd. Nearly unstoppable executing back-shoulder catches. Strong, reliable hands. Very strong after the catch — slams into tacklers, is a load to bring down and leans for extra yardage. Productive playmaker — averaged 20 yards per catch in 2013 and showed up in big games (18-566-5 vs. Alabama and Auburn). Good blocker. Physically dominant and tough. Will be a 21-year-old rookie.

Weaknesses: Monotone mover with pedestrian speed — cannot separate vertically or pull away from the pack. Unsudden acceleration. Stiff hips. Will have to make a living in traffic at the next level — will struggle to separate vs. quick-twitch NFL cornerbacks. Did not run a full route tree and could require patience learning the nuances of refined route running. Backyard element to his college success — must become savvier instead of depending on superior size and improvisational production. Can be hotheaded and lose control of his emotions. Basketball was first love.

Future: A prep hoopster with shooting-guard size, Evans combined with Johnny Manziel to form one of the most dominant quarterback-receiver connections in the nation the last two seasons. He's a big, physical, strong-handed, West Coast possession receiver with playmaking ability who projects as a No. 2 in the pros where he will make his money as a chain mover and red-zone target.

Draft projection: First-round pick.

Scout's take: "He has deceptive speed. He's still a No. 2 in the league. I will say this — he made that quarterback. If you look at all the circus catches he makes down the field, it's unbelievable how much he bails out Johnny Football. If you have a quarterback that can't see over the pocket and likes to just heave the ball up in an area, Evans is the guy you want on the receiving end. He'll make an inaccurate quarterback look good."

WR [Z] BENNIE FOWLER, #13

MICHIGAN STATE   ▶ GRADE: 5.03

Ht: 6-1 1/4 | Wt: 217 | Sp: 4.52 | Arm: 32 | Hand: 9 1/2

History: Michigan native who also competed in track, won a state long jump championship and a state basketball championship. Missed five games during his junior season because of a broken collarbone. Redshirted in 2009 while dealing with a stress fracture in his foot. Appeared in 13 games in '10 (one start) and recorded 14 receptions for 175 yards (12.5-yard average) and a touchdown. Also returned 15 kickoffs for 336 yards (22.4). Scratched 2-20-0 (10.) in '11, but was limited to five games (foot). Recovered a blocked punt in the end zone for a touchdown against Wisconsin. Started 7-of-13 games in '12 — five as the third receiver, one at "Z" and one at "X" — and tallied 41-524-4 (12.8). Started 8-of-13 games in '13, catching 36-622-6 (17.3). Also had 16 career rushes for 102 yards (6.4) and a touchdown. Did not play against Purdue (hamstring).

Strengths: Looks the part with excellent size. Shows the ability to track and adjust. Extends to snatch throws away from his body. Strong and productive after the catch. Good leaping ability. Flashes playmaking ability. Has special-teams experience. Untapped potential.

Weaknesses: Needs to get functionally stronger and play with more physicality. Lacks elite top-end speed to separate vertically. Route running needs refinement. Average suddenness in and out of breaks. Lets some throws into his body and drops have been an issue. Intermittent intensity. Has underachiever traits — motivation and work ethic should be examined.

Future: Big, talented, underachieving flanker who showed signs of life as a senior after injuries and inconsistency plagued his previous seasons. Is still rough around the edges and questionable hands and passion for the game could prevent him from reaching his ceiling.

Draft projection: Priority free agent.

WR (F)-KR AUSTIN FRANKLIN, #4

NEW MEXICO STATE ▶ GRADE: 5.10

Ht: 5-10 5/8 | Wt: 189 | Sp: 4.58 | Arm: 31 1/4 | Hand: 10

History: Played receiver, defensive back and kick returner in addition to playing basketball as a Texas prep. Played all 12 games in 2011 and caught 32 balls for 508 yards (15.9-yard average) and three touchdowns. Started all 12 games at the "Z" receiver in '12, totaling 74-1,245-9 (16.8). Sat out '13 spring practice as well as the first four games of the season because of academics — returned to play eight games, starting the final six at the "H" receiver, and led the team in receiving for the second straight season with 52-670-7 (12.9). For his career, returned 29 kickoffs for 605 yards (20.9) and 12 punts for 1 yard (0.8). Also carried 28 times for 130 yards (6.4) and zero touchdowns. *Strengths:* Accelerates smoothly off the line and chews up ground with long strides. Sinks his hips and is sudden out of breaks to create separation. Slippery underneath. Quick, soft hands to catch off his frame. Catches in stride. Has springs to elevate and highpoint. Creates after the catch and turns short throws into long gains — darts upfield quickly, dances past tacklers in space and shows long speed. Has experience covering kicks. *Weaknesses:* Is lean and needs to bulk up. Lined up in the slot and was not required to defeat press coverage. Ran an abbreviated route tree and needs refinement in this area. Prone to concentration drops. Questionable in traffic. Limited physicality and run strength. Underpowered blocker. Reception numbers were inflated by bubble screens. Does not project as an impact kick returner. Did not face NFL-caliber cornerbacks. *Future:* A lean, speedy, finesse slot receiver, Franklin missed the first four games of the season (academics), but pulled in 44 catches and scored 6 TDs in the final five games of the season, showing speed, quickness and some playmaking ability. Is raw, but has developmental value. *Draft projection:* Priority free agent.

WR (F)-RS JEREMY GALLON, #21

MICHIGAN ▶ GRADE: 5.24

Ht: 5-7 1/2 | Wt: 185 | Sp: 4.48 | Arm: 29 1/2 | Hand: 9 3/8

History: Two-time all-stater who played quarterback, running back and safety as a Florida prep. Redshirted in 2009. Appeared in 12 games in 2010 when he caught four balls for 49 yards (12.2-yard average) and a touchdown while returning 27 kickoffs for 589 yards (21.8) and 10 punts for 43 yards (4.3).

Did not play against Ohio State (shoulder). Played all 13 games (one start) in '11, catching 31-453-3 (14.6) with 3-46 (15.3) on kickoffs and 19-192 (10.1) on punts. Gave way to a two-tight end formation against Air Force. In '13, was the Wolverines' leading receiver for the second straight season and established a UM single-season record for receiving yards — started 12-of-13 games (gave way to two-tight end formation against Ohio State) and produced 89-1373-9 (15.4), with 6-32 (5.3) on punt returns. Set a Big Ten single-game record for receiving yards when he posted 14-369-2 against Indiana. Also had 16 career rushes for 102 yards (6.4) and zero touchdowns. *Strengths:* Fine route savvy to read coverage and uncover in zones. Good hand-eye coordination. Runs hard with good balance and vision after the catch. Outstanding production. Identifies with the game and is very passionate about it. Has return experience. *Weaknesses:* Short with a limited catching radius. Lacks top-end speed to separate vertically or run away from a crowd (consistently tracked down from behind). Not a natural hands catcher and will often body the ball. Lacks dynamic run skills for an undersized receiver. Much of his production results from schemed bubble screens and lateral tosses. Underpowered blocker. Will be a 24-year-old rookie. *Future:* Stocky, strong slot receiver with more of a running back's build, Gallon possesses the hands, zone awareness and toughness to fend for a job in the pros. Lacks the top-end speed desired as a kick returner, but shows enough burst to warrant an opportunity fielding punts. *Draft projection:* Late draftable pick. *Scout's take:* "He's a little slot receiver. He makes the game look easy. He's strong and compact. He's built almost more like a running back. I like him."

WR (F) RYAN GRANT, #3

TULANE ▶ GRADE: 5.12

Ht: 6-0 3/8 | Wt: 199 | Sp: 4.64 | Arm: 31 | Hand: 9 5/8

History: Prepped in Texas. As a true freshman in 2009, appeared in nine games and recorded nine receptions for 39 yards (4.3-yard average) and a touchdown. Started 6-of-12 games in '10, tallying 33-515-4 (15.6). Started one game in '11, but was granted a medical hardship because of season-ending hernia injury. Returned to start all 12 games in '12, snagging 76-1,149-6 (15.1). Led the team in receiving for the second year in a row in '13 when he started 12-of-13 games (gave way to two tight ends against Syracuse) and produced 77-1,039-9 (13.5).

Strengths: Good size. Smooth accelerator off the line. Good flexibility to sink his hips. Tracks throws and shows terrific body control to adjust. Impressive hands catcher — quick, soft mitts. Makes NFL-caliber catches, snatching throws out of the air away from his body. Determined runner with the ball in his hands. Nice upfield quickness to pick up yards after the catch. Good field awareness.

Weaknesses: Could stand to improve functional strength and physicality. Can be jammed and rerouted at the line. Pedestrian speed. Is an unpolished route runner and does not consistently separate — drifts into patterns neglecting deception and does not snap off breaks. Limited route tree. Marginal blocker. Appears lackadaisical at times — intermittent intensity, urgency and compete level. Questionable courage to work the middle of the field.

Future: Productive, monotone, unrefined, enigmatic mid-major receiver with one of the best pair of hands in the draft, though he comes with concerning tweener traits he will have to overcome. Lacks ideal speed and physicality to survive outside and lacks ideal suddenness and toughness to thrive inside. Workout numbers will be critical.

Draft projection: Priority free agent.

WR [X] MATT HAZEL, #84

COASTAL CAROLINA   ▶ GRADE: 5.17
Ht: 6-1 | Wt: 198 | Sp: 4.49 | Arm: 31 3/8 | Hand: 9 1/8

History: Prepped in South Carolina. As a true freshman in 2010, played 11 games (three starts) and caught 20 balls for 276 yards (13.8-yard average) and five touchdowns. Missed the season opener against West Virginia (illness). Started 9-of-11 games in '11, tallying 32-488-6 (15.3). Started all 13 games in '12 and posted 61-799-8 (13.1). Started all 14 games in '13 and produced 70-990-9 (14.1). Hurt his shoulder against Hampton and did not play against Elon. Led the Chanticleers in receiving his final three seasons. Owns CCU career and single-season receptions records. Was the third player in school history to participate in the East-West Shrine Game, joining Jerome Simpson (Vikings) and Josh Norman (Panthers).

Strengths: Good functional football-playing speed. Accelerates off the line and can create separation. Tracks the deep ball well, contorts his body in the air and can make difficult catches look easy. Can create after the catch

and make the first defender miss on bubble screens out of the slot. Willing blocker — displays surprising toughness for his size to mix it up with linebackers. Fared well vs. better competition (see South Carolina). Comes from a very supportive family and has strong personal and football character. The game is very important to him.

Weaknesses: Not physically strong with a lean body build, small hands and short arms. Can be knocked off routes by tight press coverage. Average strength and elusiveness after the catch. Looks for a landing spot before contact (hears footsteps). Alligator arms appear in traffic and bodies the ball along the sideline. Shows some tightness in his body coming out of breaks and routes could use more refinement.

Future: A smooth, fluid, athletic small-school receiver with the hands, body control and concentration to earn a roster spot and develop into a solid contributor.

Draft projection: Fifth- to sixth-round pick.

Scout's take: "He might be a riser coming out of the Shrine (all-star) game. He made some plays. He was one of the guys who stood out. ...He's a little bit raw, but he is athletic. He is a little bit of a stick and his skinny frame show up. He has pretty good hands and concentration. He will highpoint the ball. He has good balance and body control. I thought he would be a late rounder."

WR [F] ROBERT HERRON, #6

WYOMING   ▶ GRADE: 5.20
Ht: 5-9 1/8 | Wt: 193 | Sp: 4.47 | Arm: 30 1/2 | Hand: 9 3/4

History: Last name is pronounced "HUR-on." Los Angeles native who also starred on the track as a prep, recording a 10.5-second 100 meters. As a true freshman in 2010, played 10 games (one start) and tallied six receptions for 57 yards (9.5-yard average) and zero touchdowns. Did not play against Utah (ankle) or Colorado State (concussion). Started 8-of-12 games played in '11, snagging 43-379-3 (8.8). Did not play against Boise and did not start the final two games against Colorado State and Temple. Started all eight games played in '12, managing 31-657-8 (21.2). Did not play against Toledo and Cal Poly because of a shin injury, then suffered a hamstring pull against Nevada and sat out against Air Force. Started all 12 games in '13 and hauled in 72-937-9 (13.0). Split his time between running back and receiver his first two seasons — rushed 54 times in his career for 310 yards (5.7) and zero touchdowns.

Strengths: Good athlete. Exceptional

straight-line timed speed — can accelerate and get on top of DBs vertically. Quick-footed. Above-average hands. Has return capability (despite not being used as a returner because of offensive value).

Weaknesses: Does not play fast. Marginal toughness — does not like crossing the middle or extending across his frame. Drifts in his routes. Short-arms the ball. Does not adjust to or track the deep ball well. Lacks physical strength and is jarred on contact after the catch. Carries the ball loosely. Disinterested blocker, especially on the backside. Regularly matched up vs. inferior competition. Has been dinged a lot and long-term durability is a concern.

Future: Very diminutive, outside receiver with the timed speed to threaten the field vertically and potentially contribute in the return game. Needs to prove he can bow up against better competition and is more than a track athlete.

Draft projection: Fifth- to sixth-round pick.

Scout's take: "(Herron) has mid-round developmental potential. He has upside. I did a lot of work on him. He is a track guy. ... A lot of (scouts) were buzzing about him (at the Senior Bowl). Everyone says he will run fast and clock in the 4.3's. I don't see that play speed. You might see it with track spikes. He is showing better speed here than I saw on tape. He looks better in one-on-one's than he did in team. I don't think he likes traffic."

WR ⟨Z⟩-KR **CODY HOFFMAN**, #2

BYU   ▶ GRADE: 5.07

Ht: 6-3 7/8 | Wt: 223 | Sp: 4.64 | Arm: 33 1/4 | Hand: 9 3/4

History: Father, Derrick Ramsey, was a tight end with the Raiders and Patriots (1978-1985). Redshirted in 2009. Started 10-of-13 games in '10 and recorded 42 receptions for 527 yards (12.5-yard average) and seven touchdowns, while returning 15 kickoffs for 380 yards (25.3). Missed time during '11 spring practice because of torn rib cartilage, then tore the right labrum in his right shoulder during training camp. In the fall, started all 13 games and caught 61-943-10 (15.5). Set a school single-season record for kickoff returns and yards with 36-879 (24.4), including a 93-yard score against Central Florida. Started all 13 games in '12, hauling in 100-1,248-11 (12.5) with 3-72 (24.0) on kickoffs. Suffered a separated shoulder against San Jose State. After playing two seasons with a torn labrum, had it surgically repaired and sat out '13 spring practice. In the fall, started all 11 games played and posted 57-894-5 (15.7). Sat out the season opener against Virginia

(hamstring) and was suspended against Middle Tennessee State for a violation of team rules. Was the Cougars' leading receiver his final three seasons. Owns BYU's all-time records for receptions (260), receiving yards (3,612), receiving touchdowns (33) and all-purpose yards (5,105).

Strengths: Outstanding size with long arms. Extends outside his frame and can snag throws outside his body. Wide catching radius. Deceptively quick coming out of breaks. Has NFL pedigree. Experienced, four-year starter. Played through a shoulder injury during 2011 and '12 seasons. Is tough and durable.

Weaknesses: Comes off the line too gingerly and will struggle beating NFL press coverage. Limited agility to shake defenders releasing and does not create in space. Monotone route runner. Many of his catches are contested (minimal separation). Does not play to his size in the run game — uses too much finesse as a blocker. Average athlete with limited burst and explosion. Average leaping ability, as verified by a 27 1/2-inch vertical jump and 8'10" broad jump, the lowest of any receiver at the Combine. Must learn what it means to be a pro and could benefit from committing more to the craft.

Future: A big, outside-the-numbers possession receiver with good length and hand-eye coordination to fend for a roster spot as a No. 4 or No. 5 receiver.

Draft projection: Late draftable pick.

Scout's take: "I gave him a free-agent grade. He is soft, and he can't run (fast). He doesn't make our team."

WR ⟨F⟩-KR **JOSH HUFF**, #1

OREGON   ▶ GRADE: 5.28

Ht: 5-11 1/4 | Wt: 206 | Sp: 4.51 | Arm: 31 1/4 | Hand: 9 3/8

History: Prepped in Texas. Wore jersey No. 4 as a true freshman in 2010 when he played all 13 games (two starts) and caught 19 balls for 303 yards (15.9-yard average) and three touchdowns with 23 kickoff returns for 567 yards (24.7). Strained his left knee during '11 spring practice, then had his left foot in a walking boot during fall camp. On the season, started 10-of-12 games played and managed 31-430-2 (13.9) receiving with 8-174 (21.8) on kickoff returns. Suffered an ankle injury in the season opener against LSU — missed games against Nevada and Southwest Missouri State and did not start his first two games back. Was arrested in March '12 and charged with driving under the influence of marijuana, driving without a license and speeding, though he was ultimately acquitted. In the fall, started all 11 games played, recording 32-493-7 (15.4). Hurt his left knee against Fresno State and sat out against Tennessee Tech and Arizona. Started all 13 games in '13 and totaled 61-890-7 (14.6) with 11-252 (22.9) on kickoffs. Suffered a head injury against Stanford.

Strengths: Nice size with a lean, tight-skinned body. Very athletic with natural balance and body control. Good speed and a fluid stride. Soft, quick hands to extend and snatch throws off his frame. Makes contested grabs. Can take a hit and hang on. Settles in zone pockets. Creates after the catch — competitive, elusive and strong. Playmaking ability — averaged 18.4 yards per catch as a senior. Gets after it as a blocker — works to position, fit and sustain. Desirable temperament — determined, tough and confident. Has special-teams experience returning and covering kicks. Works hard and wants to be coached.

Weaknesses: Could stand to get stronger. Was not pressed at Oregon. Lacks elite explosion and top speed to pull away vertically. Limited route tree. Could stand to refine his route running. Lets some throws into his body and tends to trap some. Not a go-up-and-get-it guy (average leaping ability). Is relatively naïve through no fault of his own and off-field maturation is a work in progress. Could require emotional support and professional mentorship in order to avoid the pitfalls of NFL trappings.

Future: Smooth, competitive, versatile receiver with an impressive skill set which translates well to the evolution of NFL offenses. Can work at flanker or slot and has potential to become a No. 2 or No. 3 receiver in a system incorporating spread concepts. Is the type of player you root for, having persevered through an adverse upbringing and lingering baggage, which forced him to mature the hard way. Would be best served landing in a close-knit locker room with a nurturing position coach.

Draft projection: Fifth- to sixth-round pick.

Scout's take: "I liked him. He's probably more of a slot receiver or a team's third (receiver). He's good looking, but he's not very big. He is built more like a running back and used like one. They line him up as a slot receiver, motion him and hand off on counters and sweeps. He has inconsistent hands — that's the big thing. He made some key drops against Stanford. He was crying that game because he dropped a first down that could have brought them back closer to scoring. He's a good kid. He has above average finishing speed. I put him in the fifth round."

WR [F] ALLEN HURNS, #1

MIAMI (FLA.)   ▶ GRADE: 5.10
Ht: 6-1 1/4 | Wt: 198 | Sp: 4.58 | Arm: 32 | Hand: 9 1/4

History: Prepped in Florida — missed most of his senior season because of a torn left meniscus. Was a special-teams player as a true freshman in 2010 (wore jersey No. 80) when he recorded four tackles. Started 7-of-12 games played in '11 — recorded 31 receptions for 415 yards (13.4-yard average) and four touchdowns. Missed '12 spring practice while recovering from surgery to repair a torn labrum. Started 8-of-11 games played in the fall, catching 28-314-4 (11.2). Did not play against Bethune-Cookman (concussion) and broke his left thumb against Virginia. Led the Hurricanes in receiving in '13 when he produced 62-1,162-6 (18.7) in 13 games (11 starts).

Strengths: Good length and competitive speed. Runs hard after the catch. Adjusted well to frequent errant throws.

Weaknesses: Narrow-framed and non-physical. Struggles to separate against tight man coverage. Lacks polish and precision in his routes. Average burst out of his breaks. Is not a burner — limited long speed. Soft blocker.

Future: An underneath, zone receiver, Hurns emerged as the Hurricanes' top go-to receiver as a senior. Runs a lot of simple, stationary, short-to-intermediate routes and could have a more difficult time shaking NFL cornerbacks.

Draft projection: Late draftable pick.

Scout's take: "He does not have a lot of twitch or long speed. He plays 4.6. He is productive for his size and the way he catches, but there is no special quality to hang your hat on. He is a late-rounder."

WR [X] JEFF JANIS, #82

SAGINAW VALLEY STATE   ▶ GRADE: 5.34
Ht: 6-2 7/8 | Wt: 219 | Sp: 4.42 | Arm: 32 1/2 | Hand: 9

History: Also played basketball as a Michigan prep. Broke a finger on his left hand as a senior, causing him to switch to running back — returned to the field with a cast up to his left elbow. Redshirted in 2009. Started 6-of-10 games played in '10 and caught nine balls for 130 yards (13-yard average) and a touchdown. Started 8-of-11 games in '11, tallying 48-968-14 (20.2). Set SVSU single-season records for catches and receiving yards in '12 when he started all 11 games and piled up 106-1635-17 (15.4). Was Great Lakes Intercollegiate Athletic Conference Offensive Back of the Year in '13 when he totaled 83-1,572-14 (18.9) in 12 contests.

Strengths: Exceptional measurables and

leaping ability — will test through the roof. Accelerates into routes quickly and can separate vertically and uncover underneath working short-to-intermediate zones. Terrific production — carves up lesser competition and creates chunk plays. Good red-zone target. Exceptional work ethic. Outstanding football character. Very passionate about the game. Has a 37 1/2-inch vertical jump, posted a 3.98-second 20-yard shuttle (fourth-best among receivers) and a 6.64-second 3-cone time.

Weaknesses: Has very small, inconsistent hands — will cradle the ball and use his body. Is not a nuanced route runner. Does not attack the ball in the air and will give up some break points. Not strong after the catch and will look for a soft landing spot. Can be fazed by traffic. Regularly faced Division II competition. Not a consistent blocker — does not play to his size.

Future: A Division II standout with rare measurables and production, Janis must prove that he can translate his small-school success to the field against better competition.

Draft projection: Third- to fourth-round pick.

Scout's take: "On paper, he looks like a first-round pick. On tape, I was expecting to see more polish. He's not going to be instant coffee. There's still going to be a learning curve."

WR [F] CHANDLER JONES, #89

SAN JOSE STATE ▶ GRADE: 5.09
Ht: 5-8 5/8 | Wt: 180 | Sp: 4.50e | Arm: 29 | Hand: 8 5/8

History: Father, Mike, played receiver for the Vikings and Saints (1983-89), coached in NFL Europe and currently works as Tennessee State's offensive coordinator. Chandler is a Los Angeles native who also ran track in high school. Redshirted in 2009. Played all 13 games in '10, starting three, and had 54 receptions for 474 yards (8.8-yard average) and a touchdown. Started 9-of-12 games in '11, catching 61-566-2 (9.3). Played all 13 games in '12, starting three, and produced 54-691-11 (12.8). Started 11-of-12 games in '13 (gave way to extra tight end in season opener) — led Spartan receivers and set a SJSU single-season touchdown record with79-1,356-15 (17.2). Also had 18 career carries for 116 yards (6.4) and a touchdown. Notched 17 career tackles on special teams. Owns SJSU career marks for receptions (248) and touchdown receptions (29). One of two players in NCAA history to score a touchdown rushing, receiving and by fumble recovery in the same game (Hawaii, '11). Team captain.

Strengths: Has a feel for where to settle in zone coverage. Shows toughness to catch in traffic. Confident and competitive.

Weaknesses: Is short with very short arms and small hands. Not exceptionally fast for a smaller receiver. Average creativity and limited strength after the catch. Production inflated by lateral passing game and porous defenses.

Future: Smallish, productive slot receiver who plays bigger than his size and flashes the short-area quickness and zone awareness to compete for a job. Small hands and lack of physicality are limiting factors.

Draft projection: Priority free agent.

WR [F] T.J. JONES, #7

NOTRE DAME ▶ GRADE: 5.35
Ht: 5-11 5/8 | Wt: 188 | Sp: 4.49 | Arm: 30 5/8 | Hand: 10

History: Born in Winnipeg, Canada. Father, the late Andre Jones (died in June 2011), was a defensive end on the 1988 ND national championship team. Uncle, Philip Daniels, was a 14-year NFL defensive end with the Seahawks, Bears and Redskins (1996-2010), and currently works as the Director of Player Development for the Redskins. Cousin, DaVaris Daniels, is a receiver for the Fighting Irish. Godfather, Raghib "Rocket" Ismail, starred as a receiver and return man for the Irish (1988-90) before a pro career with the CFL's Toronto Argonauts (1991-92) and NFL's Raiders, Panthers and Cowboys (1993-2001). T.J. prepped in Georgia. As a true freshman in 2010, started 7-of-12 games played and recorded 23 receptions for 306 yards (13.3-yard average) and three touchdowns. Did not play against Utah (concussion). Started 12-of-13 games in '11, snagging 38-366-3 (9.6). Started 11-of-13 games in '12, catching 50-649-4 (13.0). Was the Irish's leading receiver in '13 when he produced 70-1,108-9 (15.8) while returning 14 punts for 106 yards (7.6) in 13 games (seven starts). Team captain.

Strengths: Fluid movement with good balance and body control. Releases cleanly and accelerates off the line. Excellent route runner. Sinks his hips and gets in and out of cuts cleanly to create separation. Adjusts to throws and has soft, reliable hands. Exhibits field awareness and is quarterback friendly. Quick and slippery after the catch. Comes from football family. Durable and experienced. Mature, likeable, intelligent team captain.

Weaknesses: Could stand to add some body armor and improve functional strength. Average physicality. Lacks elite top-end speed. Not exceptionally explosive, nor is he a go-up-and-get-it guy. Limited kick-return experience.

Future: Athletic, smooth-moving, polished receiver who runs crisp routes, has terrific hands and boasts NFL bloodlines. Balanced skill set, dependability and versatility will be valued at the next level, where he could be a productive No. 2 or No. 3 receiver in a sophisticated passing system. Arrow is ascending.

Draft projection: Third- to fourth-round pick.

Scout's take: "He is ideal in the slot. That's where he is going to make his mark."

WR [Z, F] JARVIS LANDRY, #80 (JUNIOR)
LSU   ▶ GRADE: 5.60
Ht: 5-11 1/2 | Wt: 205 | Sp: 4.60e | Arm: 31 3/4 | Hand: 10 1/4

History: Cousin of 49ers defensive tackle Glenn Dorsey, who starred at LSU (2004-07). Highly sought after recruit out of Louisiana. Suffered a stress fracture in his foot in the summer of 2011. As a true freshman in the fall, saw limited action in 14 games (one start) and scratched four receptions for 43 yards (10.8) and zero touchdowns. Added 11 tackles on special teams. Played all 13 games in '12 (one start), producing 56-573-5 (10.2) with nine special-teams tackles. Was the Tigers' leading receiver in '13 — started 10-of-13 games and racked up 77-1,193-10 (15.5). Was bothered by a foot injury in October. Strained his right hamstring running the 40-yard dash at the Combine and only ran one route in drills. Team captain.

Strengths: Good balance and body control. Savvy route runner — uses stems and nods and works back to throws. Confident hands-catcher — snatches throws off his frame. Extends and high points. Attacks throws and wins "50-50" balls. Makes some spectacular, acrobatic grabs. Good concentration and toughness over the middle. Does not go down without a fight after the catch. Willing blocker. Lined up outside and inside. Likes to compete and it shows. Has special-teams experience covering kicks.

Weaknesses: Has a fairly lean frame — could stand to bulk up and get stronger in order to combat the jam. Lacks elite explosiveness and top-end speed — does not have an extra gear to take the top off. Average line release, acceleration and suddenness. Could struggle to separate vs. quick-twitch cornerbacks. Large percentage of catches are contested. Lacks ideal height and is not a great leaper. Started just 12 career games.

Future: Polished, quarterback-friendly, sure-handed possession receiver with a flair for the highlight-reel catch. Could be an effective No. 3 option, capable of lining up as a "Z" or slot, working short-to-intermediate and beating zone coverage.

Draft projection: Second- to third-round pick.

Scout's take: "I know the bad 40 (time) at the Combine created a sour taste, but he pulled up short with a tight hammy. He plays faster than the 4.77 he ran. He's a legit high-4.5 guy. He runs fast as he needs to run. He has good competitive playing speed. I love his toughness. ... He does make some drops. He is a No. 2 receiver, and not a bad one."

WR [Z] CODY LATIMER, #3 (JUNIOR)
INDIANA   ▶ GRADE: 5.24
Ht: 6-2 1/2 | Wt: 215 | Sp: 4.55e | Arm: 32 5/8 | Hand: 9 5/8

History: Basketball was primary sport as an Ohio prep — played receiver, defensive back and kick returner in his two seasons as a football player. Appeared in eight games as a true freshman in 2011 (two starts) and had 12 receptions for 141 yards (11.8-yard average) and two touchdowns. Did not play against Illinois and missed the final three games because of hernia surgery. Started 10-of-12 games in '12, recording 51-805-6 (15.8). Was the Hoosiers' leading receiver in '13 when he posted 72-1,096-9 (15.2) in 12 starts. Did not work out at the Combine because of a left foot injury (medical exclusion).

Strengths: Very good size. Shows a jab step to get into routes cleanly and is equipped to combat the jam. Can use his frame and physicality to create separation on slants and "post-up" throws (strength was evidenced by benchpressing 225 pounds 23 times at the Combine, leading all receivers and besting some lineman. Nice catch radius — extends to snag throws off his body. Soft, dependable hands. Nice strength after the catch. Good blocker — subdues cornerbacks, shields, stalks and sustains. Improved steadily over three years as a starter.

Weaknesses: Is high-cut and shows some lower-body stiffness in his route running. Average burst off the line. Not a quick-twitch athlete — could struggle to shake loose from more athletic corners. Lacks foot speed to separate vertically. Is straightlinish after the catch and will not make anyone miss. Marginal special-teams utility. Football was not his first love.

Future: A prep basketball standout, Latimer is a well-built, sure-handed, West Coast possession receiver whose hardwood background is evident in his leaping ability, body control and hand-eye coordination. Lacks ideal explosiveness, gear change and flexibility. Could be effective running slants and making contested catches to beat zone coverage and succeed in the red zone. Has a ceiling as a No. 3.

Draft projection: Fourth- to fifth-round pick.

WR [F, X, Z] MARQISE LEE, #9 (JUNIOR)

USC   ▶ GRADE: 6.23

Ht: 5-11 3/4 | Wt: 192 | Sp: 4.46 | Arm: 31 3/4 | Hand: 9 1/2

History: Highly recruited Parade All-American who starred as an all-purpose football player, basketball player and track competitor as a California prep. Also competed as a sprinter and long jumper for the USC track team. Made an immediate impact as a true freshman in 2011 when he was named Pac-12 Freshman Offensive Co-Player of the Year — started 8-of-12 games and produced 73 receptions for 1,143 yards (15.7-yard average) and 11 touchdowns with 10 kickoff returns for 285 yards (28.5), including an 88-yard score against Washington. Teaming with Bills '13 second-rounder Robert Woods for the second year, totaled 118-1,721-14 (14.6) in 13 starts, garnering the Biletnikoff Award, Paul Warfield Award and Pac-12 Offensive Player of the Year. Was the Trojans' leading receiver for the second year in a row in '13 when he managed 57-791-4 (13.9) receiving, 10-164 (16.4) on kickoffs and 8-46 (5.8) on punts. Did not play against Arizona, Utah and Colorado because of knee and shin injuries. Also had 24 career rushes for 146 yards (5.5) and zero touchdowns. Owns or shares 24 USC records and three conference records. Team captain.

Strengths: Very good athletic ability. Is a nifty runner after the catch — can navigate through traffic and create with the ball in his hands. Can shift into top gear and run by tacklers — terrific acceleration and short-area burst. Fine route runner — understands how to set up defensive backs and has an innate feel for coverage. Understands how to manipulate man and zone coverage and can create separation when he needs to uncover. Very good hand-eye coordination. Tracks the deep ball very well — has a knack for running underneath it. Attacks the ball and plucks it out of the sky. Very good competitive, functional playing speed. Has game-breaking return ability — exceptional vision and traffic burst.

Weaknesses: Average size and run strength. Does not break many tackles. Was slowed by nagging injuries, and body is not built to withstand a lot of punishment. Can do a better job securing the ball through traffic — has shown a tendency to flag the ball. Long-term durability could become an issue.

Future: An extremely motivated, dynamic, playmaking receiver, Lee's junior season was plagued by shoulder, knee and leg injuries and a revolving door at head coach, where he cycled through three. Showed all the traits desired in a No. 1 receiver early in his career and has overcome a lot of adversity in his life to get to this point.

Draft projection: First-round pick.

Scout's take: "(Lee) is really talented. He didn't put up big numbers, but he is smooth, explosive, can change gears. He is a cinch first-rounder. The only thing I didn't like were the concentration drops. He will snatch the ball outside his frame and extend and pluck the ball out of the air and then he'll have some easy drops on simple routes. He does it at practice too. He still has good hands. He is going to catch eight out of 10, and five of them will be 'wow' catches. ... I think he could be a No. 1 receiver in the league."

WIDE RECEIVERS

WR [FI-PR] ERIK LORA, #88

EASTERN ILLINOIS ▶ GRADE: 5.10
Ht: 5-10 3/8 | Wt: 203 | Sp: 4.51 | Arm: 29 5/8 | Hand: 9 1/2

History: Lightly recruited Florida prep. Wore jersey No. 22 his first two seasons. As a true freshman in 2009, recorded 23 receptions for 320 yards (13.9-yard average) and two touchdowns in 12 games (one start). Started 9-of-10 games played in '10 and snagged 50-478-2 (9.6). Did not play against Central Arkansas. Sat out the '11 season while recovering from a herniated disc in his back and torn labrum in his hip. In '12, set the FCS single-season receptions record and was the Ohio Valley Conference Offensive Player of the Year after starting all 12 games at inside receiver and racking up 136-1,664-12 (12.2). Was the Panthers' leading receiver for the third straight season in '13 when he started 12-of-13 games played at IR and posted 123-1,544-19 (12.6). Did not start against Tennessee-Martin (gave way to a fullback). In his career, rushed 21 times for 180 yards (8.6) and zero touchdowns, returned 24 punts for 224 yards (9.3), including a score, and returned eight kickoffs for 144 yards (18.0). Also completed 3-of-4 pass attempts (75 percent) for 53 yards with two touchdowns and zero interceptions. Teamed with Walter Payton Award winning quarterback Jimmy Garoppolo.

Strengths: Highly competitive. Solid football IQ. Good coverage recognition and field awareness to uncover — has a knack for getting open and continuing to work free. Catches on contact and without breaking stride. Runs hard after the catch. Carries a swagger. Outstanding productivity (career leader). Has punt return experience.

Weaknesses: Has a non-descript body with short arms. Not a blazer. Could struggle to separate vs. man coverage in the pros. Lacks strength to beat tight press coverage or factor as a blocker. Limited speed and elusiveness to create after the catch. Can be tracked down from behind. Not explosive or dynamic in the return game to create big plays. Durability has been an issue — missed sophomore season after having hip surgery.

Future: A tough, instinctive, crafty slot receiver with very reliable hands. Has benefitted from a high-octane, dink-and-dunk spread passing game featuring a lot of quick-hitting routes. Must prove he can stay healthy and create separation vs. better competition to carve a niche.

Draft projection: Late draftable pick.

Scout's take: "Two words — Tim Toone. (Selected 255th overall as Mr. Irrelevant by the Detroit Lions in 2010.)"

WR [X, H] MARCUS LUCAS, #85

MISSOURI ▶ GRADE: 5.10
Ht: 6-3 3/4 | Wt: 218 | Sp: 4.58 | Arm: 33 5/8 | Hand: 9 3/8

History: Highly recruited three-sport athlete (basketball, track) out of Missouri. Saw very limited action in 10 games in 2010, catching three balls for 23 yards (2.3-yard average) and zero touchdowns. Played all 13 games in '11, starting three at the "X" receiver, and tallied 23-414-5 (18.0). Led Tigers receivers in '12 when he started 6-of-12 games and caught 46-509-3 (11.1), though he was demoted in favor of Bud Sasser the second half of the season. Started all 14 games at the "Y" receiver in '13, snagging 58-692-3 (11.9).

Strengths: Outstanding size and body length. Has good hands. Tough to enter traffic and catch on contact. Will do dirty work between the hashes. Has H-back potential.

Weaknesses: Shows only one gear and struggles to pop out of breaks or separate with quickness. Long strider with build-up speed. Is not strong or creative after the catch and is easily corralled.

Future: A lean, long-limbed, rare-sized, possession receiver, Lucas lacks starter-quality positional traits and does not play big, yet, with continued development, offers intrigue to teams as a developmental H-back.

Draft projection: Late draftable pick.

Scout's take: "No. 85 is a tweener. He's big and tough, but he can't separate. He'll probably have to be a flex tight end. He is not like Delanie Walker, but he has a good body. He's not a slouch."

WR [Z, F] JORDAN MATTHEWS, #87

VANDERBILT ▶ GRADE: 5.80
Ht: 6-3 1/8 | Wt: 212 | Sp: 4.47 | Arm: 33 1/4 | Hand: 10 3/8

History: Cousin of Hall of Famer Jerry Rice. Receiver-defensive back who also played basketball as an Alabama prep. Played all 52 games of his career. As a true freshman in 2010, started 10-of-12 games and caught 15 balls for 181 yards (12.1-yard average) and four touchdowns. Started all 13 games and paced Commodore receivers each of the next three seasons — produced 41-778-5 (19.0) in '11; 94-1,323-8 (14.1) in '12; and 112-1,477-7 (13.2) in '13. Rewrote the VU receiving records and owns Southeastern Conference records for career receptions (262) and receiving yards (3,759). Team captain.

Strengths: Good length. Big zone target. Good form as a route runner. Sinks his hips and pops out of breaks. Concentrates, tracks and adjusts. Soft hands and sticky fingers. Has leaping ability to compete in the air. Opens up his stride in the clear and shows nice long speed. Good field awareness. Gives effort as a blocker. Competes and plays with intensity. Tough and intelligent. Lined up outside and inside and has punt-return experience. Team captain and four-year starter with record-setting production.

Weaknesses: Could stand to bulk up his frame. Adequate line release. Fairly linear. Not a quick-twitch athlete. Does not show elite explosion to separate vertically. Lets some throws into his body and is not immune to concentration drops. Limited creativity and elusiveness after the catch. Can be moody and has some diva in him.

Future: A relative of Jerry Rice, Matthews departs Vanderbilt as the most productive pass catcher in SEC history. He's a tall, narrow-framed, West Coast possession receiver with soft hands, a professional approach and the versatility to line up inside or outside and become a solid No. 2 or No. 3. High-floor prospect.

Draft projection: Second- to third-round pick.

Scout's take: "I think he is a solid third-rounder. I am going to (grade) him inside. He's big, physical enough, handles contact well enough and has good hands. He's big and strong. He kind of reminds of the guy the Saints found late (Marques Colston). I know some scouts that put him in the first round. If he ends up running a lot better, I'll push up my grade. If he runs worse, I won't float him down much. He's still a good complimentary player. I don't think he'll ever be a No. 1 (receiver)."

WR IX, ZI **DONTE MONCRIEF**, #12 (JUNIOR)

MISSISSIPPI   ▶ GRADE: 5.85
Ht: 6-2 3/8 | Wt: 221 | Sp: 4.39 | Arm: 32 3/8 | Hand: 9 1/8

History: Highly recruited Mississippi prep who also played basketball and won a pair of long jump state championships. As a true freshman in 2011, started all 12 games at split end and recorded 31 receptions for 454 yards (14.6-yard average) and four touchdowns. Was the Rebels' leading receiver in '12 when he started 12-of-13 games (gave way to extra tight end against Texas) and snagged 66-979-10 (14.8). Started all 13 games in '13 and posted 59-938-6 (15.9).

Strengths: Terrific size. Smooth accelerator — jets off the line, eliminates cushion and has speed to stretch the field vertically. Good balance and body control. Can stem his pattern and leverage defenders. Drives off cornerbacks and creates separation. Knows where the sticks

are. Outstanding leaping ability to elevate and pluck throws out of the air. Flashes playmaking ability. Able to sidestep the first tackler and pick up chunk yards after the catch. Gives effort as a blocker to engage and seal. Has experience going head-to-head with NFL-caliber cornerbacks. Will be a 21-year-old rookie and has upside. Tied for the longest broad jump (11'0") among receivers at the Combine.

Weaknesses: Needs to sharpen his route running. Inconsistent ball reactions, particularly in traffic — better running through or under passes. Does not always play to his size — gets outmuscled for "50-50" balls and is still coming into his own as a dependable go-up-and-get-it guy. Average hand strength. Tends to trap some throws against his body and occasionally drops catchable balls. Could be more physical. Average elusiveness and open-field electricity. Showed he could be contained — seven games of 60 yards or less as a junior.

Future: Big, physically gifted "X" receiver with deep speed, leaping potential and playmaking ability. Could emerge a No. 1 or No. 2 receiver in a vertical passing offense, and his best football is in front him. Solid Combine showing elevated draft standing.

Draft projection: Top-50 pick.

Scout's take: "He got a third-round grade back from the (NFL's advisory) committee. I thought he came on strong down the stretch, and got better as the season went on. He has a lot of ability to work with."

WR IZ, FI **KEVIN NORWOOD**, #83

ALABAMA   ▶ GRADE: 5.34
Ht: 6-2 | Wt: 198 | Sp: 4.48 | Arm: 32 1/8 | Hand: 10

History: Prepped in Mississippi. Redshirted in 2009. Saw very limited action in 13 games in '10 and caught three balls for 56 yards (18.7-yard average) and a touchdown. Played in 11 games in '11 and snagged 11-190-0 (17.3). Sat out against North Texas and Arkansas (right ankle). Played through turf toe in '12 — started 11-of-13 games played at the "Z" receiver for the national champs, contributing 29-461-4 (15.9). Sat out versus Western Carolina (precautionary). Started 7-of-12 games played at the "Z" in '13 and caught 38-568-7 (14.9). Did not play against Colorado State (ankle). Team captain.

Strengths: Solid build. Good hands and concentration — extends outside his frame and makes the difficult catch. Fine route savvy — sells his routes with stems and nods. Understands how to get open. Good sideline awareness — dots the "i." Established rapport with the quarterback is noticeable (is the first receiver sought on broken plays) and keeps working to come free. Very solid personal and football character. Trustworthy, accountable and dependable.

Weaknesses: Has short arms. Does not pop out of his breaks or create separation with burst and acceleration. Struggles some defeating the jam. Can show more urgency as a blocker in the run game. Breaks few tackles after the catch.

Future: Quicker-than-fast possession receiver with trusted hands a quarterback cherishes in critical situations. Could develop into a reliable, third-down option route runner. Is best with free releases in the slot.

Draft projection: Fourth- to fifth-round pick.

Scout's take: "Norwood doesn't have a lot of speed to him. Some scouts have him (graded) as a free agent. I think he's a later pick. He can be productive enough because he is a decent enough route runner and has good enough hands. ... He's climbing. I would think about him in the third (round). He won't get out of four."

WR [FI-RS] SOLOMON PATTON, #83

FLORIDA   ▶ GRADE: 5.10

Ht: 5-9 1/4 | Wt: 173 | Sp: 4.55e | Arm: 29 7/8 | Hand: 9 1/4

History: Highly recruited out of Alabama, where he also ran track in high school. Was arrested in August 2010 and charged with misdemeanor alcohol possession. Was a reserve/special-teams player his first two seasons — played 23 games 2010-11, totaling seven receptions for 62 yards (8.9-yard average) and zero touchdowns. Added 11 coverage tackles. In '12, appeared in the first eight games before suffering a season-ending broken left arm injury against Georgia. Was the Gators' leading receiver in '13 — played the "Z," started 8-of-12 games and produced 44-556-6 (12.6). Team captain. Was voted team MVP and honored with the Iron Gator Strength and Conditioning Award as well as the team's Courage Award. For his career, rushed 31 times for 217 yards (7.0) and zero touchdowns, returned 39 kickoffs for 1,079 yards (27.7), including a score, and returned three punts for 84 yards (28.0), including a score.

Strengths: Good short-area burst and acceleration. Adjusts well to the thrown ball and stabs it out of the air. Extends outside his frame and catches the ball cleanly. Quick to turn upfield and displays fine vision and run instincts to create and elude tacklers. Is very tough for his size and can withstand a hit.

Weaknesses: Small framed and lacks run strength. Small catching radius. Gets overwhelmed in the run game as a blocker and barely gets in the way.

Future: Tiny, athletic playmaker with the toughness, burst and acceleration to factor readily in the return game and offer a flair as a receiver. Good hands and ability to create some magic with the ball overcompensate for marginal size. Can be effective on bubble screens, reverses and quick tosses.

Draft projection: Priority free agent.

Scout's take: "He won't get drafted. He goes as an undrafted free agent. We wouldn't waste a pick on a one-dimensional smurf."

WR [FI-PR] WALT POWELL, #9

MURRAY STATE   ▶ GRADE: 4.90

Ht: 5-11 3/8 | Wt: 189 | Sp: 4.62 | Arm: 31 5/8 | Hand: 9 1/2

History: Brother, Brandon Williams, was a 49ers third-rounder in 2006. Wore jersey No. 82 his first two seasons. As a true freshman in 2010, saw limited action in all 11 games and caught three balls for 16 yards (5.3-yard average) and zero touchdowns. Took ownership of the Racers' "Z" receiver in '11 when he started 7-of-11 games and produced 45-584-5 (13.0). Established MSU single-season receiving records in '12 — started all 11 games and racked up 94-1213-10 (12.9). Added 23 kickoff returns for 604 yards (26.3) and 19 punt returns for 301 yards (15.8), including two scores. Started all 10 games played in '13, totaling 66-837-13 (12.7) receiving and 11-346 (31.5), including a score, on kickoffs. Suffered a foot injury and was sidelined the final two games of the season against Tennessee State and Eastern Kentucky. Was arrested in October and charged with 4th degree assault (domestic violence) and theft by unlawful taking (less than $500) stemming from an incident at the Calloway County Fairgrounds — ultimately charges were dropped when a grand jury found insufficient evidence. Was the Pacers' leading receiver three straight years. Team captain.

Strengths: Loose lower body. Good balance and short-area quickness. Slippery after the catch — can elude the first tackler and dart to daylight. Shows confidence and a knack for finding creases as a returner — four scores the last two seasons. Productive three-year starter. Smart and competitive. Two-time team captain with terrific intangibles — cares about the game and works at his craft.

Weaknesses: Has a thin build and short arms. Needs to get stronger — ill-equipped to combat press coverage. Not an explosive, quick-twitch athlete. Average hands and foot speed. Route running needs refinement. Underpowered blocker.

Future: Lean, short-armed, smoother-than-sudden receiver/return man who will need the benefit of a free slot release given his pedestrian speed and strength. Intangibles and return skills will have to carry him, as he lacks distinguishable athletic traits.

Draft projection: Priority free agent.

WR [X]-PR TEVIN REESE, #16

BAYLOR   ▶ GRADE: 5.17

Ht: 5-10 1/2 | Wt: 163 | Sp: 4.46 | Arm: 31 5/8 | Hand: 8 5/8

History: Also starred in track as a Texas prep — high school teammate of Lache Seastrunk. Greyshirted in 2009. Worked as an inside receiver for the Bears. Played all 13 games in '10, starting four, and recorded 45 receptions for 401 yards (8.9-yard average) and zero touchdowns. Started 7-of-13 games in '11 and caught 51-877-7 (17.2). Played all 13 games in '12, starting the final 12, and snagged 53-957-9 (18.1). Non-start was season opener against SMU when the Bears began with two tight ends. Started 8-of-9 games played in '13, managing 38-867-8 (22.8) before he broke his right wrist against Oklahoma — missed four games and did not start against Central Florida in the Fiesta Bowl. Also had 11 career rushes for 136 yards (12.4) and zero touchdowns.

Strengths: Boasts freakish athleticism, including rare leaping ability. Explodes off the line. Fast and sudden. Turns over fluid stride with length and frequency. Stretches the field vertically. Tracks and adjusts to throws and displays terrific body control. Catches easily — snatches throws out of the air. Good short-area quickness. Darts upfield after the catch. Playmaking ability — averaged 19.4 yards per catch the last three seasons. Paced all receivers at the Combine with a 41-inch vertical jump and tied for the longest broad jump (11'0").

Weaknesses: In desperate need of NFL weight training and nutrition — is rail thin with small hands (weighed the lightest of any Combine participant). Can be jammed and re-routed at the line. Questionable toughness to consistently work the middle. Outmuscled in a crowd and struggles to make contested catches. Dabbled in track and is fairly straightlinish. Marginal blocker. Durability is a concern — has been dinged up and is not built to withstand the physicality of the NFL game.

Future: Thin, underdeveloped, confident, field-fast receiver with soft hands. Was a playmaker in a prolific spread offense. Will have to be a slot receiver given his dependence on a free release, but does not have an ideal skill set to work inside and could require patience.

Draft projection: Fifth- to sixth-round pick.

Scout's take: "He is tiny. He looks like an Ethiopian long-distance runner. He's really thin. He is a No. 4 receiver. He can't (escape) press coverage. He'd have to be inside really."

WR [X] PAUL RICHARDSON, #3 (JUNIOR)

COLORADO   ▶ GRADE: 5.27

Ht: 6-0 3/8 | Wt: 175 | Sp: 4.41 | Arm: 32 5/8 | Hand: 8 7/8

History: Father, Paul Sr., played at UCLA and had a cup of coffee in the NFL. Cousin, Shaquille Richardson, played cornerback at Arizona (2010-13). Paul Jr. starred in football, basketball and track as a California prep. Originally signed with UCLA in 2010, but was dismissed by then-head coach Rick Neuheisel after he was arrested, along with Shaquille and another incoming freshman, for theft — allegedly stole a female student's backpack from a storage locker. Moved on to Colorado, where he played all 12 games in the fall, starting four, and recorded 34 receptions for 514 yards (15.1-yard average) and six touchdowns. In '11, caught 39-555-5 (14.2) in nine starts — missed four October contests and was hampered the rest of the season because of a torn left MCL. Missed the '12 season after tearing his left ACL in April. Returned to start all 12 games in '13, leading CU receivers with 83-1,343-10 (16.2). Was bothered by a right ankle sprain (sustained against Arizona) in November. Team captain.

Strengths: Jab steps and accelerates into routes. Fluid and field fast. Chews up ground with long strides. Stretches the field vertically and can run under deep throws. Can drive off corners, break off and work back to the quarterback. Can extend to pluck off his frame. Shows he's capable of making the spectacular grab. Productive despite a poor supporting cast. Has a 38-inch vertical jump.

Weaknesses: Is very lean. Needs to bulk up and get stronger. Has been injured and durability could be an issue. Vulnerable to the jam. Does not separate consistently — needs to become a more refined, deceptive route runner. Average burst out of breaks. Lets some throws into his body and drops throws he shouldn't. Gets outmuscled at the catch-point for the ball. Limited run strength. Underpowered blocker.

Future: Very lean, narrow-framed, finesse "X" receiver who made an immediate impact at Colorado before knee injuries derailed his progress. Measurables will go a long way in determining his ultimate draft value, and his success at the next level is dependent upon his ability to make plays in the vertical passing game. Has a boom-or-bust element. Size and durability are question marks.

Draft projection: Third- to fourth-round pick.

Scout's take: "He is going to have to make his living outside the numbers. I don't think he'll stay in one piece working the middle. He has some freakish athletic ability, and he'll win most footraces."

WR IZ, FI ALLEN ROBINSON, #8 (JUNIOR)
PENN STATE   ▶ GRADE: 5.70
Ht: 6-2 5/8 | Wt: 220 | Sp: 4.59 | Arm: 32 | Hand: 9 1/2

History: Also played basketball as a Michigan prep. As a true freshman in 2011, saw very limited action in 11 games and caught three balls for 29 yards (9.7-yard average) and zero touchdowns. Started all 12 games in '12 and produced 77-1,013-11 (13.2). Was the Nittany Lions' leading receiver for the second straight year in '13 when he started 11-of-12 games and totaled 97-1,432-6 (14.8). Non-start was season opener against Syracuse when PSU opened with three tight ends. First player since at least 1985 to lead the Big Ten in receptions and receiving yardage in consecutive seasons.

Strengths: Excellent size. Good line release — defeats press. Sinks his hips, breaks off sharply and creates separation. Works back to the ball. Climbs the ladder — has elevation and body control to contort and make plays in the air. Turns short throws into chunk plays — gets upfield quickly and shows shiftiness, vision and run strength. Executed a full route tree in a pro-style offense. Highly productive — totaled 174-2,445-17 (14.0) in last two seasons. Will be a 21-year-old rookie. Recorded a 39-inch vertical jump.

Weaknesses: Lacks elite top-end speed — needs double moves to separate vertically and gets tracked down from behind. Occasionally tracking and leap timing are off. Is more confident in his hands outside the numbers or in the air than he is over the middle. Traps throws against his body and double-catches some. Tends to cradle throws or go down to the ground. Swings the ball loosely as a runner. Can improve physicality and sustain as a blocker.

Future: The Big Ten's leading receiver the last two seasons, Robinson is a big, fluid, outside receiver with a nice combination of "above-the-rim" prowess and run-after-catch ability. Offers possession skills, playmaking ability and red-zone utility to develop into a solid No. 2 option.

Draft projection: Second- to third-round pick.

Scout's take: "I don't like his demeanor. When you see he is not getting the ball, you see antics. I do like his size. He is like Anquan Boldin that way. He is a power receiver."

WR IFI-RS JALEN SAUNDERS, #8
OKLAHOMA   ▶ GRADE: 5.22
Ht: 5-8 7/8 | Wt: 165 | Sp: 4.44 | Arm: 30 | Hand: 8 7/8

History: Also ran track as a California prep. Began his college career at Fresno State in 2010, where he played all 13 games (one start) and had 30 receptions for 462 yards (15.4-yard average) and three touchdowns. Added 32 kickoff returns for 738 yards (23.1). Started 8-of-13 games in '11, snagging 50-1,065-12 (21.3). Following '12 spring practice, transferred to Oklahoma because he did not like the way he was being used in new head coach Tim DeRuyter's offense. Once eligible, he started 8-of-9 games for the Sooners and produced 62-829-3 (13.4). Started all 13 games in '13, totaling 61-729-8 (12.0). Also returned 31 career punts for 465 yards (15.0), including three scores.

Strengths: Light on his feet with a fluid stride. Good balance and body control. Nifty, conscientious route runner. Has speed and twitch to separate vs. man coverage — sinks his hips with ease and pops out of breaks. Quick, soft hands. Slippery after the catch. Eludes the first tackler and can turn a short throw into a long gain if he gets a step. Three punt-return TDs in 25 returns at OU — eludes the first wave, runs to daylight and can take it the distance.

Weaknesses: Marginal size. Cannot play outside — is easily knocked off course and needs a free release. Lets throws into his body. Small catch radius. Lacks elite top-end vertical speed, especially for his size (averaged just 12.0 yards per catch as a senior). Outmuscled in a crowd. Limited run strength. Lets throws into his body. Weak blocker — gets ragdolled outside. Durability could be a concern — is not built to take a pounding.

Future: A Fresno State transfer, Saunders is a lightweight, quicker-than-fast, competitive slot receiver and punt returner. Will always have size limitations, but has the hands, suddenness, polish and moxie to be a useful piece for a creative offensive coordinator able to free him up. Return ability adds to value.

Draft projection: Fifth- to sixth-round pick.

Scout's take: "He is a team's fifth receiver and punt returner. He's not strong. He has to be in the slot, but he's not an ideal slot receiver because he is too small. So the question becomes — what do you do with him? He had two touchdown returns on punts, but they were both short returns, and nothing he did made it happen. He was first-team all-conference as a punt returner, but second as a receiver. It kind of reminded me of Ace Sanders, but better. I was not a Sanders' fan."

WR [F] WILLIE SNEAD, #3 (JUNIOR)

BALL STATE   ▶ GRADE: 5.16
Ht: 5-11 | Wt: 195 | Sp: 4.62 | Arm: 33 | Hand: 10 1/4

History: Prepped in Michigan, where he played for his father and was the AP's Division 5-6 Player of the Year as a dual-threat quarterback. As a true freshman in 2011, started 4-of-11 games and had 28 catches for 327 yards (11.7-yard average) and two touchdowns. Started 12-of-13 games in '12 and piled up 89-1148-9 (12.9). Started all 13 games in '13, producing 106-1,516-15 (14.3).

Strengths: Controlled mover with nice balance. Gets in and out of breaks cleanly. Runs crisp routes — shows some savvy and subtle physicality to work himself open. Tracks and adjusts very well. Has soft, sure hands and catches naturally. Good concentration to make contested catches. Confident and competitive. Excellent two-year production.

Weaknesses: Lacks ideal height. Fairly monotone — does not have explosive speed to separate vertically. Too many catches are contested. Lacks wiggle to elude tacklers and create after the catch. Did not face top-notch competition.

Future: Productive, dependable, fairly polished possession receiver with natural receiving skills. Lacks ideal size and horsepower to thrive outside, but his sure hands give him a chance to compete for a role as a chain-moving, short-to-intermediate slot receiver.

Draft projection: Late draftable pick.

WR [F]-PR JOSH STEWART, #5

OKLAHOMA STATE   ▶ GRADE: 5.14
Ht: 5-9 7/8 | Wt: 178 | Sp: 4.69 | Arm: 30 | Hand: 9 3/8

History: Has a son. New Orleans native who relocated to Dallas because of Hurricane Katrina. Lost his mother and older brother in a car accident when he was just a baby, then was present when an accidental gunshot killed his father when he was five. Also played basketball as a Texas prep. Was a reserve as a true freshman in 2011 — played all 13 games and caught 19 balls for 291 yards (15.3-yard average) and two touchdowns. Also returned 13 kickoffs for 261 yards (20.1). Started 10-of-13 games in '12, amassing 101-1,210-7 (12.0). Was the Cowboys' leading receiver for the second straight season in '13 when he started 10-of-12 games played and posted 60-703-3 (11.7). Sprained his left ankle against Kansas and sat out against Texas. Also had 26 career punt returns for 438 yards (16.8), including a pair of scores.

Strengths: Good balance and body control. Runs routes with tempo and gear change to create separation. Nice stop-and-start quickness in short area. Flexible lower half to get in and out of breaks cleanly and execute speed outs and double moves. Shifty and slippery. Tracks and adjusts to throws very well. Quick hands. Attacks throws in the air. Experienced working from the slot. Can flip field position as a punt returner — makes one move to elude the first wave and runs to daylight. Confident and mentally tough. Pleasing, coachable and well-liked.

Weaknesses: Size is just adequate — lacks ideal height. Needs to bulk up and get stronger. Struggles to get off the jam and can be rerouted by more physical defensive backs. Lacks elite top-end speed to separate vertically. Ran an abbreviated route tree. Limited run strength. Underpowered blocker. Ordinary playmaking ability — averaged less than 12 yards per catch from 2012-13. Production decreased as a junior.

Future: Small-framed, quicker-than-fast slot receiver and punt returner. Is not uniquely electric, and will have to get his foot in the door on special teams. Stewart would have benefited from another year of college development, but is the type you root for, having persevered through tragedy and adversity.

Draft projection: Priority free agent.

WR [X] DEVIN STREET, #15

PITTSBURGH   ▶ GRADE: 5.23
Ht: 6-2 7/8 | Wt: 198 | Sp: 4.54 | Arm: 33 3/8 | Hand: 9 1/4

History: Prepped at Bethlehem (Pa.) Liberty, where he went to three state title games (one win) and excelled in track and field. Redshirted in 2009. Played all 13 games in '10, starting four, and caught 25 balls for 318 yards (12.7-yard average) and two touchdowns. Sustained a concussion during '11 fall camp. In the fall, started all 13 games and snagged 53-754-2 (14.2). Was charged (via mailed summons) with simple assault and conspiracy in November after a student told police he was hit in the head during a confrontation with Street and two other players — ultimately the charge was reduced to disorderly conduct, and Street was given community service. Was the Panthers' leading receiver for the second straight season in '12 when he started all 13 games and totaled 73-975-5 (13.4). In '13, managed 51-854-7 (16.7) in 10 starts — hurt his right shoulder against Virginia Tech and sat out against Old Dominion, then injured his elbow against Syracuse and missed the final two games against Miami and Bowling Green. Also rushed 11 times in his career for 77 yards (7.5) and zero touchdowns. Owns the school's career receptions mark (202). Team captain.

Strengths: Has excellent length and room for added bulk. Chews up ground with long strides. Is a big target underneath with a sizable catch radius. Shows natural receiving skills to track, concentrate and adjust. Soft, dependable hands to extend and pull in a throw off his body. Uses his big frame to post up defensive backs. Nice field awareness. Lined up outside and inside. Solid personal and football character. Productive, 40-game starter. Team captain.

Weaknesses: Has a thin build and could stand to pack on body armor — durability could be an issue. Needs to get stronger, particularly to improve his release vs. the jam. Builds to speed and is not a threat to take the top off. Leggy and fairly straight-linish — does not pop out of breaks or separate with quickness. Inconsistent route runner. Not aggressive or physical as a blocker. Can be more cognizant of ball security — carries loosely and swings the ball away from his body. Limited special-teams utility.

Future: Pitt's all-time leading pass catcher, Street is a narrowly built, long-levered, smooth-muscled receiver whose best assets are his length and hands. Needs to incorporate more physicality into his overall game, but has the ability to be an effective zone beater and red-zone target.

Draft projection: Fourth- to fifth-round pick.

WR [X] L'DAMIAN WASHINGTON, #2

MISSOURI   ▶ GRADE: 5.20
Ht: 6-3 7/8 | Wt: 195 | Sp: 4.44 | Arm: 33 3/8 | Hand: 9

History: Father was shot and killed in 1996 and his mother died from complications of a blood clot during one of his basketball games sophomore year of high school in Louisiana. Redshirted in 2009. Played 12 games in '10 (one start) and scratched five receptions for 35 yards (4.8-yard average) and zero touchdowns. A reserve again in '11, had 20-364-3 (18.2) in 13 games. Started all 12 games in '12 — first six at "Z" receiver, final six at "X" receiver — and tallied 25-443-2 (17.7). Started all 14

games at the "Z" in '13, producing 59-692-3 (11.9). Dealt with turf toe on his left foot the final five games of the season. Team captain.

Strengths: Very good body and arm length. Outstanding timed speed. Can threaten vertically and has explosive, big-play ability. Very competitive. Emotional leader driven to succeed. Very hard worker. Willing blocker.

Weaknesses: Classic body-catcher with small, skillet hands — consistently smothers and traps the ball. Does not track the deep ball well and adjustments look unnatural. Very inconsistent hand placement. Has a very skinny build and plays small in the run game — does not finish blocks. A bit straight-linish — not elusive after the catch. Tends to build to speed. Does not show a good feel for zones. Disappears for stretches. Could stand to improve beating the jam.

Future: A speed merchant with raw catching skills, Washington is still developing as a football player and has the type of determination to become a success story if he continues to refine his hands and work at the craft.

Draft projection: Fifth- to sixth-round pick.

Scout's take: "He's a straight-line speed guy with terrible hands. He drops a lot of balls — he does not know how to adjust his hands. He is so skinny. He plays small — he don't block. He's does not have immediately explosive acceleration. I thought he was a height-weight-speed guy. He's not even a B catcher. He's probably a C catcher. Someone will like him because of his speed, but the ball will have to be dropped right in his belly. Man he is a scary catcher — if the ball goes anywhere outside his frame, he has no hand placement and is flailing on balls that should have been caught."

WR [Z, F, X] SAMMY WATKINS, #2 (JUNIOR)

CLEMSON   ▶ GRADE: 7.25
Ht: 6-0 3/4 | Wt: 211 | Sp: 4.43 | Arm: 32 | Hand: 9 5/8

History: Brother, Jaylen, played cornerback at Florida (2010-13). Sammy was an elite recruit out of Florida, where he also won the AA state title in the 200 meters and finished second in the 100 meters. In 2011, was just the fourth first-year freshman in NCAA history to garner AP first-team All-America recognition, joining Herschel Walker, Marshall Faulk and Adrian Peterson — started 10-of-13 games and produced 82 receptions for 1,219 yards (14.9-yard average) and 12 touchdowns. Hurt his right shoulder against Wake Forest and sat out against North Carolina State. In May '12 was charged with two counts of misdemeanor possession when he was pulled over and found to have marijuana and pills he didn't have a prescription for (expunged upon completion of pre-trial intervention). In the fall, served a two game suspension before starting 7-of-10 games played and managing 57-708-3 (12.4) opposite Texans '13 first-rounder DeAndre Hopkins . Did not play against Boston College (abdominal virus) and was knocked out of the Chick-fil-A Bowl against LSU on the second play (right ankle). Started 12-of-13 games in '13, racking up 101-1464-12 (14.5), including 16-227-2 against Ohio State in the Orange Bowl. For his career, also returned 60 kickoffs for 1,376 yards (22.9), including a score, and returned punts 9-23 (2.6). Added 52 rushes for 339 yards (5.3) and a touchdown. Owns 23 Clemson records, including career receptions (240), receiving yards (3,391) and touchdowns (27, tied with Hopkins).

Strengths: Exceptional football playing speed — can flat out fly and take the top off a defense. Has world-class track speed. Extends outside his frame and plucks the ball. Outstanding body control and agility. Tracks the ball well over his shoulder and is a natural hands-catcher who can make an average quarterback look good. Consistently turns 2-yard gains into 15-yard chunks — possesses big-time playmaking ability and is very effective creating in the open field on bubble screens and quick-hitting short/lateral tosses. Superb run-after-the-catch ability. Good burst out of his cuts to separate. Has game-breaking return ability and is a threat to score every time he touches the ball. Has a strong support structure (mother moved to Clemson following Watkins' 2012 drug arrest and he has steered clear of any trouble). Will be a 21-year-old rookie.

Weaknesses: Production results heavily from a gimmicky offense. Routes could use some more polish. Does not consistently work the middle of the field. Could improve field awareness. Is still immature and could require some time to acclimate to an NFL playbook. Could stand to improve ball security and do a better job fielding punts.

Future: A legitimate No. 1-caliber receiver who stepped onto the field as a true freshman and made an immediate, game-changing impact. Was slowed by injuries as a sophomore, but responded with a strong junior season and capped his career as one of the most impactful receivers in school history. Has rare speed, soft hands and the big-play ability to challenge NFL defensive backs as a rookie.

Draft projection: Top 10 cinch.

Scout's take: "The best player in the draft is Sammy Watkins. He has a skill set where he can do everything. He can stretch the field even though he didn't get a chance to do it. He has quick feet and suddenness to create. Can come out of the backfield, play the slot, play outside. He is quick enough to avoid press and strong enough to beat press. …If you are talking about a pure athlete who can do it all — I think it is him. There is nothing he cannot do well."

WR [F]-KR ALBERT WILSON, #2

GEORGIA STATE ▶ GRADE: 4.75
Ht: 5-9 3/8 | Wt: 202 | Sp: 4.43 | Arm: 30 3/8 | Hand: 9 1/8

History: Played quarterback as a Florida prep. As a true freshman in 2010, appeared in 10 games and had 19 catches for 294 yards (15.5-yard average) and two touchdowns with 22 kickoff returns for 618 yards (28.1), including a score. Sat out against Lambuth (hamstring). Started 6-of-9 games played in '11, recording 37-772-6 (20.9) receiving, 13-239 (18.4) on kickoffs and 13-155 (11.9) on punts. Missed two games while nursing a hamstring injury. Started 10-of-11 games in '12, totaling 48-947-7 (19.7) receiving, 29-751-1 (25.9) on kickoffs and 10-94 (9.4) on punts. Was GSU's leading receiver for the third straight year in '13 when he started all 12 games and amassed 71-1177-8 (16.6) receiving, 31-730 (23.5) on kickoffs and 15-125 (8.3) on punts. Also had 47 career rushes for 331 yards (7.0) and a touchdown. Team captain.

Strengths: Has a strong, compact build. Very good timed speed and leaping ability. Will catch in a crowd and can make the first tackler miss. Nice run vision after the catch. Can take a hit and pop back up. Tracks the ball well over his shoulder. Has a feel for finding lanes in the return game. Continually improved and outstanding overall multipurpose production as a runner, receiver and return man.

Weaknesses: A bit straight-linish and unsudden out of his breaks. Limited strength to beat the jam and avoid the hold-up. Inconsistent hands-catcher. Has carried a sense of entitlement and is still learning what it means to be a pro. Could require some additional maintenance.

Future: Short, squatty, Sun Belt Conference standout utility threat with potential to compete for a job as a slot receiver and return man in the pros.

Draft projection: Priority free agent.

TIGHT ENDS

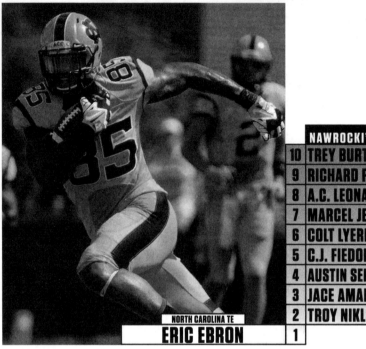

NORTH CAROLINA TE
ERIC EBRON

NAWROCKI'S **TOP 10**	
10	TREY BURTON
9	RICHARD RODGERS
8	A.C. LEONARD
7	MARCEL JENSEN
6	COLT LYERLA
5	C.J. FIEDOROWICZ
4	AUSTIN SEFERIAN-JENKINS
3	JACE AMARO
2	TROY NIKLAS
1	

EDITOR'S NOTE:
Y — In-line blocker
F — Slot, receiving role
H-Back — Move role

TE [F] JACE AMARO, #22 (JUNIOR)

TEXAS TECH ▶ GRADE: 5.55

Ht: 6-5 3/8 | Wt: 265 | Sp: 4.74 | Arm: 34 | Hand: 9

History: Also played basketball as a Texas prep. Was a reserve as a true freshman in 2011 when he caught seven balls for 57 yards (8.1-yard average) and two touchdowns in 12 games. Was arrested in March '12 for credit card fraud, though charges were later dropped. In the fall, started 6-of-7 games played — three at tight end, one at "H," one at "Y," one at "Z" — and managed 25-409-4 (16.4). Missed the last six regular-season games after taking a hit against West Virginia which caused a lacerated spleen, fractured rib and internal bleeding. Was ejected from Meineke Car Care Bowl against Minnesota for throwing a punch. Set an FBS record for receiving yards by a tight end in '13, though he was used primarily as an inside receiver — started 10-of-13 games and piled up 106-1352-7 (12.8).

Strengths: Exceptional size with a well-proportioned build. Releases cleanly into routes. Enough foot speed to stretch the seam. Functional hands to extend and catch. Gives effort as a move blocker and can block out defensive backs. Flashes nastiness. Historic one-year production.

Weaknesses: Was used as a slot receiver and does not show the functional strength and body power to match up with NFL defensive linemen. Is unsudden (average acceleration) and lacks elite top-end speed. Upright, unrefined route runner — shows hip and ankle stiffness in and out of breaks. Struggles to consistently separate. Fairly straight-linish after the catch, as confirmed by an average three-cone time (7.42 seconds) at the Combine. Ordinary run strength. Production was inflated by scheme and poor pass defenses. Labored to catch the ball at the Combine and really struggled to consistently haul it in.

Future: Very productive, finesse, detached tight end who racked up exceptional production as a junior when he was essentially deployed as an inside receiver for the Red Raiders. Will be best utilized in a similar role in the pros.

Draft projection: Second- to third-round pick.

Scout's take: "His body looks like he has never lifted a weight in his life. He's not a blocker, but he is a tough (expletive). I love his toughness. You see him kick the (expletive) out of people when he does block. He got kicked out of a game for punching a DB. He mauls them into the ground. As he was mauling the kid, he was punching him in the face last year and got suspended in the season opener because of it."

TE [Y] ALEX BAYER, #82

BOWLING GREEN   ▶ GRADE: 5.00

Ht: 6-3 7/8 | Wt: 257 | Sp: 4.77 | Arm: 33 3/4 | Hand: 9 5/8

History: Also played baseball as an Ohio prep. Redshirted in 2009. In '10, caught 22 balls for 298 yards (7.8-yard average) and a touchdown in 12 games (four starts). Started all 39 games the next three seasons — totaled 20-242-2 (12.1) in '11 (12 games); 36-410-3 (11.4) (13 games); and 37-593-4 (16.0) in '13 (14 games). Team captain.

Strengths: Very good size. Good base and knee bend as an in-line blocker. Functional wham blocker. Reliable short-area receiver. Hauls in off-target throws. Brings tenacity to the field and keeps working to pick off defenders. Respected, team captain. Very durable, experienced, three-year starter.

Weaknesses: One-gear route runner — creates minimal separation and lacks the route savvy, suddenness and acceleration to beat tight man coverage. Not elusive after the catch. Gives up too much surface area releasing. Limited explosion as an in-line blocker.

Future: Try-hard, effort blocker with enough athletic ability and blocking strength to fend for a No. 3 'Y' role, where he could bring the most value as a move blocker.

Draft projection: Priority free agent.

TE [Y] ROB BLANCHFLOWER, #87

MASSACHUSETTS   ▶ GRADE: 5.11

Ht: 6-4 1/8 | Wt: 256 | Sp: 4.85e | Arm: 33 3/4 | Hand: 9 5/8

History: Tight end-defensive end as a Massachusetts prep. Redshirted in 2009. Played all 11 games in 2010, starting four, and caught 21 balls for 179 yards (8.5-yard average) and three touchdowns. Was arrested in March '11 for OUI and possession of a fake ID. Started 8-of-11 games in '11, catching 18-208-1 (11.6). Started all 10 games played in '12 and tallied 43-464-2 (10.8). Did not play against Western Michigan and Bowling Green State (leg). In '13, started 5-of-6 games played and managed 27-313-3 (11.6), though he was bothered by a

bilateral sports hernia injury that prevented him from practicing, sidelined him for six games and medically excluded him from any workouts at the Combine. Team captain.

Strengths: Outstanding size. Competitive run blocker — drives his legs and works to finish. Tough. Functional pass protector. Lays out for the ball and will sell out his body to make difficult catches. Good career production — exits school as career receiving leader for a tight end. Smart. Solid special-teams temperament. Respected leader and two-time team captain. Four-year starter.

Weaknesses: Average athletic ability. Can improve beating the jam. Not a quick or savvy route runner. Rounds out of his breaks and can do a better job selling routes with stems and nods. Creates little separation. Takes what he is given after the catch — limited creativity and elusiveness. Inconsistent hands. Regularly matched up vs. lesser competition. Will be a 24-year-old rookie.

Future: A tough, scrappy competitive 'Y' tight end, Blanchflower was slowed by injury as a senior. However, he possesses the grit to factor in-line in the run game and can become a solid base-blocking No. 3 tight end and short-area receiving option.

Draft projection: Late draftable pick.

H-BACK-TE [F] TREY BURTON, #8

FLORIDA   ▶ GRADE: 5.20

Ht: 6-2 1/8 | Wt: 224 | Sp: 4.62 | Arm: 31 | Hand: 9 3/8

History: Dual-threat quarterback who also played basketball as a Florida prep. As a true freshman in 2010, started 11-of-13 games and tallied 32 receptions for 210 yards (6.6-yard average) and a touchdown. Started 7-of-13 games in '11, recording 19-149-1 (7.8). Did not play against Kentucky (herniated disc). Started 7-of-12 games in '13 and produced 38-445-1 (11.7). Was used as a tight end, H-back/wing back, fullback, receiver and quarterback by the Gators — also had 153 career carries for 720 yards (4.7) and 16 touchdowns and completed 11-of-17 pass attempts (64.7 percent) for 103 yards with zero touchdowns and an interception. Team captain. Did not perform bench press test at the Combine because of a left AC joint sprain.

Strengths: Very good athlete. Natural hands-catcher. Catches in stride and adjusts very well to the flight of the ball. Keeps working to uncover and has a good feel for zones. Good route runner. Sets up defensive backs and can create some separation out of his breaks. Can make the first tackler miss and is fairly elusive. Versatile and has played every offensive skill position. Football smart — understands offensive concepts and how the pieces fit together like a former quarterback. Outstanding personal character and will represent a team with class. Is tough and durable and will play through pain. Willing, effective special-teams contributor. Highly competitive team player.

Weaknesses: Has short arms and is very undersized for a tight end. Lacks run strength and does not power through tackles or create much yardage after contact. Marginal blocking strength and overall length to sustain and can be overwhelmed. Lacks top-end speed to mismatch safeties. Recorded a 30-inch vertical jump at the Combine.

Future: A savvy, athletic, undersized H-back who was utilized in a flexed receiving role in the Gators' offense. Has the athletic traits to earn a living working detached out of the slot as an 'F' tight end. Can offer a creative offensive coordinator a versatile jack-of-all-trades gimmick weapon.

Draft projection: Fourth- to fifth-round pick.

Scout's take: "I graded him as a receiver because he plays it more. He is not a true tight end. I put him in the fifth (round). Other teams have him as a free agent. He catches the ball well."

H-BACK-WR ANTHONY DENHAM, #8
UTAH ▶ GRADE: 4.80
Ht: 6-4 1/2 | Wt: 235 | Sp: 4.71 | Arm: 33 3/8 | Hand: 10 1/2

History: Never met his father, was taken away from his mother by social workers and placed in foster care when he was 11 and has family members who turned to gangs. Also lettered in basketball (two) and track (one) as a California prep. College receiver spent two years at East Los Angeles (CA) College — recorded 49 receptions for 1,189 yards (24.3-yard average) and 16 touchdowns in 2009 and 40-475-7 (11.9) in '10. Signed with Utah in '11, injured his hamstring during fall camp and redshirted. Missed '12 spring ball because of a broken thumb. In the fall, appeared in 11 games, tallying 11-135-0 (12.3). Started 10-of-12 games in '13 and totaled 24-291-2 (12.1).

Strengths: Outstanding size and overall length (body and arms). Can climb the ladder to secure the ball. Effective outside-the-numbers/red-zone target.

Weaknesses: Marginal play speed. Does not sell his routes and gives up break points. Struggles to beat the jam, and most catches are contested. Does not keep working to uncover or show much awareness for zones. Disinterested, lackadaisical blocker. No special-teams value.

Future: Long-limbed, high-cut possession receiver must learn what it means to be a pro to stand a chance to realize his potential. Very raw size prospect. Was invited to the combine as a tight end and proving he could project to the position in spring workouts could enhance his draft status.

Draft projection: Priority free agent.

TE [Y] JOE DUN DUNCAN, #9
DIXIE STATE ▶ GRADE: 5.05
Ht: 6-2 5/8 | Wt: 268 | Sp: 4.79 | Arm: 32 3/8 | Hand: 10 1/2

History: Also played basketball and baseball as a California prep. Walked on at Sacramento State in 2008, but suffered a microfracture in his right femur, forcing him to redshirt. Transferred to El Camino (CA) Junior College, where he played four games in '09 and scratched two catches for 14 yards (7-yard average) and one touchdown. Played eight games in '10, recording 13-211-3 (16.2). Signed with Division II Dixie State in order to play with his brother, Jake, a Red Storm linebacker. Was the leading receiver in '11 — started all 10 games and produced 64-949-9 (14.8). Did not play against Azusa Pacific (left MCL sprain). Went for arthroscopic surgery on his right knee prior to '12, at which time doctors discovered the cartilage had not properly reattached to the bone after his previous microfracture procedure. Another surgery was required, sidelining him for the season. Returned to start all 10 games played in '13, leading DSU receivers with 71-1045-13 (14.7). Did not play in the season finale against Central Washington (hamstring), then broke his left foot attempting a box jump during post-season training that excluded him from performing at the Combine.

Strengths: Big, soft hands and adjusts very well to the ball — outstanding hand placement and catching radius. Good muscularity and weight-room strength — benchpressed 225 pounds a TE-best 35 times at the Combine. Very good coverage recognition — feels his way through zones and finds open areas. Will drop his shoulder and barrel through contact. Flashes some power running after the catch. Respected, vocal, emotional team leader and it shows. Extremely smart. Outstanding football IQ. Football is extremely important to him. Emergency kicker and long-snapper. Superb production for a tight end.

Weaknesses: Average arm length and foot speed. Benefited heavily from facing inferior competition (able to separate vertically vs. small, slow defensive backs). Unsudden route runner. Not distinguished as an in-line blocker and plays down to the competition. Very inconsistent second-level blocker — does not sustain or finish. Will be a 25-year-old rookie. Durability is a concern — had multiple surgeries on his right leg.

Future: Stands out against lesser competition and could have made a statement in postseason all-star competition to solidify his draft standing. However, he broke his foot training for the Senior Bowl and only showed to interview. Age and injury history can diminish his value, but he possesses the intelligence, leadership traits and versatility desired at the bottom of a roster. Long-snapping ability could be his ticket.

Draft projection: Late draftable pick.

TE [F, Y] ERIC EBRON, #22 (JUNIOR)

NORTH CAROLINA   ▶ GRADE: 6.40

Ht: 6-4 3/8 | Wt: 250 | Sp: 4.58 | Arm: 33 1/4 | Hand: 10

History: Prepped in North Carolina. As a true freshman in 2011, appeared in 10 games (one start) and tallied 10 receptions for 207 yards (20.7-yard average) and a touchdown. Did not play in the Independence Bowl against Missouri (academics). Started 11-of-12 games in '12, catching 40-625-4 (15.6). In '13, set the Atlantic Coast Conference single-season record for yards by a tight end — started 11-of-13 games and totaled 62-973-3 (15.7), breaking Vernon Davis' ACC record for receiving yards. Hurt his right shoulder and was limited against Old Dominion. Strained his right hamstring on his second 40 attempt at the Combine and did not perform shuttles or drills.

Strengths: Releases cleanly and accelerates into patterns. Outstanding athletic ability and receiving skills. Threatens every level. Advanced route runner. Pierces the seam and is a mismatch vs. man coverage — regularly bested defensive backs. Terrific quickness, agility, balance and body control. Catches cleanly off his frame. Makes one-handed grabs look routine. Wide catching radius. Catches on the move and has an extra gear to pile up yards. Excellent production. Will be a 21-year-old rookie.

Weaknesses: Lacks ideal bulk. Can improve as a blocker, both in-line and on the move — could stand to improve technique, physicality and finish. Not equipped to lock horns with NFL defensive ends. Inconsistent adjusting to and fitting on moving targets. Could stand to play with more consistent intensity and focus. Makes the occasional concentration drop. Ordinary touchdown production.

Future: Highly athletic, highly productive "F" tight end loaded with upside and mismatch capability. Possesses the speed, movement skills, hands and run-after-catch skills to emerge as a playmaking weapon in the pros, though has room to continue developing as a blocker.

Draft projection: First-round pick.

Scout's take: "He's a big-time talent — no doubt about it. He looks the part. He has really good hands and movement skill. He will step inside and battle and shows the footwork to control the edge. He is going to be a complete, all-around tight end. I already put a middle-of-the-first-round grade on him and he keeps getting better. He might go in the top 10. He's better than all the first rounders I've done in recent years — (Brandon) Pettigrew, (Coby) Fleener, (Tyler) Eifert. Vernon Davis is special. He's not better than Vernon."

TE [Y] C.J. FIEDOROWICZ, #86

IOWA   ▶ GRADE: 5.48

Ht: 6-5 1/2 | Wt: 265 | Sp: 4.76 | Arm: 33 | Hand: 10 1/4

History: Given name is Colton John. Last name is pronounced "feh-DOR-uh-wits." Saw limited action in all 13 games as a true freshman in 2010 and did not record any receiving stats. Played all 13 games in '11, starting five, and caught 16 balls for 167 yards (10.4-yard average) and three touchdowns. Started all 12 games in '12, producing 45-433-1 (9.6). Started 12-of-13 games in '13, snagging 30-299-6 (10.0). Was replaced in the starting lineup by Ray Hamilton against Minnesota. Said head coach Kirk Ferentz: "Ray has been playing well as has C.J. It was more a matter of giving Ray an opportunity based on how he has been performing in games and practice."

Strengths: Outstanding size and big hands. Carries his weight well. Has size to widen the hole or seal defensive ends. Good balance and body control for his size. Surprising lower-body flexibility to sink his hips to run sharp-angle routes. Has stature and enough speed to threaten the seam. Understands how to use his frame and physicality to create subtle separation. Makes athletic hands catches off his frame. Sizable catch radius. Shows toughness and concentration in traffic. Lowers his shoulder to deliver a blow after the catch. Can line up in-line or split out. Smart and durable.

Weaknesses: Has average, build-up speed. Not elusive after the catch. Can improve as a move blocker and develop more of a mean streak to finish blocks. Average production. Could stand to adopt a more blue-collar work ethic when people aren't watching — is not a self-starter and has been able to cruise on his rare size and natural ability.

Future: Big-framed, linear and dependable, Fiedorowicz looks the part and has balanced skills to become a legitimate "Y" tight end in the pros. Is an asset as a competitive blocker and as a sure-handed, underneath receiver. Draft status could benefit from an average tight end crop.

Draft projection: Third- to fourth-round pick.

Scout's take: "He is a middle-round pick. He is a true blocking Y. He power-cleans almost 400 pounds and is a freak in the weight room. I wish I saw more hip snap on tape. His weight room numbers don't always convert to the field. He's robotic. His father is a big power-lifter."

TE [Y] CROCKETT GILLMORE, #10

COLORADO STATE   ▶ GRADE: 5.12

Ht: 6-5 7/8 | Wt: 260 | Sp: 4.89 | Arm: 33 3/4 | Hand: 10 3/8

History: Receiver-defensive end who also wrestled, played basketball and ran track as a Texas prep. As a true freshman in 2010, injuries to other players forced a switch from tight end to defensive end in August — tallied 11 tackles, two for loss and a sack in nine games played (wore jersey No. 99). Moved back to tight end during '11 spring practice, and was the Rams' leading receiver in '11 when he started all 12 games and recorded 45 receptions for 468 yards (10.4-yard average) and four touchdowns. Started 10-of-11 games played in '12, managing 19-263-2 (13.8). Did not play against Hawaii (torn left labrum). Started all 14 games in '13 and caught 47-577-2 (12.3). Did not lift at the Combine because of a strained left elbow.

Strengths: Has a good compact frame with long arms and very big hands. Scrappy, competitive blocker — latches on and plays through the whistle. Good finisher. Natural hands catcher. Catches in a crowd and will shake off a hit and run through contact. Rises to a challenge and matched up well as a base blocker vs. Alabama's Adrian Hubbard. Functional positional, pass protector — gets in the way. Very durable.

Weaknesses: Underdeveloped lower body with limited overall weight-room strength. Not a nuanced route runner to create separation and lacks polish releasing off the line (pinballed too easily). Limited suddenness and burst out of his breaks. Marginal creativity after the catch. Lacks top-end speed to threaten the seam. Has been a bit of a china doll and long-term durability requires evaluation. Recorded a 1.77-second 10-yard time, tied for slowest among tight ends at the Combine.

Future: A try-hard, developmental blocker capable of catching on as a No. 3 tight end with continued improvement in the weight room. Possesses above-average base blocking ability, hands and foot speed to carve a role.

Draft projection: Late draftable pick.

Scout's take: "He catches the ball okay. He's an above-average blocker. His biceps look bigger than his lower body. He looks like he does a lot of beach workouts. He's kind of a china doll. ...I can see him stick as a team's third tight end. I thought he jumped out a little bit at the Senior Bowl and had a good game."

H-BACK XAVIER GRIMBLE, #86 (JUNIOR)
USC   ▶ GRADE: 5.10
Ht: 6-4 1/4 | Wt: 257 | Sp: 4.94 | Arm: 33 5/8 | Hand: 10 1/4

History: Cousin of 2013 Browns first-rounder Barkevious Mingo, who starred at LSU. Grimble was a Parade and USA Today All-American who won football and basketball state titles at Bishop Gorman in Las Vegas. Redshirted in '10 after he hurt his ankle during fall camp. Started 7-of-12 games in '11 and recorded 15 receptions for 144 yards (9.6-yard average) and four touchdowns. Started 9-of-

13 games in '12 and snagged 29-316-5 (10.9). Missed time during '13 spring practice because of a fractured rib. In the fall, started 6-of-13 games and caught 25-271-2 (10.8). Sprained his shoulder against Arizona, then sprained his ankle against Notre Dame and missed the Utah contest. Did not lift at the Combine because of a right shoulder injury or perform any running because of a strained left calf.

Strengths: Has a nice frame for the position — room to pack on bulk. Can work the middle of the field, take a hit and maintain possession. Solid hands — can extend to catch and is a reliable short-to-intermediate receiver. Has the look of a throwback with the ball in his hands — rumbles downfield and is a load to bring down. Shows willingness as a blocker and potential to be functional with improved strength and technique.

Weaknesses: Needs to get stronger and could use more glass in his diet. Average balance. Narrow-based, underpowered, in-line blocker — gets manhandled and tossed aside. Releases tall and mechanically — too easily jammed and rerouted. Linear mover who builds to speed. Has been dinged up and durability could be an issue. Recorded a 26 1/2-inch vertical jump, lowest of any tight end at the Combine. Recorded a 4.85-second 20-yard shuttle time at his pro day, demonstrating poor agility.

Future: Big-framed, underpowered, underachieving tight end who did not live up to expectations at USC and made a curious decision to forgo his final season of eligibility despite producing a modest 25-271-2 (10.8) during an injury-affected 2013 campaign. Has size and enough athletic ability and hands to warrant developmental consideration.

Draft projection: Priority free agent.

TE [Y] NIC JACOBS, #88 (JUNIOR)
McNEESE STATE   ▶ GRADE: 5.00
Ht: 6-4 3/4 | Wt: 269 | Sp: 4.85e | Arm: 34 1/8 | Hand: 10

History: Tight end-defensive end who prepped in Louisiana. Began his college career at LSU (wore jersey No. 84), where he redshirted in 2010 and did not record receiving stats in '11 (10 games). Played nine games in '12 (one start) and tallied five receptions for 58 yards (11.6-yard average) and zero touchdowns. Was suspended for the Tigers' final four games for a violation of team rules. Transferred to I-AA McNeese State for the '13 season, starting 12-of-13 games and catching 32-453-4 (14.2). Strained his right pectoral muscle during the bench-press test and did not work out at the Combine.

Strengths: Outstanding size with a good frame — possesses enough girth to block inline. Effort blocker — works to position and tries to run his feet on contact. Effective move blocker — shows good awareness and reactions to adjust to and fit on targets. Functional short receiver — generally catches what he should and offers a short-to-intermediate target.

Weaknesses: Could stand to improve weight room and functional football-playing strength. Tight hips and stiff ankles. Pedestrian foot speed — does not threaten the seam. Will struggle to create separation vs. man coverage. Limited after the catch. Does not generate power through his lower half. Could stand to improve his blocking technique — tends to bend at the waist. Does not physically dominate FCS competition.

Future: An LSU transfer, Jacobs is a monotone, inline-blocking "Y" tight end lacking any distinguishable trait for the pro game. Will have to excel as a blocker to stick as a No. 3.

Draft projection: Priority free agent.

TE [Y] MARCEL JENSEN, #89

FRESNO STATE ▶ GRADE: 5.26
Ht: 6-5 3/4 | Wt: 259 | Sp: 4.84 | Arm: 34 7/8 | Hand: 9 7/8

History: Defensive end who also played basketball as a California prep. Signed in 2008 and grayshirted. Arrived with a broken right leg and redshirted in '09. Was listed as a defensive lineman in '10 when he appeared in two games. At tight end in '11, played 10 games (one start) and recorded two catches for 16 yards (8-yard average) and a touchdown. Added three blocked kicks. Did not play against North Dakota (left knee sprain) and missed games against San Jose State and San Diego State (left calf). Started 8-of-13 games in '12 and caught 20-339-4 (17.0). Started 9-of-13 games in '13 and tallied 26-353-3 (13.6). Strained his groin during Senior Bowl practice.

Strengths: Passes the eyeball test with outstanding size, including vines for arms. Big target. Smooth off the line for his size. Surprising speed to stretch the field. Can use physicality and his frame to outmuscle smaller DBs. Can adjust to throws and has good hands. Turns upfield with a head of steam. Gets after it in the run game — engages with leverage and works to position, sustain and finish. Lines up in-line and flexed. Smart and coachable. Arrow pointing up. Has a 35-inch vertical jump.

Weaknesses: Needs to get stronger — has untapped body power and potential as an in-line blocker. Shows some hip tightness in his route running. Is more advanced with linear routes than sharp-breaking patterns. Ordinary creativity and elusiveness. Relatively raw — still honing technique and developing positional instincts and nuances. At times looks like he's processing too much. Average production. Will

be a 24-year-old rookie. Recorded a pedestrian 20-yard shuttle (4.69 seconds), slowest among all tight ends at the Combine.

Future: Athletic, long-armed, ascending talent who did not play a starring role in a run-and-gun, receiver-dominated spread offense, but has raw physical tools to develop into a balanced "Y" tight end. Should only get better and has potential to become an asset in the running game and a mismatch in the passing game.

Draft projection: Fifth- to sixth-round pick.

Scout's take: "The Fresno tight end is stiff and cannot bend very well. He flashes blocking ability — he's 270 — but he does not bend. You can find those guys late or as free agents all over the place. They are a dime a dozen. He has little quickness or acceleration — he's not very athletic when turns up field. He stumbles."

TE [F] REGGIE JORDAN, #89

MISSOURI WESTERN ▶ GRADE: 5.18
Ht: 6-2 7/8 | Wt: 240 | Sp: 4.77 | Arm: 32 1/4 | Hand: 9 5/8

History: Won a state championship as a Missouri prep. Redshirted in 2009 and saw very limited action in four games in '10. Played all 12 games in '11 and caught six balls for 83 yards (13.8-yard average) and two touchdowns. Started all 25 games the next two seasons — recorded 23-230-11 (10.0) in '12 (14 games) and 23-366-4 (15.9) in '13 (11 games).

Strengths: Good speed to threaten the seam. Flashes the ability to bury defenders as a blocker — rides them off the screen and has shown the ability to dominate lesser competition. Can extend and pluck the ball outside his frame and create big plays.

Weaknesses: Average arm length. Not a polished route runner — runs very imprecise routes. Does not sink his hips, get in and out of breaks quickly or sell his routes to create separation. Marginal coverage recognition and feel for zones — runs into coverage. Plays too upright and does not run strong after the catch. Timed speed does not translate to the field and is still learning how to convert his strength to the field. Has struggled to gain and maintain weight.

Future: Developmental H-back with the raw tools to excite a tight ends coach. Many of his flaws are correctable and could blossom with continued refinement.

Draft projection: Late draftable pick.

TE [F] A.C. LEONARD, #1 (JUNIOR)

TENNESSEE STATE ▶ GRADE: 5.22
Ht: 6-2 3/8 | Wt: 252 | Sp: 4.51 | Arm: 33 | Hand: 9 1/4

History: Highly recruited Florida prep who began his college career at University of Florida. As a true freshman in 2011 (wore jersey No. 81), played nine games (four starts) and recorded eight receptions for 99 yards (12.4-yard average) and zero touchdowns. Tore his left meniscus in fall camp and was a non-factor the first eight weeks. Was suspended in February '12 — was arrested and charged with misdemeanor battery after a woman alleged he shoved her, grabbed her by the hair and threw her out of their apartment. Was sentenced to six months probation, paid $628 in court costs and underwent anger management counseling. Then was cited in May for driving with a suspended license. Transferred to TSU the following summer. In '12, started 8-of-10 games played and caught 51-733-6 (14.4). Did not play against Southeast Missouri. Started 6-of-12 games played in '13 and managed 34-441-5 (13.0). Did not play against Austin Peay and Butler.

Strengths: Releases quickly into routes. Relatively loose athlete with nice balance. Good speed to stretch the seam and separate on crossers. Soft hands — can extend to catch off his frame. Shakes tacklers and creates yards after the catch. Flashes mismatch and playmaking ability. Lined up all over the field. Led all tight ends at the Combine with a blazing 1.51-second 10 time and 4.5-second 40 time.

Weaknesses: Marginal size, bulk and strength to block in-line. Will be overpowered by NFL defensive ends — struggles to sustain, lets defenders cross his face and is not a finisher. Could stand to sharpen his route running and field awareness. Swings the ball loosely away from his body and fumbled three times in 2013. Marginal competition. Character, maturity and stability need to be investigated.

Future: A highly-recruited Florida transfer, Leonard is an athletic, one-dimensional, "move" tight end with good hands and run-after-catch ability. Must prove trustworthy, and will go as far as his receiving ability takes him.

Draft projection: Fifth- to sixth-round pick.

Scout's take: "Someone will take a flier on him after he ran the way he did at the Combine. I didn't think he played to it consistently. He's a project. He'll take some time to figure it out. He's raw."

TE [F] COLT LYERLA, #15 (JUNIOR)

OREGON   ▶ GRADE: 5.33

Ht: 6-3 7/8 | Wt: 242 | Sp: 4.61 | Arm: 32 3/4 | Hand: 10 1/4

History: Grew up poor in an unstable environment. Parents divorced when he was nine — mother was on disability and unable to provide adequate structure, discipline and guidance, oftentimes relying on coaches to keep Colt in line, according to a September 2012 article in the Oregonian. Father disappeared for eight months (fled to Hawaii) during Colt's high school years and missed all his games from his sophomore year on. Consequently, Colt skipped

stretches of class and was absent for meetings and practices, incurring suspension. Native Oregonian who won a state title and garnered all-state recognition as both a running back and linebacker. Ended a tumultuous recruiting process by committing to Oregon and then-head coach Chip Kelly. As a true freshman in 2011 (wore jersey No. 32), tallied seven receptions for 147 yards (21-yard average) and five touchdowns in 12 games. Missed the first week of '12 fall camp (undisclosed). On the season, started 9-of-13 games and contributed 25-392-6 (15.7). In March '13, tweeted a YouTube link of a video claiming the Sandy Hook Elementary school shooting tragedy was a conspiracy. He followed up by tweeting, "The parents of the kids that supposedly died in the Sandy Hook situation are liars." Started three of the Ducks' first four games in the fall and scratched 2-12-0 (6.0) — did not play against Tennessee (stomach flu, according to Lyerla, "circumstances," according to head coach Mark Helfrich), was suspended against Colorado for violating team rules, then quit the team on Oct. 6. Had his driver's license suspended Oct. 11 after getting four driving tickets in two years, then was arrested Oct. 23 for cocaine possession (pleaded guilty) after undercover officers reportedly spotted him snorting cocaine in a car in a Eugene, Oregon parking lot. Did not perform 3-cone drill because of groin injury.

Strengths: Good athlete. Fluid route runner. Very good body control. Adjusts easily to the ball. Can create in the open field with very good run skills. Natural hands. Good catching radius. Functional blocker with enough playing strength to sustain. Highly competitive and determined to prove critics wrong. Is smart and hardworking. Recorded a 39-inch vertical jump to pace all tight ends at the Combine.

Weaknesses: Lacks ideal bulk strength to block in-line. Overly emotional and prone to outbursts following a dysfunctional childhood that offered little direction and much confusion related to a divorce. Not a disciplined team player. Off-the-field issues linger. Drops were too consistent (see West Virginia). Only benchpressed 225 pounds 15 times.

Future: An extremely athletic receiving tight end, Lyerla was overshadowed by the play of emerging freshman Johnny Mundt and litany of issues (suspensions, drugs, academics). Has overcome a lot of adversity stemming back to his youth and defied the odds to become an impactful performer. Possesses elite physical talent, but his history could easily knock him down several rounds and off many NFL draft boards. Would benefit tremendously from a coach willing to serve as a strong father figure and an established, veteran locker room with a positional leader able to take him under his wing the way Kyle Long did at Oregon.

Draft projection: Third- to fourth-round pick.

Scout's take: "Lyerla's past and background will always be a concern. I know he works out like a phenom and you love the athletic talent. I'd guess he's going to be off three-quarters of the team's boards. He will fall just like (Aaron) Hernandez did, but in Aaron's case, he was actually 'cleaner' with no documented arrests. Lyerla would be a great value in the third (round), but it's too risky for us."

TE [Y] ARTHUR LYNCH, #88

GEORGIA ▶ GRADE: 5.10

Ht: 6-4 5/8 | Wt: 258 | Sp: 4.82 | Arm: 32 1/2 | Hand: 10 1/8

History: Highly recruited tight end-defensive end who migrated from Massachusetts. As a true freshman in 2009, appeared in 11 games (one start) and recorded two catches for 17 yards (8.5-yard average) and zero touchdowns. Was redshirted in '10 in order to preserve a year of eligibility. Was used exclusively as a blocker in '11 when he played all 14 games (one start). Started 13-of-14 games in '12 and contributed 24-431-3 (18.0). Started 11-of-12 games in '13 and caught 30-459-5 (15.3). Bruised his ribs against Florida and sat out against Appalachian State. Team captain.

Strengths: Good size. Functional short-to-intermediate target. Can adjust to throws and extend to catch. Strong and competitive after the catch. Willing to engage and compete as an in-line blocker. Has special-teams experience. Hardworking and football smart. Tough and durable. Team captain.

Weaknesses: Needs to develop more finishing strength — not yet ready to match physically 1-on-1 with NFL defensive ends. Can improve his base and leverage. Average quickness off the line. Pedestrian foot speed. Tight hips. Unsudden — cannot separate. Shaky hands (too many drops). Needs to improve his route running. Straight-linish after the catch. Thinks he's better than he is. Will be a 24-year-old rookie.

Future: Big, competitive, inconsistent tight end lacking special traits for the NFL game. Will have to dedicate himself as a blocker to have a chance to stick as a No. 3.

Draft projection: Late draftable pick.

Scout's take: "I liked his competitiveness. I didn't see any foot quickness. He ended up finishing the season stronger than he started. I gave him a PFA grade and could see him make it for his blocking effort and competitive nature more than his receiving skill. For us, I don't think he can beat out our No. 3 tight end. He reminded me of the Western Kentucky kid (Jack Doyle) that went undrafted last year."

H-BACK JAKE MURPHY, #82 (JUNIOR)

UTAH   ▶ GRADE: 5.10
Ht: 6-4 | Wt: 249 | Sp: 4.79 | Arm: 31 3/4 | Hand: 10

History: Father, Dale, played 18 years in the major leagues, winning back-to-back NL MVP awards with the Atlanta Braves (1982-83). Brother, Shawn, was drafted by the Dolphins in the fourth round of the 2008 draft. Jake, a high school receiver/safety, also played baseball and basketball as a Utah prep. Originally signed with BYU in '08 before serving a two-year LDS mission in Australia. Upon returning a semester earlier than expected, he was without a scholarship and did not want to grayshirt. Moved on to Utah, where he redshirted in '10. Played 10 games in '11, starting two, and had five catches for 64 yards (12.8-yard average) and a touchdown. Did not play against Washington (knee). Started 5-of-12 games in '12 and caught 33-349-4 (10.6). Started 7-of-8 games in '13 and pulled in 25-417-5 (16.7). Broke his wrist against UCLA, had surgery and missed four games.

Strengths: Dependable short-to-intermediate receiver. Adjusts to throws and has good, quick hands for a tight end — catches off his body. Functional as a back-side hinge blocker or move blocker. Has athletic bloodlines — father is 1982-83 National League MVP Dale Murphy.

Weaknesses: Lethargic release. Can be jammed up and rerouted off the line of scrimmage. Average speed. Stiff movement. Unrefined route runner — tends to drift. In-line blocking needs work. Gets overpowered at the point of attack. Could stand to play with more intensity. Ordinary production. Is not especially strong for an overaged prospect. Will be a 25-year-old rookie (served a two-year LDS mission).

Future: Overaged, fairly athletic tight end/H-back who grew out of the receiver position. Missed four games as a junior because of a broken wrist and made a premature decision to leave school early in order to support his wife and daughter. Sure hands are his only standout trait.

Draft projection: Late draftable pick.

Scout's take: "He didn't interview very well. He didn't understand a lot of football concepts. He's raw. He did not come across as confident. He spoke softly. He should have stayed in school another year."

TE [Y] JORDAN NAJVAR, #18

BAYLOR   ▶ GRADE: 4.85
Ht: 6-5 7/8| Wt: 256 | Sp: 4.93 | Arm: 32 1/4 | Hand: 10

History: Prepped in Texas, where he led the state's tight ends in receiving as a senior when he caught 52 balls for 787 yards (15.1-yard average and three touchdowns. Originally signed with Stanford — redshirted in 2009, but transferred instead of vying for positioning on the Cardinal's depth chart which included Coby Fleener (Colts), Levine Toilolo (Falcons), Zach Ertz (Eagles) and Ryan Hewitt. Sat out '10 per NCAA transfer rules. Served primarily as a blocker in Baylor's spread offense. Started 8-of-13 games in '11 and snagged 15-146-2 (9.7). Played all 13 games in '12, starting three, and caught 10-80-2 (8.0). Started 8-of-12 games played in '13 and contributed 10-85-0 (8.5). Injured his back against Buffalo and sat out against Louisiana-Monroe.

Strengths: Terrific size. Functional seal, "move" or "wham" blocker. Can stay frontal long enough to keep his quarterback clean in the quick game. Lined up inline and in the backfield. Catches the low-difficulty, short-to-intermediate passes he should. Produced the best 60-yard shuttle time (12.02 seconds) among tight ends at the Combine.

Weaknesses: Has short arms. Average foot speed. Stiff movement — cannot separate vs. man coverage. Does not play to his size. Poor in-line blocker — gets overpowered at the point of attack. Limited grip strength to sustain. Minimal receiving production (not a natural catcher). Clocked the slowest 40-time (4.98 seconds) among tight ends at the Combine and only benchpressed 225 pounds 18 times.

Future: Big, smart Stanford transfer who was used primarily as a blocker in an explosive offense, though he does not excel in this area or in the receiving game. Could be startled by the body power of NFL defensive ends, and has a ceiling as a No. 3 tight end.

Draft projection: Priority free agent.

TE [Y] TROY NIKLAS, #85 (JUNIOR)

NOTRE DAME   ▶ GRADE: 5.65
Ht: 6-6 1/2 | Wt: 270 | Sp: 4.80e | Arm: 34 1/8 | Hand: 10

History: Highly recruited two-way lineman/tight end out of Anaheim (CA) Servite, where he won a state title. Nephew of Hall of Famer Bruce Matthews. Played outside linebacker as a true freshman in 2011 when he played 12 games (one start) and collected 20 tackles, one-half for loss and zero sacks. Did not play in the Champs Sports Bowl against Florida State. Converted to tight end and backed up Bengals '13 first-rounder Tyler Eifert in '12 — started 7-of-13 games and tallied 5 catches for 75 yards (15-yard average) and a touchdown. Took on a more prominent role in '13 when he started all 13 games and produced 32-498-5 (15.6). Elected not to run the 40-yard dash at the Combine.

Strengths: Outstanding size with a well-proportioned, muscular build. Big target over the middle and in the red zone. Athletic with flexible hips and knees to run the full tight end route tree. Bursts into routes and stretches the seam. Good hands. Has playmaking ability. Lined up flexed and in-line. Good potential as a blocker. Bends his knees, shuffles and fans rushers wide. Works well in tandem and can combo block effectively. Takes care of his body and maintains low body fat. Has NFL bloodlines.

Weaknesses: Work in progress as an in-line blocker — lacks ideal base strength, grip strength and overall body power. Bends at the waist and falls off some blocks. Route running needs refinement. Is still learning to use his frame advantageously — inconsistent traffic player. Lacks elite top-end speed. Average elusiveness and creativity after the catch. Could stand to play with more physicality and become a better finisher.

Future: A converted DE/OLB who emerged from the shadow of Bengals 2013 first-rounder Tyler Eifert, Niklas is the latest in a strong line of NFL tight ends produced by Notre Dame. He boasts an intriguing combination of size, athleticism, receiving ability and blocking ability to develop into a bona fide, balanced, No. 1 tight end. Has played tight end for just two years and is clearly ascending.

Draft projection: Second- to third-round pick.

Scout's take: "He reminds me a little bit of Martellus Bennett, but he was a better blocker. Niklas is very raw in that area. I still think someone will take a shot at him in the second (round). …I think teams are trying to float some misinformation on him already, hoping he will fall to the third."

H-BACK JACOB PEDERSEN, #48

WISCONSIN   ▶ GRADE: 5.10
Ht: 6-3 1/2 | Wt: 238 | Sp: 4.89 | Arm: 31 3/4 | Hand: 9

History: Last name pronounced "PED-er-sen." Won a state football championship, played basketball and competed in track and field as a Michigan prep. Redshirted in 2009. Played all 13 games in '10, starting four, and caught eight balls for 132 yards (16.5-yard average) and two touchdowns. Missed time during '11 spring practice because of a broken right foot. Played all 14 games each of the next two seasons — caught 30-356-8 (11.9) in '11 (seven starts) and 27-355-4 (13.1) in '12 (10 starts). Started all 12 games played in '13, totaling 39-541-3 (14.1). Did not play against Ohio State (left MCL sprain). Caught the most touchdowns (17) by a tight end in school history.

Strengths: Used inline, in motion, in the backfield and as lead blocker. Gets off the line cleanly (smoother than sudden). Does

the dirty work and is willing to mix it up inside — displays leverage, knee bend and competitiveness. Effective move blocker. Very good personal and football character.

Weaknesses: Has short arms and small hands. Lacks ideal bulk strength. At a size disadvantage vs. NFL defensive ends. Ordinary acceleration and foot speed, especially for his size. Does not threaten the seam and lacks suddenness to separate vs. athletic defenders. Lets throws into his body and is not strong-handed. Average strength and elusiveness after catch. Does not exhibit fullback-caliber pop on contact to consider for conversion. Has a 28 1/2-inch vertical jump.

Future: A valued component of the Wisconsin offense, Pedersen lacks the girth to line up as an in-line tight end, but could function as a complementary H-back capable of deploying in multiple spots and catching short-to-intermediate passes in the play-action passing game.

Draft projection: Fifth- to sixth-round pick.

Scout's take: "He's just a guy. I'd be interested in him after the draft. I thought the other tight end there had more upside."

TE [Y] RICHARD RODGERS, #11 (JUNIOR)

CALIFORNIA   ▶ GRADE: 5.20
Ht: 6-4 | Wt: 257 | Sp: 4.87 | Arm: 32 5/8 | Hand: 10 1/8

History: Father, Richard Sr., was involved in "The Play" in the 1982 Cal-Stanford game, and currently serves as the special teams coordinator for the Carolina Panthers. Richard Jr. was a receiver-defensive end who also played basketball as a Massachusetts prep. Recruited as a tight end, committed to Cal and then-head coach Jeff Tedford. Saw very limited action in 2011 (13 games). Started 6-of-11 games played in '12 and caught 20 balls for 288 yards (14.4-yard average) and a touchdown. Did not play against Ohio State (ankle) and played the final three games of the season with torn ligaments in his right foot. Had surgery to repair a torn labrum and sat out '13 spring practice. In the fall, played 11 games and pulled in 39-608-1 (15.6). Injured his left thumb against Arizona, had surgery and did not play against USC.

Strengths: Good balance and body control. Dependable short-to-intermediate receiver. Can snatch throws off his body and make contested grabs. Has potential as a move blocker. Showed dedication and discipline re-shaping his body as a junior. Coach's son.

Weaknesses: Tight hips. Average speed and suddenness — dull in/out of breaks and struggles to separate vs. more explosive safeties. Unrefined route runner. Straightlinish after the catch. Started just 11 games in three seasons.

Future: Rodgers' career arc was affected by

Cal's coaching turnover, as the former high school receiver was recruited as a tight end by Jeff Tedford's staff and bulked up to 275 pounds as a sophomore when he was out of shape, in part because of a torn labrum and torn foot ligament. As a junior, Rodgers shed 30 pounds and shifted to inside receiver for Sonny Dykes, enabling him to show his more natural "F" tight end skills. Is an unpolished product, but could be a better pro than college player.

Draft projection: Fourth- to fifth-round pick.

TE [Y] AUSTIN SEFERIAN-JENKINS, #88 (JUNIOR)
WASHINGTON   ▶ GRADE: 5.50

Ht: 6-5 1/2 | Wt: 262 | Sp: 4.70e | Arm: 33 3/4 | Hand: 9 3/4

History: Highly recruited out of Washington where he also played basketball in high school. As a true freshman in 2011, started 10-of-13 games and caught 41 balls for 538 yards (13.1-yard average) and six touchdowns. Started all 13 games in '12 and hauled in 69-852-7 (12.4). Was arrested March '13 for DUI following a late-night car accident (blood-alcohol level was 0.18) — pleaded guilty, paid a $695 fine and was sentenced to 364 days in jail, 363 of which were suspended. Also was suspended for the season opener against Boise State. Broke his right pinkie finger during fall camp and had surgery to insert a pin in the finger. On the season, started all 12 games played and won the Mackey Award — snagged 36-450-8 (12.5) while establishing UW career records most receptions (146), receiving yards (1,840) and touchdown catches (21) by a tight end. Also played 17 games for the Huskies basketball team as a freshman. Combine examination revealed a stress fracture in his right foot which required surgery and precluded working out.

Strengths: Looks the part. Has outstanding size and stature — presents a big target and dwarfs defensive backs. Uses physicality to create separation and can post up in the red zone. Athletic — spent time on the UW basketball team. Terrific movement skills and receiving ability for a big man. Surprising foot speed and agility — stretches the seam. Adjusts to throws and has soft hands. Has potential to be an effective in-line blocker — has size and core strength to seal defensive ends.

Weaknesses: Could stand to sculpt his physique and get functionally stronger. Work-in-progress as an in-line blocker. Not an explosive athlete. Ordinary release. Builds to speed. Tight hips. Does not pop out of breaks. Limited elusiveness after the catch. Receptions and yards fell off by nearly 50 percent as a junior. Character and stability need to be looked into.

Future: An intriguing height-weight-speed prospect, Seferian-Jenkins has all the tools to be a legitimate No. 1 tight end in the NFL, though he has to maintain focus and consistency and continue improving as a blocker. Has good core strength to develop into a functional, all-around tight end if he learns to get after it in the run game. Suspect quarterback play dipped production as a senior.

Draft projection: Second- to third-round pick.

Scout's take: "He is a basketball dude — what everyone is trying to get at tight end. He has that Gronkowski-type basketball build. The quarterback sprays the ball and they don't have much outside him at receiver, so they can double-down on him. He started since he was a freshman and had success early. He has had some issues that I don't know if we'll be able to get past."

TE [Y] D.J. TIALAVEA, #91
UTAH STATE   ▶ GRADE: 4.80

Ht: 6-3 1/2 | Wt: 267 | Sp: 4.75e | Arm: 33 5/8 | Hand: 9 1/4

History: Last name is pronounced "Tee-al-uh-vah-uh." Two-way lineman and tight end who earned three letters in both basketball and baseball as a Utah prep. Was recruited as a defensive lineman — redshirted in 2009 and saw very limited action in '10 (nine games). Switched to tight end in '11 and started 6-of-13 games, catching seven balls for 74 yards (10.6-yard average) and a touchdown. Started 7-of-12 games played in '12 and had 6-31-1 (5.2). Did not play in the season opener against Southern Utah. In '13, started 4-of-6 games played and managed 17-93-3 (5.5) before having season-ending surgery to repair a broken right foot. Father, Don, passed away in November '13. Did not perform any workouts at the Combine because of a foot injury.

Strengths: Well-built, muscular blocker. Good arm length and overall mass. Can get in the way as a blocker. Efficient cut blocker. Functional short-area receiver.

Weaknesses: Has small hands. Spends more time on the ground than he should — lunges and overextends too much. Does not play big and feet do not run on contact. Very undisciplined route runner. Marginal release — easily pinballed and knocked off his path. Is not quick or urgent into his routes.

Future: Looks like Tarzan, but plays like Jane and must learn how to convert his natural strength to the field to earn his way in the NFL. Has raw moldable tools to be groomed as a developmental H-back or move tight end. Will require patience.

Draft projection: Priority free agent.

OFFENSIVE LINEMEN

NAWROCKI'S TOP 10

MARCUS MARTIN	10
SEANTREL HENDERSON	9
JA'WUAN JAMES	8
CYRUS KOUANDJIO	7
JOEL BITONIO	6
GABE JACKSON	5
ZACK MARTIN	4
TAYLOR LEWAN	3
JAKE MATTHEWS	2
	1

AUBURN OT
GREG ROBINSON

C MATT ARMSTRONG, #56

GRAND VALLEY STATE ▶ GRADE: 5.14

Ht: 6-2 1/8 | Wt: 302 | Sp: 5.32 | Arm: 33 | Hand: 10 5/8

History: Two-way lineman who also excelled in track and field as a Michigan prep. Redshirted in 2008. Started 11-of-13 games played in '09 — one at left tackle, four at left guard and the final six at center. Sustained a concussion midseason which kept him out of two games and prevented him from starting three others. Started all 12 games played in '10 (seven at right tackle, five at center). Did not play against Lake Erie (right quad). Sat out '11 — tore cartilage in his left knee and required bone graph surgery. Started all 12 games in '12, including 11 at right guard and one at center. Moved to the pivot in '13, started all 15 games and won the Division II Rimington Award as the nation's top center. Had surgeries after the season to remove bone spurs in his ankle and tighten his shoulder joint. Strained his right quad running the 40-yard dash at the Combine and did not lift because of a right shoulder injury. Also competed in track at field (throws) at GVSU.

Strengths: Has large hands. Good strength. Nice snap-and-step quickness. Works his hips and maneuvers to gain positioning. Can bend and slide. Can combo block and step to the second level. Smart, aware and competitive. Has played all along the offensive line. Four-year starter.

Weaknesses: Size is just adequate and does not look the part. Fleshy midsection. Could struggle to drop anchor vs. powerful widebodies. Not explosive. Plays short-armed. Hand use needs work — does not punch or jolt defenders. Latches on and stalemates rather than driving his man off the line. Has been dinged up. Marginal competition. Will be a 24-year-old rookie.

Future: Average-sized, smart, strong, scrappy, decorated Division II center who lacks exceptional athletic traits for the pro game. Faces a big jump in competition, but has a chance to stick as a swing backup if his versatility translates. Also competed in track and field (throws shot put), which affected his year-round football training.

Draft projection: Late draftable pick.

OLG-OLT JOEL BITONIO, #70

NEVADA ▶ GRADE: 5.75

Ht: 6-4 1/4 | Wt: 302 | Sp: 4.97 | Arm: 33 7/8 | Hand: 9 5/8

History: Prepped in California where he also

played basketball and competed in shot put. Redshirted in 2009, earning Offensive Scout Team Player of the Year. Was a reserve and special-teams contributor in '10 (14 games). Started all 38 games at tackle 2011-13. Team captain.

Strengths: Plays with vinegar and seeks to bury defenders — nasty finisher who runs his feet on contact and consistently blocks defenders off the screen. Extremely tough and durable. Highly versatile — can play any position on the line. Outstanding personal character and football character — work ethic, leadership and responsibility are all exemplary. Produced the best 10-yard split (1.69 seconds) and 20-yard split (2.80) of any offensive lineman at the Combine.

Weaknesses: Tends to shoot his hands wide and needs to improve placement — too grabby. Slips off blocks and could stand to play more under control. Operated heavily out of a 2-point stance and might need to get acclimated to playing with his hand in the dirt. Average knee bend in pass protection.

Future: An undersized college left tackle who projects best to the inside in the pros. Displays the tenacity, leg drive and mean streak that is highly coveted by OL coaches and could drive up his draft status. Could require some initial patience moving inside, yet possesses the skill set, intelligence and desire to successfully convert.

Draft projection: Second- to third-round pick.

Scout's take: "I think (Bitonio) is an inside guy. He is not a tackle. He dominates more at the position than (Chiefs first-round pick Eric) Fisher did and he went No. 1 overall. He was just two inches taller and longer. …Watch him run a linebacker down 40 yards down the field after a fumble vs. San Diego State. That one play defines what the kid is about."

C-OG RUSSELL BODINE, #60 (JUNIOR)
NORTH CAROLINA ▶ GRADE: 5.32
Ht: 6-3 1/8 | Wt: 310 | Sp: 5.18 | Arm: 32 1/2 | Hand: 10

History: Last name is pronounced "BO-dine." Prepped at Fork Union (VA) Military Academy, where his father is a teacher. Redshirted in 2010. Was a backup in '11 — played nine games, including two starts as an injury replacement. Started all 25 games 2012-13.

Strengths: Carries a load in his punch and plays with vinegar. Can seal and turn defenders in the run game to create small creases. Plays with a mean streak and likes to finish blocks. Is aggressive working up to the second level and efficient cutting linebackers. Rugged competitor. Stout anchor in pass protection. Versatile and has seen action at center and guard. Excellent weight-room strength — benchpressed 225 pounds 42 times to lead all participants at the Combine.

Weaknesses: Stiff-bodied. Plays short-armed and overextends. Average agility. Is late to switch off blocks. Relies too much on his upper-body strength. Mechanics deteriorate the farther he is asked to travel. Slow to adjust to counter moves. Produced the slowest 3-cone time (8.29 seconds) of any offensive lineman at the Combine.

Future: A top-heavy, barrel-chested, thick-bodied, short-area blocker, Bodine plays with a gritty football demeanor. Swing-interior versatility adds to his value.

Draft projection: Third- to fourth-round pick.

Scout's take: "I was not all fired up watching (Bodine) the first time. He is a bubble three (third-rounder) for me, and I didn't love him. I liked him early on, but the more you watch, the more you see the stiffness. He's not quick, but he is powerful in the upper body. There's not a 'wow' factor. I was surprised he came out, but there are never a lot of quality centers in the draft."

OLG CONOR BOFFELI, #59
IOWA ▶ GRADE: 4.80
Ht: 6-4 1/8 | Wt: 298 | Sp: 5.29 | Arm: 32 | Hand: 9 3/8

History: Last name is pronounced "bo-FELL-ee." Won a pair of state championships and lettered in basketball and baseball as an Iowa prep. Redshirted in 2009. Was a reserve 2010-11, seeing very limited action in seven games over two seasons. Injuries opened the door at the end of the '12 season when he started the final three games at left guard. Started all 13 games at left guard in '13.

Strengths: Understands angles and positioning. Can shuffle, slide and mirror defenders in pass protection. Good football intelligence and work habits. Plays hard and competes. The game is important to him. Versatile.

Weaknesses: Small-framed with marginal arm length and a narrow base. Average athlete. Sets tall. Not strong or explosive at the point of attack to move defenders. Is late to reach and cut off defenders. Spends too much time on the ground. Overwhelmed by Minnesota DL Ra'Shede Hageman. Only a one-year starter. Benchpressed 225 pounds only 21 times, the fewest of any guard at the Combine.

Future: Raw, light-framed zone blocker ideally suited for a role as a swing interior backup in a slide-movement protection scheme. Has the smarts and versatility to battle for a roster spot.

Draft projection: Priority free agent.

OLT JUSTIN BRITT, #68
MISSOURI ▶ GRADE: 5.18
Ht: 6-5 7/8 | Wt: 325 | Sp: 5.19 | Arm: 33 1/2 | Hand: 10 1/4

History: High school left tackle who also captured a state wrestling title, going 45-0 as a senior. Redshirted in 2009 and saw limited action as a reserve in '10 (13 games). Started all 13 games at LT in '11. Suffered a Jones Fracture in his left foot in July '12, but healed in time to start the first nine games of the season — six at right tackle, three at LT — before suffering a season-ending torn right ACL injury. Started all 14 games at LT in '13.

Strengths: Solid build with a stout base and long torso. Quick enough to cut off the outside rush and give help where it is needed. Recognizes the blitz and displays good enough agility to adjust to movement. Good work ethic. Very good weight-room strength — cleans nearly 400 pounds.

Weaknesses: Operates out of a two-point stance in a spread-option offense. Falls off blocks and does not finish. Very average sustain. Limited body control and recovery speed. Late to reach the block point on the second level. Does not create movement in the run game. Gives too much ground in pass protection.

Future: College left tackle with enough length and foot quickness to handle the blind side in a pinch, but is more ideally suited for the right side and could be best suited for a swing backup role. Has played nearly every position on the line and could add depth as a positional, wall-off blocker.

Draft projection: Late draftable pick.

OLG DAKOTA DOZIER, #78

FURMAN   ▶ GRADE: 5.36
Ht: 6-3 5/8 | Wt: 313 | Sp: 5.41 | Arm: 33 7/8 | Hand: 9 7/8

History: Two-way lineman who also wrestled as a California prep. Redshirted in 2009. Manned left tackle all four years for the Paladins. In '10, became the first freshman offensive lineman to start in 14 years, starting 10-of-11 games. Sustained a sprained ankle against The Citadel and did not start against Wofford. Started all 11 games in '11. Started all nine games played in '12 — sprained his left MCL against Chattanooga and sat out against Georgia Southern and Elon. Healthy in '13, started all 14 games. Team captain.

Strengths: Outstanding overall body mass and thickness, especially in the lower body. Strong power base with a very stout anchor. Locks down and dominates lesser competition in pass protection (pancake machine). Plays with vinegar and finishes blocks. Rose to the occasion vs. better competition (see LSU). Plays with good knee bend and generates movement off the ball. Experienced, four-year starter.

Weaknesses: Raw hand technician. Footwork is not clean. Shuffles instead of kicksliding and can get overextended attacking defenders. Carries his hands low and does not replace them. Oversets and gives up inside counters. Rolls slowly to the second level under control and can be beaten to the block point by speed. Can get complacent and play down to the competition level.

Future: Small-school college left tackle best suited to kick inside in the pros. Has the girth and enough athletic ability to compete as a guard or center and ornery football disposition desired in the trenches. A tough, gritty, road grader capable of paving the way in the run game, Dozier will require some technique refinement in pass protection, yet possesses clear starter potential with continued development. Draft status could ascend if he proves he can play center.

Draft projection: Third- to fourth-round pick.

Scout's take: "Some other (scouts) on the road have pushed that big tackle from Furman all the way up to the third round. I think it's too rich. He is a small-school guy. I think he's too short to stay outside. He's athletic to be pretty good in a year or two. I think there'll be an adjustment period needed. Some thought he could play left tackle — I didn't see that."

ORT LAURENT DUVERNAY-TARDIF, #66

McGILL (CAN.) UNIVERSITY   ▶ GRADE: 5.33
Ht: 6-5 | Wt: 321 | Sp: 5.00e | Arm: 33 | Hand: 11

History: Name is pronounced "loh-RON DOOVER-nay-TAR-dif." Quebec native. Played as a defensive lineman in 2010, starting 3-of-6 games played. Converted to offensive tackle and started all 26 games 2011-13. Two-time team captain bulked up approximately 65 pounds since his freshman season. Honored with McGill University's 1938 Champions Award for combining leadership with athletic prowess and academic excellence. Has designs on being a doctor — maintained a 3.9 GPA in the Ph. D. program, and the coaching staff reduced his practice commitments in order to accommodate his stringent academic workload. Is rated as the top prospect in the 2014 Canadian Football League draft according to the CFL Scouting Bureau. Participated in the East-West Shrine Game.

Strengths: Looks the part with outstanding upper-body strength and massive quads. Stout anchor in pass pro. Violent shock in his punch. Plays with a nasty temperament and seeks to bury defenders into the ground. Aggressive run blocker — runs his feet on contact and plays beyond the whistle. Is physically and mentally tough and will play through pain (fought through a torn left labrum injury as a senior and never took himself out of a game or missed time). Highly intelligent (in medical program) and football smart. Can take concepts from the board to the field.

Weaknesses: Raw technician. Lunges overaggressively and loses positioning. Can learn to play under more control and take better angles. Average recovery speed vs. inside counters. Lets defenders into his body and does not replace his hands — slow to re-load after initial strike (though he was playing thru a shoulder injury). Will need to adjust to playing a yard off the ball (Candaian rules) and getting into blocks more quickly.

Future: Tough, gritty, smart battler who transformed from an impactful 250-pound three-technique as a freshman. Made a successful conversion to left tackle as a sophomore and has grown to be a dominating Canadian 315-pound left tackle expected to be the first pick of the CFL Draft. Projects best inside in the pros and could prove to be the best product delivered from Canada's developmental system since Israel Idonije. Will require refinement, but has the physical tools and temperament that cannot be taught.

Draft projection: Fourth- to fifth-round pick.

OLG KADEEM EDWARDS, #73

TENNESSEE STATE ▶ GRADE: 5.24
Ht: 6-4 1/4 | Wt: 313 | Sp: 5.22 | Arm: 35 1/2 | Hand: 9 1/2

History: Won a state title as a Florida prep. Manned left guard all four years. As a true freshman in 2010, started 9-of-10 games played. Did not play against Austin Peay and did not start against North Carolina A&T. Started all 10 games played at LG in '11, missing just the season finale against Jacksonville State because of a left ankle sprain. Started all 11 games in '12. Started 12-of-13 games played in '13 — did not play against Austin Peay and did not start against Eastern Illinois.

Strengths: Outstanding size — built low to the ground with a thick trunk and vines for arms (big wingspan). Generates movement in the run game and seeks to bury defenders. Surprising balance and straight-line foot speed — steps to the second level easily. Has crude tools to work with. Motivated and coachable.

Weaknesses: Could stand to shed some bad weight. Gets lax with his technique. Needs to play with more consistent pad level. Needs to work on a more efficient short punch. Lets his feet stall. Thick, tight hips — struggles to maneuver and snap is limited. Is not sudden or explosive — more push than pop. Lets defenders cross his face. Intermittent urgency. Does not dominate physically inferior competition.

Future: A soft-spoken, thickly built, long-armed FCS prospect, Edwards is a raw base blocker who must make significant strides with his technique, ratchet up his play-to-play intensity and learn to play with power.

Draft projection: Priority free agent.

ORG MATT FEILER, #72

BLOOMSBURG ▶ GRADE: 4.90
Ht: 6-5 7/8 | Wt: 330 | Sp: 5.37 | Arm: 32 | Hand: 9 1/2

History: Two-way lineman out of Pennsylvania. Was a reserve in 2010, seeing limited action in 11 games. Started all 11 games at left guard in '11. Moved to left tackle and started all 25 games 2012-13.

Strengths: Outstanding size. Good upper-body strength. Can control and steer blockers when he gets his hands on them. Flashes pop in his punch.

Weaknesses: Not a natural bender. Limited explosion and balance. Spends too much time on the ground. Marginal arm length and agility to cut off the rush and handle edge speed. Late to hit a moving target.

Future: Top-heavy, thick-bodied, short-armed plodder best in a phone booth. College left tackle who needs to move inside for a man-blocking, power-based offensive line to fend for a roster spot in the pros.

Draft projection: Free agent.

ORT CAMERON FLEMING, #73 (JUNIOR)

STANFORD ▶ GRADE: 5.22
Ht: 6-4 7/8 | Wt: 323 | Sp: 5.36 | Arm: 34 | Hand: 9 7/8

History: Also lettered in basketball as a Texas prep. Redshirted in 2010. Started all 11 games played at right tackle in '11 — did not play against Oregon or Oregon State (ankle). Started all 28 games at RT 2012-13.

Strengths: Big body. Strong hands. Can down block and generate movement in the run game. Agile enough to run out of his kick-slide and push rushers wide. Shows alertness and reactions to combo block and pass off stunts. Three-year starter in a pro-style offense. Very intelligent.

Weaknesses: Thick, tight hips. Needs to improve footwork. Can be impatient in pass protection. Tends to bend at the waist. Could be stressed by quicker rushers. Average sustain. Does not generate power through his core, and lack of explosion confirmed in 23 1/2-inch vertical jump. Balance and coordination wanes on the second level — struggles connecting with moving targets. Does not consistently block through the whistle and could become a better, nastier finisher.

Future: Big, thickly built, experienced right tackle who graduated with a degree in aeronautics and astronautics and entered the draft early despite standing to benefit from another year of seasoning on The Farm. Has size and smarts to stick in a power/slide-protection scheme, but needs to make strides with his functional strength, technique and aggressiveness. Could be tried inside.

Draft projection: Fourth- to fifth-round pick.

OLG ZACH FULTON, #72

TENNESSEE ▶ GRADE: 5.27
Ht: 6-4 5/8 | Wt: 316 | Sp: 5.16 | Arm: 33 1/4 | Hand: 10 1/4

History: Brother, Xavier, played at Illinois, was drafted in the fifth round of the 2009 draft by the Buccaneers and currently plays in the CFL. Prepped in suburban Chicago. Manned right guard for the Vols. Played 12 games as a true freshman in '10, starting five — did not play against Ole Miss (left ankle). Started all 12 games in '11. Suffered a stress fracture in his left leg in the offseason. In the fall, started 11 games — suffered high ankle sprain, MCL sprain and bone bruise to his left leg against Alabama, forcing him to sit out against South Carolina. Started all 12 games in '13.

Strengths: Looks the part with good overall size and mass. Strong enough to anchor in pass protection. Flashes thump on contact and ability to down block and seal run lanes. Started 40 games in the SEC and has experience locking horns with NFL-caliber defensive tackles. Has raw traits to develop. Coachable pleaser and will appeal to offensive line coaches. Good teammate.

Weaknesses: Does not breathe fire or impose his will. Still learning how to generate power through his core. Has heavy legs and could stand to improve footwork. Is a soft puncher and tends to overextend. Needs to improve grip strength and sustain. Struggles to engage linebackers in space. Awareness is lacking — not ideally suited to shift to center. Struggles to connect with moving targets. Has a history of ankle injuries. Recorded the slowest 20-yard shuttle (5.18 seconds) of any Combine participant.

Future: Physically impressive, moldable right guard prospect with a good soldier's attitude to go along with untapped physical ability, though his tape falls short of his intangibles at this stage of his development. Could be a pet project for an offensive line coach confident he can turn Fulton into an effective mauler.

Draft projection: Fourth- to fifth-round pick.

Scout's take: "Scouts are all over the board on him, from the seventh (round) to the fifth to the second (round). I thought he was a fifth-round type player. I think he has ideal size and girth. He's not explosive or quick-footed. He's never able to dislodge a defender off the line of scrimmage. He plays with very little push and leg drive. He's more of a solid backup type. I went in there hoping to see a third-rounder. He shows some flashes but the majority of the time he is very average. He's not athletic enough to play center — that limits him."

OLG RYAN GROY, #79

WISCONSIN ▶ GRADE: 5.25
Ht: 6-4 5/8 | Wt: 316 | Sp: 5.14 | Arm: 33 1/4 | Hand: 10 3/8

History: Wisconsin native. Redshirted in 2009. Set a UW record by playing all 54 games of his career. Played 13 games in '10, starting two at fullback (wore jersey No. 47). Played 14 games in '11, starting four — three at left guard, one at center. Started all 14 games in '12 — 12 at LG, two at left tackle. Started all 13 games at LG in '13.

Strengths: Terrific size. Very football smart. Plays with awareness. Has enough strength to hold his ground. Can lean and seal when he has an angle. Surprisingly effective pulling and working to the second level. Competes and gives consistent effort. Three-year starter. Respected by teammates and coaches — solid work ethic and character.

Weaknesses: Needs to develop better hip snap. Average initial quickness, athletic ability and pop on contact. Has heavy legs and tends to bend at the waist. Needs to improve punch and grip strength. Struggles adjusting to and fitting on moving targets.

Future: Big, durable, blue-collar guard who is generally effective despite lacking exceptional physical traits. As a starter, is the type you look to replace, but could be serviceable backup in a slide-protection scheme given his size, intelligence and functional anchor.

Draft projection: Fourth- to fifth-round pick.

ORG JON HALAPIO, #67

FLORIDA ▶ GRADE: 4.95
Ht: 6-3 1/2 | Wt: 323 | Sp: 5.34 | Arm: 33 5/8 | Hand: 10 1/4

History: Two-way lineman as a Florida prep. Appeared in three games in 2009, but hurt his shoulder and was granted a medical redshirt. Started 7-of-12 games played at right guard in '10 when he split starts with Maurice Hurt. Did not play against Mississippi State (broken finger). Started all 26 games at RG 2011-12. Missed '13 spring practice (meniscus), then tore pectoral muscle in July — sat out the first two games before starting the final 10 at RG (reportedly played through an 80 percent pectoral tear). Suffered an eye injury requiring stitches against Tennessee. Team captain.

Strengths: Naturally thick with big hands. Can drive block and is effective when he has an angle. Functional anchor. Provides adequate three-step drop protection. Has a warrior's mentality — plays hurt. Made 43 career starts.

Weaknesses: Tightly wound — struggles reacting to movement, changing direction and recovering. Does not generate power through his hips. Poor contact balance. Empties the chamber with initial punch and cannot recoil. Hands and feet do not work in unison. Opens the gate in pass protection. Unsudden to clear his feet and pull. Limited blocking range. Tied for the lowest vertical jump (211/2 inches) of any offensive lineman at the Combine.

Future: A hulking short-area guard whose best traits are intangible. Is most effective in a phone booth, but too often looks like he requires max effort to provide adequate blocking. Best chance to stick will be in a slide-protection scheme.

Draft projection: Priority free agent.

Scout's take: "Everyone said he played better last year. I couldn't warm up to him on the school call. He's just a plodder."

C JONOTTHAN HARRISON #72

FLORIDA   ▶ GRADE: 5.24

Ht: 6-3 1/2 | Wt: 304 | Sp: 5.09 | Arm: 33 3/8 | Hand: 9 7/8

History: High school teammate of former Gator and current Buccaneer Jeff Demps. Redshirted in 2009. Primarily a reserve/special-teams contributor in '10 when he played all 13 games, drawing his first start at right tackle against Penn State in the Outback Bowl. Started all 13 at center in '11 (played left guard against South Carolina). Started all 25 games at center 2012-13. Hurt his right elbow against Vanderbilt in '12. Was ejected from the '13 Arkansas game for accidentally touching an official — Harrison claimed he was complaining about defenders using racist language. Team captain.

Strengths: Outstanding size and arm length with good overall body thickness. Plays with fine balance and knee bend. Sits to anchor and can stop a charge. Matches up well vs. size and power. Strong run blocker — can generate some movement. Sets the protections and makes the line calls. Keeps his head on a swivel — shows awareness to switch off blocks and pick up the blitz and handle stunts. Good work ethic. Well-respected, articulate team player.

Weaknesses: Average athletic ability. Could stand to improve sustaining and finishing blocks. Lets quick penetrators cross his face. Average recovery speed once beat. Lacks ideal foot quickness and agility to pull and cut off linebackers at the second level. Can do a better job replacing his hands (tends to grab). Can learn to keep emotions in check — ejected from Arkansas game (2013) for unsportsmanlike conduct (bumped an official).

Future: Very good-sized mauler functions well in a phone booth. Possesses the strength and power to match up vs. big bodies. The farther he is asked to move, the more he will struggle and would be best in a man-blocking power scheme.

Draft projection: Fourth- to fifth-round pick.

ORT SEANTREL HENDERSON, #77

MIAMI (FLA.)   ▶ GRADE: 5.62

Ht: 6-7 1/8 | Wt: 331 | Sp: 5.04 | Arm: 34 5/8 | Hand: 10 1/2

History: Prepped at St. Paul (MN) Cretin-Derham, where he won a state championship and participated in basketball and track field. Was the first lineman to win USA Today's High School Offensive Player of the Year. Also was Parade's Player of the Year as well as the nation's consensus No. 1 offensive tackle recruit, drawing offers from coast to coast. Originally signed with USC, but asked for and was granted his release after the NCAA handed down sanctions stemming from the Reggie Bush investigation. Joined Miami in July '10, starting 9-of-12 games played at right tackle — did not start the season opener against Florida A&M, did not play against Ohio State and did not start against Pittsburgh. Also did not start the Sun Bowl against Notre Dame (stomach virus). Had off-season sciatica nerve surgery and was suspended for the '11 opener against Maryland — on the season, started 3-of-8 games played at RT. Was suspended for the beginning of '12 spring practice. Following a funeral, was involved in a car accident and sustained a concussion — missed the first 12 practices of fall camp and sat out the season opener against Boston College. Played 11 games, starting the final seven at RT. In '13, started 8-of-12 games played at RT. Was suspended against Georgia Tech. Revealed at the Senior Bowl that college suspensions stemmed from failed drug tests.

Strengths: Looks every bit the part with a rare-sized body that will make offensive line coaches drool — broad-shouldered, big-boned, well-proportioned and thickly built. Athletic bender. Light-footed kick slide. Is a day trip to get around — long arms aid recovery and enable him to push rushers wide of the pocket. Thwarts rushers with a heavy punch and sturdy base. Locks on and controls. Walls off and seals. Widens the hole. Gets to the second level with ease. Passes off stunts.

Weaknesses: Weight-room strength is not special given his size. Needs to strengthen his core — affects body control, contact balance, sustain and finish. Spends too much time on the ground. Technique lapses — needs to play with more consistent bend and leverage. Gets in trouble when his feet stall and is slow to shift his weight. Labors to execute reach blocks and is stressed by quick inside moves — occasionally lets defenders cross his face. Struggles adjusting to moving targets in space. Should be more powerful than he is. Uneven performance. Underachiever traits. Suspect maturity, dependability and decision-making — is easily led astray and was suspended multiple times.

Future: Monster-sized, long-armed, physical specimen with the raw talent to emerge as a dominating NFL right tackle in any type of blocking scheme. Failed to live up to expectations in college as a result of tumultuous career marred by tragedy, suspensions, injuries and benchings. High-risk, high-reward wild card who must convince decision-makers he's worth gambling on. Has already been removed from many draft boards and must be paired with a veteran position coach nuanced in managing undisciplined, high-maintenance players.

Draft projection: Second- to third-round pick.

Scout's take: "Physically, he's a first-round

talent. That is one big man with movement skills. He's a mountain of a man. He's similar to (Chargers 11th overall pick) D.J. Fluker, but he's a better foot athlete. I put him in the third round because of some of his issues, but if you can get to the kid, he has a chance to be a really good right tackle. He could fall further once everyone gets done doing all of their (character) work. It's just a lack of consistency that drives people crazy."

OLT JAMES HURST, #68

NORTH CAROLINA   ▶ GRADE: 5.39

Ht: 6-5 1/4 | Wt: 296 | Sp: 5.30e | Arm: 33 3/4 | Hand: 10 1/8

History: Highly recruited out of suburban Indianapolis — chose UNC over offers from Alabama, Florida, Georgia, Ohio State and Notre Dame, among others. Enrolled early and took ownership of the left tackle position as a true freshman in 2010 — played all 13 games, starting the final 12, and graded out at 83 percent with 33 knockdowns. Started all 13 games in '11 and graded out at 88 percent. Started all 11 games played in '12, grading out at nearly 90 percent. Did not play against Idaho (undisclosed injury). Had off-season shoulder surgery. In '13, started all 13 games before suffering a broken left fibula against Cincinnati in the Belk Bowl — did not work out at Combine.

Strengths: Very good size. Smart and instinctive — understands angles. Good leg drive as a run blocker — is tough and aggressive. Competes hard and flashes some nastiness. Plays with a chip on his shoulder. Alert to see the blitz and feel stunts and switch off blocks. Experienced, four-year starter. Works hard and the game is very important to him.

Weaknesses: Average athletic ability and agility. Tends to lunge, bend at the waist and get overextended. Is heavy-footed and struggles to adjust to quick, inside counters. Gets jarred, knocked off balance and at times collapsed and lifted off the ground by power-leverage rushers. Tends to shoot his hands wide of his target in pass protection and will give up the edge. Is late to reach the second level and connect in space. Has a fast metabolism and some trouble maintaining weight. Tied for the lightest offensive lineman at the Combine.

Future: A wide-bodied, overachieving, college left tackle more ideally suited for the right side in the pros. Is football smart, gritty and competitive enough to eventually enter a starting lineup, but would be an ideal backup swing tackle on a strong offensive line and might even benefit from kicking inside where he'd have help on each side.

Draft projection: Fourth- to fifth-round pick.

Scout's take: "I wasn't all fired up about him. I think he is going to be a solid backup-type player. If you needed him to come in and play — he could get you through. He's slow-footed and really struggles with speed and handling speed to power. He's better when he has time to set. He's an average athlete playing left tackle and it shows."

C-OLG GABE IKARD, #64

OKLAHOMA   ▶ GRADE: 5.23

Ht: 6-3 5/8 | Wt: 304 | Sp: 5.16 | Arm: 33 1/8 | Hand: 9 5/8

History: Last name is pronounced "EYE-curd." High school tight end-defensive end who won five state championships (three basketball, two football) at Oklahoma prep powerhouse Bishop McGuiness. Redshirted in 2009. Played all 14 games in '10, starting the final 12 at left guard and logging 72 knockdowns. Started all 13 games in '11, including seven at center, six at LG. Started all 12 games played at center in '12 — did not play against Baylor (concussion). Missed part of '13 spring practice with a broken finger on his right hand. Started all 13 games at center in the fall when he was awarded the Wuerffel Trophy (exemplary community service with athletic and academic achievement) and Lee Roy Selmon Spirit Award (academic excellence, community service) and was a finalist for the Campbell Trophy ("Academic Heisman") and Rimington Trophy (nation's top center).

Strengths: Good grip strength. Uses his hands well to control and steer defenders. Highly intelligent. Plays smart. Sets the protections and makes line calls. Tough and dependable. Experienced, four-year starter. Outstanding work habits. Exceptional character. Charismatic, humble, well-grounded leader. Versatile. Produced the best 20-yard shuttle time (4.37 seconds) and 3-cone time (7.30 seconds) of any offensive lineman at the Combine.

Weaknesses: Is on the ground a lot. Limited athlete. Average play strength. Can be overwhelmed by size and struggle to cut off speed. Could stand to do a better job finishing blocks. Only benchpressed 225 pounds 22 times at the Combine.

Future: A functional positional blocker who lacks the foot quickness, athletic ability and strength desired in a starter, yet consistently finds a way to get the job done and overcome his physical limitations. Intelligence and intangibles are off the charts and could allow him to capture and hold onto a starting job. The sum is better than the parts.

Draft projection: Fifth- to sixth-round pick.

Scout's take: "He is not very strong and I don't like his balance. He's smart, tough and everything you want from that standpoint, but he'll struggle to match up physically at our level."

OFFENSIVE LINEMEN

ORG GABE JACKSON, #61

MISSISSIPPI STATE   ▶ GRADE: 5.85

Ht: 6-3 1/4 | Wt: 336 | Sp: 5.51 | Arm: 33 3/4 | Hand: 10

History: Played for his father as a Mississippi prep. Redshirted in 2009. Started all 52 games of his career at left guard 2010-13. Did not give up a sack his last two seasons. Two-time captain.

Strengths: Exceptional girth with long arms and a thick lower body. Fundamentally sound with advanced technique. Quick out of his stance. Good anchor. Strong, efficient punch (can pop and recoil). Keeps his hands inside and controls defenders. Mirrors in pass protection. Walls off running lanes. Understands positioning and angles. Athletic enough to short pull effectively — nice balance and body control for a big man. Good eyes, awareness and reactions. Smart and tough. Durable four-year starter. Professional makeup.

Weaknesses: Lacks explosive power to shock defenders. Does not blow defenders off the ball in the run game. Average overall athletic ability and lateral agility. Is unsudden and lacks elite recovery quickness. Occasionally fails to dig his heels in and gives ground vs. strong bull rushes. Stressed to cut off fast-flowing linebackers. Recorded the slowest 20-yard split (3.28 seconds) and tied for the slowest 40-time (5.63 seconds) of any player at the Combine.

Future: Big, thickly built, relatively nuanced blocker who brings a steadying presence to the interior offensive line. Dependability and effectiveness blocking for pass and run combined with sterling intangibles, including football intelligence, make him capable of starting as a rookie and holding down a position for years to come.

Draft projection: Top-50 pick.

Scout's take: "He's a short-area mauler. I worry about his foot speed. He's a little bit like the Alabama kid (Chance Warmack) last year. He's strong and powerful, but he's going to get exposed outside a confined area at our level."

ORT JA'WUAN JAMES, #70

TENNESSEE   ▶ GRADE: 5.70

Ht: 6-6 | Wt: 311 | Sp: 5.34 | Arm: 35 | Hand: 9 7/8

History: Prepped in Georgia. Enrolled in January 2010 and immediately took ownership of the right tackle position. Started all 49 games of his career (2010-13), setting a school record for career starts by an offensive lineman. Sprained his knee during Senior Bowl practice.

Strengths: Outstanding size, girth and overall body mass. Good hand placement. Can steer and control blockers once he gets his hands on them. Very patient pass protector. Matches up very well vs. size and power (see Alabama). Battle-tested, experienced four-year starter in the SEC. Outstanding personal and football character. Very smart, mature and highly respected.

Weaknesses: Raw footwork. Has a lot of heaviness in body and can improve sustain. Lumbers to the second level and struggles to cut off and adjust to moving targets. Does not roll off the ball with power and generate strength or movement in the run game.

Future: Big, strong, heavy pass protector with good balance, anchor strength and hand use to handle power and speed. Does not affect the run game the same way and almost appears more destined for the left side in the pros. Has instant-starter potential.

Draft projection: Second- to third-round pick.

Scout's take: "I thought he was hands-down the best offensive linemen of any in the Southeast. ... Some people have Ju'Wuan James going in the first. I don't think he will. The issue for me is the strength and power he can generate. ... He's (Tennessee's) best prospect. He is the hardest worker on an underachieving line."

OLG-C WESLEY JOHNSON, #67

VANDERBILT   ▶ GRADE: 5.26

Ht: 6-5 3/8 | Wt: 297 | Sp: 5.16 | Arm: 33 1/8 | Hand: 10 1/4

History: Nashville native who won a state championship and competed in track and field (throws) as a prep. Redshirted in 2009. Started all 12 games at left tackle in '10. Started all 13 games in '11 — seven at center, four at LT, two at left guard. Started all 26 games at LT 2012-13, allowing just two sacks. Two-year captain.

Strengths: Quick out of his stance. Natural bender with athletic, coordinated movement. Light on his feet and can work his hips. Keeps his hands inside and can pop and recoil. Shuffles, slides and mirrors. Gets to the second level with ease and can wheel around the edge as a puller. Durable, versatile 51-game starter — has experience playing all across the line. Highly respected, passionate, no-nonsense vocal leader.

Weaknesses: Average length. Is not built for power. Needs to bulk up and get functionally stronger. Light anchor — stressed by power rushers. Does not jolt defenders with his hands. Average explosion/pop on contact. Inconsistent connecting with moving targets and fitting on linebackers. Has had difficulty filling out his frame and maintaining weight.

Future: Experienced, intelligent, competitive, athletic, strength-deficient zone blocker. Has everything you want intangibly and has developmental value, but has to make significant strength gains and perfect his technique to survive against longer, more powerful NFL defensive ends. Has worked out as a center in the spring and might be most natural inside.

Draft projection: Fourth- to fifth-round pick.

ORT CYRUS KOUANDJIO, #71 (JUNIOR)

ALABAMA   ▶ GRADE: 5.75

Ht: 6-5 3/4 | Wt: 322 | Sp: 5.59 | Arm: 35 5/8 | Hand: 10 1/4

History: Last name is pronounced "KWON-joe." Parade All-American and elite recruit out of Maryland's DeMatha Catholic. Was a reserve as a true freshman in 2011 when he appeared in eight games before suffering a season-ending torn left ACL and MCL against Tennessee. Started all 26 games at left tackle 2012-13. Issues about arthritic knee condition were reported.

Strengths: Excellent body mass with extremely long arms. Uses his length to push rushers wide — day trip to run the arc on. Has the ability to drop anchor and stymie the bull rush. Can latch onto, control and maul his man. Can hook and seal or widen the hole in the running game. Flashes the ability to bury defenders. Will be a 21-year-old rookie and has clear potential — is physically gifted with raw, moldable tools.

Weaknesses: Has heavy legs and lacks ideal foot quickness for blind-side protection. Footwork and hand use have to be coached up — looks clumsy at times. Carries his hands low. Struggles to subdue counters and gets beat across his face — limited lateral quickness and needs to strengthen power step and inside punch. Average contact balance — too often bends at the waist and slides off blocks. Inconsistent clearing his feet through traffic and spends too much time on the ground. Labors to cut off fast-flowing linebackers and sustain on the second level. Could stand to develop more of a mean streak. Tied for the slowest 40-time (5.63 seconds) of any participant at the Combine.

Future: Massive, long-limbed, inconsistent, overhyped college left tackle whose sheer dimensions, raw tools and high ceiling are far more appealing than his snap-to-snap performance at this stage of his development. Has enough length and anchor strength to survive on the left side, though he will never be a dancing bear, and he projects more ideally as a bulldozing right tackle in a power scheme.

Draft projection: Top-50 pick.

Scout's take: "He looks the part, but he leaves you wanting more too. He tends to play short-armed and a little top heavy and lets guys into his body. He is not a great puncher. He sets his hands late. I don't see a lot of snap to him. In pass pro, he handles the outside rush and can handle the speed-to-power transition because he can sink his (butt) and is hard to run through. He's not a real powerful type — he tends to fall off blocks way too much. I'm not sure I would touch him in the first round. When I was in the school, he was really struggling. (The coaches) try to sell him hard, but it's hard to really bite. A lot of (scouts) are talking about him in the third round."

C TYLER LARSEN, #58

UTAH STATE   ▶ GRADE: 5.20

Ht: 6-3 5/8 | Wt: 313 | Sp: 5.25e | Arm: 31 1/2 | Hand: 9 1/4

History: Married. Brother, Cody, played defensive tackle at Southern Utah, and latched on with the Ravens as an undrafted free agent in 2013. Tyler was a two-way lineman who also lettered in basketball as a Utah prep. Appeared in two games as a freshman in 2009, but strained his left MCL and redshirted. Started all 51 games at center 2010-13. Played through a herniated disc injury in '12, had post-season surgery and sat out '13 spring practice while recovering. Rimington finalist in '13, the third straight year he earned first-team All-Western Athletic Conference honors.

Strengths: Excellent size — sheer mass to wall off. Generally holds his ground. Can sit and anchor and replace his hands. Good awareness. Consistent gun snaps. Was a rock for the Aggies — started 51 career games.

Weaknesses: Has short arms and struggles to sustain. Not explosive or powerful. Very average athleticism and flexibility to maneuver and torque. Limited lateral quickness to slide and recover. Too easily tossed aside and cannot recover. Slow-footed — struggles to cut off fast flowing linebackers. Not a nasty mauler. Measured the shortest wingspan of any offensive lineman at the Combine.

Future: Big, experienced, wall-off zone blocker with a ceiling as a serviceble starter, though questionable versatility detracts from his appeal in a league offering few center-only spots. Has to be a masterful technician given his short arms and pedestrian athleticism.

Draft projection: Fourth- to fifth-round pick.

Scout's take: "He is big, but he has short arms and it allows (defenders) to get into his body. It knocks him back some."

OLT CHARLES LENO JR., #78

BOISE STATE   ▶ GRADE: 5.25

Ht: 6-3 7/8 | Wt: 303 | Sp: 5.20e | Arm: 34 3/8 | Hand: 10 1/8

History: High school offensive tackle-defensive end out Oakland, Calif., where he also lettered in basketball. Redshirted in 2009. Appeared in 10 games as a reserve in '10. Started all 13 games at right tackle in '11. Started all 26 games at left tackle 2012-13.

Strengths: Outstanding arm length. Solid base in pass protection and can bump, steer and mirror. Understands fit and positioning. Can work up to the second level with ease. Flashes pop in his punch. Very durable, experienced three-year starter.

Weaknesses: Lacks substance in pass protection and can be moved off a spot and walked back to the quarterback. Tends to bend at the waist, overextend and lose positioning — average recovery speed. Carries his hands too low and does not shoot them with violence. Is stressed by speed and struggles to cut off the rush. Does not play strong and catches too much.

Future: Long-armed, soft-bodied college left tackle most ideally suited for a role as a versatile, swing backup in a zone-blocking scheme. Has not learned how to translate his athletic ability and explosion to the field, yet possesses enough length, agility and untapped talent to find a role for a patient offensive line coach. Could warrant interest inside as a guard or center where he has help on each side. Similar to Packers OT Marshall Newhouse.

Draft projection: Fifth- to sixth-round pick.

OLT TAYLOR LEWAN, #77

MICHIGAN ▶ GRADE: 6.18

Ht: 6-7 | Wt: 309 | Sp: 4.87 | Arm: 33 7/8 | Hand: 9 1/4

History: Prepped in Arizona, where he transferred to Chaparral High as a senior and won a state championship while playing offensive line for the first time (defensive end previously). Redshirted in 2009. In '10, overtook upperclassman Mark Huyge in Week Four — started nine of the final 10 games at left tackle, sitting out against Wisconsin (head). Started all 39 games at LT 2011-13, winning the Big Ten Rimington-Pace Offensive Lineman of the Year award his last two seasons. Team captain. Was invited, but did not participate in the Senior Bowl.

Strengths: Accomplished, four-year starter vs. Big Ten competition. Clean kickslide in pass protection. Good knee bend, footwork and recovery quickness to handle outside speed and inside counters. Very good balance — is seldom on the ground. Is quick climbing to the second level to reach linebackers. Plays with intensity and the game is very important to him. Tough and very durable. Produced the best 40-yard time (4.79 seconds) and broad jump (9'9") of any offensive lineman at the Combine.

Weaknesses: Is not a gritty, physical finisher. Has a lean lower body and does not explode on contact. Can be inverted by power and does not carry a load in his hands. Could do a better job recognizing and adjusting to the outside blitz. Quirky personality that can be easily misunderstood.

Future: An experienced, finesse left tackle with the length, agility and temperament to hold down a starting job for a long time. Is nuanced in pass protection and would fit best in a slide-lateral movement, bucket-stepping, zone-based blocking scheme. Similar in mold to Patriots 2011 17th overall selection Nate Solder. Outstanding Combine performance could elevate his draft status.

Draft projection: Top-15 pick.

Scout's take: "He is not very big genetically in the lower body. Everyone is saying he is a top pick. He graded out at the bottom of the first for me. ... He is a little bit different. Not all the coaches will like his personality. But he is tough. He loves the game."

ORG BRANDON LINDER, #65

MIAMI (FLA.) ▶ GRADE: 5.26

Ht: 6-5 5/8 | Wt: 311 | Sp: 5.34 | Arm: 34 1/2 | Hand: 10 1/4

History: Won a state championship at Florida prep power St. Thomas Aquinas. As a true freshman in 2010, played 12 games and had five starts as an extra blocker in UM's "jumbo" personnel package. Started all 12 games at right guard in '11. Was sidelined by a cracked rib during '12 fall camp, but started all 12 games. Missed '13 spring practice with a left PCL sprain. Was the Hurricanes' offensive MVP in the fall, starting all 13 games, including 10 at RG and three at right tackle.

Strengths: Terrific size. Engages with urgency and works to gain positioning. Can lean and seal. Good hand placement. Functional anchor when his base and posture are technically sound. Ideal makeup to battle in the trenches. Plays with his head on a swivel — alert to threats. Nasty finisher. Outstanding personal and football character. Smart vocal leader. Tough, durable and experienced (42 career starts).

Weaknesses: Adequate athlete. Limited explosion — cannot overpower defenders. Plays short-armed (average sustain). Tends to lunge and slip off blocks. Body control and contact balance wane in space and on the move. Is late to cut off linebackers and struggles the farther he has to go.

Future: Big, experienced, highly competitive, short-area base blocker at his best in a phone booth. Lacks ideal power and athleticism, but has football intelligence, leadership traits and a bulldog's mentality. Should earn a spot as an interior backup initially, but brings grit to the line and has the makeup to outplay his draft position.

Draft projection: Fourth- to fifth-round pick.

c COREY LINSLEY, #71

OHIO STATE　　　　▶ GRADE: 5.18
Ht: 6-2 5/8 | Wt: 301 | Sp: 5.03 | Arm: 32 | Hand: 9 7/8

History: Prepped in Ohio where he also was a state champion discus thrower and state champion and All-American shot putter. Played through a shoulder injury as a senior. Redshirted in 2009. Appeared in six games as a reserve in '10 and 10 games as a reserve in '11. Started all 12 games at center in '12 despite hurting his foot against Illinois in early November. Had it surgically repaired and sat out the following spring. Started all 14 games at center in '13. Team captain.

Strengths: Stout base. Works to re-anchor. Jolting punch. Strong upper body to latch onto and control defenders in short area. Generates movement in the run game. Understands angles and positioning. Excellent weight-room strength — bench-presses 500 pounds and squats a small house. Smart and dependable. Communicated all the line calls and checks. Is tough and will play hurt. Hardworking team captain with leadership traits.

Weaknesses: Has short arms. More strong than explosive — doesn't roll his hips and blow nose tackles off the ball. Falls off blocks when he bends at the waist. Pedestrian foot athlete — slow to cut off linebackers, labors to pull and lacks lateral quickness to recover when beaten. Stressed by quicker rushers. Tied for the lightest offensive lineman at the Combine.

Future: Strong-bodied, heavy-handed, short-area mauler who anchored one of the nation's most physical, productive rushing attacks. Has athletic limitations, but compensates with strength, smarts and competitiveness. Has the makeup to overachieve, and could increase his value by proving versatile enough to back up at guard.

Draft projection: Late draftable pick.

ORG SPENCER LONG, #61

NEBRASKA　　　　▶ GRADE: 5.26
Ht: 6-4 5/8 | Wt: 320 | Sp: 5.25e | Arm: 33 1/8 | Hand: 10 3/4

History: Native Nebraskan. Walked on and redshirted in 2009. Did not see action in '10. Stepped into the lineup in '11, starting all 13 games at right guard. Played through a torn right meniscus in '12, starting all 14 games at RG. In '13, started the first six games at RG before tearing his right MCL against Purdue and undergoing season-ending surgery and did not work out at the Combine because of it (medical exclusion). Elected not to lift at the Combine because of a appendectomy. Team captain.

Strengths: Very solidly built with a good frame. Good leg drive — can create a push in the run game and position-sustain. Solid in pass protection — good anchor, shadow and mirror. Good base and balance — controls and steers defenders. Flashes some nastiness. Intense, competitive battler. Smart and instinctive. Lunchpail worker will do a lot of extras and is very ambitious and driven to succeed. Excellent weight-room strength — can squat a small house. Good versatility — has played inside and outside. Very tough and played much of final two seasons through knee injuries. Possessed the biggest hands of any offensive linemen at the Combine.

Weaknesses: Average athlete. Is tight-ankled and heavy-legged — lumbers to the second level. Labors to cut off the inside rush. Struggles to adjust and pick off linebackers and is not efficient pulling and trapping.

Future: Big, tough, physical, ornery blocker with starter-quality positional traits and intangible qualities. Is best in a phone booth, where he excels as a run and pass blocker, and is smart and savvy enough to contribute outside in emergency situations.

Draft projection: Fourth- to fifth-round pick.

OLT CORNELIUS "LUKE" LUCAS, #78

KANSAS STATE　　　　▶ GRADE: 5.16
Ht: 6-8 3/8 | Wt: 316 | Sp: 5.33 | Arm: 36 3/4 | Hand: 10

History: New Orleans native. Redshirted in 2009. A reserve/special-teams contributor 2010-11, appeared in 12 games in each season. Started all 13 games at left tackle 2012-13.

Strengths: Rare length (body and arms) with a wingspan of a small aircraft — led all Combine participants at 881/8-inches. Fairly light on his feet for as big as he is and overall length allows him to recover to inside counters.

Weaknesses: Thin-framed. Lacks weight-room and functional football-playing strength. Not stout at the point of attack. Plays too upright and is not a natural knee bender. Not explosive and does not generate power through his lower body. Marginal finisher. Struggles to cut off the wide rush. Just a two-year starter.

Future: Exceptionally sized, underpowered, developmental positional wall-off blocker lacking ideal foot quickness to handle edge speed and the grit and toughness desired to match up vs. power. Needs to spend more time in the weight room and develop his core strength. Could be most ideally suited for a swing-backup-tackle role and has upside to be groomed, with traits better suited for the right side.

Draft projection: Late draftable pick.

OLG-OLT-C ZACK MARTIN, #70
NOTRE DAME   ▶ GRADE: 6.18
Ht: 6-4 1/4 | Wt: 308 | Sp: 5.20e | Arm: 32 7/8 | Hand: 9 1/2

History: Won a pair of state championships at Indianapolis Bishop Chatard. Redshirted in 2009. Started all 13 games in '10, including 11 at left tackle and two at right tackle. Started all 39 games at LT 2011-13. Two-time captain's 52 career games are the most in school history. Did not run the 40 at the Combine (tight hamstring).

Strengths: Engages quickly. Flexible and light on his feet. Can work his hips and maneuver. Good blocking posture — bends his knees, sits in his stance and can shuffle, slide and mirror. Good hand placement (can pop and recoil). Seals running lanes. Can combo block and fit on linebackers. Athletic to pull and trap. Passes off stunts and is alert to blitzers. Started all 52 games of his career. Played well against Alabama in the BCS Championship and was MVP of the Pinstripe Bowl. Sparkling intangibles. Highly respected, hardworking leader who does all the right things. Two-time captain.

Weaknesses: Lacks ideal length to stay outside in the pros — relatively small wingspan. Not a pure road grader who rolls off flat-backed and buries defenders. Could be stressed by bigger, more powerful defensive tackles. Can improve balance and sustain on the second level. Does not have experience at guard. Could stand to bulk up in preparation for a move inside.

Future: Athletic, smart, competitive, dependable college left tackle whose length dictates a move inside, where he has plug-and-play ability in a zone-blocking scheme. One of the cleanest prospects in this year's draft.

Draft projection: First-round pick.

Scout's take: "He's fun to watch. He's easy on the eyes. He'll get beat at times, but he has such a good feel for angles and leverage and uses his hands so well that it's not easy to beat him. There's not much not to like about the guy."

C-OG MARCUS MARTIN, #66 (JUNIOR)
USC   ▶ GRADE: 5.60
Ht: 6-3 3/8 | Wt: 320 | Sp: 5.25e | Arm: 34 | Hand: 10

History: Prepped at Crenshaw (Calif.) High, where he won two L.A. City championships. Cracked the lineup as a true freshman in 2011, starting the final 10 games at left guard. Started 10-of-12 games at left guard in '12. Moved to center in '13 and started all 13 games played — dislocated his left knee cap and sustained a high left ankle sprain against UCLA, knocking him out of the Las Vegas Bowl against Fresno State. Team captain. Did not perform at the Combine because of left knee injury (medical exclusion).

Strengths: Naturally thick and wide-bodied. Walls off and seals defenders. Can work his hips to maneuver and seal. Athletic enough to step to the second level. Plays with his head on a swivel. Good anchor ability in pass protection — can dig his cleats in the ground vs. big-bodied pluggers and match size with size. Three-year starter with experience at guard and center. Was a 20-year-old junior.

Weaknesses: A bit knock-kneed and pigeon-toed with herky-jerky movement. Soft puncher. Gets top-heavy and bends at the waist. Average initial quickness, balance and sustain. Ordinary hip snap — power element missing. Limited lateral agility and recovery ability. Struggles to connect with moving targets. Is not a strong finisher or an aggressive go-getter. Does not dominate the way he is capable. Only benchpressed 225 pounds 23 times at the Combine.

Future: Outstanding-sized, barrel-chested finesse pivot with center-guard versatility. Grades out highly as a position-sustain blocker and possesses untappped strength and power in his body. Lacks desirable grit, toughness and finishing strength to maximize his talent and is stronger than he plays. Has instant-starter potential as a center or right guard, but could stand to benefit from some time to be groomed.

Draft projection: Second- to third-round pick.

Scout's take: "Of all the centers, USC's is the best of all of them. If he had any kind of finish or nasty and pushed anyone around, he would go higher. He's more finesse than mauler. He can get his body on (defenders) — he just does not get much push."

OLT-OLG-C JAKE MATTHEWS, #75
TEXAS A&M   ▶ GRADE: 7.20
Ht: 6-5 1/2 | Wt: 308 | Sp: 5.06 | Arm: 33 3/8 | Hand: 9 7/8

History: Son of Hall of Famer Bruce Matthews. Uncle, Clay Matthews Jr., was a Pro

Bowl linebacker for the Browns; cousin, Clay III, is an All-Pro linebacker for the Packers; and cousin, Casey, is a linebacker for the Eagles. Jake was a USA Today and Parade All-American. Played 10 games as a true freshman in 2010, starting the final seven at right tackle. Started all 26 games at RT 2011-12. In '13, replaced Jaguars first-rounder Luke Joeckel at left tackle and started all 13 games. Team captain.

Strengths: Big, strong, athletic, natural bender. Exceptional technician. Explosive six-inch punch — quick, active hands. Outstanding base, balance, body control and hand placement. Drives defenders off the ball — outstanding run blocker. Explosive hip snap. Takes good angles to the second level. Plays with very good awareness — shows very good athletic ability flipping his hips and adjusting to moving pockets with a jitterbug quarterback. Keen to recognize and quick to adjust to the blitz. Strong finisher — displays a mean streak and seeks to finish. Has long-snapping experience. Hails from football royalty family — third-generation NFLer. Tough competitor. Very focused and determined. Humble and grounded. Outstanding all-around character. Film junkie. Started in the SEC for 3-plus seasons. Extremely durable — missed no time to injuries.

Weaknesses: Arm length appears too short — limited reach and extension. Operated in a spread offense. Can do a better job sustaining (though was presented with a near-impossible task of knowing where the pocket would be to protect). Has only one year of experience at left tackle.

Future: Smart, tough, versatile franchise left tackle capable of playing all five positions on the line. Can plug into a starting lineup immediately and will play a long time at a consistently high level. One of the safest picks in the draft, Matthews' best position might even be center.

Draft projection: Top-10 pick.

Scout's take: "The A&M tackle is the best that I have seen this year. Even watching some of the games last year — I think he was better than (Luke) Joeckel, and I loved Joeckel. He reminds me a lot of the guy the Jaguars drafted second overall — Tony Boselli. They have similar body types. You can play him any position you want. I'd love to have him. He's one of the best I've seen. Factor in the bloodlines — he's a can't miss."

ORT JACK MEWHORT, #74

OHIO STATE ▶ GRADE: 5.55
Ht: 6-6 | Wt: 309 | Sp: 5.38 | Arm: 34 | Hand: 9 3/4

History: Ohio native. Was a reserve as a true freshman in 2010 when he appeared in 10 games. Started all 13 games in '11 — the first five at left guard, the final eight at right guard. Suffered two broken ribs (when teammate Carlos Hyde slammed into him) against Nebraska, but did not miss any games. Was temporarily suspended from team activities in June '12 after being arrested for public urination (pleaded guilty to disorderly conduct). Started all 26 games at left tackle 2012-13. Team captain.

Strengths: Good size. Engages with urgency. Reestablishes the line of scrimmage in the run game. Can drive block, widen the hole and seal lanes. Stout base — good anchor strength. Plays with a load in his hands to jar defenders. Locks on and controls. Good enough feet to slide and mirror. Alert to stunts and blitzes. Versatile. Has an ideal temperament for the trenches — breathes fire. Smart, tough and competitive. Three-year starter. Is passionate about the game and works at his craft. Highly respected vocal leader.

Weaknesses: Has a soft midsection. Stronger than he is explosive. Lacks ideal length and foot quickness for the left side (not a dancing bear). Vulnerable to strong bull rush when he gets tall and narrow-based. Occasionally gets top-heavy and slips off blocks. Average blocking range. Tight hips and ankles show when he pulls or climbs to the second level. Struggles to cut off fast-flowing linebackers. Lets his pads rise outside the phone booth. Recorded a very ordinary 1.92-second 10-yard split at the Combine, indicating average short-area quickness for the left side.

Future: Thickly built, physical, highly competitive lineman who manned left tackle competently in college, but is better suited for the right side in the pros. Has starter-caliber strength, athleticism and technique supplemented with desirable intangibles. Versatility to play guard or left tackle in a pinch adds to value.

Draft projection: Second- to third-round pick.

Scout's take: "(Mewhort) is a right tackle to me. He's tough and ornery. He'll fall off some blocks and get overextended, but he's tough, tough, tough. He'll be very good in the run game. Carlos Hyde picked up a lot of yards running behind him."

ORT MORGAN MOSES, #78

VIRGINIA ▶ GRADE: 5.30

Ht: 6-6 | Wt: 314 | Sp: 5.36 | Arm: 35 3/8 | Hand: 9 7/8

History: Virginia native and Parade All-American. Was a non-qualifier out of high school and attended Fork Union (VA) Military Academy in 2009. Played 11 games in '10, starting six of the final seven at right tackle. Sprained his left ankle during '11 fall camp, but started all 13 games at RT. Started 11-of-12 games at left tackle in '12 — did not start against Wake Forest (undisclosed injury) and sprained his ankle against North Carolina. Started all 12 games at LT in '13. Did not lift at the Combine because of a left shoulder injury (medical exlusion).

Strengths: Has outstanding size and vines for arms — sheer mass and length makes it difficult for rushers to run the arc on him. Has strength to anchor. Wins with his hands. Pulls with a head of steam and can eliminate defenders when he has a bead. Logged 43 career starts.

Weaknesses: Plays too tall and needs to drop anchor more consistently. Heavy on his feet and tends to bend at the waist. Lethargic shifting his weight — stressed by speed and quickness and cannot recover when beaten. Limited hip snap and is not sudden or explosive. Does not breathe fire — plays smaller than his size in the run game and does not seek to bury defenders. Weight has fluctuated and conditioning needs to be monitored closely. Recorded the slowest 10-yard split (2.08 seconds) of any participant at the Combine and tied for the lowest vertical jump (211/2 inches) among all offensive linemen.

Future: Big, long-armed leaner with sheer size and length and enough movement skill to function at an adequate level on the right side, though his high-maintenance conditioning, intermittent intensity and uneven performance turns off some teams. Developmental project.

Draft projection: Fourth- to fifth-round pick.

Scout's take: "Once (Moses) gets his hands on you, it's all over. He's got great length and he knows how to use it. I like his six-inch punch. Where he gets in trouble is handling quickness and speed. He has no recovery (speed) once he gets beat off the ball."

C MATTHEW PARADIS, #65

BOISE STATE ▶ GRADE: 5.02

Ht: 6-2 5/8 | Wt: 306 | Sp: 5.34 | Arm: 32 3/8 | Hand: 9 7/8

History: Grew up on an Idaho farm. Played eight-man football in high school, won a state championship and was named Idaho's 1A Player of the Year award. Also won a state discus championship and played basketball. Tore his left ACL in 2007. Was lightly recruited, walked on and grayshirted in '08. Redshirted as a defensive tackle in '09, earning Scout Team Defensive Player of the Year recognition. Saw action in just one game in '10. Earned a scholarship going into '11 when he converted to center and played eight games, drawing one start as an injury replacement. Stepped into the lineup and started all 25 games at center 2012-13.

Strengths: Plays on his feet with good balance. Generates movement in the run game. Seeks to bury defenders. Strong 6-inch punch. Good hand placement. Firm base in pass protection. Plays with leverage to bend and slide. Alert to stunts and blitzes. Tough and competitive. Terrific intangibles, including leadership traits — humble, hardworking and highly respected.

Weaknesses: Is not big-framed and body is nearly maxed out. Could stand to improve weight-room strength. Average athlete for the position. Might be stressed by larger, more powerful wide-body nose tackles. Falls off blocks when he bends at the waist. Questionable long-term durability (hip).

Future: A converted defensive lineman and former walk-on, Paradis is a stoutly built, intelligent, hard-nosed overachiever who will make it difficult for coaches to cut him.

Draft projection: Priority free agent.

OLT-OLG MATT PATCHAN, #71

BOSTON COLLEGE ▶ GRADE: 5.18

Ht: 6-6 1/4 | Wt: 302 | Sp: 4.97 | Arm: 33 | Hand: 9 3/8

History: Father was an offensive tackle at Miami (1983-87) and was drafted by the Eagles in the third round of the 1988 draft. Matt was a USA Today All-American and highly regarded defensive end-left tackle out of Florida. Suffered soft tissue damage in May '08 when he was shot in the shoulder — was a bystander at a park when a man shot into a crowd. In the fall, began his college career at the University of Florida, where he was recruited as a defensive lineman and played 11 games (one start), recording seven tackles, one tackle for loss and 1 1/2 sacks. Switched to offensive tackle in '09 — played the first four games before suffering a torn right ACL injury (received a medical hardship, preserving a year of eligibility). Was sidelined in '10 after fracturing his right wrist during fall camp (had a second surgery in November). Played 12 games in '11, starting the final seven at right tackle — did not play in the Gator Bowl against Ohio State (back). Tore a pectoral muscle during summer lifting and missed the '12 season. Transferred to BC to play for Steve Addazio, his position coach at UF, and was healthy enough to start all 13 games at left tackle for the Eagles.

Strengths: Fires out of his stance. Effective with an angle. Good foot speed when asked to pull or get to the second level. Functional kickslide. Flashes a strong punch. Aggressive and competitive. Has tools to work with. Led all offensive linemen at the Combine with a 33 1/2-inch vertical jump.

Weaknesses: Short arms. Lacks ideal bulk and core strength — lengthy injury history has stunted physical development. Gets walked back. Limited hip snap — does not generate power. Hand use needs work. Inconsistent leverage. Bends at the waist. Balance issues. Inconsistent body control on the move — struggles to connect and sustain. Has underachiever traits and thinks he's better than he is. Will be a 24-year-old rookie.

Future: A Florida transfer, Patchan's lone season at BC was the first of his career in which he was a healthy, full-time starter. He's a tall, stiff, linear, zone blocker whose relatively short wingspan dictates a shift to guard, though he isn't ideally suited for the interior given his core strength deficiency and wobbly base. Practice-squad candidate who must dedicate himself to the weight room and the practice field and tap into the raw ability that made him a highly sought after recruit in order to have longevity.

Draft projection: Late draftable pick.

ORT ANTONIO RICHARDSON, #74 (JUNIOR)

TENNESSEE ▶ GRADE: 5.58
Ht: 6-5 3/4 | Wt: 336 | Sp: 5.31 | Arm: 35 | Hand: 10 1/4

History: Nicknamed "Tiny".Tennessee native. Appeared in all 12 games as a true freshman in 2011, primarily on special teams. In '12, stepped into the lineup and started all 12 games at left tackle. Had off-season knee surgery and missed '13 spring practice. In the fall, started all 12 games at LT.

Strengths: Looks the part with long arms and outstanding overall size and mass to cover up defenders in the run game and generate a push. Good strength to anchor vs. power and possesses enough brute strength to hold his ground even when he locks his legs. Is not easily moved and can position-sustain. Bends fairly well for as big as he is and is agile enough to handle speed.

Weaknesses: Is not a finisher and carries underachiever tendencies, displaying inconsistent effort and technique. Rises out of his stance and relies too much on his natural power, letting defenders walk him back. Plays too passively and gives more ground than he should. Is late to reach the second level and gives up instead of peeling back to pick off another defender. Hand use is very raw — not active and does not replace. Could require some

time to assimilate a playbook.

Future: A big, strong, athletic college left tackle who might be more naturally suited for the right side in the pros, Richardson is agile enough to protect the blind side if he learns to become a better hand technician. Has the look of a Pittsburgh prototype and compares favorably to Steelers 2011 second-round pick Marcus Gilbert. Has clear, unrefined starter traits.

Draft projection: Second- to third-round pick.

Scout's take: "He's big, long and has upside, but he doesn't learn well. He's not a tough kid. Oregon outquicked him all day long. I worry about what kind of edge he has. For as big and long-armed as he is, he's not really strong or powerful. He's a finesse guy. I thought he did a solid job against Clowney (in 2012) and was expecting more. He's a third-rounder for me."

OLG CYRIL RICHARDSON, #68

BAYLOR ▶ GRADE: 5.40
Ht: 6-4 3/4 | Wt: 329 | Sp: 5.36 | Arm: 34 5/8 | Hand: 9 1/2

History: New Orleans native who moved to Texas after Hurricane Katrina. Redshirted in 2009. Played 12 games in '10, starting four at left guard. Did not play against Texas. Moved to left tackle in '11 and started all 13 games, grading at 80.8 percent with 70 knockdowns. Started 12-of-13 games at left guard in '12, grading out at 89.8 percent with 105 knockdowns. Lone non-start was against Kansas when he was suspended for the first half by the Big 12 Conference for kicking an Iowa State player in the groin. Was an Outland Trophy finalist in '13 when he started all 13 games at left guard, grading out at 89 percent with 89 knockdowns. Was the Big 12 Offensive Lineman of the Year (coaches) his final two seasons.

Strengths: Outstanding size and girth with legitimate strength. Sturdy base and heavy anchor — squats a small house and is dependable in pass protection. Can work his hips and gain positioning in the run game. Walls off and seals. Packs a jolting punch and plays with a load in his hands — latches on, controls and steers. Wins in a phone booth and can manhandle smaller linemen. Enough balance, coordination and foot speed to pull and trap effectively. Has played tackle and guard. Conditioned in an up-tempo, no-huddle offense.

Weaknesses: Bad body — has a fleshy midsection and could stand to shed some bad weight. Lateral agility and recovery quickness are just adequate. Gets in trouble when his feet stall or he bends at the waist (slips off blocks). Intermittent intensity — does not play violently or impose his will physically as often as he should. Could stand to become more of a nasty finisher. Has underachiever traits. Questionable motivation and passion for the game.

Future: Massive road grader with grown-man strength which enables him to reestablish the line of scrimmage in the run game and thwart the rush. Versatility to play right tackle adds to value and he has plug-and-play capability in a power scheme, though bust factor cannot be ignored.

Draft projection: Third- to fourth-round pick.

Scout's take: "He is an underachiever. He scares me. He's a backup for me. He has a bad body. He plays the game lazy. I found myself yelling at him on tape. Then again, there was one time when he tosses his hand out and blasts someone with his punch. He is capable when he wants to, but it's going to be difficult to get it out of him. He needs some time to digest what he sees. That's part of why he struggled so much at the Senior Bowl. He can't find the guys he is supposed to eventually block. You can see it if the defense lines up in a blitz package or multiple front. He can't handle a zone scheme. There's going to be a huge learning curve. If you take him too early, it's going to put too much pressure on him."

c WESTON RICHBURG, #70

COLORADO STATE   ▶ GRADE: 5.32
Ht: 6-3 3/8 | Wt: 298 | Sp: 5.11 | Arm: 33 3/8 | Hand: 9 1/4

History: Also played basketball and threw the discus as a Texas prep. Tore his right ACL in high school and did not play his sophomore and junior seasons. Redshirted in 2009. Started all 12 games in '10 — first three at strong-side guard, final nine at center. Started all 12 games at '11, including the first nine at center before breaking a bone in his right (snapping) hand against San Diego State — stayed in the lineup by playing left tackle the next two games and right guard in the final contest. Started all 26 games at center 2012-13. Team captain established a new school record with 50 career starts.

Strengths: Good snap-and-step quickness. Maneuvers to gain positioning. Good mobility — gets out of the chute quickly as a puller and demonstrates nice body control. Good awareness. Energetic and aggressive temperament. Durable, 49-game starter. Vocal team leader with outstanding intangibles.

Weaknesses: Lacks ideal girth and could be stressed by widebody nose tackles. Average hip snap — lacks body power to blow defensive tackles off the ball. Lacks elite athleticism to execute reach blocks. Can improve grip

strength to better control defenders (average sustain) — slides off some blocks. Inconsistent contact balance, especially at the second level where he can be more efficient connecting and fitting.

Future: Adequate-sized, smart, experienced, competitive center who commanded the offensive line, made all the calls and was a team leader for the Rams. At worst, should stick as a backup, but has developmental value and starter potential in a zone scheme. Could help himself by proving versatile enough to back up at guard.

Draft projection: Third- to fourth-round pick.

Scout's take: "He played better last year than he did when I saw him this year."

OLT GREG ROBINSON, #73 (SOPH-3)

AUBURN   ▶ GRADE: 7.60
Ht: 6-5 | Wt: 332 | Sp: 4.92 | Arm: 35 | Hand: 10

History: Highly recruited out of Louisiana, where he was a state champion shot putter. Redshirted in 2011. Started 11-of-12 games played at left tackle in '12 — was benched against Alabama A&M. In '13, started all 14 games at left tackle for the national runners-up. Has a right meniscus surgery on his medical record. Left school early to support his family — lost his father in April '13, his mother struggles to make ends meet and he has four siblings, two of which were incarcerated for selling drugs.

Strengths: Has long arms and excellent overall body mass. Outstanding run blocker with the strength and power to wash down half of the line. Creates a surge and generates power from his lower body. Good get-off and body control. Excellent reach-blocking, chipping and releasing to the second level. Very good balance in his set and is quick to cut off the rush. Can maneuver his hips, shuffle, slide and mirror. Has a strong punch and replaces his hands. Very athletic in vertical sets.

Weaknesses: Could stand to refine his technique in pass protection and do a better job finishing blocks. At times will quit after contact and let defenders come underneath or get over the top — handwork is too passive. Developing eyes and awareness vs. the blitz — still learning how to adjust to overload pressure and could improve switching off blocks. Aggressively overextends and occasionally loses balance and falls off blocks.

Future: Big, strong, athletic, overpowering left tackle with the raw potential to become a premiere, franchise left tackle. Is only a third-year sophomore and two-year starter and still must improve his hand use, footwork and technique. However, he is undeniably gifted and capable of walking into a starting-left-tackle job in the pros and paving the way in the run game.

Draft projection: Top-10 pick.

Scout's take: "I think Robinson is a helluva run blocker — one of the best coming out in recent years. He is not overly powerful where he is going to drive a guy into the ground. But he does get push and movement more than most people do. His pass sets and pass pro is what I have a problem with. He does not have a great secondary punch. That's why he loses the edge and why he can get beat in pass protection. It's all technique. It's easier to teach pass blocking than run blocking. That is why you see in my eyes later-round guys able to play tackle in the NFL."

OT MICHAEL SCHOFIELD, #75

MICHIGAN ▶ GRADE: 5.37
Ht: 6-6 1/2 | Wt: 301 | Sp: 5.02 | Arm: 34 | Hand: 9 5/8

History: Prepped in suburban Chicago, where he also ran 110m hurdles his first two years in high school. Redshirted in 2009. Was a reserve/special-teams contributor in '10, appearing in all 13 games. Started 10-of-13 games at left guard in '11. Started all 26 games at right tackle 2012-13.

Strengths: Good run blocker — drives his legs on contact and generates some power through his lower body. Can steer, control and lock down defenders once he gets his hands on them. Good playing demeanor — gets after it and seeks to finish. Is tough-minded and hardworking. Gritty competitor.

Weaknesses: Not an explosive drive blocker who can clear holes with regularity. Average foot quickness. Tends to overextend and lunge in-line and on the move. Marginal reactive quickness and recovery speed for the outside. Exposed by edge speed (see Michigan State vs. Shilique Calhoun) — cannot cut off the wide rush and struggles to handle quick, inside counters. Late to reach the second level.

Future: Quick-footed college right tackle with experience playing on the inside and offers versatility as a utility swing backup. Possesses eventual-starter potential, but could always be restricted by athletic limitations and leave teams desiring better.

Draft projection: Third- to fourth-round pick.

ORG ANTHONY STEEN, #61

ALABAMA ▶ GRADE: 5.24
Ht: 6-3 3/8 | Wt: 314 | Sp: 5.35e | Arm: 30 1/2 | Hand: 9 1/8

History: Two-way lineman who also snapped as a Mississippi prep. Redshirted in 2009. Appeared in all 13 games in '10, starting the final two games of the regular season at right guard as an injury replacement for Rams '13 fifth-rounder Barrett Jones. Played all 13 games in '11, starting nine at RG — sustained a concussion against Ole Miss and did not start against Tennessee or LSU, then gave way to Alfred McCullough in the final two games against Auburn and LSU. Started all 14 games at RG in '12. Started all 11 games played in '13 — did not play against Colorado State (concussion) and surgery to repair a partially torn left labrum knocked him out of the Sugar Bowl against Oklahoma as well as the Senior Bowl and Combine.

Strengths: Reliable pass protector. A 500-pound bench-presser and it shows — jars defenders with his punch. Efficient run blocker. Is quick to set and gain positioning. Works up to the second level quickly and is agile enough to wall off and seal linebackers and safeties. Dominated LSU's Anthony Johnson. Hardworking and coachable. Tough competitor. Very durable.

Weaknesses: Does not look the part — has a deceptive, dumpy-looking frame with a lot of weight concentrated in his trunk. Can do a better job sustaining at the second level. Not a consistent finisher. Catches a lot — tends to let defenders into his body and could stand to improve extension. Possessed the smallest hands and shortest arms of any offensive linemen at the Combine.

Future: Scrappy, competitive, try-hard, tough guy who does not always look pretty, but consistently finds a way to get the job done. An efficient zone blocker, Steen understands angles and leverage. He could be ideally suited for a zone-based ground game such as the Eagles, Seahawks or Packers.

Draft projection: Third- to fourth-round pick.

Scout's take: "Steen is okay. I graded him as a middle-round guy. He belongs in the fifth. He is stiff. His 29-something last spring and it was corrected at the beginning of the year to 33. Then he shows up at the Combine and measured short again. He's sort of a stiff guy. I think the arm length is really going to hurt him. A lot of teams won't touch him for that reason."

C JAMES STONE, #64

TENNESSEE ▶ GRADE: 5.10
Ht: 6-3 5/8 | Wt: 306 | Sp: 5.18 | Arm: 33 7/8 | Hand: 10 1/8

History: Two-way lineman as a Tennessee prep. As a true freshman in 2010, started 8-of-12 games played, including five at center, three at left guard. Started 7-of-9 games played in '11 — first six at center, then at left guard

OFFENSIVE LINEMEN

against Alabama before he was benched in favor of freshman Marcus Jackson. Started all 24 games at center 2012-13.

Strengths: Agile enough to slide and cut off penetrators. Good arm length for the position — able to extend. Has played some guard. Quick to the second level. Is intelligent and sets protections. Has been an experienced, durable four-year starter in the Southeastern Conference.

Weaknesses: Deficient core strength. Limited push and power. Stiff lower body. Inconsistent leverage and contact balance — overextends, falls off blocks and gets tossed aside. Not a finisher. Only benchpressed 225 pounds 22 times at the Combine.

Future: Stiff-legged, underpowered, bump-and-steer zone blocker who will struggle to match up against the size and power of NFL defensive tackles. Best chance to stick will be as a swing interior backup in a slide-protection scheme. Left-hander who snaps right-handed and gun-snaps left-handed.

Draft projection: Late draftable pick.

Scout's take: "He's a 7-PFA for me. He has played two positions — center this year and guard last year — so he's a dual position player. Most thought I was little high in the 7th. He's a stick-and-sit type. He's not powerful. He struggles to handle quickness. He's not quick to work hands. I see him as more of a PFA."

C-OG BRYAN STORK, #52

FLORIDA STATE   ▶ GRADE: 5.15
Ht: 6-3 7/8 | Wt: 315 | Sp: 5.30e | Arm: 32 1/4 | Hand: 10 1/8

History: Played tight end as a Florida prep. Redshirted in 2009. Appeared in 10 games in '10, starting four at right guard. Missed two games (mono). Started 10-of-12 games played in '11, including eight at center, two at left guard — did not play against Boston College and did not start against Miami (migraines), then suffered a finger injury against Florida which became infected and nearly required amputation. Started all 13 games played at center in '12. Sat out against Savannah State (neck). Was limited during '13 fall camp while recovering from toe surgery. On the season, started all 13 games played at center for the national champs and won the Rimington Trophy as the nation's top center. Did not play against Wake Forest (ankle). Did not participate in any physical testing at the Combine because of injuries to his left knee and both shoulders (medical exclusion).

Strengths: Excellent size. Has shown he can handle big-bodied cloggers. Maintains good positioning and can slide, shuffle and seal off defenders. Solid anchor in pass protection. Uses his hands well to control defenders. Understands angles and leverage. Athletic enough to chip and work up a level. Good competitor. Has played guard and center and offers interior versatility. Good football intelligence. Lunchpail worker. The game is important to him.

Weaknesses: Has short arms and stiff hips. Lumbering movement skill — can be late to reach the second level. Dips his head and grabs. Tends to play tall and can be bulled into the backfield when he rises straight up. Not explosive — cannot sink his hips and roll off the ball in the run game to move defenders. Average functional strength. Benefited from playing alongside two very talented guards that helped cover up deficiencies.

Future: Good-sized, bump-and-steer blocker ideally suited for a zone-blocking, slide-protection scheme. Smart, tough technician capable of serving as an interior swing backup and could eventually fend for a starting job as a pivot. Will be best developed by a patient, respectful position coach.

Draft projection: Fifth- to sixth-round pick.

Scout's take: "I didn't like Stork. He is pretty good at being a fit type guy. When he has to match up against better defensive tackles with more explosiveness, they will just lock his (butt) out. He's sort of a stiff guy – will get clashed and shoved backwards. You have to remember — he is surrounded by some pretty good players there. They have four linemen that could all come out next year and will all probably go in first three rounds of the draft."

OLG XAVIER SU'A-FILO, #56 (JUNIOR)

UCLA   ▶ GRADE: 5.70
Ht: 6-4 1/8 | Wt: 307 | Sp: 5.04 | Arm: 33 3/8 | Hand: 9 3/8

History: Parade All-American who won three state titles at Provo (UT) Timpview and was the state's 4A Offensive Player of the Year as a senior. In 2009, was the first true freshman offensive player in UCLA history to start the start the season opener — started all 13 games at left tackle. Did not play the next two years while serving a two-year LDS mission in Alabama and Florida. Upon returning, started all 14 games at left guard in '12. Started all 13 games in '13, including seven at left guard, six at left tackle. Won the Morris Trophy, which is given to the most outstanding offensive lineman in the Pac-12 as voted on by the conference's defensive linemen. Was also voted the Bruins' offensive MVP. Team captain.

Strengths: Quick out of his stance. Effective

pass blocker — can bend his knees, extend and mirror in short area. Generates movement in the run game. Can work his hips and maneuver to gain positioning. Good foot athlete. Can pull, trap, combo block and step to the second level. Durable three-year starter. Has played guard and tackle.

Weaknesses: Lacks ideal length. Missed two years of strength training while serving a LDS mission and has a bad body. Could stand to play with better pop and power in his hands. Bends at the waist, gets overextended and falls off blocks. Heavy-legged — slow to shift his weight and adjust to stunts and quick inside moves. Gets beat across his face. Needs to play with better awareness — gets short-circuited by complicated defensive movement. Struggled mightily at left tackle.

Future: Does not look the part and was miscast when forced to play left tackle for the Bruins, but Su'a-Filo is more effective than he is pretty. Projects best at left guard, where he has starter-caliber ability in a power scheme, though he is athletic enough to appeal to zone teams, too.

Draft projection: Second- to third-round pick.

Scout's take: "He is awful at left tackle. He is playing there out of need. Watch one game of him at guard — put on the Cal game. He has one of the ugliest bodies I've seen this year, but if you get past his body, he can be a starter in the league. He looks like almost a reject playing left tackle. I could beat him inside with a cross-face, inside counter with two bad hips. He is bad on the edge. He is a one-position starter."

C TRAVIS SWANSON, #64

ARKANSAS   ▶ GRADE: 5.50

Ht: 6-5 | Wt: 312 | Sp: 5.24 | Arm: 33 1/8 | Hand: 10

History: Prepped in Texas. Redshirted in 2009. Started all 50 games at center 2010-13. First two-time captain in Razorback history.

Strengths: Functional base in pass protection. Can work his hips and seal and execute combo blocks. Aware and alert — good in-line reactions. Durable and battle-tested — started all 50 games of his career and has experience locking horns with NFL-caliber defensive tackles. Highly respected two-time captain. Intelligent vocal leader with outstanding football character.

Weaknesses: Needs to bulk up his frame and get stronger. Limited push, power and explosion — too often content to stalemate. Does not play with a load in his hands. Tends to bend at the waist, lean and fall off blocks. Spends too much time on the ground. Struggles to sustain on the second level. Center only. Produced the fewest

reps (20) of 225 pounds of any lineman at the Combine.

Future: Experienced, dependable pivot who lacks starter-caliber power and athleticism. Lack of versatility hurts his chances, and he will have to survive on smarts, leadership and competitiveness.

Draft projection: Third- to fourth-round pick.

Scout's take: "I put Swanson in the fifth round. He's a little undersized. He's a center only and they do not go as high. I don't think he can play guard. ...The coaches there love him and think he's somewhere in between the two they had at Wisconsin. One went in the first to Dallas (Travis Frederick) and the other (Peter Konz) to Atlanta in the third."

OLG-OLT BRANDON THOMAS, #63

CLEMSON   ▶ GRADE: 5.45

Ht: 6-3 1/4 | Wt: 317 | Sp: 5.07 | Arm: 34 3/4 | Hand: 10 1/2

History: South Carolina native. Tore his ACL as a high school senior in 2008. Redshirted in '09. Appeared in 10 games as a reserve in '10. Took over the left guard spot in Week Four in '11— started 10-of-13 games played (nine at LG, one at left tackle). Yielded start to David Smith against South Carolina. Started all 26 games at left tackle 2012-13. Team captain tallied 98 knockdowns in his career.

Strengths: Good size with very long arms and big hands. Quick out of his stance. Knee bender with good balance and body control. Solid base. Places his hands inside and can pop and recoil. Strong-handed puncher with good grip strength once he latches on. Athletic, efficient mover. Light on his feet to step to the second level or pull. Can maneuver and throw his hips in the hole. Climbs to the second level. Three-year starter who played tackle (two-time first-team All-ACC at left tackle). Held his own against Jadeveon Clowney without help.

Weaknesses: Power element missing. Limited hip snap — not a road-grading mauler. Susceptible to bull rush when he sets tall. Could stand to improve lateral slide and inside punch to shut down strong inside moves. Inconsistent second-level sustain. Is better with simple assignments and effectiveness wanes in space. Can do a better job playing with his head on a swivel. Still learning what it means to prepare like a pro.

Future: Strong-bodied, dependable gap blocker who played left tackle in college but will likely slide inside in the pros. Showed improvement as a senior and has the potential to be a long-term fixture at left guard. Ability to play tackle in a pinch adds to value.

Draft projection: Third- to fourth-round pick.

Scout's take: "I liked the Clemson kid

(Brandon Thomas). I put him in the late third (round). He was disappointing at the Senior Bowl. I thought he struggled. Look at the South Carolina game vs. Clowney, and he does a better job against him than anyone. He went through the majority of the game single-blocking Clowney. He got beat a few times, but everyone else chipped and used a tight end to stop him. Thomas was was open-ended vs. Clowney and did a decent job."

OLT BILLY TURNER, #77

NORTH DAKOTA STATE   ▶ GRADE: 5.24
Ht: 6-4 7/8 | Wt: 315 | Sp: 5.16 | Arm: 34 | Hand: 10

History: Father, Maurice, was a running back and kick returner drafted in the 12th round of the 1983 draft by the Vikings — played 27 games with the Vikings, Packers and Jets (1984-85, 1987). Half brother, Brian Kehl, is a seven-year NFL linebacker. Billy also played baseball as a Minnesota prep. As a true freshman in 2010, stepped into the lineup in Week Three, starting 12-of-13 games played at right tackle. Suffered a torn right thumb ligament in '11 fall camp — sat out the season opener, but started all 14 games played at left tackle. Started all 30 games at LT 2012-13. Won three straight I-AA national championships.

Strengths: Big hands and nice length. Light on his feet. Flashes strength in his punch. Tries to run his feet on contact. Is athletic enough to fan the rush when all his moving parts are coordinated. Aware to handle stunts. Energetic playing temperament — competes and blocks to the whistle. Four-year starter for the nation's preeminent I-AA program. Smart, hardworking and dependable. Has NFL bloodlines.

Weaknesses: Needs to improve his core strength and fortify his base. Plays too tall and narrow-based — pad level fluctuates. Does not explode on contact. Footwork and technique need refinement. Carries his hands low. Tends to overextend and bend at the waist. Average contact balance and body control. Slides off blocks. Struggles to clear his feet as a puller. Inconsistent connecting and sustaining on the second level.

Future: Big-framed, raw, aggressive FCS standout who flashes a nice combination of foot quickness, punch strength and nastiness to warrant consideration as a project. Has a bit of a bull-in-a-china-shop element at this stage of his career, but has moldable tools and could develop into a swing backup.

Draft projection: Fourth- to fifth-round pick.

Scout's take: "I thought he struggled at the Senior Bowl. You wouldn't expect it to be instant coffee. He's intriguing."

OG-C TRAI TURNER, #56 (SOPH.-3)

LSU   ▶ GRADE: 5.52
Ht: 6-2 5/8 | Wt: 310 | Sp: 4.94 | Arm: 34 | Hand: 9 1/2

History: New Orleans native. As a high school freshman, was asked to provide depth as a varsity reserve, but refused because he thought he was better than the starters. Separated his shoulder in the first game of his senior season and had surgery after the season. Redshirted in 2011. Played 12 games in '12, starting the final seven at right guard in place of Josh Williford, whose career was cut short by concussions. Started all 13 games at RG in '13. Suffered an ankle contusion against Auburn, but did not miss any starts. Totaled 115 career knockdowns. Did not perform the shuttles at the Comine because of a hip flexor injury.

Strengths: Good overall body mass. Walls off defenders and generates movement in the run game. Can latch on and keep defenders at bay. Has experience locking horns with NFL-caliber defensive tackles, both in SEC games and practice. Will be a 21-year-old rookie. Registered the best 10-yard split (1.73 seconds), 20-yard shuttle (4.44 seconds) and the only sub-5-flat 40 time of all guards at the Combine.

Weaknesses: Lacks ideal length. Has thick hips and a fleshy midsection, which affects his ability to maneuver, position and fit. Ordinary hip snap. Has balance issues. Tends to bend at the waist and let his weight drift over his toes. Body control wanes the farther he travels. Technique needs work.

Future: Turner is a squarely built interior blocker built for road grading, though he has not demonstrated the ability to dominate as a third-year sophomore draft entrant. Could obviously have used another year of college experience, but has size and run-blocking potential in a power-running scheme. Could prove to be a better center than guard and offers swing interior versatility.

Draft projection: Third- to fourth-round pick.

Scout's take: "I can't see him getting out of the third round after the way he ran at the Combine. He's too big and athletic. Some people are talking about him higher. When you look at the untapped potential, there's some reason to get excited. He has a lot of upside."

ORG-C JOHN URSCHEL, #64

PENN STATE   ▶ GRADE: 5.27
Ht: 6-3 | Wt: 313 | Sp: 5.29 | Arm: 33 | Hand: 10 3/8

History: Prepped in Buffalo where he also competed in track and field. Redshirted in 2009 and saw limited action in three games in '10. Did not start in '11, but played 396 snaps in 13 games. Started all 24 games at right guard 2012-13. Team captain. Winner of the Campbell

Trophy as the nation's premier college football scholar athlete ("Academic Heisman") — earned a master's degree in mathematics (4.0 GPA), taught undergraduates at PSU and was published in a scientific journal.

Strengths: Highly intelligent — will be successful with or without football. Engages quickly. Good leverage, balance and body control. Works his feet and hips to position and seal. Can pull and trap and work up to the second level very quickly. Protects with awareness. Shuffles, slides and mirrors. Three-year starter. Sparkling intangibles. Well-versed in a pro-style offense having played for newly minted Texans coach Bill O'Brien.

Weaknesses: Lacks ideal size and plays short-armed. Functional strength is just adequate — gets pushed back. Is not explosive or powerful. Lets defenders cross his face and struggles to reach. Athletic ability is average.

Future: Underpowered, quick-footed, scrappy, zone blocker with the smarts, movement skill and competitive zeal to emerge as a very efficient pro. Displays the quickness highly desired at the pivot and might prove to be best at center.

Draft projection: Fourth- to fifth-round pick.

OLG CHRIS WATT, #66

NOTRE DAME   ▶ GRADE: 5.40
Ht: 6-2 5/8 | Wt: 310 | Sp: 5.25e | Arm: 32 3/4 | Hand: 9 1/2

History: Suburban Chicago native prepped at Glenbard West, where he was a USA Today and Parade All-American. Had surgery to repair a torn labrum after his senior season and redshirted in 2009. Backed up Chris Stewart at right guard in '10, appearing in all 13 games (117 snaps). Started all 26 games at left guard 2011-12. In '13, started all 11 games played at LG — tore his right PCL against Air Force and did not play against Navy, then tore his right MCL against Stanford. Was sidelined for the Pinstripe Bowl against Rutgers as well as the Senior Bowl.

Strengths: Engages quickly and runs his feet on contact. Effective with an angle and can swing his hips in the hole. Generates movement in the run game and works to finish blocks. Good bend and balance — plays on his feet. Sound fundamentals in pass protection. Strong, active hands to punch and control defenders. Can shuffle and slide. Good mobility. Works well in tandem. Smart and alert. Praised for his toughness and blue-collar work ethic. Three-year starter.

Weaknesses: Lacks ideal arm length and does not have large hands. Needs more sand in his pants. Susceptible to bull rush when powerful tackles get into his frame. Average athlete.

Inconsistent connecting with moving targets in space. Missed his final bowl game after suffering a knee injury.

Future: Good-sized, physical, competitive, bump-and-steer technician with starter-caliber ability in multiple schemes. Has a desirable temperament for the position and is a projectable, low-risk prospect.

Draft projection: Third- to fourth-round pick.

Scout's take: "I watched five games and didn't see him give up a sack. I dinged him for making only one mental mistake. He's got all everything you want intangibly — the makeup and toughness. I think he'll play a long time in the league."

OLG DAVID YANKEY, #54 (JUNIOR)

STANFORD   ▶ GRADE: 5.50
Ht: 6-5 5/8 | Wt: 315 | Sp: 5.48 | Arm: 34 | Hand: 9 1/2

History: Born in Sydney, Australia. Prepped in Georgia. Appeared in two games as a true freshman in 2010, but suffered a season-ending injury. Started all 13 games at left guard in '11. Won the Morris Trophy as the Pac-12's most outstanding offensive lineman in '12 when he started all 14 games at left tackle. Saw action at six positions — both tackles, both guards and two different tight end spots vs. Oregon State in 2012. Started 13 games at LG in '13. Missed the Washington game after his father, David, died in Roswell of cardiac arrest. Team captain.

Strengths: Very good size — has sheer mass to lean, wall off or cover up defenders. Solid base in pass protection — gets his hands on rushers, anchors and slides to fan pressure. Effective short puller. Durable three-year starter. Has played guard and tackle. Smart and dependable.

Weaknesses: Average hip snap — does not roll off the ball and overpower defenders. Stiff, lumbering movement. Needs to improve contact balance, particularly on the move — tends to get out over his skis and slip off blocks. Could struggle to corral quicker interior defenders — lacks ideal athleticism, lateral suddenness and recovery ability.

Future: Big, physical, smart, serviceable offensive guard who will not score many style points, but generally gets the job done. Has starter-caliber ability and fits best in a power scheme that takes advantage of his size and pulling ability.

Draft projection: Third- to fourth-round pick.

Scout's take: "I like the guard at Stanford. He is stiff-ankled and stiff-legged. He's not a natural bender. I wish his movement skills were better. ...He's smart. He works angles. He can create some movement. He'll play in the league."

DEFENSIVE LINEMEN

SOUTH CAROLINA DE
JADEVEON CLOWNEY

NAWROCKI'S **TOP 10**	
10	**ANTHONY JOHNSON**
9	**DANIEL McCULLERS**
8	**ED STINSON**
7	**TIMOTHY JERNIGAN**
6	**KONY EALY**
5	**LOUIS NIX III**
4	**RA'SHEDE HAGEMAN**
3	**AARON DONALD**
2	**STEPHON TUITT**
1	

EDITOR'S NOTE:
3T — Three-technique
5T — Five technique
NT — Nose tackle

5T-3T JAY BROMLEY, #96

SYRACUSE　　　　　▶ GRADE: 5.32

Ht: 6-3 1/8 | Wt: 306 | Sp: 5.06 | Arm: 33 1/2 | Hand: 9 1/4

History: Has overcome many obstacles in life — biological mother abandoned him shortly after birth; father was charged with murder when he was 5 months old; and his grandmother, who took care of him for the first 13 years of his life, died the summer before he started high school. The New York prep earned four letters in football and a scholarship from Syracuse. Appeared in 12 games as a true freshman in 2010 and had eight tackles. Played in 12 games in '11, including 10 starts at defensive tackle, and had 32 tackles, 5 1/2 tackles for loss and 1 1/2 sacks. Started 11 of Syracuse's 13 games at nose tackle in '12 (the team started a fifth defensive back in the other two games), tallying 39-5 1/2-2 1/2 with one batted pass. Blocked a West Virginia field goal attempt in the New Era Pinstripe Bowl. Broke out in '13, starting 13 times and recording 42-14 1/2-1 1/2 with three forced fumbles. Led the team in tackles for loss and sacks. Team captain.

Strengths: Good combination of size and movement skills. Flashes quick get-off and the ability to hold his ground against the run. Can work half a man, get skinny enough to penetrate the gap and closes with some steam when he has a direct bead on the QB. Is active and gives effort in pursuit. Strong tackler when he's able to wrap up ball carriers. Coachable and hardworking.

Weaknesses: Small hands. Pad level fluctuates. Average eyes and diagnostic ability. Does not play with pop or power in his hands to shock or discard blockers. Moved by double teams. Bland pass rusher (inflated sack numbers). Has tweener traits. Tepid intensity level — could use more glass in his diet.

Future: Well-built, inconsistent interior defender with enough strength, athleticism and pass-rush ability to contribute in a rotational role. Best fits as a 4-3 defensive tackle, but could appeal to teams running a hybrid scheme given his potential to be used as a five-technique.

Draft projection: Fourth- to fifth-round pick.

Scout's take: "I think he's a bit underrated. He has some versatility. He's scheme-diverse. There is some hidden value there. ... You see him play the nose and three-technique. I didn't think he could be a five-technique for us. He is a player that is active, not dominating. He will run and chase. He has pretty good pursuit and effort. I gave him a sixth-round grade and thought he was a tweener. He's not creative to make plays as a pass rusher. He is a solid complimentary type player."

NT RYAN CARRETHERS, #98

ARKANSAS STATE ▶ GRADE: 5.15

Ht: 6-13/8 | Wt: 337 | Sp: 5.47 | Arm: 31 3/4 | Hand: 9 3/8

History: The Nashville-area prep led his school to three consecutive championship games. Also lettered in wrestling. Redshirted in 2009. Appeared in 10 games in '10 as a reserve defensive lineman and had six tackles, zero for loss and zero sacks. Played in all 13 games in '11, moving into the starting lineup for the final six games at nose guard — had 29-3-1 1/2. Started all 13 games at nose tackle in '12, recording 68-3 1/2-1. Broke out in '13, starting 13 times at nose tackle and tallying 93-8-4 with two blocked field goals. Lined up at fullback against Western Kentucky and rumbled into the end zone for a 1-yard score. Completed his career in dramatic fashion in the GoDaddy Bowl against Ball State, blocking a game-tying 38-yard field goal attempt as time expired.

Strengths: Big and thick with outstanding weight-room strength — maintains low body fat, squats a small house and benchpressed 225 pounds 32 times at the Combine. Has sheer mass and natural girth to dig in and hold his ground vs. double teams. Has a wrestling background and understands leverage. Has two-gap ability. Heavy tackler. Nice effort for a big man. Tough and durable. Solid personal and football character — is devoted to his craft and has a professional approach to the game.

Weaknesses: Lacks ideal height. Has short arms and small hands. Average initial quickness. Heavy-legged with limited range. Inconsistent contact balance at the point of attack — rooted out of the hole more often than he should be. Needs to improve hand use — quickness, placement and shed timing. Marginal pass-rush value. Stamina has to be monitored. Not a workout warrior — across the board was one of the worst Combine performers, including a 7-foot, 2-inch broad jump and 8.29-second

3-cone drill, both Combine worsts.

Future: Stoutly built, NFL-strong interior defender who was a literal and figurative anchor for the Red Wolves despite playing for four different head coaches. Could make a living occupying blocks and clogging run lanes as a two-down, rotational nose tackle in an odd front.

Draft projection: Fifth- to sixth-round pick.

DLE-3T WILL CLARKE, #98

WEST VIRGINIA ▶ GRADE: 5.20

Ht: 6-6 1/8 | Wt: 271 | Sp: 4.77 | Arm: 34 5/8 | Hand: 9 7/8

History: Played defensive line and tight end as a Pennsylvania prep. Redshirted in 2009. Saw his first West Virginia action in '10, playing in four early games and collecting two tackles, one-half tackle for loss and zero sacks. Suffered a high ankle sprain against Marshall and missed the remainder of the year. Moved into a starting role in '11 and recorded 34-5-2 with one pass batted away in 13 games (11 starts). Was the listed starter at defensive end in seven games and at defensive tackle in four contests. Registered a sack in the Orange Bowl against Clemson. Was a starting defensive end in '12 and had 26-6 1/2-1 with three passes batted in 12 games (11 starts). Missed one game with a right MCL sprain. Started all 12 games for the Mountaineers at defensive tackle in '13 and recorded 49-17-6 with three passes batted and one forced fumble.

Strengths: Has a long, athletic, muscular frame. Very good movement skills for his size. Flashes the ability to penetrate or stack and shed. Gives effort in pursuit and ranges to make tackles. Solid personal and football character — has leadership traits. Smart and coachable. Durable three-year starter.

Weaknesses: Does not play to his size — plays too tall and does not generate power through his core. Shrivels against double teams and is too easily uprooted. Needs to play with better pop and power in his hands. Linear, vanilla rusher — does not have a variety of moves to defeat and accelerate off blocks.

Future: Looks the part with desirable length and musculature to warrant consideration as a developmental five-technique in a one-gapping 3-4 scheme or base end in a 4-3 front, though he will have to make significant strides with his technique and improve his run defense to be more than just a guy.

Draft projection: Late draftable pick.

Scout's take: "He did a solid job in the Shrine game. He is very long and has some rush talent."

DE-OLB JADEVEON CLOWNEY, #7 (JUNIOR)

SOUTH CAROLINA   ▶ GRADE: 7.50

Ht: 6-5 1/4 | Wt: 266 | Sp: 4.53 | Arm: 34 1/2 | Hand: 10

History: His first name is pronounced "juh-DEV-ee-uhn." Was USA Today's National Defensive Player of the Year, a Parade Magazine All-America selection and the state of South Carolina's "Mr. Football" in 2010, finishing his storied senior season with 162 tackles, 29 tackles for loss and 29 1/2 sacks with 11 forced fumbles and five defensive touchdowns. Also played part-time at running back. Arrived on campus in '11, appearing in 13 games (one start) as a true freshman and tallying 36-12-8 with one pass batted and five forced fumbles. Was selected as the SEC's Freshman of the Year. Finished sixth in the Heisman Trophy voting in '12 and was the SEC's Defensive Player of the Year after registering 54-23 1/2-13 with two passes batted and three forced fumbles in 12 starts at defensive end. Was just the second Gamecock sophomore to earn unanimous all-America honors, joining George Rogers (1980). Set school single-season records in tackles for loss and sacks and a school single-game mark with a 4 1/2-sack performance against Clemson. Missed one game, sitting against Wofford to rest an ailing foot. In 11 games in '13, he had 40-11 1/2-3 with four passes batted and one forced fumble. Missed two games with injuries (bone spurs in foot, muscle strain near rib area). Had a pair of well-publicized speeding citations in December '13 (going 110 mph in a 70 zone and 84 mph in a 55 zone). Concluded his three-year college career with 47 tackles for loss, 24 sacks and nine forced fumbles in 36 games.

Strengths: Looks every bit the part with long arms (big wing span) and large hands. Athletic marvel with raw explosive power and rare speed for his size. Is physically tough and will battle through injuries. Can collapse the corner with ease and rag-dolls blockers. Highly disruptive — creates a lot of pressure and flushes production to his teammates. Can split the double team and closes in a hiccup. Plays with leverage and power in his hands — converts speed into power and bulls blockers into the backfield. Disrupts a quarterback's vision with long arms and can bat down balls. Seldom leaves the field. Flashes playmaking ability and can produce athletic feats in a category with few others before him. Posted a 37 1/2-inch vertical jump and 10-foot, 4-inch broad jump at the Combine. Versatile — lines up everywhere along the line and can win with strength, power, quickness and speed. Has the personality of a pleaser and does not like to disappoint coaches or teammates.

Weaknesses: Is more thinly built in the lower body. Inconsistent technician. Has a tendency to play tall. Down-to-down effort lacks consistency. Lacks discipline on and off the field and has had to be managed closely since he arrived on campus. Needs to learn what it means to be a pro. Plays in spurts and is too much a of flash player — does not consistently dominate like he could. Is still immature and finding his way — too much of a follower.

Future: A physical specimen with a rare size-speed combination, Clowney was not as impactful as a junior while playing through injuries and being forced to deal with opposing offenses that fully accounted for him with extra chip protection. Was a 20-year-old junior affected by turnover on the defensive coaching staff. Could benefit tremendously from a stable positional coach and strong, veteran mentor on the defensive line who will hold him accountable, show him the way and serve as a fatherly figure. Is one of the most unique talents in the draft and could easily be a double-digit sack producer in the pros from either end. Is every bit worthy of the first overall pick — will immediately upgrade a defensive line and improve the production of those around him.

Draft projection: Top-10 pick.

Scout's take: "He's kind of a scary guy when you think about drafting him in the top-5. He has all the talent in the world, but he is a flash player. There is a lack of consistency in his play. … There are a lot of similarities to Mario Williams. The single biggest (factor) for (Clowney) to be successful — he needs a good coach. I spent a lot of time with him. I think he is a good kid. Jason Pierre Paul went 14 and fell into the right system — guys like that are difficult to find. Regardless of what everyone says about Mario Williams, he still had 13 sacks this year."

5T DEANDRE COLEMAN, #91

CALIFORNIA   ▶ GRADE: 5.40

Ht: 6-4 3/4 | Wt: 314 | Sp: 4.77 | Arm: 34 3/8 | Hand: 10 1/4

History: Parade All-American out of Seattle. Following a 2009 redshirt season, he saw his first college action in '10 as a reserve defensive lineman and had 18 tackles, three tackles for loss and zero sacks with one pass batted in 12 games. Appeared in 13 games in '11, starting twice at defensive end in December, and contributed 19-6-2. Played in all 12 games (11 starts) in '12 and recorded 48-8 1/2-3 with one pass batted. Was the listed starter in nine games at defensive end and two games at defensive tackle. Started all 12 games at nose tackle in '13 and had 40-9-2 1/2 with one pass batted. Recorded Cal's first safety since 2008 (tackle in end zone against Washington State). Team captain. At the Combine, hurt his right knee running the 40-yard dash and did not work out.

Strengths: Outstanding arm and body length and overall size. Is not easily moved off a spot. Can anchor vs. the double team and clog lanes. Very tough and durable. Plays through injuries. Versatile and has experience lining up anywhere along a "30" front.

Weaknesses: Not an accomplished pass rusher — hand use is unrefined and displays minimal acceleration and closing burst. Has to figure out how to work half a blocker. Tends to rise straight up out of his stance and stays blocked too long. Limited playing range. Lacks urgency. Has a hearing impairment in one ear.

Future: A very big, strong, two-gapping plugger ideally suited to stack the corner of an odd front. Will make a living digging his feet in the dirt and defending the run.

Draft projection: Third- to fourth-round pick.

Scout's take: "I gave him a grade as a situational starter. He's a kid who is half deaf, the kind of guy you root for. He's not really impressive on film. He plays like a lot of the other big slugs with size — the Jason Hatcher's and Allen Bailey's and Alex Carrington's. There were not a lot of (scouts) in our meetings that were high on him, but it's not easy to find guys like that. Those type of guys go in the third round."

DLE **SCOTT CRICHTON**, #95 (JUNIOR)

OREGON STATE ▶ GRADE: 5.42
Ht: 6-2 7/8 | Wt: 273 | Sp: 4.84 | Arm: 32 3/4 | Hand: 10 1/8

History: His last name is pronounced "CRY-ton." His parents are both from Western Samoa. The Washington prep enrolled at Oregon State and redshirted as a freshman in 2010. Earned the starting job at right defensive end in '11 and had 74 tackles, 14 1/2 tackles for loss and six sacks with three passes batted and a school-record six forced fumbles in 12 games. Ranked first among the nation's freshman class in tackles for loss and sacks. Moved over to the left defensive end spot in '12 and appeared in 13 games (12 starts), recording 44-17 1/2-9 with three passes batted and one forced fumble. Had a three-sack contest against Washington State. Missed spring practice in '13, rehabilitating from off-season shoulder

surgery. In 13 starts at left defensive end in the fall, he tallied 47-19-7 1/2 with three passes batted and three forced fumbles. Concluded his career as the Beavers' all-time leader in forced fumbles (10) and ranked third in sacks (22 1/2). Revealed at the NFL Combine that he elected to leave school one year early to support his struggling family; his mother works two jobs and his father still works despite having a leg amputated.

Strengths: Put together — has a well-proportioned, muscular build with long arms and big hands. Good burst off the snap. Flashes power. Can shoot his hands, extend and get under a tackle's pads. Generally plays on his feet. Nice closing speed when he has a bead. Strong tackler. Tries for the strip (10 career FFs). Productive three-year starter.

Weaknesses: Needs to play with lower pad level — tends to rush upright and defend too tall against the run. Dominated by double teams. Needs to cultivate pass-rush moves and counters — does not have a plan. Shows overall body stiffness — struggles to dip and bend the corner with leverage or flexibility. Gets sucked inside and loses contain. Loafs on the back side. Has tweener traits — lacks ideal athleticism for the right side and bulk for the left side. Inexperienced playing in reverse.

Future: Strong, athletic, raw defensive end prospect who would have been better served returning for his senior season. Despite being rough around the edges at this stage of his development, Crichton shows in flashes and has power potential as a 4-3 defensive end. Could require patience.

Draft projection: Second- to third-round pick.

Scout's take: "He is going to be pretty good. He's raw, just with no technique. He has no idea what he is doing. He needs to be coached up. He is strong and can run. He has that Samoan strength with big hands. He doesn't look like he is as big as he is because he is solid all over. He played around 260, but he has a frame to easily carry 275 by the Combine or his pro day."

3T-DLE **AARON DONALD**, #97

PITTSBURGH ▶ GRADE: 6.32
Ht: 6-0 3/4 | Wt: 285 | Sp: 4.68 | Arm: 32 5/8 | Hand: 9 7/8

History: Native Pennsylvanian. Played all 13 games as a true freshman in 2010, recording 11 tackles, three tackles for loss and two sacks with two passes batted in a reserve role. Saw action in 13 games in '11, playing every down lineman position in the 3-4 scheme, and registered 47-16-11 with four passes batted and

one forced fumble. Finished second in the Big East Conference in sacks and tackles for losses despite not starting until the final five weeks of the campaign (defensive end). In '12, he had 64-18 1/2-5 1/2 with two passes batted and one forced fumble in 12 starts. Led the conference in tackles for losses. Missed the Gardner-Webb game after his right knee was scoped. Was honored with numerous awards during his all-America campaign at defensive tackle in '13, tallying 59-28 1/2-11 with three passes batted, four forced fumbles and one blocked extra point in 13 starts. Team captain was the first Pitt defensive player to earn unanimous all-America honors since Hugh Green in 1980. Also was the recipient of the Bronko Nagurski Award, the Outland Trophy and the Rotary Lombardi Award. Was the NCAA leader in tackles for loss.

Strengths: Quick off the snap. Plays with natural leverage. Gets under pads and into gaps and is highly disruptive penetrating. Explosive in short area — recorded a 1.64-second 10-yard split at the Combine. Good foot athlete — redirects well and can work the edges and loop and stunt. Flexible enough to zone drop in short area. Plays with awareness and consistently locates the ball. Closes hard and fast. Keeps working to the ball. Disruptive penetrating ability. Outstanding career production. Tough and competitive with terrific personal and football character. Ran the fastest 40-yard dash by a defensive tackle

and the Combine and pumped 225 pounds 35 times. Was unblockable in Senior Bowl one-on-one drills.

Weaknesses: Marginal height and frame is nearly maxed out. Hands are more active than strong — could play with more pop and power. Overpowered in the run game and ground up by double teams. Gets snared and controlled by bigger, longer blockers. Not a two-gap player. Has some tweener traits — lacks ideal length and bend to play outside.

Future: Short, scrappy, instinctive, highly productive defensive penetrator who does not look the part, but inspires confidence he can be an exception to the rule. Is the type you root for and has the first-step quickness, athleticism and motor to emerge as a havoc-wreaking three-technique in a fast-flowing 4-3 scheme such as the one deployed in Dallas, Chicago and Tampa Bay.

Draft projection: First-round pick.

Scout's take: "I thought he was a second-rounder. He might have pushed himself into the first round (at the Senior Bowl). He is kicking everyone's (butt). He plays like a rolling ball of butcher knives. ... He is your classic, prototype three-technique. He's (Tampa Bay 1999 15th overall pick) 'Booger' McFarland. That's who he is. He's a building block for the Tampa-2 teams. (Tampa head coach) Lovie (Smith) and (Cowboys defensive coordinator) Rod (Marinelli) will be arm-wrestling for a way to land this kid. He's small, but he's special."

DLE-DT KONY EALY, #47 (JUNIOR)

MISSOURI   ▶ GRADE: 5.75

Ht: 6-4 | Wt: 273 | Sp: 4.92 | Arm: 34 1/4 | Hand: 9 1/2

History: His name is pronounced "COE-nee EE-lee." Was an all-state player in both football and basketball as a Missouri prep. Weighed 207 pounds when he arrived at Mizzou in 2010, redshirting as a freshman. Played in all 13 games in '11, including a start at defensive end at Baylor, and had 16 tackles, three tackles for loss and one sack. Moved into the starting lineup at defensive end in '12, seeing action in 12 games (10 starts) and recording 37-10-3 1/2 with seven passes batted and one forced fumble. Was a first-team all-SEC selection in '13, starting all 14 games and totaling 43-14 1/2-9 1/2 with six passes batted, one interception and three forced fumbles. Scored his first college touchdown on a 49-yard interception return against Indiana.

Strengths: Is long and has a big, projectable frame with room for added bulk. Quick off the snap. Loose athlete. Moves like a linebacker — 6.83-second 3-cone drill paced defensive lineman at the Combine. Plays on his feet. Runs the arc — dips his shoulder, bends the corner and gets home. Closes fast on the quarterback. Can spin off blocks, redirect and chase the quarterback. Crashes down the line and ranges in pursuit. Flexible and coordinated to zone-drop. Has upside.

Weaknesses: Needs more time in the weight room. Still developing positional instincts and awareness to blocking schemes. Pad level is too high. Exposes his frame and gets locked up. Does not convert speed to power. Unrefined hand use, counters and pass-rush moves. Needs to learn to use his length advantageously. Does not provide enough resistance at the point of attack. Crumbles vs. double teams.

Future: Big, athletic, ascending, pass-rush talent with the size, burst and flexibility to pressurize the edge as a right defensive end. Is not a finished product, particularly as a run defender, but should only become more disruptive as his strength, technique and savvy catch up with his natural physical ability. Could also draw looks as a 3-4 rush linebacker.

Draft projection: Second- to third-round pick.

Scout's take: "Ealy doesn't have a lot of production, but he is talented. He is actually really disappointing for how good he looks and the traits that he possesses. I will give him a decent grade for someone else. He's too up and down in everything he does. He's just not an aggressive, find-it player. His motor does not run high. He's big, athletic and has good speed, not great speed. He's a rep guy. He's going to need a lot of reps. He has more bust written on him than make it. He's quick, athletic, can bend and has enough strength. You can check off all the boxes."

3T DOMINIQUE EASLEY, #2

FLORIDA   ▶ GRADE: 5.40

Ht: 6-1 3/4 | Wt: 288 | Sp: 4.90e | Arm: 32 7/8 | Hand: 9 3/4

History: Has a son born in November 2012. Highly recruited out of New York. Enrolled at Florida in 2010 and played in five games as a true freshman, recording four tackles, zero for loss and zero sacks. Was limited all year by an ankle injury. Earned a starting defensive tackle spot in '11 and played in 12 games, recording 37-7 1/2-1 1/2 sacks. In October, he was allegedly involved in an altercation with former Alabama football player Reggie Myles. After an investigation, the University of Florida Police Department recommended he be charged with misdemeanor battery, but the State Attorney's Office declined to press charges. In the regular-season finale against Florida State, he tore the ACL in his left knee and missed playing in the Gator Bowl. Returned to the field in '12 and started 11 games at defensive end, recording 26-8 1/2-4 with one pass batted. Missed two games with a sprained meniscus. Started the first three games of '13 at defensive tackle and had 5-2-0. His season was cut short when he ruptured his right ACL and medial meniscus in a non-contact practice drill. Team captain.

Strengths: Has natural leverage to give blockers fits. Explodes off the snap — thrusts into gaps and wins with suddenness. Plays on his feet. Quick, active paws — shoots his hands and locks out. Disruptive penetrating ability. Relentless and energetic. Excellent pursuit effort — doesn't quit on plays and chases outside the box and downfield. Has played inside and outside. Works hard in the weight room.

Weaknesses: Lacks ideal length and bulk. Could stand to get functionally stronger. Has short arms and can be neutralized by larger linemen. Cannot be counted on to two-gap. Average production. Can be overaggressive and lose sight of the ball. Durability is a concern — both knees have required ACL surgery.

Future: Undersized, explosive, athletic, high-motor three-technique whose junior season was cut short in Week 3 by a knee injury. Injury history will likely affect his draft stock, but when healthy, he shows the ability to disrupt the backfield and pressure the quarterback. Fits best in an aggressive scheme in which he could use his quickness to slant, stunt and shoot gaps.

Draft projection: Third- to fourth-round pick.

Scout's take: "(Easley) is coming off a big injury. He is a little undersized. He's an under-tackle who has to win on quickness and get-off. I don't think he'll fit a 3-4 (front). He can change the game a little bit with his movement. They say he has really settled down and matured since he became a father — he seems to have a better work ethic and is more structured than the kid that used to sleep in meetings when he arrived. He hurt his left knee two years ago and his right knee this season. The good thing is, these guys keep healing quicker and quicker."

DRE-ROLB KASIM EDEBALI, #91

BOSTON COLLEGE   ▶ GRADE: 5.10
Ht: 6-2 | Wt: 253 | Sp: 4.79 | Arm: 32 3/4 | Hand: 9 1/2

History: The native of Hamburg, Germany, arrived in the United States in 2007 as part of the USA Football International Student Program; although he had played American football (he was a tight end for the German under-19 national team at the 2006 European Championships), he spoke limited English. After playing for a New Hampshire prep school for two years, he enrolled at Boston College and redshirted as a freshman in 2009. Played in 13 games in '10, including four starts at defensive end, and had 13 tackles, 1 1/2 tackles for loss and zero sacks with one pass batted. Started 12 games in '11 and had 27-1/2-0 with five passes batted. In 11 starts in '12, he registered 59-7 1/2-1 1/2 with four passes batted and one forced fumble. Missed the Clemson game with a shoulder injury. Had a solid senior season in '13, starting all 13 games and tallying 67-14-9 1/2 with five passes batted and three forced fumbles. Team captain.

Strengths: Good get-off. Shows an arm-over to defeat tackles. Has some disruptive ability to penetrate gaps. Reads plays and locates the ball. Uses his arms to create room to operate. Good motor in pursuit — forces runs outside and chases to the boundary. Strong tackler. Tries to disrupt passing lanes. Intelligent and articulate. Hardworking, well-respected with a professional approach to the game. Three-year starter.

Weaknesses: Lacks ideal size. Overpowered at the point of attack. Pops up off the snap. Needs to develop pass-rush moves and use his hands more violently. Average flexibility, foot speed and change of direction — exposed in space and shows when he runs the arc. Power element missing. Will be a 24-year-old rookie.

Future: German-born, high-motor, effort-based pass rusher who could warrant developmental consideration as a situational 4-3 rush end or stand-up 3-4 linebacker. Is not a natural, physically gifted hunter, but football smarts, competitiveness and effort give him a chance.

Draft projection: Late draftable pick.

NT JUSTIN ELLIS, #70

LOUISIANA TECH   ▶ GRADE: 5.10
Ht: 6-1 1/2 | Wt: 334 | Sp: 5.27 | Arm: 33 | Hand: 10 1/8

History: Lettered for three years in football and track, competing in the shot put, as a Louisiana prep. Redshirted in 2009. During camp in '10, he cracked a bone in his left foot and missed the first eight games of the season. Appeared in each of the final four contests and had four tackles, one-half tackle for loss and zero sacks. Was Louisiana Tech's starting nose tackle in '11, recording 29-3 1/2-1 with one pass batted in 13 games (11 starts). During the season, he had his right shoulder scoped, although he didn't miss any action. Was limited to just nine games (two starts) in '12, missing three full games with a right ankle sprain, and had 21-0-0 with one pass batted and two forced fumbles. Recorded his best college season as a senior in '13, starting all 12 games and tallying 48-5 1/2-1 1/2 with one pass batted.

Strengths: Good anchor strength — is seldom inverted or moved off a spot. Can stack the line and occupy blockers.

Weaknesses: Short with short limbs and a lot of extra concentrated weight in his midsection. Limited athlete. Tires easily and tends to stand straight up and get caught on blocks (marginal extension). Does not show violence in his hands. Is not a pass rusher. Has missed time with foot and ankle injuries associated with excessive weight that he has struggled maintaining.

Future: Round-bodied, short-armed plugger with enough anchor strength to hold the point and clog the middle on a shade in a 4-3 front. Must prove he can manage his weight and stay healthy to earn a spot in the NFL.

Draft projection: Late draftable pick.

DLE-LOLB IK ENEMKPALI, #41

LOUISIANA TECH ▶ GRADE: 5.05

Ht: 6-0 3/4 | Wt: 261 | Sp: 5.01 | Arm: 33 1/8 | Hand: 9 3/4

History: His name is pronounced "EYE-KAY IN-em-PALL-ee." His full name is Ikemefuna Chinedum Enemkpali. His parents were born in Nigeria. The Texas prep helped lead his school to the state playoffs during his two years as a starter. Enrolled at Louisiana Tech and redshirted in 2009; was part of the same freshman class as defensive line mate Justin Ellis. Saw action in 11 games (10 starts) at defensive end in '10 and had 36 tackles, six tackles for loss and 2 1/2 sacks. Missed one game with a sprained ankle. In April '11, he was arrested following an off-campus incident and was subsequently charged with disturbing the peace and battery of a police officer. Was initially suspended by the team, but was reinstated before the season began. In 13 games that fall, he recorded 33-7 1/2-3 1/2 with one forced fumble. Started all 12 game at RDE in '12 and totaled 32-7 1/2-6 with one pass batted and one forced fumble. In 12 starts at right defensive end in '13, he tallied 47-11-5 1/2 with one pass batted and two interceptions. Was one of two linemen in the country to have two interceptions, picking off passes against North Carolina State and North Texas.

Strengths: Very thickly built. Flashes shock and violence in his punch. Highly competitive, plays hard and motor runs hot. Keeps battling to the quarterback. Gave Texas A&M OLT and 2013 No. 2 overall pick Luke Joeckel fits in '12. Superb football character — the game is very important to him. Film junkie. Tough and physical.

Weaknesses: Below-average height. Ultra-stiff and overly muscled, negating his quickness, speed and lateral agility. Green eyes and instincts — gets outflanked too easily, is consistently late off the ball and can improve his snap anticipation and get-off quickness. Marginal hip flexibility. Lacks variety of pass-rush moves and gets hung up on blocks too easily. Can create better extension and improve hand use to swat, shed and disengage. Does not consistently convert speed to power. Benchpressed 225 pounds only 19 times at the Combine.

Future: A strong, tenacious, tightly wound leverage-power rusher most ideally suited for a 3-4 outside linebacker role. Will require patience to develop. Has a high-collision special-teams temperament to contribute in coverage if he can learn to unlock his hips. Best chance will come in Blitzburgh.

Draft projection: Priority free agent.

Scout's take: "Stiff, stiff, stiff."

DT EGO FERGUSON, #9 (JUNIOR)

LSU ▶ GRADE: 5.44

Ht: 6-27/8 | Wt: 315 | Sp: 5.15e | Arm: 315 | Hand: 10 3/4

History: Spent the first three years of high school in Maryland before transferring to Hargrave Military Academy as a senior. Redshirted in 2010. Spent his first two seasons at LSU backing up Eagles 2013 third-rounder Bennie Logan. Saw action in 13 games in '11 and managed 13 tackles, 1/2 tackle for loss and zero sacks with one batted pass. Did not play against Mississippi State. Came off the bench again in '12 and posted 14-1-0 with a pass batted down in 13 contests. Moved into the starting lineup in '13, logging 58-3 1/2-1 with three batted passes in 12 starts at defensive tackle. Was not allowed to travel to Tampa for the Outback Bowl for medical reasons. Did not work out at the Combine because of a right ankle injury (medical exclusion).

Strengths: Good size, foot speed, balance and athletic ability. Flashes the ability to stack, locate and shed. Bends his knees, redirects efficiently and has good range for a 300-pounder — flows well laterally. Nice closing speed. Had disruptive potential.

Weaknesses: Needs to get stronger through his core and base. Needs to quicken his hands and use them more violently. Raw counters and pass-rush moves. Power element is missing. Spends too much time idled at the line of scrimmage. Does not dominate single blocks and gets beat up by double teams. Limited two-gap ability. Disappears for long stretches. Only a one-year starter with minimal behind-the-line production.

Future: Athletic, raw, developmental three-technique with clear upside, though he is inexperienced, aimless and unrefined at this stage of his development. Needs more glass in his diet and simply does not impact games the way he should. Is likely to test well and be drafted higher than his performance dictates in the hopes a defensive line coach can tap into his potential.

Draft projection: Third- to fourth-round pick.

Scout's take: "He looks just like you'd draw them up. He is big and athletic. You're going to have to be patient with him though, and I wonder if the light will ever go on."

3T-5T RA'SHEDE HAGEMAN, #99

MINNESOTA   ▶ GRADE: 6.00
Ht: 6-5 7/8 | Wt: 310 | Sp: 5.02 | Arm: 34 1/4 | Hand: 10 1/4

History: Has a son. Name is pronounced "ruh-SHEED HAYG-men." Grew up in foster homes before being adopted at the age of 7 by a Minnesota couple. Highly recruited tight end who also won a basketball state championship. Stayed home to play for the Gophers in 2009, where he redshirted and was switched to the defensive line. Appeared in eight games as a reserve in '10 and managed five tackles, zero tackles for loss and zero sacks. Suspended for the last four games of the season for academic issues. Logged 13-3 1/2-2 with one forced fumble in 13 games as a reserve in '11. Arrested in May '12 while trying to break up a bar fight and charged with disorderly conduct. The charges were later dropped. Became a starter at defensive tackle in the fall and recorded 35-7 1/2-6 with two batted passes and one forced fumble in 12 starts. Named the team MVP in '13 after leading the team with 13 tackles for loss with 38-13-2 with eight batted passes, his first career interception and a pair of blocked kicks —field goal vs. UNLV and an extra point against Western Illinois in 13 starts. Team captain.

Strengths: Long and well-proportioned. Intriguing height-weight-speed ratio and natural athleticism. Flashes the ability explode off the ball, jolt blockers and disrupt the backfield. Terrific movement, flexibility and range. Loose ankles. Can work the edges. Able to redirect and chase athletically. Fierce tackler. Workout all-star with rare leaping ability for his size (35 1/2-inch vertical) — benchpressed 225 pounds 32 times at the Combine. Disrupts passing lanes. Has a "wow" factor at his best. Has immense upside.

Weaknesses: Wide gap between physical ability and performance on tape. Green eyes, instincts and understanding of blocking schemes. Motor idles. Too often lets his pads rise and exposes his frame. Does not play to his length. On skates vs. double teams. Hand use needs work. Unsophisticated counters and pass-rush moves. Aimless pass rusher in need of a plan. Minimal, inflated sack production. Still learning to convert speed to power. Does not dominate single blocking. Is rotated heavily. Needs more glass in his diet. Could require simple assignments. Motivation and coachability should be examined more closely. Will be 24-year-old rookie. Has a glaring bust factor.

Future: A raw, converted tight end with a basketball background, Hageman is a big, athletic, finesse three-technique with intriguing dimensions and movement skills who fits best in an aggressive, one-gap scheme where he could fire into gaps. Will probably be restricted to nickel pass-rush duty initially until the game slows down for him, but has impact potential if he ever figures it out. Is still maturing, having endured a harrowing childhood to get to where he is today, and would be best served landing in a structured environment with veteran mentorship. Classic boom-or-bust prospect.

Draft projection: Top-40 pick.

Scout's take: "He is too big and athletic. Those guys all go. You just have to coach them. He's raw as (heck). You don't think Rex or Rob Ryan would want to coach that dude? We played Sheldon Richardson this year. You can run at him. He just jumps around working edges. He plays the same way as a jumbo end. ... (Hageman) is going to go higher than where I am going to put him. I would like to put him at the top of three, knowing the projection is that he is going in the first round. Really, honestly, my vision is late three-early fourth. There's no way he makes it that far, but that's where he grades the way he played this year. There is too much inconsistency and not enough production."

5T-DT TAYLOR HART, #66

OREGON   ▶ GRADE: 5.22
Ht: 6-61/8 | Wt: 281 | Sp: 4.95e | Arm: 32 3/4 | Hand: 10 1/8

History: Engaged to a former Duck volleyball player. Prepped in Oregon. Also played basketball. Redshirted in 2009 and fractured his right hand. Saw action in 12 games as a reserve defensive lineman in '10, managing 18 tackles, two tackles for loss and two sack with one batted pass. Did not play in the BCS National Championship game against Auburn. Posted 44-3-2 1/2 with two batted passes, one forced fumble and a blocked kick in 14 starts at defensive tackle in '11. Made the switch to defensive end in '12, playing in all 13 contests (12 starts, all but Stanford) and logged 36-11-8 with three batted passes and one forced fumble. Named the team's co-MVP after registering 75-6-3 1/2 with five batted passes and three forced fumbles in 13 starts. Made the first five starts at DE and the remaining seven at DT. Broke his left foot while training in January '13 and missed the Senior Bowl and did not work out at the Combine.

Strengths: Terrific size and length. Good eyes and awareness. Plays on his feet. Holds his ground at the point. Gains extension and can stack and shed. Collapses the pocket. Good range and pursuit effort. Closes hard. Strong wrap tackler (very good production) — snares ball carriers and drags them to the turf. Good soldier who falls in line willingly and has clean character. Three-year starter.

Weaknesses: Could stand to add bulk to his frame and get functionally stronger. Average athlete. Not explosive. Ordinary get-off — takes short initial steps and exposes his frame off the snap. Needs to play with more consistent pad level. Fairly linear rusher. Limited shoulder flexibility to dip and bend the edge. Stiffness shows in space.

Future: Big-framed, smart, active, high-effort player who willingly does the dirty work and will make it difficult for coaches to cut him. Best chance to stick could be as a five-technique, but could also draw interest as a developmental left end. Has the makeup to surprise if he learns to play with power.

Draft projection: Fourth- to fifth-round pick.

Scout's take: "He has to be a 3-4 defensive end, but he's a backup or No. 3. He is a non-athlete. He's a tough overachiever, a guy that paid his dues. He has a stance like a frog. He is stiff. He cannot rush the passer. Maybe he has okay strength — I'd say borderline at best. I was surprised he was at the Senior Bowl."

DT KERRY HYDER, #91

TEXAS TECH ▶ GRADE: 4.90

Ht: 6-2 1/2 | Wt: 290 | Sp: 5.11 | Arm: 33 1/2 | Hand: 9 3/4

History: His cousin, Chris Houston, is a cornerback for the Detroit Lions. Redshirted in 2009. Saw action in 11 games in '10, making two starts at defensive tackle (first two games) and one start vs. Baylor at left defensive end, and recorded 13 tackles, 3 1/2 tackles for loss and two sacks with two batted passes. Missed two games with a strained hamstring. Started all 12 games at DT in '11, leading the team in tackles for loss, and logged 42-5-1 1/2 with three batted passes. In '12, posted 56-14-5 1/2 with four batted down passes in 13 starts at nose tackle. Again, led the squad in TFL's in '13 with 65-11 1/2-2 with one batted pass, three forced fumbles and two blocked kicks in 13 starts at nose tackle. Blocked a field goal against Oklahoma and a punt vs. Oklahoma State. Team captain.

Strengths: Thick through his trunk. Stout

against the run — drops his base and holds his ground. Excellent hand use — shoots his hands and jolts defenders. Strong, active paws to disengage. Gives effort in pursuit. Strong wrap tackler. Competes against double teams. Tough, durable, three-year starter. Has a professional work ethic.. Recorded an exceptional 4.33-second 20-yard shuttle time, tops among defensive tackles at the Combine.

Weaknesses: Bad-bodied. Size and length are just adequate — does not have ideal build. Not explosive — ordinary get-off. Very average foot athlete, especially for his size. Top-heavy movement — shows some lower-body stiffness and struggles to redirect efficiently. Production is effort-based. Could stand to shed some bad weight and improve his conditioning and stamina. Production is fabricated against lesser competition in garbage time.

Future: Undersized, thickly built, active defensive lineman with tweener traits. Lacks ideal explosiveness and flexibility, but his hand use, competitiveness and motor could enable him to fight for a spot as a rotational three- or five-technique.

Draft projection: Priority free agent.

Scout's take: "His body looks like Fred Sanford's. It's not pretty. He has some production, but a lot of it is fabricated. You rarely see it on tape, and it comes against garbage."

DRE-ROLB JACKSON JEFFCOAT, #44

TEXAS ▶ GRADE: 5.15

Ht: 6-3 | Wt: 247 | Sp: 4.63 | Arm: 33 7/8 | Hand: 9 5/8

History: His father, Jim Jeffcoat, won two Super Bowls with the Dallas Cowboys, and is currently an assistant coach at Colorado. Highly recruited Texas native who also lettered in basketball (four years) and ran track (three times). Saw action in 2010 as a true freshman, making two starts at defensive end, and posted 15 tackles, six tackles for loss and 2 1/2 sacks with one batted pass. Sprained his ankle against Nebraska and missed the next four games. Led the team and finished third in the Big 12 in tackles for loss in '11 after logging 71-21-8 with three batted passes in 13 contests (12 starts at the Buck position – hybrid DE/LB). Only non-start was against Baylor, when Texas opened in the dime package. Suffered a ruptured left pectoral muscle against Texas A&M in November but put surgery off until January. Had a monster game against California in the Holiday Bowl with 8-3-2. Did not participate in '12 spring practice while recovering from surgery. Returned in the fall and started the first six games at the Buck position, recording 31-11-4 with one batted pass and two forced fumbles. Had a fumble return touchdown against West Virginia – his first career points. Continued his run of serious injuries when he ruptured his right pectoral muscle against Oklahoma and underwent season-ending surgery October 19. Still finished second on the club in TFL and sacks despite only seeing action in six games. Returned in '13 and won the Hendricks Award after pacing the Longhorns defense with 86-22-13 with three batted passes, his first career interception vs. Iowa State, two forced fumbles and one blocked kick in 13 contests. Team captain.

Strengths: Good body length and size-speed ratio. Flashes some quickness and shock in his hands to swat and control blockers. Football smart. Solid instincts and overall sack production. Has NFL pedigree. Has a 36-inch vertical jump and recorded a 6.97-second 3-cone drill, second-best among defensive lineman at the Combine.

Weaknesses: Needs more time in the weight room, as evidenced by 18 benchpress reps at the Combine, and has a very underdeveloped lower body. Tight hips. Has been slowed by injuries throughout his career and it has affected his physical development. Lacks the base strength to set the edge. Gets rooted out of the hole vs. the double team. Cannot drop his hips and turn the corner. Very inconsistent effort — average competitiveness and desire.

Future: Developmental 3-4 rush-linebacker prospect with the pedigree and sack production to warrant interest. However, Jeffcoat will need to get stronger and improve vs. the run to ever become more than a backup.

Draft projection: Late draftable pick.

Scout's take: "He has skinny legs. He is underdeveloped. He's a 3-4 rush guy. He is not an end. He can't set the edge. He's not strong. He has some quickness, but he's stiff in the hips. He can't drop his hips and turn the corner. You can have him. ...The Steelers and Ravens and the zone-blitzing teams can get away with guys who are more stiff on the edges. That's where he'll land."

NT TIMMY JERNIGAN, #8 (JUNIOR)

FLORIDA STATE   ▶ GRADE: 5.70
Ht: 6-1 5/8 | Wt: 299 | Sp: 5.06 | Arm: 31 5/8 | Hand: 9 5/8

History: Highly recruited Florida prep. The true freshman saw action in all 13 games as a reserve in 2011 and led interior linemen with 30 tackles, six tackles for loss and 2 1/2 sacks. Was sidelined during '12 spring practice with a sprained MCL and slight meniscus tear. Backed up Cowboys 2013 seventh-rounder Everett Dawkins for a second straight season in the fall, logging 45-8-1 1/2 in 13 games with two starts. His '13 spring practice was cut short by an ankle injury. Was healthy in the fall and had 63-11-4 1/2 in 14 starts at nose tackle, his only season as a starter. Led the Noles in tackles for loss. Battled an illness in the National Championship game against Auburn and had nine tackles.

Strengths: Strong for his size and clogs the middle. Has disruptive ability. Bends his knees and plays with leverage. Able to stack, locate and shed. Wraps and rips down ball carriers. Coordinated hands and feet. Is difficult to engage — has quick, active paws. Can slap, rip and swim to beat blockers and turns up the heat on passing downs. Good foot athlete for his size — changes direction well, gives effort in pursuit and ranges outside the box. Will be a 21-year-old rookie.

Weaknesses: Has a fleshy midsection. Lacks ideal height and overall body length. Average get-off. Can be overpowered at the point or neutralized when bigger, longer blockers get into his frame. Limited two-gap ability. Average playing range. Stiff-legged and does not change direction easily, as confirmed by 4.84-second 20-yard shuttle time at the Combine (tied for slowest among DTs). Could stand to improve his stamina. Was a rotational player prior to junior season.

Future: Slightly undersized, stoutly built, country-strong run stopper with the ability to drop anchor inside an odd front and develop into a solid, 3-4 movement nose tackle. Strength is his calling card despite his relatively modest size.

Draft projection: Top-50 pick.

Scout's take: "I don't see it. There are others in our building that have high grades on him and think he is really good. Some of these young guys are telling me how good he is. If you think he can rush, I will come back and play linebacker tomorrow (in my 60's). He is very stiff-hipped. He has a strong anchor. He's yoked up solid as a rock. He doesn't have any pass-rush ability. I didn't think he was a very good athlete. How many sacks did he have? People think he is a special three-tech. He is stiffer than stiff and hasn't had any production."

NT ANTHONY JOHNSON, #90 (JUNIOR)

LSU ▶ GRADE: 5.55
Ht: 6-2 1/2 | Wt: 308 | Sp: 5.24 | Arm: 33 | Hand: 10 3/8

History: Prepped in New Orleans where he was the consensus No. 1 defensive tackle prospect in the country. Was a Parade All-America selection and the 2010 Louisiana Gatorade Player of the Year. Saw action in all 14 games as true freshman and recorded 12 tackles, three tackles for loss and one sack as a reserve defensive lineman. Logged 30-10-3 with two pass breakups in 13 games (three starts at left defensive tackle) in '12. Moved into the starting lineup in '13 and recorded 35-9-3 with one batted pass and one interception in 13 starts at DT. Shed more than 30 pounds since his freshman year in an effort to get quicker.

Strengths: Looks the part — big and well-proportioned. Quick get-off. Plays on his feet. Excellent movement skills and foot speed. Knee bender who redirects and accelerates efficiently for a big man. Flashes strength to stack and shed single blocks. Good closing burst to the quarterback. Was a 20-year-old junior — has moldable, raw tools and upside.

Weaknesses: Plays tall and short-armed — too easily turned and washed. Weak base and lackluster compete vs. double teams. Hand use needs work — spends too much time flailing at the line of scrimmage. Does not consistently convert speed to power. Unsophisticated pass rusher — needs to cultivate moves and develop a plan. Disappears for stretches. Started just 16 career games. Weight has fluctuated. Has underachiever traits. Character and stability need to be investigated. Disappointing Combine performance.

Future: Thick, athletic, overhyped defensive tackle who shows in flashes, but leaves evaluators wanting more. Was not as impactful in a starting role as a junior as he was in a wave role as a sophomore. Fits best in an even front stacking the point, though he's not instant coffee. A boom-or-bust prospect.

Draft projection: Second- to third-round pick.

Scout's take: "I thought he underachieved this year. I liked what I saw more a year ago. His character is one that you're going to have to look into."

5T-DT DaQUAN JONES, #91

PENN STATE ▶ GRADE: 5.40
Ht: 6-3 3/4 | Wt: 322 | Sp: 5.34 | Arm: 33 1/2 | Hand: 9 5/8

History: His first name is pronounced "DAY-qwan." Was a highly recruited offensive lineman as a New York prep. Also lettered in basketball and track. Enrolled at Penn State in 2010 and initially was going to redshirt as a freshman, as he was held out of the Nittany Lions' first four games. His play in practice got him on the field, though, and he saw action in the final nine games, recording six tackles, two tackles for loss and one sack. Was forced to play defensive end against Illinois when three ends were injured in the contest. Saw action in all 13 games as a backup defensive tackle in '11, registering 8-0-0. Moved into the starting lineup in '12 and had 22-2-1/2 with one pass batted in 12 games (11 starts). Had a strong senior year in '13 after dropping 15 pounds in the off-season, starting 12 times and recording 56-11 1/2-3. Team captain.

Strengths: Big body — looks the part. Fires off the snap and engages quickly. Is difficult to displace and has a strong upper body. Able to control blocks and locate the ball. Plays with a load in his hands — presses blockers, extends and discards. Generates a strong bull rush and collapses the pocket. Is athletic and redirects well for a big man. Flashes disruptive ability and dominates at times, creating production for teammates. Scheme versatile. Has upside.

Weaknesses: Takes some plays off and occasionally loafs on plays away from him. Could stand to develop counters and pass-rush moves. Does not threaten the edges. Does not accelerate off blocks and closing burst is just average. Can do a better job protecting his legs. Weight and conditioning have fluctuated.

Future: Big, strong-bodied interior force who shed weight and improved his stamina as a senior, displaying NFL-caliber physicality in the trenches. Has been inconsistent in the past, but if the light has come on, Jones' combination of size, power and movement enables him to play as a 4-3 one-technique or 3-4 five-technique.

Draft projection: Second- to third-round pick.

Scout's take: "He didn't look very natural at the Combine moving around. I was expecting to see better. He looked more disruptive on tape than athletic."

NT ZACH KERR, #94

DELAWARE ▶ GRADE: 5.10
Ht: 6-1 3/8 | Wt: 326 | Sp: 5.08 | Arm: 32 7/8 | Hand: 9 3/4

History: Two-way lineman won a state title as a Maryland prep. Started the 2008-09 school year at Fork Union (Va.) Military Academy prep school before enrolling at Maryland in January '09, where he participated in spring practice. Saw limited action in seven games as a freshman, recording two tackles. Missed time with a concussion. Played in 13 games as a reserve defensive lineman in '10 and had 21 tackles, one-half tackle for loss and zero sacks. Was also used as a goal-line fullback on offense. Did not play in '11, as he transferred to Delaware. Earned a starting spot with the Blue Hens in '12, starting 11 games at right defensive tackle and recording 27-4 1/2-1 with one pass batted. Intercepted a pass at the line of scrimmage against William & Mary and ran 47 yards for a touchdown. Started all 12 games in '13, tallying 57-5 1/2-3 1/2 with two passes batted and two forced fumbles. Team captain.

Strengths: Has a solid frame with long arms. Good lower-body power — can collapse the pocket and walk blockers back to the quarterback when he comes off the ball low. Secure tackler. Regularly splits the double team and can stack the point vs. single blocks. Likes the weight room and works to improve.

Weaknesses: Short. Limited agility. Tends to wear down, takes some plays off and effort wanes. Gets fooled by misdirection and can be late to locate the ball. Could stand to improve hand use as a pass rusher and shedding blocks. Regularly faced inferior competition. Has a concussion history.

Future: Thick-bodied, long-armed, powerful 3-4 nose tackle with scheme versatility to factor in a rotation for an even or odd front. Uses a lot of finesse and would be best utilized in a defense where he is allowed to slant, stunt and shoot gaps. Has moldable tools to develop.

Draft projection: Late draftable pick.

DLE-OLB AARON LYNCH, #19 (JUNIOR)
SOUTH FLORIDA   ▶ GRADE: 5.17
Ht: 6-5 | Wt: 249 | Sp: 4.69 | Arm: 34| Hand: 10 1/4

History: Highly recruited Florida prep. Began his college career at Notre Dame — played 12 games as a true freshman in 2011, starting six at defensive end, and recorded 33 tackles, seven tackles for loss and 5 1/2 sacks with two passes batted and one forced fumble. Left the team during spring practice in '12, expressing an interest to play closer to home, and transferred to South Florida. Was forced to sit out that season after his transfer waiver was denied by the NCAA. In his lone season with South Florida, he tallied 29-11 1/2-5 with one pass batted in 12 games (10 starts) in '13. Had a 44-yard fumble return for touchdown against Connecticut. Weight has fluctuated heavily, which he reportedly said stems from his use of Adderall. Did not work out at the

Combine because of a right hamstring injury (medical exclusion).

Strengths: Outstanding size, including long arms and large hands. Flashes some playmaking ability. Deceptive strength to leverage the edge. Has a giant wingspan and can corral ball carriers.

Weaknesses: Classic underachiever. Questionable effort, motor and desire. Leaves production on the field. Does not play with passion and lacks urgency. Goes through the motions. Is not a strong or creative rusher and does not create plays. Lacks concentration and focus. Will require maintenance. Weight has fluctuated a lot. Managed just 18 benchpress reps at the Combine. Did not show well at his pro day — managed just a 29-inch vertical and recorded poor times in the 3-cone drill (7.46 seconds) and short shuttle (4.61 seconds).

Future: A big, athletic prospect who displayed the most potential as a freshman at Notre Dame. Has underachieved since transferring closer to home and shedding considerable weight. Must prove motivated to reach his potential. Finished the season strong and finally showed signs of the talent he displayed as a standout freshman. Would benefit from a strong, mentoring, veteran position coach, and could land with a team like the Bengals, who have a propensity to gamble on boom-or-bust prospects, especially in the mid to late rounds when reward outweighs risk.

Draft projection: Late draftable pick.

Scout's take: "I'm not sure how much he loves the game. I wanted to put a reject grade on him. He didn't have any production or many any plays early in the games I saw. His sacks were washed to him. If you looked at my notes, the negative column was littered and I struggled to find any positives. I usually don't write guys like that."

5T-DT EATHYN MANUMALEUNA, #55
BYU   ▶ GRADE: 5.15
Ht: 6-2 1/4 | Wt: 296 | Sp: 5.16 | Arm: 32 1/4 | Hand: 10

History: His name is pronounced "EE-thin MAH-noo-MAY-lay-oo-nah." The Alaska native is married and has a son. His uncle, Robert Anae, is BYU's offensive coordinator. His cousin, Brandon Manumaleuna, was a fullback with the Rams, Chargers and Bears from 2001-2010. As a Utah prep, he was a two-way starter and helped lead his team to a state championship. Enrolled at BYU in 2007 and started all 13 games at nose tackle as a true freshman, recording 25 tackles, three tackles for loss and one sack with one pass batted. In the Las Vegas Bowl against UCLA, he blocked a potential game-winning field goal attempt as time expired. Served a two-year mission to Oklahoma City before returning to the football field in '10, appearing in 13 games (eight starts) and registering 27-3-2 1/2 with one pass batted and one interception. Started four games at left defensive end and four at nose guard. Made all 13 starts at right DE in '11 and had 33-0-0. In what was supposed to be his final season in '12, he started the first four games at left DE before suffering a season-ending injury – tearing the patella tendon in his left knee. Had opened the year 11-4-2 with a pass batted and one forced fumble, starting in front of Lions 2013 first-round pick Ziggy Ansah. Was granted a medical redshirt by the NCAA. Returned in '13 and made 13 starts at nose tackle, tallying 25-3-1 with one pass batted. Concluded his career having appeared in a school-record 56 games.

Strengths: Good strength, balance and body control. Lines up in a flexible stance and engages quickly. Generally holds his ground. Has two-gap ability. Shoots his hands to stack, locate and shed. Can press his man and walk him back to cave the pocket. Moves very well for a big man, especially laterally — can pick 'em up and put 'em down in chase mode. Senses screen. Strong wrap tackler. Has NFL bloodlines.

Weaknesses: Lacks ideal length and bulk — can be locked up by larger blockers. Is not a quick-twitch, power player. Marginal sack production — one-dimensional rusher who could stand to develop counter moves. What you see is what you get — will be a 25-year-old rookie.

Future: Thick, stout, overaged defensive lineman with functional strength, awareness and competitiveness to provide depth and effective run defense. Is scheme-versatile, having played tackle and end in a hybrid front, and could be used as a 4-3 tackle or 3-4 five-technique. Good soldier.

Draft projection: Late draftable pick.

DLE-LOLB KAREEM MARTIN, #95

NORTH CAROLINA ▶ GRADE: 5.44

Ht: 6-5 7/8 | Wt: 272 | Sp: 4.72 | Arm: 35 | Hand: 10

History: Played football and basketball as a North Carolina prep. Played in 11 games (starting the first three at defensive end) as a true freshman in 2010 and had 16 tackles, 1 1/2 tackles for loss and zero sacks with one pass batted. Moved into the starting lineup for good in '11 and tallied 40-7-4 with six passes batted, starting 13 games from the right

DE position. Started all 12 games in '12 and recorded 40-15 1/2-4 with three passes batted and one forced fumble. Had at least one tackle for loss in 10 different games. In '13, he tied for eighth among FBS players in sacks, finishing the year 82-21 1/2-11 1/2 with three passes batted and three forced fumbles in 13 starts. Team captain.

Strengths: Has very long arms. Good eyes and recognition — senses screens, locates the ball and understands contain. Strong-handed to punch and extend. Good short-area burst. Uses his length to force his way into gaps. Flashes power potential. Nice closing speed. Wrap tackler. Football smart. Durable three-year starter. Solid personal and football character with leadership traits. Showed explosion at the Combine, recording a 10-foot, 9-inch broad jump (tops among defensive linemen) and a 35 1/2-inch vertical jump.

Weaknesses: Needs to bulk up and get functionally stronger. Has tapered legs and is not stout at the point of attack — does not generate power through his lower half and is too easily displaced. Pad level fluctuates. Needs to improve as a hands fighter. Can do a better job protecting his legs. Average get-off — pops up off the snap and initial steps are unthreatening. Rush lacks variety. Does not accelerate off blocks or consistently bend the corner. Occasionally loafs on the back side. Tweener traits.

Future: Big, narrow-framed, long-levered defensive lineman who shows flashes of potential as a developmental, 4-3 left end, though he needs to fortify his base as a run defender and hone his technique as a pass rusher.

Draft projection: Fourth- to fifth-round pick.

Scout's take: "(Martin) is really intriguing. He had a really good game against Pittsburgh. There were some inconsistencies with him taking plays off. I was hemming and hawing about where to grade him. I thought he was a sixth-rounder the first time I went through. I wound up sticking him at the top of the fourth. He got better late in the season."

5T-DT JOSH MAURO, #90

STANFORD ▶ GRADE: 5.09

Ht: 6-5 7/8 | Wt: 271 | Sp: 5.21 | Arm: 33 | Hand: 9 1/2

History: His last name is pronounced "MORE-owe." Born in St. Albans, England, the Texas prep moved to defensive end as a senior after playing linebacker and quarterback. Also lettered in basketball. Enrolled at Stanford in 2009 and redshirted.

DEFENSIVE LINEMEN

Was utilized in eight games as a reserve defensive lineman in '10 and had seven tackles and one pass batted. Played in all 13 games as a reserve in '11 and recorded four tackles, two tackles for loss and two sacks with one pass batted. Was a key reserve in '12, seeing action in 13 games and totaling 19-7-5. Entered his redshirt senior campaign in '13 with no career starts and began the year second on the depth chart, but moved into the starting lineup in Week 3 due to injuries and never looked back. Recorded 51-12 1/2-4 with one pass batted, one interception and two forced fumbles. Made his first college start – in his 35th Stanford game – September 21 against Arizona State and had two tackles, one sack and a 25-yard interception return. Missed one game with a leg injury.

Strengths: Big, well-built, projectable frame with little excess weight. Likes to play and it shows — intense competitor. Is strong enough to anchor down and set the edge. Can neutralize the double team. Plays bigger than his size. Experienced in a pro-style, 3-4 front. Tough and durable. Good weight-room work ethic.

Weaknesses: Has never been a full-time starter. Mechanical, robotic movement. Needs to add some more bulk and bulk strength. Is a bit top-heavy. Minimal pass-rush ability. Still growing into his body and learning how to use his hands. Marginal foot quickness — late to the outside. Limited athletic ability to create penetration.

Future: English-born, high-motor, developmental five-technique with intriguing growth potential. Has generated solid production from a wave role and could continue to be molded into a solid fencepost for a 3-4 front. Draws semblances to a young Brett Keisel, drafted in the seventh round by the Steelers in 2002, and has the makeup to play a long time in an unsung role occupying blockers and defending the run.

Draft projection: Sixth- to seventh-round pick.

Scout's take: "He's so stiff he hurts me when he changes direction. That's what is going to be most difficult to overcome. How many ultra-stiff guys stick in the league? Usually they flame out pretty fast."

NT DANIEL McCULLERS, #98

TENNESSEE   ▶ GRADE: 5.65
Ht: 6-6 3/4 | Wt: 352 | Sp: 5.50e | Arm: 36 5/8 | Hand: 11

History: The North Carolina prep began his college career at Georgia Military College in 2010, weighing nearly 400 pounds when he arrived on campus. As a freshman, he appeared in eight games and had 27 tackles, four tackles for loss and three sacks with four passes batted, one interception and one forced fumble. Became a top junior college recruit in '11, recording 37-9-2 in 10 games. Transferred to Tennessee in '12 and won the starting nose tackle job in camp, registering 39-5 1/2-1 with one pass batted, one forced fumble and one blocked kick in 12 games (seven starts). Started 12 games in '13 and had 33-4 1/2-1/2 with one blocked kick. Did not run at the Combine because of a strained right hamstring.

Strengths: Rare size with vines for arms, an enormous wingspan and exceptional mass to occupy space and hold up multiple blockers — has clear two-gap potential. Looks every bit the part with a relatively lean build for a 350-pounder — carries his weight well with some muscle definition and good overall body thickness. Can overpower zone blockers with sheer size. Very durable and has not missed any games to injury throughout his career.

Weaknesses: Lets his pads rise (first move is up), gets outleveraged and does not hold his ground as well as a man his size should. Gets turned out of the hole and sealed. Duck-footed short-stepper with limited play range — does not make plays outside the box. Average body power to roll his hips and generate torque. Limited pass-rush potential (confirmed by 1.5 career sacks) — is late off the ball, does not collapse the pocket and stays blocked too long. Must improve his hand use to disengage. Exited high school pushing 400 pounds and weight has fluctuated in the past.

Future: A big-boned, short-area plugger with some underachiever tendencies, McCullers has raw tools that could become special if he learns to harness the innate strength in his body and pairs with a DL coach who can refine his mechanics.

Draft projection: Second- to third-round pick.

Scout's take: "He's probably the biggest defensive tackle I have ever seen. He looks like a Greek god. You want more than a body-beautiful guy that doesn't do anything for you. What someone has to explain to me is why the 270-pound guy is playing the nose. What does that tell you? ... He is a wildcard because he looks so good. I would think he would be the kind of guy you want to draft late. If his (signing) bonus check is not much and he has to play to get paid, maybe it gives him incentive. I wouldn't take and pay without getting something back from him. What is fourth-round salary and bonus — it's not a lot compared to the top. That's where I'd feel comfortable with him."

DLE TEVIN MIMS, #99

SOUTH FLORIDA ▶ GRADE: 4.90

Ht: 6-4 | Wt: 260 | Sp: 4.94 | Arm: 33 1/2 | Hand: 9 3/8

History: The Texas prep had shoulder surgery before his senior season to repair a torn labrum. Began his college career at Texas in 2009 and saw action in five games as a reserve defensive lineman, recording three tackles, one-half tackle for loss and zero sacks. Requested to redshirt in '10 after he re-aggravated his shoulder during fall drills. Transferred to Navarro (TX) Junior College for the '11 season, tallying 19-7-4 with three passes batted in nine games. Returned to the Division I level in '12, landing at South Florida and tallying 35-3 1/2-2 with one forced fumble in 11 starts at right defensive end. Did not play in the season finale due to an undisclosed injury. Was USF's defensive MVP in '13 after posting 40-6-1 1/2 in 10 games (eight starts). Missed two games with an ankle injury. Strained his left hamstring at the Combine and did not perform shuttles.

Strengths: Flashes upfield quickness. Uses his arms to create room to work. Good closing speed. Gives effort in pursuit, chases plays from behind and tries to deliver a blow when he arrives. Is tough and will play hurt.

Weaknesses: Average eyes and instincts — see-and-go reactor. Inconsistent, often delayed get-off. Needs to play with better leverage — exposes his frame off the snap and gets overpowered against the run. Does not use his hands violently. Vanilla pass rusher. Marginal sack production. Motivation and work ethic should be looked into. Recorded a 27 1/2-inch vertical jump.

Future: A junior-college product, Mims was an undersized college rush end, though he recorded just 3.5 sacks in 21 games at USF and is actually at his best during the latter portion of the play when he kicks into pursuit mode. Best chance will come as developmental, situational 4-3 right end or stand-up rush linebacker, though he must turn up the heat more consistently to stick.

Draft projection: Priority free agent.

DLE-3T ZACH MOORE, #90

CONCORDIA (MN) ▶ GRADE: 5.24

Ht: 6-5 1/2 | Wt: 269 | Sp: 4.84 | Arm: 33 3/4 | Hand: 9 5/8

History: Has a daughter. Prepped in the Chicago Public League, but was not a Division I qualifier, and landed at Division II Concordia-St. Paul in Minnesota. As a true freshman in 2009, played in eight games (one start) and recorded 16 tackles, three tackles for loss and two sacks with one forced fumble. Moved into the starting lineup in '10 and had 42-12-10 with one forced fumble in nine games. Was academically ineligible in '11. Returned to start 11 games in '12, tallying 39-21-14 with one pass batted, one interception and two forced fumbles. In '13, registered 33-9 1/2-7 with three passes batted and two forced fumbles in 11 starts. Was a finalist for the Cliff Harris Division II Player of the Year Award. Two-time captain was the first Concordia player to be invited to the NFL Combine.

Strengths: Looks the part with NFL stature, length and musculature. Is athletic and flexible with nice explosion for his size — recorded a 10-foot, 3-inch broad jump and 33 1/2-inch vertical jump at the Combine. Quick off the snap. Flashes the ability to gain extension and play off blocks. Gives effort in pursuit and ranges to make tackles. Good closing speed. Snares ball carriers. Averaged a sack per game in college. Has experience in a 4-3 and 3-4. Dedicated, hardworking and coachable. Mentally tough guy who has beaten the odds and persevered to get to this point. Has moldable tools and upside.

Weaknesses: Needs to get functionally stronger. Still learning to convert speed to power and does not physically dominate marginal competition. Green eyes and instincts to locate and diagnose. Plays too tall and needs to learn how to grow roots defending the run. Washed by double teams. Hand use and pass-rush moves need to be developed. Will be a 24-year-old rookie.

Future: Raw, physically gifted, Division II standout with untapped potential given his combination of size, length and movement skills. Will have defensive line coaches drooling in workouts, and has the dimensions and athleticism to warrant consideration as a draftable, developmental investment with positional versatility to play defensive end or three-technique in an even front or five-technique in an odd front. Could be tried as a linebacker.

Draft projection: Fourth- to fifth-round pick.

Scout's take: "He has a long way to go. I don't think he really knows how good he can be. There's no doubt he has tools to work."

NT LOUIS NIX III, #9 (JUNIOR)

NOTRE DAME   ▶ GRADE: 5.90

Ht: 6-2 3/8 | Wt: 331 | Sp: 5.42 | Arm: 33 | Hand: 9 7/8

History: Highly recruited out of Florida, where he also played basketball. Redshirted in 2010. Moved into the starting nose tackle role in '11, recording 45 tackles, 4 1/2 tackles for loss and one-half sack with one pass batted in 13 games (11 starts). Had a breakout campaign in '12, playing in 13 games (11 starts) and registering 50-7 1/2-2 with five passes batted and one forced fumble. Led all Irish defensive linemen in tackles. In '13, he started the first seven games – but then played just once over the final six weeks due to a left knee injury. Tallied 27-2-0 with two passes batted. Underwent surgery in late November to repair a torn meniscus (Dr. James Andrews). Did not benchpress at the Combine (pectoral).

Strengths: Outstanding size. Commands a double team and has two-gap ability. Good quickness off the snap. Has press strength and power to push blockers into the backfield. Shows disruptive ability when his battery is charged. Flashes an arm-over. Redirects well for a big man. Nice pursuit effort. Strong wrap tackler. Scheme versatile.

Weaknesses: Can play with better leverage against double teams. Does not dominate single blocking. Needs to improve hand use — punch impact, counter moves and shed timing. Limited pass-rush value (minimal sack production). Can do a better job protecting his legs — is not as strong on his pegs as you'd expect and spends too much time on the ground. Conditioning and stamina will have to be monitored — takes plays off and weight has fluctuated.

Future: Despite standing to benefit from a more dominant senior season in South Bend, Nix, who already graduated, opted to forgo his final year of eligibility in order to provide for 13 siblings. He does not enter the NFL with momentum, having coped with knee tendinitis before season-ending surgery to repair a torn left meniscus, and too often his gregarious personality and media hype overshadowed his performance. However, if the massive interior defender taps into his power more consistently, Nix has ample mass, strength and athleticism to anchor a "30" front as a space-eating, block-occupying run stuffer.

Draft projection: Top-40 pick.

Scout's take: "He's very smart. He challenges authority a little bit. He's not going to respond to hard coaching well if he thinks his coach is phony. ...He did not have the year everyone was expecting. He won't be for everyone."

5T JEOFFREY PAGAN, #8 (JUNIOR)

ALABAMA   ▶ GRADE: 5.21

Ht: 6-3 1/2 | Wt: 310 | Sp: 5.00e | Arm: 33 | Hand: 9 5/8

History: The North Carolina prep overcame a severe knee injury, missing a portion of his senior season with two torn ligaments in his right knee which required surgery. Played in six games as a true freshman for Alabama in 2011 and recorded four tackles. Was a valuable reserve defensive lineman in '12, appearing in all 14 games for the national champions. Had 23 tackles, four tackles for losses and 1 1/2 sacks with one forced fumble. Moved into the starting lineup in '13 and tallied 34-3 1/2-2 in 12 starts at defensive end. Missed a mid-season contest against Georgia State because of a sprained shoulder.

Strengths: Good size. Can occupy blocks and squeeze running lanes. Strong hands to press and tug free. Can push the pocket. Heavy tackler. Played multiple techniques in a pro-style, hybrid defensive scheme.

Weaknesses: Thick, tight hips — cannot work the edges. Gets blown off the ball by double teams. Needs to play with better extension, refine his hand use, develop counters and quicken his shed timing. Heavy-legged when required to redirect. Limited pass-rush value. Only a one-year starter. Average production — did not make splash plays.

Future: Thickly built, relatively nondescript contributor who decided to forgo his senior season despite never establishing himself as a force. Has size and strength to warrant developmental consideration as a five-technique, but lacks exceptional traits and will have to commit to handling the dirty work to have longevity.

Draft projection: Fourth- to fifth-round pick.

Scout's take: "The trainer tells you Pagan didn't play well early in the year, but he played better at the end with the shoulder harness. I'm thinking, from what I just got done watching, the dude played worse at the end of the year. I don't know why he came out early. He needs shoulder surgery, he's not getting it done, he's not going to work out at the pro day tomorrow and he's not working out in April. If he doesn't get his shoulder done, he could fall all the way out of the draft."

3T TENNY PALEPOI, #91

UTAH ▶ GRADE: 5.27

Ht: 6-1 1/2 | Wt: 298 | Sp: 5.11 | Arm: 30 1/2 | Hand: 9 7/8

History: His last name is pronounced "pah-lay-poy." Married with two kids. Is one of 14 children. One of his brothers, Anton, was a defensive lineman with the Seahawks, Broncos and Cardinals from 2002-2005. His father, Tony, played for the Samoan Rugby team. The Utah prep began his college career at Snow (UT) College in 2009 and recorded 58 tackles, five tackles for loss and five sacks in 11 games. Was redshirted in '10 after tearing the MCL in his left knee. Returned to the gridiron in '11 and had 49-10-2 in 10 games. Transferred to Utah in '12 and played in 12 games (three starts) at defensive tackle, tallying 21-3-2. Had a solid campaign as a senior in '13, totaling 53-9 1/2-4 1/2 with one forced fumble in 12 starts. Team captain.

Strengths: Good initial quickness, athletic ability and hip snap to shoot gaps and disrupt the backfield. Displays fine body control and agility. Good closing speed. Square tackler with some explosive knock-back body power. Pumped 225 pounds 32 times at the Combine. Can throw his hips in the hole and create penetration. Solid production. Has NFL pedigree — brother, Anton, played four seasons in the league. Carries a passion for the game. Well-grounded and mature. Contributes on special teams (personal punt protector).

Weaknesses: Not physically impressive — is short with short arms and a relatively thin lower body. Limited extension — struggles to disengage from blocks and can be engulfed by the double team. Lacks lead in his pants and can be moved. Average anchor strength — too easily controlled and sealed off in the run game. Instincts are developing.

Future: A quick, athletic penetrator best working in a single-gap, heavy-movement, stunting front. Flashes the ability to disrupt and could be effective working in a rotational role.

Draft projection: Fourth- to fifth-round pick.

Scout's take: "He has some quickness that intrigues you. His issue is going to be his arm length. How many guys are playing at a high level with short arms. Most get injured or don't do much at our level."

NT MIKE PENNEL, #99

COLORADO STATE-PUEBLO ▶ GRADE: 5.00

Ht: 6-4 1/4 | Wt: 332 | Sp: 5.23 | Arm: 33 3/8 | Hand: 9 7/8

History: The Colorado prep began his collegiate career at Scottsdale (AZ) Community College in 2010, where he had 34 tackles, 10 tackles for loss and one sack with one pass batted and two forced fumbles in nine games. Earned junior college all-America honors in '11 after recording 37-13-2 with one pass batted and one forced fumble in nine games. Went to Arizona State in '12, but saw action in only five early season games, tallying 4-0-0. Was suspended twice in less than a month by head coach Todd Graham — the second time indefinitely for a Twitter rant — in his lone season at ASU. Transferred to Division II Colorado-State Pueblo in '13 and had 36-6-3 with four passes batted and three forced fumbles in 12 games.

Strengths: Rare size and body mass. Looks the part with a well-distributed frame and carries his weight well for a 350-pounder. Is seldom moved off a spot. Can lock out and walk back blockers with sheer brute strength. Flashes some violence in his hands. Strong short-yardage/goal-line plugger.

Weaknesses: Gets hung up on blocks too easily and can't split the double team. Plays flat-footed. Limited explosion, quickness and agility to shoot gaps or make plays behind the line of scrimmage. Plays with limited knee bend and tends to stand tall. Could stand to do a better job protecting his legs. Did not dominate vs. lesser competition. Has been disciplined for not following rules and must prove committed.

Future: A massive run-stuffing space-occupier with the bulk to plug the middle or function outside in a traditional 3-4 front. His calling card will be defending the run on early downs.

Draft projection: Priority free agent.

3T KELCY QUARLES, #99 (JUNIOR)

SOUTH CAROLINA ▶ GRADE: 5.22

Ht: 6-3 3/4 | Wt: 297 | Sp: 5.03 | Arm: 33 1/4 | Hand: 9 3/8

History: His father, Buddy, was an offensive lineman for South Carolina from 1984-1987. Kelcy was a Parade All-American as a South Carolina prep. Attended Fork Union (Va.) Military Academy prep school before enrolling at South Carolina. Played in 12 games as a true freshman in 2011, starting the last six games at defensive tackle, and had 28 tackles, two tackles for loss and zero sacks. Started all 11 games in which he appeared in '12 and recorded 38-8-3 1/2. Was suspended by coach Steve Spurrier for punching an LSU player. Also missed a game with a sprained shoulder. Saw action in 12 games (11 starts) in '13, tallying 39-13 1/2-9 1/2 with one pass batted. Missed one game with a concussion.

Strengths: Good size and initial quickness. Long arms and strong upper body — can press and extend to create operating space. Flashes the ability to walk guards back. Is fairly light on his feet and shows nice closing burst to the quarterback. Good pursuit effort when his battery is charged. Heavy tackler. Excellent sack production, particularly for an interior defender — 9 1/2 sacks ranked second nationally among defensive tackles.

Weaknesses: Narrow-based. Gets upright off the snap. Lets his pads rise and gets controlled or washed. Struggles to fight through blocks. Chewed up by double teams. Does not generate powerful hand violence. Could stand to get in better shape and improve his stamina. Posted a meager 23 1/2-inch vertical jump at the Combine. Production was inflated — had plays flushed to him, benefiting from attention paid to Jadeveon Clowney. Character needs to be evaluated very closely.

Future: Thickly built, long-armed, defensive tackle who was not as consistently dominant as his numbers or accolades suggest. Has enough quickness, strength and enough pass-rush ability to develop into a rotational three-technique in the pros, but could have benefited from another year of SEC competition.

Draft projection: Fourth- to fifth-round pick.

Scout's take: "He had a bunch of production, but tell me where it comes from. He is an absolute stiff. He does not have a sterling reputation. I have a free-agent grade on him for someone else. I hope someone bites earlier."

5T-DLE KALEB RAMSEY, #96

BOSTON COLLEGE   ▶ GRADE: 5.00

Ht: 6-3 | Wt: 293 | Sp: 5.05e | Arm: 32 7/8 | Hand: 9 3/4

History: Also played tight end and was an all-state basketball player as a Pennsylvania prep. Saw action in seven games as a freshman in 2008 and posted six tackles, zero tackles for loss and one sack. Logged 11-0-2 in seven contests (two starts at right tackle and one at left) in '09. Missed five games because of leg injuries. Appeared in 11 games, starting 10 at left defensive tackle, in '10 and recorded 39-7 1/2-2 1/2 with one pass batted down. Was suspended for unspecified reasons against Notre Dame and missed the Virginia game with a hip injury. Did not participate in '11 spring practice while recovering from left shoulder surgery. In the fall, started the season opener against Northwestern but injured his left foot and sat out the season

with plantar fasciitis (was granted a medical hardship, preserving eligibility). Started the first two games in '12, tallying 4-1/2-0, before a left calf tear sidelined him for the season. Obtained a sixth year of eligibility in '13 — shifted to defensive end and started 8-of-10 games played, collecting 28-4-2. Did not start against Florida State or Miami, and missed three games in November while nursing a hamstring injury. Did not perform at the Combine because of a right calf injury (medical exclusion).

Strengths: Good read-and-react skills. Shows stack strength to press and extend. Good initial quickness — bursts off the snap and has disruptive ability. Plays on his feet, is athletic and bends well for his size. Can redirect and chase. Gives effort in pursuit. Strong tackler. Has played inside and outside. Benchpressed 225 pounds 36 times at the Combine, tops among defensive linemen.

Weaknesses: Durability is a red flag — is fragile and has missed a multitude of games the last five seasons because of head, hip, shoulder, foot, knee and calf injuries. Inconsistent pad level. Needs to improve hand violence and dexterity to disengage more quickly. Linear rusher. Could stand to play with more intensity snap to snap. Ordinary production. Will be 25-year-old rookie.

Future: A sixth-year senior, Ramsey has the physical tools to serve in a rotational role as an aggressive five-technique or 4-3 left end, though his injury history and long-term durability concerns limit his value and could scare teams off.

Draft projection: Priority free agent.

3T-5T CARAUN REID, #11

PRINCETON   ▶ GRADE: 5.35

Ht: 6-2 1/8 | Wt: 302 | Sp: 4.91 | Arm: 33 | Hand: 10 1/2

History: The New York prep enrolled at the Ivy League school in 2009 and played in 10 games as a true freshman, tallying 32 tackles, 4 1/2 tackles for loss and one-half sack with four passes batted. Saw action at both nose tackle and defensive end. Tore his left pectoral muscle in the '10 season opener at Lehigh and missed the rest of the campaign. Underwent surgery after the season. Returned in '11 and recorded 68-16-7 with three passed batted and one forced fumble and three blocked kicks in 10 games (nine starts). Led all Ivy League linemen in tackles. Started nine games in '12 and had 40-9 1/2-5 with one pass batted, one forced fumble and three blocked kicks. Missed the Penn game with a concussion. Was a finalist for the Ivy League Defensive Player of the Year award in '13 after registering 26-11-6 1/2 with one pass batted in 10 starts, helping lead Princeton to a conference title. Team captain was just the second Princeton player ever to be invited to the Senior Bowl.

Strengths: Very quick off the ball. Disruptive shooting gaps and working half a blocker. Active and energetic — feet are always running. Plays hard and competes. Very good sack production from the interior (20.5 career sacks). Good intelligence. Is very young (entered college as 17-year-old freshman) and still growing into his body — has physical upside. Good length and hand-eye coordination — 7 career blocked kicks.

Weaknesses: Tends to stand straight up, negating his quickness and power out of the gate. Is not stout and can be waylaid by the double team. Marginal upper-body strength (diminished from 2011 pectoral surgery). Shows little feel for blocking pressure and can be late to locate the ball. Can do a better job protecting his legs. Pushed around too easily. Durability issues have crept up throughout his career.

Future: A quick, agile, tilted nose who is effective slanting and stunting and working his way into the backfield. Has kicked outside in passing situations and has the tools to pique the interest of aggressive, one-gapping, 3-4 fronts such as the Jets, Steelers or Ravens as a five-technique. Developmental talent with raw traits to mold.

Draft projection: Fourth-round pick.

Scout's take: "I thought he was outmatched in (Senior Bowl) practice, and he ended up with two sacks in the game. That tells me it's a great day for defensive linemen. It's tougher for an offensive linemen coordinating protection in those games. You have guys who never played inside before being tried at guard or being switched from the left side to the right side. That's not easy, especially in this kind of setting."

DRE-ROLB CHRIS SMITH, #42

ARKANSAS ▶ GRADE: 5.31
Ht: 6-1 | Wt: 266 | Sp: 4.71 | Arm: 34 1/8 | Hand: 9 1/2

History: Was a top defensive recruit as a North Carolina prep, helping his school to back-to-back state titles and a 30-game winning streak. Enrolled at Arkansas in 2010 and played in six games as a true freshman, recording three tackles and one pass breakup. Appeared in all 13 games (three starts) in '11 and had 31 tackles, six tackles for losses and

3 1/2 sacks with one pass batted. Moved into the starting lineup at left defensive end in '12 and recorded 52-13-9 1/2 with four passes batted and one forced fumble. Was arrested in October after missing a court date for a speeding ticket (64 mph in a 45 zone); when he failed to appear, a warrant was issued (he was released on $415 bond). Made 12 starts in '13 and tallied 36-11 1/2-8 1/2 with one pass batted. Team captain.

Strengths: Long arms. Very good take-off, burst and closing speed — wins with quickness and effort. Plays hard with good urgency and runs to the ball. Good finishing speed and hustle in backside pursuit. Gradually improving strength. Likeable personality with natural leadership traits. Has a 37-inch vertical jump.

Weaknesses: Lacks functional playing strength and can be controlled easily when big-bodied blockers get their hands on him (see Alabama). Struggles to split the double team. Not a nuanced pass rusher — reliant on upfield speed too much. Can do a better job diagnosing the run more quickly and shedding blocks.

Future: A weakside pass rusher who could most ideally project to the rush linebacker position in the pros for a 3-4 front, Smith graded more highly as a junior than he did as a senior, yet possesses the tools to earn a starting job in the pros in multiple schemes. Versatility is a plus.

Draft projection: Third- to fourth-round pick.

Scout's take: "He stood out to me more as a junior than he did as a senior. He's best when he has a clear path. I question how well he plays the run. He might be better for the 3-4 teams as a linebacker."

DRE-ROLB-PRS MARCUS SMITH, #91

LOUSVILLE ▶ GRADE: 5.39
Ht: 6-3 | Wt: 251 | Sp: 4.68 | Arm: 34 | Hand: 10

History: Played quarterback as a Georgia prep. Converted to linebacker as a true freshman in 2010 — saw action in nine games (one start) and recorded three tackles, one tackle for loss and zero sacks. Started at outside linebacker in the season opener against Kentucky before spending the rest of the year as a reserve/special teams player. Moved to defensive end in '11, seeing action in 10 games (five starts) and totaling 12-6 1/2-5 1/2 with one pass batted and two forced fumbles. Missed three games with an ankle injury. Took over as the starting left defensive end in '12 and posted 29-7-4 with two passes batted, one interception and two forced fumbles in 13 starts. Caught two-point conversion passes against Kentucky and Missouri State. Was the American Athletic Conference's Defensive Player of the Year in '13, starting 13 games and recording 42-18 1/2-14 1/2 with three passes batted, four forced fumbles and a blocked kick.

Strengths: Nice bend, balance and body control. Good pass-rush ability and potential. Quick first step. Coordinated hands and feet. Athletic and agile — can stunt and loop. Flashes a spin move. Shows burst to close and get home. Moves well laterally. Gives effort in pursuit and ranges all over the field. Operated from 2- and 3-point stance. Solid character. Is coachable and has improved steadily.

Weaknesses: Lacks ideal length — plays short-armed and can be locked up by larger blockers. Short initial steps. Still crafting a wider array of counters and pass-rush moves. Still learning to convert speed to power. Work in progress as a run defender. Does not set a hard edge and can do a better job using his hands to disengage quicker. Needs to become a more violent hands fighter. Limited experience playing in reverse.

Future: A high school quarterback turned pass rusher who broke out with 14.5 sacks as a senior, Smith projects as a pass-rush specialist or 3-4 right outside linebacker in the pros. Should contribute initially on passing downs and has eventual starter potential as his game becomes more well-rounded.

Draft projection: Third- to fourth-round pick.

Scout's take: "If you're talking about pure pin-your-ears-back-and-go, he can get off the rock. I like his first two steps."

NT-5T SHAMAR STEPHEN, #59

CONNECTICUT   ▶ GRADE: 5.42

Ht: 6-5 | Wt: 309 | Sp: 5.26 | Arm: 33 1/8 | Hand: 10

History: His last name is pronounced "STEF-an." The defensive lineman also lettered in basketball as a New York prep. Redshirted in 2009. Made his college debut in '10 and was a regular member of the defensive front all year, recording 27 tackles, four tackles for loss and two sacks in 12 games (eight starts). Appeared in all 11 games in '11 and was 17-1-0 with one pass batted. In '12, he sprained his right MCL during preseason drills and missed two games. After returning from the injury, he played in 10 games (nine starts) and totaled 26-2-0 with four passes

batted. Underwent surgery after the season to clean up a right shoulder labrum issue. In '13, he started all 12 games at defensive tackle and tallied 60-10-3 with one pass batted and one blocked kick. Team captain.

Strengths: Terrific size. Very athletic for a big man. Generally plays on his feet. Occupies blocks. Flashes the ability to lock out and reestablish the line of scrimmage. Has raw tools to work with. Scheme versatile. Solid personal and football character.

Weaknesses: Lethargic get-off. Average eyes, instincts and recognition (doesn't sense screen). Needs to go to school on blocking schemes and learn to fight pressure. Could stand to play with more violence in his hands — feels his way through plays instead of imposing force. Linear, vanilla rusher (just five career sacks). Moved by double teams. Compete level leaves something to be desired. Disappears for stretches.

Future: Big, athletic, raw interior defender with underachiever traits who had a fairly nondescript career at UConn, but has crude physical tools for a defensive line coach to mold. Developmental prospect who potentially fits in a 4-3 or as a 3-4 five-technique.

Draft projection: Third- to fourth-round pick.

Scout's take: "I like him. I think he can play three-technique for us. I think he will wind up being a third-round guy. He is just raw. He can move. He's very athletic. Defensive line coaches will fall in love with him. He's huge and athletic. He's just raw."

5T-DLE ED STINSON, #47

ALABAMA   ▶ GRADE: 5.65

Ht: 6-3 1/4 | Wt: 287 | Sp: 4.90e | Arm: 33 3/4 | Hand: 9 3/8

History: Has a daughter. Redshirted in 2009. Saw his first college action in '10, recording 14 tackles, zero for loss and zero sacks in nine games (two starts). Although he didn't make any starts in '11, he was a key part of the defensive line rotation for the national champions. Played in all 13 games and had 19-5-1 with one pass batted and one forced fumble. Started all 14 games in '12, tallying 30-8 1/2-3 to help the Crimson Tide repeat as national champs. In 13 starts in '13, he had 42-2-1 1/2 with one pass blocked. Did not participate at the Senior Bowl or Combine (groin).

Strengths: Very good arm and body length. Outstanding strength at the point of attack. Big stout, power base and superb press strength to set the edge and walk blockers back to the quarterback. Very stout vs. the run. Possesses pop and power in his hands and jolts blockers on contact. Plays square to the line and controls blockers with ease. Physical, drive-through tackler. Extremely tough, hardworking and ultra-competitive. Very well-conditioned with outstanding endurance.

Weaknesses: Average foot speed. Has some stiffness in his body. Plays a bit flat-footed. Not sudden to get off blocks. Limited burst and explosion to reach the outside — can secure speed backs. Will require some patience absorbing a game plan.

Future: Long-framed, long-armed, prototype five-technique capable of kicking inside and manning the nose. Very impressive strength and power. Can play anywhere along a "30" front. An underrated cog in a defense, Stinson could play a long time in the league and may never receive his due outside the building.

Draft projection: Second- to third-round pick.

Scout's take: "He's sort of a stiffer guy. He has really good strength and can play the point and lock it down. He does a really good job there, but he's not a true stack-and-shed guy to make plays or sudden to get off blocks and attack the ball. He's just really good and sitting and holding down his spot. He is a great fit for a 3-4 defense. He's hard to knock off a spot."

DT WILL SUTTON, #90

ARIZONA STATE ▶ GRADE: 5.34
Ht: 6-0 1/2 | Wt: 303 | Sp: 5.36 | Arm: 31 1/4 | Hand: 10

History: His father, Mickey, was a defensive back/punt returner with the Rams, Packers and Bills from 1986-1990. Will prepped in California. Saw action in 12 games (two starts) as a true freshman in 2009, recording 17 tackles, three tackles for loss and one sack with one forced fumble. Was academically ineligible in '10. In his return to the gridiron in '11, he appeared in all 13 games (12 starts) and had 33-5 1/2-2 1/2 with one pass batted. In '12, tallied 64-23 1/2-13 with five passes batted and three forced fumbles in 12 games (11 starts). Missed one game with a toe injury. Started all 14 games in '13 and had 48-13 1/2-4 with three passes batted and one interception. Back-to-back Pac-12 Defensive Player of the Year. Team captain.

Strengths: Very good athlete. Good body control and balance. Feels blocking pressure and finds the ball quickly. Effective spin move. Shoots gaps and makes plays behind the line. Flattens down the line and can range to the sideline. Strong tackler and athletic enough to string down backs in space. Outstanding career sack production (20.5) from the interior.

Weaknesses: Short. Questionable competitiveness and desire — motor runs hot and cold. Will disappear for stretches. Has some underachiever traits and work ethic has a lot of area for improvement. Average strength at the point of attack. Can be turned and rooted out of the hole by the double team. Can improve hand use and develop more of a pass-rush arsenal. Poor timed speed.

Future: Bulked up and added a lot of bad weight as a senior, negating his initial burst and diminishing his production, yet still showed enough quickness off the ball. Played at a more natural weight and was noticeably a step quicker in 2012. Fits best as an under tackle in an even front and would be best playing close to 290 pounds. Would benefit tremendously from a disciplined nutrition regimen.

Draft projection: Fourth- to fifth-round pick.

Scout's take: "I saw Will Sutton live last year at 285 (pounds). I was thinking he is a (warrior). When he stayed in school, I did not see him again in person until the Senior Bowl. I said to myself, 'That is not the same guy.' Holy (cow). He looked like he was trying to eat his way out of the league. I'm not sure what you do with him now. He could drop like a rock. ... If someone can get him playing like he was as a junior again, you could have something special. He put on too much bad weight too fast, and he's still trying to get back to what he was."

NT ROBERT THOMAS, #98

ARKANSAS ▶ GRADE: 4.75
Ht: 6-1 1/4 | Wt: 327 | Sp: 5.25e | Arm: 33 7/8 | Hand: 10

History: The Oklahoma prep began his college career at Coffeyville (KS) Community College in 2010. Played in 11 games and recorded 51 tackles, 17 tackles for loss and five sacks with two passes batted and one forced fumble. Transferred to Arkansas in '11 and appeared in 12 games (five starts) that fall, tallying 23-2 1/2-1. Missed one game with a leg injury. In '12, he saw action in all 12 games (two starts) and had 18-5-2 1/2. Started the first seven games of '13, managing 31-6-3 1/2 suffering a season-ending broken left leg against South Carolina. Had surgery in October, but was not recovered by the Combine. Team captain.

Strengths: Has good body mass. Can keep blockers occupied, fight the double team and control gaps. Plays hard and competes. Is a respected team leader.

Weaknesses: Round-bodied. Struggles to play off or split the double team. Limited short-area range and closing burst. Gets stuck in place and struggles to disengage blocks. Lacks power to walk back blockers or generate a push.

Future: A heavy-bodied, short-range, effort player, Thomas did not finish the season after breaking a bone in his leg. Can fend for a role as a rotational wave backup in the pros. Practice-squad candidate.

Draft projection: Free agent.

3T-5T KHYRI THORNTON, #98

SOUTHERN MISSISSIPPI   ▶ GRADE: 5.15
Ht: 6-2 5/8 | Wt: 304 | Sp: 5.03 | Arm: 32 1/2 | Hand: 9 1/2

History: Played defensive tackle and fullback as a Florida prep. Attended Hargrave Military Academy in Virginia for one year. Originally committed to South Florida, but was denied entry to the school despite meeting NCAA qualifying requirements. Enrolled instead at Southern Mississippi, redshirting in 2009. Played all 13 games in '10 and recorded 17 tackles, five tackles for loss and 2 1/2 sacks. In '11, he appeared in 14 games, starting seven at defensive tackle, and tallied 24-9-1 1/2 with one pass batted and one forced fumble. Was Southern Miss' primary defensive tackle in '12, playing in 12 games (11 starts) and totaling 36-9 1/2-1 with one pass batted, one interception and one forced fumble. Started 11 games in '13 and had 39-6 1/2-1/2. In the Golden Eagles' home finale November 23 against Middle Tennessee, he suffered a deep bone bruise to his right leg that caused some internal bleeding and was not able to play the following week. Team captain.

Strengths: Flashes shock in his hands. Solid anchor strength. Versatile and lines up all along the front. Flashes speed and short-area burst to flatten down the line and close to the ball. Three-year starter.

Weaknesses: Has short arms and small hands. Could do a better job working off blocks, creating separation and protecting his legs. Tends to wear down and tire late in games and effort wanes. Needs to develop more pass-rush moves — stays blocked too long. Relies too much on his upper-body strength. Can be late to locate the ball and needs to do a better job of feeling blocking pressure and anticipating. Misses a lot of tackles. Minimal sack production.

Future: Has the size, brute strength and

enough agility to warrant interest as a developmental, rotational five-technique in an aggressive, zone-blitzing scheme such as the Jets, Ravens or Steelers. Versatility is a plus.

Draft projection: Late draftable pick.

Scout's take: "He'll pick his spots at times. They play him all over. I wish he were a little bit longer. He's interesting though."

5T-3T STEPHON TUITT, #7 (JUNIOR)

NOTRE DAME   ▶ GRADE: 6.35
Ht: 6-5 1/2 | Wt: 304 | Sp: 5.05e | Arm: 34 3/4 | Hand: 10

History: His name is pronounced "stuh-FON TOO-it." Highly recruited out of Georgia. As a true freshman in 2011, played nine games (three starts) and collected 30 tackles, three tackles for loss and two sacks with one pass batted. All Non-starts were coach's decisions. Moved into a starting defensive end role in '12, tallying 47-13-12 with one pass batted, three forced fumbles and one blocked kick in 13 starts. Returned a fumble 77 yards for a touchdown against Navy. Required off-season surgery to repair a hernia. Underwent hernia surgery in the offseason. In '13, he started all 13 games and had 49-9-7 1/2 with two passes batted, one interception and one forced fumble. Picked off an errant pass in the end zone for a touchdown against Michigan. Pulled out of NFL Combine drills after a medical scan revealed a Jones fracture in his left foot, necessitating surgery.

Strengths: Looks the part — has prototypical dimensions for a five-technique. Long-armed to play off blocks. Holds his ground at the point of attack. Can stack and shed. Has excellent movement skill for a man his size. Plays on his feet. Coordinated and in control of his body. Knee bender able to flatten or redirect efficiently. Strong wrap tackler. Scheme and position versatile — played end and tackle in even and odd fronts. Notched 20.5 sacks in 28 career starts. Disrupts passing lanes. Did 31 benchpress reps at the Combine.

Weaknesses: Monotone edge rusher — not a quick-twitch athlete (average get-off quickness). Can play with more consistent leverage. Hip and shoulder stiffness shows when he attempts to bend the corner. Can do a better job shooting his hands with authority to jolt blockers. Needs to become a better hands fighter and develop pass-rush moves. Can play with more violence. Average intensity and relentlessness.

Future: Hulking, long-armed, physically gifted defensive lineman with desirable size, strength, athleticism and versatility to appeal as a five-technique or as a defensive tackle or base end in a 4-3. Gained approximately 20 pounds as a junior and was not in peak condition, but has disruptive upside.

Draft projection: First-round pick.

Scout's take: "He's big, long and athletic. He's exactly how you draw them up. The injuries slowed him down this year. You throw on last year's tape and he was a beast. He just needs to get healthy. I'd love to have him."

DLE GEORGE UKO, #90 (JUNIOR)
USC   ▶ GRADE: 5.05
Ht: 6-2 5/8 | Wt: 284 | Sp: 4.99 | Arm: 33 1/4 | Hand: 10 1/8

History: Parade All-American as a California prep. Redshirted in 2010. Was part of the defensive line rotation in '11, seeing action in 12 games (two starts) and recording 18 tackles, 1 1/2 tackles for loss and 1 1/2 sacks with one pass batted and two forced fumbles. Was a full-time starter in '12, posting 31-9-5 with one pass batted and one forced fumble. Started three at defensive tackle and one at left defensive end before moving to the nose tackle spot for the final nine games. Recovered a fumble in the end zone for a touchdown at UCLA. Made all 14 starts at right defensive end in '13 and tallied 36-7-5 with one forced fumble. Did not perform the shuttles at the Combine because of a back injury.

Strengths: Plays with leverage and generally stays on his feet. Flashes the ability to shoot his hands inside, extend and stack. Nice versatility, having played end and tackle.

Weaknesses: Average foot athlete with lower-body stiffness. Exposes his frame and struggles to escape. Needs to develop counters and pass-rush moves — hands are more active than forceful. Does not dominate single blocks. Has tweener traits — lacks ideal bulk and anchor for DT and ideal speed and flexibility for DE. Disappears for stretches. Managed just 18 benchpress reps at the Combine.

Future: Good-sized defensive lineman who shows in flashes, but not enough to justify leaving school early, as he looked very average against strong offensive lines. Could warrant late-round consideration as a developmental base end.

Draft projection: Late draftable pick.

5T-3T BRENT URBAN, #99
VIRGINIA   ▶ GRADE: 5.32
Ht: 6-6 5/8 | Wt: 295 | Sp: 4.95e | Arm: 295 | Hand: 9 3/4

History: Grew up in suburban Toronto. Also played basketball and hockey his first two years in high school, but committed to football as an upperclassman. Redshirted in 2009. Tore his left ACL in the spring of '10, and saw very limited action in three games in the fall. Played all 13 games in '11 and was credited with 15 tackles, 2 1/2 for loss and zero sacks — battled a wrist injury and had it surgically repaired after the season. Started all 12 games at defensive end in '12, recording 20-2 1/2-2 with two passes batted and one forced fumble. Returned a fumble 16 yards for a touchdown at Virginia Tech. Dealt with a high ankle sprain in '13, starting eight games (and missing four) and totaling 40-11 1/2-1 with an NCAA-leading nine passes batted. Was forced to withdraw from the Senior Bowl due to recurring issues with the ankle, then was a medical exclusion at the Combine (knee). Was drafted by the Hamilton Tiger-Cats in the second round (15th overall selection) of the 2013 CFL Draft.

Strengths: Looks the part — has stature on the defensive line thanks to a long, well-proportioned physique with relatively little body fat. Has ideal dimensions for an odd front and has a large wingspan that enables him to disrupt passing lanes (nine PBUs in eight games as a senior). Engages quickly off the snap, jolts blockers and gains extension. Can stack and shed or press single blocking and generate push. Flashes disruptive ability. Can slide inside as a nickel rusher to cave the pocket.

Weaknesses: Limited lower-body strength to anchor vs. double teams. Shows some stiffness through his shoulders and torso. Still developing recognition and instincts. Still learning blocking schemes and how to fight pressure. Needs to improve hand use (quickness and violence). Has to concentrate on keeping his pad level low — gets uprooted and washed when he plays too tall. Linear, vanilla pass rusher (recorded just three career sacks). Relatively inexperienced. Grew up in a Canadian hockey town and has a mellow disposition that might not sit well with some people.

Future: Tall, angular, late-blooming five-technique prospect with the body type sought by teams employing odd fronts. Should only get bigger, stronger and more polished. If so, has potential to grow into an impact lineman. Broken foot bone suffered in freak accident prior to Senior Bowl could hinder his draft status.

Draft projection: Third- to fourth-round pick.

Scout's take: "I heard some second-round grades on the kid passing through in the fall. He was under the radar. The injury won't help him, but he could turn out to be a steal if he makes it to the fourth. I don't see him falling any lower. We'd pluck his card if he were there."

DRE-OLB-TE LARRY WEBSTER, #99

BLOOMSBURG   ▶ GRADE: 5.35
Ht: 6-5 3/4 | Wt: 252 | Sp: 4.58 | Arm: 33 1/2 | Hand: 10 1/8

History: His father, Larry, was an NFL defensive lineman from 1992-2002 with the Dolphins, Browns, Ravens and Jets. The Maryland native turned to football before the 2012 season after playing four years of basketball (2008-2012) for Bloomsburg , a Division II school in Pennsylvania. Finished his hoops career averaging 11.1 points and 7.2 rebounds per game and set a school record with 175 career blocked shots. Moved to the gridiron in the fall of '12 and had 39 tackles, 15 tackles for loss and a school-record 13 1/2 sacks with two passes batted and one forced fumble in 12 games. Also caught two passes for eight yards and two touchdowns. Had nearly identical defensive statistics in '13, tallying 49-16-12 1/2 with two passes batted and one forced fumble in 12 games. Was a finalist for the Cliff Harris Award, given annually to the top small-school defensive player.

Strengths: Very good size-speed ratio. Can win at the snap with his natural bend, hip flexibility and initial take-off quickness. Closes fast to the ball. Has NFL pedigree. Has seen action as a goal-line receiving threat and effortlessly adjusts to the ball. Posted the second-fastest 40-yard dash time (4.58 seconds) of any defensive lineman at the NFL Combine behind only Jadeveon Clowney and recorded a 361/2-inch vertical jump.

Weaknesses: Underdeveloped body. Tends to play too tall and can be run at and neutralized by power. Lacks weight-room strength and explosion and has not learned how to convert speed to power. Raw hand use — is still learning how to disengage from blocks. Average eyes and instincts — often late to locate the ball. Not a strong tackler and does not show knockback body power. Must adjust to facing better competition than he saw in the Pennsylvania State Athletics Conference.

Future: A gifted athlete with NFL pedigree and intriguing developmental tools as a speed rusher, Webster could prove to be better fit as

a flex tight end in the pros, possessing more of an offensive temperament and the size, wingspan, athletic ability and coordination to create mismatches in a similar mold as Broncos TE Julius Thomas and Browns TE Jordan Cameron exiting college with limited football experience.

Draft projection: Fourth- to fifth-round pick.

Scout's take: "He's what you call a diamond in the rough. Once you polish him up, he might be a star. He stood out in the Shrine game. He has a lot of upside. I'd like to get him late."

DLE ETHAN WESTBROOKS, #90

WEST TEXAS A&M   ▶ GRADE: 5.23
Ht: 6-3 1/2 | Wt: 267 | Sp: 4.89 | Arm: 33 1/4 | Hand: 9 5/8

History: Has a daughter. Also threw the shot put and discus as a California prep Spent the 2009 season at San Joaquin Delta JC (Stockton, Calif.), where he played in 11 games (nine starts) and attended Cosumnes River JC in Sacramento in '10 but didn't play football. Was named the MVP of the Mid-Empire Conference in '11 while playing at DE at Sacramento State. Transferred to West Texas State for the '12 season, where he was named the Division II National Defensive Player of the Year after logging 60 tackles, 28 tackles for loss and 19 1/2 sacks with two batted passes and three forced fumbles in 15 games (14 starts) at DE. Led the nation in sacks and led the conference in tackles for loss. Led the team in '13 in sacks and TFL after posting 43-19 1/2-7 with five batted passes and one forced fumble in 14 games (10 starts). Had two sacks in the East-West Shrine game to earn defensive MVP honors.

Strengths: Well put together with good size and length. Stands out against Division II competition. Has natural pass-rush ability and shows tenacity hunting QBs. Explosive off the snap — bursts into blockers. Disruptive penetrating ability. Athletic and flexible. Excellent balance and body control executing pass-rush moves. Spins off blocks. Ranges and covers ground in a hurry when his fire is lit. Stood out vs. better post-season competition.

Weaknesses: Motor runs hot and cold (disappears for stretches). Does not consistently dig in vs. the run (heart is in rushing the passer). Undisciplined eyes. Raw understanding of blocking schemes. Does not maintain rush-lane integrity. Was allowed to freelance in search of destructive plays in college and will have to adopt a more structured game in the pros. Accumulated nearly 30 penalties in two seasons at WTAMU, including 15 offsides flags.

Future: Talented, enigmatic Division II edge rusher who marches to the beat of his own drum, but has intriguing, raw, natural ability to harass quarterbacks. Wild-card prospect with diamond-in-the-rough characteristics if a defensive line coach is able to refine the technical aspects of his game and stoke his fire.

Draft projection: Late draftable pick.

Scout's take: "I'm still waiting on his tape to come in. He was highly productive last year. He struggled mentally this year. I noticed he was benched against Midwestern State and never started any playoff games. He had some production here and there. The motor and effort is where the problem was. He has some size and athletic ability to intrigue. He has some edge quickness to him, but he is really raw. I don't know where he goes. I have heard in the sixth-seventh (round range)."

DLE-3T CHRIS WHALEY, #96

TEXAS   ▶ GRADE: 5.20

Ht: 6-3 1/8 | Wt: 269 | Sp: 4.90e | Arm: 32 | Hand: 9 1/8

History: Has two children. Rushed for 6,174 yards and 79 touchdowns as a prep in Texas, where he also played basketball and ran track. Redshirted as a running back in 2009. Appeared in 12 games, but did not record stats in '10. Moved to the defensive line in spring of '11 — played in all 13 games (one start) and managed five tackles, two tackles for loss and one sack with one batted pass in the fall. Logged 22-4-0 with two batted passes and two blocked kicks (extra points vs. Wyoming and Oklahoma) in 13 games in '12. Made seven starts at nose tackle, one at defensive end and one at defensive tackle. Had his senior season cut short after nine starts at DT with a left ACL injury against West Virginia in '13. Recorded 25-5-2 with two batted passes and a 31-yard interception return vs. Oklahoma and had a 40-yard fumble return for a score against Kansas. Team captain. Was medically excluded from the Combine (knee).

Strengths: Good size-speed ratio and overall athletic ability. Is fairly athletic and light on his feet to slant, stunt and shoot gaps. Flashes disruptive ability behind the line of scrimmage. Hardworking.

Weaknesses: Marginal processing speed and reactive quickness — guesses too much and is late to find the ball. Not stout — is too easily rooted out of holes. Very green hand use — has no plan. Lacks functional playing strength

to handle the double team. Inconsistent effort. Gets pinballed too easily. Modest production.

Future: Similar to former Longhorns DT Henry Melton, Whaley is a converted running back who outgrew the position and flipped to the other side of the ball. Flashed big-time potential before suffering a season-ending ACL injury and will require some time to recover. Developmental project with intriguing upside for a patient team willing to develop him.

Draft projection: Priority free agent.

Scout's take: "I didn't hear anyone high on (Whaley) during the fall. Let me tell you though — if he comes back from the injury clean, he's kind of interesting. We'll monitor him."

DLE-3T KERRY WYNN, #56

RICHMOND   ▶ GRADE: 4.85

Ht: 6-4 7/8 | Wt: 266 | Sp: 4.97 | Arm: 31 3/4 | Hand: 9 1/8

History: The Virginia prep was a three sport athlete, lettering in football, basketball and track. Redshirted in 2009. Saw action in only three games in '10, including a start at defensive end in his first game, due to a stinger injury. Recorded nine tackles, three tackles for loss and 1 1/2 sacks. In '11, he had 32-7-4 with one forced fumble in eight starts — started the first three games and the final five contests. Missed three mid-season games with an arm injury. Led the Spiders in tackles for loss in '12 after posting 45-8-4 1/2 with five batted passes and one forced fumble in 11 starts. Finished his Richmond career in '13, logging 56-5 1/2-2 1/2 with three pass breakups in 10 starts at defensive tackle. Injured his left ankle against Gardner-Webb and missed the next two games. Team captain. Strained his hamstring running his first 40 at the Combine.

Strengths: Very good body length. Flashes some violence in his hands. Strong tackler. Very good 10-yard split time (1.68 seconds) at the Combine, where he also did 31 benchpress reps.

Weaknesses: Average playing speed and burst. Comes off the ball upright and stays blocked. Very inconsistent pad level. Late to locate and find the ball. Too easily controlled. His 7.93-second 3-cone drill was among the worst by defensive tackles at the Combine.

Future: Strong, stiff, developmental five-technique who showed improvement as a senior, but must learn how to play with more consistent pad level to have a chance.

Draft projection: Priority free agent.

LINEBACKERS

BUFFALO LB
KHALIL MACK

NAWROCKI'S **TOP 10**

10	ADRIAN HUBBARD
9	JEREMIAH ATTAOCHU
8	CHRIS BORLAND
7	DEE FORD
6	TRENT MURPHY
5	DEMARCUS LAWRENCE
4	RYAN SHAZIER
3	C.J. MOSLEY
2	ANTHONY BARR
1	

ROLB-DRE JEREMIAH ATTAOCHU, #45

GEORGIA TECH   ▶ GRADE: 5.52
Ht: 6-3 1/4 | Wt: 252 | Sp: 4.80e | Arm: 33 | Hand: 9 7/8

History: Born in Nigeria. Went to high school in Washington D.C. Played his first three seasons as a 3-4 outside linebacker for defensive coordinator Al Groh. As a true freshman in 2010, played 12 games (started Independence Bowl against Air Force) and recorded 23 tackles, four for loss and three sacks. Did not play against Wake Forest (groin). Started all 11 games played in '11, tallying 59-11 1/2-6 with two pass breakups, an interception and two forced fumbles. Did not play against Maryland and Virginia while nursing a high ankle sprain. Started all 13 games in '12, producing 69-12-10 with a pass breakup and a forced fumble. Did not play against Middle Tennessee State (chest). As a senior in '13, played defensive end in Ted Roof's 4-3 scheme and posted 45-16-12 1/2 with two passes batted down and a forced fumble. Team captain. Owns Georgia Tech's career sacks record with 31 1/2, which ranks fifth in ACC history behind Chris Slade, Reinard Wilson, Peter Boulware and Greg Ellis. Did not work out at the Combine because of a left finger injury (medical exclusion)

Strengths: Good burst off the snap. Heats up the edge and runs the arc. Quick inside move. Disruptive ability. Motor runs hot — keeps coming after the quarterback and chases hard from the back side. Moves well laterally and can zone drop. Has experience in even and odd fronts, having played defensive end and stand-up linebacker. Power-leverage potential. Mature and intelligent. Cares about the game and prepares like a pro. Arrow pointing up (will be a 21-year-old rookie).

Weaknesses: Lacks elite length, athleticism and top-end speed. Needs to get stronger. Gets knocked around at the point of attack. Controlled by larger blockers when they get their hands on him. Still developing pop and violence in his hands. Still learning to incorporate power into his rush (more effortful than powerful). Needs to cultivate his pass-rush arsenal.

Future: Georgia Tech's all-time sack leader, Attaochu is a young, heady, disruptive, relentless edge rusher who profiles as a 3-4 right outside linebacker. Should interview well, and has the look of a trustworthy, long-term starter given his pass-rush ability, motor and makeup.

Draft projection: Second- to third-round pick.

Scout's take: "I thought he struggled early, but really came on the second half of the season. I had him in the fourth (round) early. I pushed him up to the top of 3. Ninety percent of the time he is rushing. That is what he does best."

ROLB-DRE ANTHONY BARR, #11
UCLA   ▶ GRADE: 6.60

Ht: 6-4 7/8 | Wt: 255 | Sp: 4.66 | Arm: 33 1/2 | Hand: 9 3/8

History: Born in South Bend, Ind. and raised in a Notre Dame family — father, Tony Brooks, played fullback at ND and was drafted by the Eagles in the fourth round of the 1992 draft; uncle, Reggie Brooks, played running back at ND, was fifth in the '92 Heisman voting and played 41 games with the Redskins and Buccaneers (1993-96); and uncle, Cedric Figaro, played linebacker for the Irish as well as 98 games for the Chargers, Colts, Browns and Rams (1988-92, 1995-96). Anthony grew up in Los Angeles and was raised by his mother, who is part of a large extended family, including Anthony's grandparents, who were like second parents to him. Ran track and was an All-State running back in high school — amassed 1,890 yards and 20 touchdowns as a junior (dealt with hip pointers) before suffering a season-ending broken ankle injury in September of his senior season. According to Barr, he felt effects of the injury through his freshman season. Highly recruited, he spurned Notre Dame — not wanting to play receiver — and signed with UCLA and then-head coach Rick Neuheisel in order to play running back and remain close to home. As a true freshman in 2010 (wore jersey No. 2), rushed six times for 29 yards (4.8-yard average) and zero touchdowns with nine receptions for 66 yards (7.3) and zero touchdowns in 12 games, including four starts at the Bruins' F-back (hybrid running back/tight end/receiver). Started 7-of-12 games played at the F-back in '11, rushing 9-25-1 (2.8) and catching 3-16-1. Had arthroscopic surgery to repair cartilage damage in his right knee and missed three October contests. Converted to 3-4 right outside linebacker under new head coach Jim Mora Jr., then-defensive coordinator Lou Spanos and linebackers coach Jeff Ulbrich (current DC). Sustained a head injury during '12 fall camp and began the season with a cast protecting a broken left index finger. Switched to jersey No. 11, started all 14 games and ranked second nationally in sacks behind Steelers '13 first-rounder Jarvis Jones — recorded 83 tackles, 21 1/2 for loss and 13 1/2 sacks with five pass breakups, four forced fumbles, a blocked kick and a safety. Dealt a season-ending blow to USC quarterback and '13 Eagles fourth-rounder Matt Barkley. Sustained a head injury during '13 fall camp, but started all 13 games at ROLB and registered 65-20-10 with a pass breakup and five forced fumbles. Won the Lott IMPACT award and was a finalist for the Lombardi, Bednarik and Butkus awards. Team captain. Was invited, but did not participate in the Senior Bowl.

Strengths: Exceptional take-off speed, acceleration and closing burst. Makes plays effortlessly in back-side lateral pursuit. Outstanding recovery quickness to make plays (when he is out of position). Explosive striker. Can produce "wow" plays when he triggers quickly or releases cleanly and has developed a reputation for knocking quarterbacks out of games (see USC, 2012 and New Mexico State, 2013).

Weaknesses: Developing instincts — late to locate the ball and too easily fooled by play-action and misdirection. Motor runs hot and cold — does not always apply himself. Can be locked down too easily when engaged — unrefined hand use. Lacks variety of pass-rush moves and relies too much on natural speed. Average eyes, anticipation and awareness in coverage — marginal feel. Average base strength — moved off the ball too easily by tight ends (plays tall). Needs more time in the weight room — 15 bench-press reps were tied for the fewest among linebackers at the Combine.

Future: A highly disruptive, athletic specimen with the pass-rush potential to effortlessly emerge as a double-digit sack producer. Is far from a finished product and his best football is still ahead of him, yet he plays the game with more of an offensive temperament and could require some patience. Is the type of rare athlete that could even contribute as an offensive playmaker once he learns to grasp defensive concepts and the game slows down for him.

Draft projection: Top 10 pick.

Scout's take: "Barr is overrated. He does not always play hard. He is more athletic than Von Miller, but he is not a dominant (butt)kicker. ... For how long and lean he is, he can bend and drop and flip his hips. I'm not sure how instinctive he is. I realize he has not played the position long."

ROLB SHAQUIL BARRETT, #56
COLORADO STATE   ▶ GRADE: 5.20

Ht: 6-1 1/2 | Wt: 244 | Sp: 4.90e | Arm: 33 | Hand: 8 5/8

History: Married with two sons. Originally from Maryland. Attended Baltimore City College his first two years of high school before moving to Nebraska, where he won a state wrestling championship. Began his college career at Division II Nebraska-Omaha — started 10-of-11 games as a true freshman for the Mavericks in 2010 and recorded 82 tackles, 11 1/2 for loss and 8 1/2 sacks with three forced fumbles and four blocked kicks (two punts, two field goals). Transferred to CSU when Nebraska-Omaha dropped football. Was on the two-deep by the end of '11, then an injury to strong-side linebacker Mychal Sisson enabled Barrett to start the final 11 games at middle linebacker (incumbent MLB James Skelton shifted to SLB) — led the Rams in tackling by posting 99-4 1/2-2 1/2 with three pass breakups, a 52-yard interception touchdown and a forced fumble. Played defensive end in '12 when he started 10-of-12 games and produced 67-7.5-3.5 with a batted pass, a 49-yard INT TD and two forced fumbles. Did not start against Hawaii (left leg) or Boise State (ankle). Was the Mountain West Conference Defensive Player of the Year in '13 — started all 14 games at right defensive end, registering 80-20 1/2-12 with two batted passes, an interception and two forced fumbles. Sprained his ankle against San Jose State Team captain.

Strengths: Solid instincts — around the ball a lot. Flattens down the line and runs to the ball. Plays hard. Good closing speed and pursuit production. Strong tackler. Flashes power to walk back big blockers and is disciplined defending the run. Beat Alabama's Cyrus Kouandjio for a sack, using trademark rip move to come underneath. Has a knack for stripping the ball.

Weaknesses: Does not pass the eyeball test — slew-footed with stiff hips and segmented, mechanical movement skills. Lacks ideal first-step quickness to trim the corner. Near-liability in man coverage. Has wide shoulders and gets stuck on blocks too long.

Future: A tough, productive, stand-up rush linebacker who may not look pretty, but consistently gets the job done, came through in clutch situations and displayed a knack for making timely and game-changing big plays.

Draft projection: Late draftable pick.

Scout's take: "I liked him as a blitzing Pittsburgh Steelers-type outside linebacker. When you see him in person, he is short and tight in the hips and not a good athlete. He shows some power and short-area burst. He has a chance."

WLB LAMIN BARROW, #18

LSU   ▶ GRADE: 5.37

Ht: 6-1 3/8 | Wt: 237 | Sp: 4.64 | Arm: 33 3/8 | Hand: 10 3/8

History: Louisiana native. Redshirted in 2009. Was a backup "Will" linebacker and special-teams contributor his first two years. Played 12 games in '10 (started the season opener against North Carolina as an injury

replacement for Ryan Baker) and recorded 18 tackles, one-half for loss and zero sacks. Did not play against Tennessee. Played 13 games in '11 (started against Northwestern State when Baker was suspended) and tallied 17-1-0. Did not play against Tennessee. Started all 13 games at Will in '12, posting 104-7 1/2-0 with five pass breakups and a forced fumble. Was the leading tackler in '13 when he notched 91-5 1/2-1 1/2 with two pass breakups. Team captain wore jersey No. 57 prior to his senior season when he was elected to wear No. 18, signifying the player who bests represents what it means to be a Tiger.

Strengths: Knee bender. Uses his arms like flippers to ward off blocks on the move. Athletic and agile. Moves well laterally. Large hands. Can redirect and chase. Drops easily into zone coverage and shows hip swivel and range. Tough and football smart. Highly respected and hardworking team captain. Has special-teams experience and traits. Posted a 35-inch vertical leap and 10-foot, 3-inch broad jump at the Combine.

Weaknesses: Small-framed — is short and lacks ideal bulk. Lacks elite speed for his size. Average eyes and instincts. Gives ground at the point of attack. Does not play downhill or make enough plays at/behind the line — too much production is downfield. Leaves production on the field — in position but does not finish. Overruns plays (loses contain). Sucked in by play-action. Not a striker.

Future: Undersized, athletic, run-around see-and-go reactor who needs to be protected to be effective. Projects as a Will linebacker, nickel defender and special-teams contributor.

Draft projection: Fourth- to fifth-round pick.

Scout's take: "(Barrow) is an explosive athlete. I like the way he runs and rolls his hips on contact. ... He's a little bit one-dimensional. I wish he were better in coverage."

MLB CHRIS BORLAND, #44

WISCONSIN   ▶ GRADE: 5.55

Ht: 5-11 1/2 | Wt: 248 | Sp: 4.83 | Arm: 29 1/4 | Hand: 9 7/8

History: Linebacker-running back who also lettered in basketball, tennis and track and field as an Ohio prep. Was the Big Ten Freshman of the Year in 2009. Backed up weak-side linebacker Mike Taylor until Taylor was lost for the season in Week Seven — played all 13 games, starting five of the final six, and recorded 54 tackles 10 1/2 for loss and five sacks with two pass breakups, an interception, five forced fumbles and a blocked kick. Did not start against Hawaii when the badgers opened with an extra defensive back. Played through a torn left labrum, routinely dealt with his shoulder popping and had post-season surgery which sidelined him for '10 spring practice. In the fall, managed 7-2-1 in two games played — started the season opener against UNLV, hurt his left shoulder, sat out against San Jose, then re-injured the shoulder against Arizona State prompting season-ending surgery. Also had surgery in December to repair a tear in his right labrum. Was granted a medical hardship, preserving a year of eligibility. Started all 14 games at middle linebacker in '11 and totaled 143-19-2.5 with five pass breakups, two interceptions and five forced fumbles. Started all 12 games played at MLB in '12, collecting 104-10-4.5 with six pass breakups and three forced fumbles. Did not play against Ohio State and Penn State (right hamstring). Earned first-team All-Big Ten honors for the third straight season and was named the conference's Defensive Player of the Year in '13 when he led the Badgers in tackles — amassed 112-8 1/2-4 with two pass breakups and two forced fumbles in 12 starts at MLB. Strained his right hamstring against Illinois and sat out against Iowa. His 15 career forced fumbles are second-most in FBS history. Started 45 career games.

Strengths: Is built low to the ground and bends his knees. Keen eyes and instincts — has a nose for the ball. Quick to fill downhill (see goal-line play vs. Ohio State when he stuck RB Carlos Hyde in the hole and drove him back). Motor runs hot — pursues hard and seldom quits on plays. Flows well laterally. Aware in zone. Capable of bringing pressure as a blitzer. Good leaping ability. Intense competitor who loves to play and it shows. Defensive playmaker — piled up 50 career TFL and 14 FFs. Special intangibles.

Weaknesses: Is short with Tyrannosaurus rex arms — too easily neutralized (struggles to disengage). Eclipsed by larger offensive linemen. Can do a better job protecting his legs. Average explosion, tackle strength and pop on contact. Lets runners escape his grasp. Exposed in space. Has man-coverage limitations, especially against tight ends (lacks length to match up). Durability could be an issue.

Future: Short, active, athletic, instinctive tackling machine who will have to overcome physical limitations to establish himself as a dependable, long-term starter, though he has immediate special-teams ability and the makeup to push for a more prominent role.

Draft projection: Fourth- to fifth-round pick.

Scout's take: "I love the way he plays on Saturdays. I think he'll find a way to get it done on Sundays."

ROLB-DE CARL BRADFORD, #52 (JUNIOR)

ARIZONA STATE ▶ GRADE: 5.31
Ht: 6-0 3/4 | Wt: 250 | Sp: 4.76 | Arm: 30 1/4 | Hand: 9 1/2

History: Played for Toby Gerhart's father at Norco (Calif.) High, where he was a wingback in a double-wing offense. Was present in March '12 when his father, Roy, died of a heart attack. Recruited as a linebacker and redshirted in 2010. Saw action as a defensive end, linebacker and special-teams player in '11 — appeared in all 13 games, drawing the start at DE against Boise State in the Las Vegas Bowl in place of the suspended Junior Onyeali, and tallied 12 tackles, 3 1/2 for loss and zero sacks. Started all 13 games at the "Devil" position (hybrid DE/OLB) in '12, notching 81-20 1/2-11 1/2 with four batted passes, an interception and three forced fumbles. Started all 14 games in '13, recording 61-19-8 1/2 with four batted passes, an 18-yard interception touchdown and three forced fumbles. Was benched in the second half of the Oregon State contest after getting into an argument with Will Sutton that escalated into words with head coach Todd Graham on the sideline.

Strengths: Plays with urgency and beelines to the ball. Explosive — can power-clean 400 pounds and hits on the rise with power. Is effective stunting and looping. Flashes playmaking ability (see UCLA). Explosive tackler. Can play on his feet off the ball and times up the blitz well. Good hands. Athletic enough to fold back into coverage. Solid instincts and diagnose — sniffs out screens and has a feel for locating the ball quickly. Excellent leaping ability — posted a 37 1/2-inch vertical.

Weaknesses: Has a short, compact frame with very short arms and gets hung on blocks. Gets locked down by big-bodied blockers when they get their hands on him. Spins in place and lacks variety of pass-rush moves. Cannot convert speed to power. Needs to improve his hand use.

Future: An undersized college defensive end, Bradford projects to outside linebacker in a 3-4 front in the pros, where his physical dimensions and rush ability are best suited. Would profile best in an aggressive, one-gapping odd front such as the Colts, Jets, Ravens or Steelers.

Draft projection: Third- to fourth-round pick.

Scout's take: "(Bradford) did not look natural in space as a linebacker (at his pro day workout). He's a rush guy. He's best moving forward."

OLB JONATHAN BROWN, #45

ILLINOIS ▶ GRADE: 5.20
Ht: 6-0 3/8 | Wt: 238 | Sp: 5.03 | Arm: 33 | Hand: 9 3/8

History: Prepped in Tennessee, where he played linebacker and running back. Played 12 games as a true freshman in 2010 and recorded 31 tackles, one-half for loss and 1 1/2 sacks with an interception and a forced fumble. Started 11-of-12 games played at Will linebacker in '11 and was U of I's leading tackler —produced 108-6-19 1/2 with four pass breakups, an interception and a forced fumble. Was benched for the opening series against Western Michigan — said then-defensive coordinator: "For lack of a better way of saying it, we all have commitments that we have to make and he just didn't completely finish his commitment that he had to do." Kneed a Northwestern player in the groin and was suspended for the Indiana contest. Started 7-of-9 games played in '12 (nursed an ankle injury in October and did not start against Wisconsin and Michigan) and collected 59-9 1/2-2 1/2 with a pass breakup and a forced fumble before suffering a season-ending injury — pectoral muscle separated from his right shoulder, requiring surgery which sidelined him for '13 spring practice. Was Illinois' leading tackler in the fall, amassing 119-15-5 with four pass breakups, an interception and a forced fumble in 12 starts. Team captain.

Strengths: Nice arm length for his size. Athletic with good feet. Quick to shoot gaps. Natural bender who moves very well laterally. Excellent range — thrives in pursuit. Productive tackler who flashes pop on contact. Has special-teams experience. Football smart. Three-year starter. Was a 21-year-old senior.

Weaknesses: Safety size. Shoddy instincts and eye discipline. Does not play a big man's game — skirts blocks instead of taking on with force. Unschooled to blocking schemes. Leaky contain player. Loses gap integrity, takes some inaccurate angles and runs himself out of position to make plays. Effectiveness wanes in traffic. Struggles in man coverage and zone awareness is limited. Intermittent intensity and urgency. Uneven performance. Alarmingly disappointing at the Combine, raising questions about his conditioning and work ethic: totaled just 16 bench-press reps, broad jumped 8 feet, 11 inches, vertical jumped 31 inches, recorded a 7.77-second 3-cone drill, recorded a 4.56-seecond short shuttle and ran a 12.38-second 60-yard shuttle — all of which ranked at or near the bottom of linebackers.

Future: Undersized, athletic, finesse, inconsistent Will linebacker who needs to be kept clean to be effective. Small frame, deficient instincts and soft run defense likely relegate him to a backup role, and he will have to excel on special teams.

Draft projection: Priority free agent.

Scout's take: "He's a solid player. He plays faster than he times. He played through a lot of injuries as a junior. I thought he had starter potential last year, though you could see he was hobbling around a lot. I like his instincts."

MLB PRESTON BROWN, #2

LOUISVILLE   ▶ GRADE: 5.42

Ht: 6-1 1/4 | Wt: 251 | Sp: 4.86 | Arm: 33 1/2 | Hand: 10 1/4

History: Cincinnati native. Appeared in all 13 games in 2010 and recorded 10 tackles, one for loss and one sack. Played strong-side linebacker in '11 — started 11-of-13 games and produced 84-5-1 1/2. Did not start against Marshall (gave way to extra defensive back) and Syracuse. Moved to middle linebacker in '12 when he started all 13 games and racked up 109-3-0 with four pass breakups and an interception. Was the Cardinals' leading tackler for the second straight season in '13, amassing 98-12 1/2-4 1/2 with a pass breakup, three forced fumbles and a 48-yard fumble return touchdown. Did not start against UCONN (nickel).

Strengths: Outstanding size. Physical tackler. Steps downhill and attacks the run with the proper shoulder. Good eyes and instincts. Delivers some pop on contact and strikes with force. Experienced three-year starter. Good football intelligence — makes the calls and lines up a defense. Has large hands and a big wing span for his size.

Weaknesses: Shows some tightness in his movement. Struggles to carry backs and match up with athletic tight ends in man coverage. Limited depth in coverage drops — is best in small areas. Average coverage instincts. Requires some motivation.

Future: Aggressive, high-collision 'Mike' linebacker best paired with a demanding position coach who will extract the most from him.

Draft projection: Third- to fourth-round pick.

Scout's take: "I like his size and toughness. He'll step up in the hole and take on blocks and fill. He's a strong tackler. You can hear his pads clicking in practice."

MLB MAX BULLOUGH, #40

MICHIGAN STATE   ▶ GRADE: 5.25

Ht: 6-3 1/2 | Wt: 249 | Sp: 4.78 | Arm: 31 | Hand: 9 3/8

History: Michigan native who grew up in a football family — father, grandfather and two uncles played at MSU, and another grandfather and uncle played at Notre Dame. Younger brother, Riley, is a fullback for the Spartans. Max played linebacker, fullback and tight end as a Michigan prep, winning two state championships. Appeared in all 13 games in 2010 and recorded 23 tackles (13 on special teams), 1 1/2 for loss and one-half sack. Was arrested in March '11 in Colorado and charged with eluding police and underage possession of alcohol — ultimately received nine months probation. Stepped into the lineup in '11, starting all 14 games, and produced 83-18 1/2-11 with three pass breakups. Was the leading tackler in '12 — amassed 111-12 1/2-2 1/2 with four pass breakups, an interception and a forced fumble in 13 starts. Started all 13 games played in '13 and was credited with 76-9 1/2-1 1/2 with two pass breakups and a forced fumble. Was suspended for the Rose Bowl against Stanford (undisclosed). Two-time captain.

Strengths: Terrific football intelligence. Keys and diagnoses quickly, understands run fits and spills willingly. Physical — good take-on/tackle strength between the tackles. Pursues hard. Good tackler when he's able to square up ball carriers. Two-year captain with outstanding football character. Leads vocally and by example. Football is in his blood and approaches the game accordingly. Pumped 30 bench press reps, tied for most among linebackers at the Combine.

Weaknesses: Average athlete. Tight hips (exposed in space). Limited foot speed, lateral agility and range. Can be late to the perimeter. Struggles in man coverage and is stiff dropping/ turning in coverage. Non-explosive athlete — his 31-inch vertical and 9-foot, 3-inch broad jump were among the worst posted by linebackers at the Combine.

Future: Big, tough, experienced, durable, competitive 'Mike' linebacker who was a heart-and-soul type for the stingiest defense in college football. Like a coach on the field, Bullough is a throwback talent whose instincts and technique will have to compensate for athletic limitations for him to win a starting role.

Draft projection: Fourth- to fifth-round pick.

Scout's take: "He can't run very well, and he's not physical. I think he lives off his name and reputation. (The coaches) love him, but put on the tape. Someone will take him as a 3-4 Mike linebacker. He has size, but he does not play with any pop to me. ... He's a throwback type. I don't see a lot of physical talent. He's a smart overachiever who likes to play the game."

ROLB-DRE-PRS DEE FORD, #95

AUBURN   ▶ GRADE: 5.57
Ht: 6-2 1/8 | Wt: 244 | Sp: 4.61 | Arm: 32 7/8 | Hand: 10 1/4

History: Prepped in Alabama. Played all 13 games as a true freshman in 2009 and was credited with 12 tackles, 2 1/2 for loss and a sack with one interception. Played all 13 games in '10 (one start at right end) and scratched 11-2-2. In '11, managed 7-2-1 in three games before having season-ending microdisectomy surgery to repair a herniated disc in his back. Was granted a medical hardship, preserving a year of eligibility. Started 7-of-11 games played at defensive end in '12, managing 34-6 1/2-6 with a batted pass, forced fumble and blocked kick. Suffered an abdominal injury against Arkansas — did not play against Ole Miss and was hampered against Vanderbilt, Texas A&M and New Mexico State. Hurt his left

MCL during '13 fall camp — missed the first two games (Washington State, Arkansas State) and did not start against Mississippi State, but started the final 11 games and collected 29-14 1/2-10 1/2 with a batted pass and two forced fumbles. Did not work out at the Combine after he was red flagged medically stemming from previous back surgery (medical exclusion).

Strengths: Very good acceleration and burst to beat blockers off the ball. Big hands. Anticipates the snap very well and has a long second step. Plays with urgency and keeps working to the quarterback. Outstanding energy and work ethic. Athletic enough to fall in coverage and play on his feet. Beat Texas A&M RT Cedric Ogbuehi for two sacks to close out a 45-41 upset victory and finished the season strong. Respected, defensive tempo-setter — distinguished by his effort, hustle and pursuit.

Weaknesses: Undersized — thin-framed, lacks bulk and anchor strength to dig in vs. the run. Cannot convert speed to power and gets stalled if he cannot work half of a blocker. Struggles to discard blockers when locked up and gets inverted. Not comfortable moving in reverse. Has consistently been dinged with injuries and has never made it through a full season healthy. Recorded a very pedestrian 4.73-second 20-yard shuttle time at his pro day, indicative of marginal change of direction.

Future: High-motor college left defensive end perhaps suited for a rush linebacker role in the pros. Has added more than 50 pounds to his frame since arriving on campus and has demonstrated the desire, work habits and competitiveness to develop into a productive edge rusher, if he can stay healthy and is programmed to go get the quarterback only.

Draft projection: Second- to third-round pick.

Scout's take: "I don't think he will be a great outside linebacker (conversion). He sees himself as a designated pass rusher. Factor in the injury thing at the Combine that no one knew about. In the drills at his pro day, they had to keep repeating things to him. He's not smart. You need to have a plan for him. He's not a plug-and-play guy. I originally had him in the third (round). Someone will probably take him in the second and say they are going to coach the heck out of him, try to justify it that way. If you're talking about speed, twitch and power, he does have it all."

WLB KHAIRI FORTT, #11

CALIFORNIA   ▶ GRADE: 5.25
Ht: 6-2 1/4 | Wt: 248 | Sp: 4.69 | Arm: 33 5/8 | Hand: 10 1/8

History: First name is pronounced "ky-REE." Highly recruited USA Today All-American who also played lacrosse and ran track as a Connecticut prep. Suffered a sprained right

ACL and bruised tibia as a senior in 2009. Began his college career at Penn State and was a reserve/special-teams player for two seasons. Appeared in nine games in 2010 (one start as an injury replacement) and tallied 17-1/2-0. Played all 13 games in '11 and was credited with 33-6-2 1/2. Had surgery in April '12 to repair a ligament that stabilized the patella in his right knee (dealt with subluxation since ninth grade when he tore the ligament). Following the Jerry Sandusky/Joe Paterno scandal, transferred to Cal where he was eligible to play immediately, but redshirted while recovering from his knee procedure. In '13, started the first nine games at Will linebacker and produced 64-3 1/2-1/2 before suffering a season-ending biceps injury against Arizona. Strained his left hamstring during Combine drills and did not run shuttles or the 3-cone drill.

Strengths: Good size with a muscular build, including long arms and big hands. Field fast — moves like a safety. Very athletic and agile. Plays on his feet and bends naturally. Excellent lateral agility — flows smoothly and has sideline-to-sideline range. Uses his arms like flippers to play off blocks. Loose-hipped to drop into coverage and match with backs and tight ends. Has traits to excel on special teams. Bench-pressed 225 pounds 30 times, tied for most among linebackers at the Combine.

Weaknesses: Frame is nearly maxed out. Very average key-and-diagnose skills slow his play speed. Does not always trust what he sees — takes false steps and hesitates to trigger. Inconsistent run fits and field leverage. Can be stronger at the point of attack. Did not make enough splash plays. Has underachiever traits. Motivation and durability should be looked into.

Future: A better athlete than football player at this stage of his development, Fortt transferred from Penn State and played only one season at Cal before making a premature jump to the NFL. Speedy, finesse, see-and-go reactor who looks the part and has intriguing, starter-caliber athleticism to fit on the weak side in a fast-flowing 4-3 where he's freed up to chase the ball. Must sharpen his eyes and instincts to reach his potential.

Draft projection: Fourth- to fifth-round pick.

Scout's take: "He played like a second-rounder vs. Ohio State. He can run and he's fast. Other games, he looks like just a guy. He's always hurt. That's his problem."

LOLB-DLE JAMES GAYLE, #99

VIRGINIA TECH　　　　　　　▶ GRADE: 5.31
Ht: 6-3 3/4 | Wt: 259 | Sp: 4.69 | Arm: 32 3/8 | Hand: 9 5/8

History: Uncle, Shaun Gayle, was a Pro Bowl safety for the Bears (1984-95). James is a Virginia native. Played defensive end for the Hokies. Redshirted in 2009. Appeared in all 14 games in '10, starting two as an injury replacement, and tallied 13 tackles, 6 1/2 for loss and four sacks with a forced fumble. Started all 13 games in '11, collecting 38-12 1/2-7. Sprained his left ankle against Miami and sat out against Wake Forest, then re-injured the ankle early against Boston College. Started 11-of-13 games in '12, recording 43-11-5 with a batted pass. Did not start in the season opener against Georgia Tech (right ankle) or the Russell Athletic Bowl against Rutgers. Started all 13 games in '13 and notched 44-10 1/2-6 with a batted pass and forced fumble.

Strengths: Excellent height-weight-speed ratio. Looks the part and has weight-room strength. Explosive athlete with rare leaping ability for his size — posted a 37-inch vertical and broad jumped 10 feet, 2 inches. Good balance and edge burst and enough flexibility to turn the corner. Dogged in pursuit and ranges all over the field to make tackles. Flattens and crashes down the line. Strong wrap tackler. Durable three-year starter. Has NFL bloodlines (uncle, Shaun, was a Pro Bowl safety for the Bears).

Weaknesses: Average eyes and instincts. Questionable football intelligence. Short on bulk and anchor strength to play with his hand in the dirt — soft edge setter. Not equipped to shadow in man coverage and is unnatural playing in reverse. Limited scheme versatility. Could require short leash and extra reps.

Future: Explosive, high-motor see-and-go reactor whose calling card is his ability to pressure the edge. Does not play to his weight-room numbers against the run and lacks desirable length and smarts, projecting as a situational 3-4 rush linebacker.

Draft projection: Fourth- to fifth-round pick.

Scout's take: "He's a finesse, edge (rusher) that has some quickness and acceleration off the ball. He's not strong. He can't anchor. He plays hard. He can't win if you have to be honest. He does a little hand chop and dip and run — that is his signature move. He can't play in the bubble, and he is not a true defensive end. The 3-4 rush teams will like him best."

MLB JEREMIAH GEORGE, #52

IOWA STATE　　　　　　　▶ GRADE: 5.18
Ht: 5-11 1/4 | Wt: 234 | Sp: 4.91 | Arm: 31 7/8 | Hand: 9 1/4

History: Prepped in Florida. Saw very limited action 2010-11 (wore jersey No. 7) — recorded five tackles, zero for loss and zero sacks in 22 games over two seasons. Started 9-of-13 games in '12 and produced 87-4-0 with three pass breakups. Was the Cyclones' MVP in '13 when he was the Big 12's leading tackler — registered 133-12-3 1/2 with six pass breakups and two interceptions. Team captain. Pulled a hamstring running the 40-yard dash at the Combine and did not participate in positional drills, shuttle or

3-cone drill.

Strengths: Is sudden stepping downhill and flashes some shock in his hands. Plays with urgency and leaves all his energy and effort on the field. Explosive short-area burst. Very good balance and body control. Flows fast to the sideline and has the speed to cut off backs at the corner. Intense, vocal team leader. Good work ethic. Strong for his size — bench-pressed 225 pounds 28 times at the Combine. Is committed to the game and competes hard. Has the makeup of a special-teams terror.

Weaknesses: Marginal size (built like a box safety). Slew-footed. Runs around blocks and takes himself out of plays overpursuing and giving up the cutback. Not stout — can be run at. Average zone awareness. See-and-go reactor — late to trigger.

Future: Undersized, run-and-hit linebacker most ideally suited for a special-teams role. Lack of size will relegate him to a fast-flowing 4-3 under front, where he could be best on the weak side where action is funneled to him and he has a clean path to the ball.

Draft projection: Priority free agent.

WLB ANTHONY HITCHENS, #31

IOWA ▶ GRADE: 4.95

Ht: 6-0 3/8 | Wt: 240 | Sp: 4.74 | Arm: 32 1/2 | Hand: 9 1/8

History: Florida native who took initiative to move out of his biological parents' house and live with a friend's family in order to attend a better, safer school and remain focused on his football career. High school running back, linebacker and kick returner who had 3,864 career rushing yards and 52 touchdowns — earned four varsity letters in addition to playing basketball and running track. Bounced between safety, linebacker and running back as a true freshman in 2010, recording nine tackles, zero for loss and zero sacks in 10 games played. Appeared in eight games in '11, tallying 25-0-0. Missed five games because of a knee sprain. Started all 11 games at Will linebacker in '12 and notched 124-5 1/2-1. Was benched during the Purdue contest after multiple blown assignments, and did not play against Michigan (illness). Was the Hawkeyes' leading tackler and Defensive MVP in '13 — started all 13 games at Will and registered 112-13 1/2-2 with two pass breakups, an interception and two forced fumbles.

Strengths: Aggressive tackler. Flows fast to the ball (when he sees it) and has good playing range to the sideline. Plays bigger than his size and does not back down from big-bodied blockers or physical runners (see Ohio State). Fairly explosive hitter. Plays with a chip on his shoulder and is highly respected for his work ethic, makeup and overall approach. Is mentally and physically tough. Very durable despite lack of size (missed only one game in career).

Weaknesses: Is short and lacks bulk. Tends to play narrow-based and get rooted out of the hole on inside runs. Angles and anticipation could stand to improve — is late to sort out misdirection. Very average cover instincts — often is lured by play-action passing game. See-and-go reactor. Modest production for a weakside position where action is designed to be heavily funneled his way — leaves some on the field.

Future: An active, undersized, run-and-hit weakside linebacker, Hitchens is at his best in a scheme where he is protected and free to run to the ball. Has shown gradual improvement and could stand to compete for a backup role.

Draft projection: Priority free agent.

Scout's take: "There's something missing instinctually. He's a finesse guy."

LOLB ADRIAN HUBBARD, #42 (JUNIOR)

ALABAMA ▶ GRADE: 5.45

Ht: 6-6 | Wt: 257 | Sp: 4.69 | Arm: 34 1/2 | Hand: 9 1/4

History: Prepped in Georgia. Redshirted in 2010. Was a reserve "Jack" linebacker in '11 and appeared in nine games, recording nine tackles, 1 1/2 tackles for loss and zero sacks. Started 13-of-14 games at "Sam" in '12, producing 41-11-7 with a batted pass and three forced fumbles. Did not start against Mississippi State (Tide opened with the "Jack" instead of the "Sam"). Started all 13 games at SLB in '13, totaling 33-5 1/2-3 with three batted passes. Did not bench press or run shuttles or 3-cone drill at the Combine because of a deltoid strain and right hamstring strain.

Strengths: Exceptional length and overall size for a rush linebacker. Good hand strength to leverage the edge. Flashes pass-rush ability — nice bend and balance. Flattens down the line and is athletic enough to string out plays to the sideline. Is strong enough to set the edge, shed and defend the run. Good take-on strength and anchor — benchpresses tight ends. Nimble-footed enough to carry tight ends down the field (see LSU). Already graduated.

Weaknesses: Lacks elite edge speed, burst and explosion. Does not make plays and too often disappears for stretches. Instincts are still developing — can be lured by play-action and misdirection. Average career sack production (10 sacks). Has a quirky personality, inflated opinion of his ability and carries a sense of entitlement that could be difficult to manage and require a patient positional coach.

Future: A long-bodied, athletic rush linebacker with the base strength desired in a 4-3 left defensive end, Hubbard's greatest physical trait is his core functional strength and ability to leverage the edge and defend the run. Is still developing as a pass rusher and offers the scheme versatility and upside to interest any defense. Has starter traits, but has yet to reach the impact level he thinks he makes. Has upside if the light bulb comes on.

Draft projection: Third- to fourth-round pick.

Scout's take: "He flashes some pass-rush ability, but he's highly inconsistent. He makes few plays and disappears a lot. He beats to his own drum."

ILB ANDREW JACKSON, #4

WESTERN KENTUCKY　　▶ GRADE: 5.17

Ht: 6-1 | Wt: 254 | Sp: 4.85e | Arm: 32 1/2 | Hand: 9 1/2

History: Prepped in Florida. Did not play football as a sophomore in high school after he was arrested for attempted burglary — completed nine months of community service, though his high school coach contended Jackson was in the wrong place at the wrong time and took the bullet for friends. Dressed for just one game in 2010. Started all 12 games at middle linebacker in '11, producing 109 tackles, 17 for loss and 3 1/2 sacks with a pass breakup and a forced fumble. Was the Hilltoppers' leading tackler for the second straight season in '12 when he started 12-of-13 games played at MLB and posted 122-17 1/2-2 with a pass breakup and four forced fumbles. Did not start against Louisiana Lafayette. Started 10-of-11 games played at MLB in '13 and totaled 95-8 1/2-1 with two pass breakups. Did not start against South Alabama, then was suspended against Georgia State (violation team rules). Was medically excluded at the Combine.

Strengths: Thickly built, especially through his trunk and lower body. Has ideal bulk to fit inside a 3-4. Outstanding leaping ability for his size — has a 38 1/2-inch vertical. Physically strong tackler when he's able to square up and wrap. Intense, confident and competitive. Did not look out of place when WKU stepped up in competition. Productive three-year starter.

Weaknesses: Lacks ideal length. Thick, tight hips and heavy legs. Average eyes and instincts. Needs to improve hand use and shed ability. Lacks speed to track down ball carriers on the perimeter. Leaves some production on the field -- inconsistent tackler. Man-coverage limitations. Does not project as a core special-teams player. Is immature and needs to learn what it means to be professional. Weight tends to fluctuate. Suspect character needs to be investigated.

Future: A stout, physical, downhill thumper with eventual-starter potential inside a 3-4 front where he's protected and able to attack the ball. However, suspect character and work ethic make him a risky investment, and he'd be best served in a locker room with a strong veteran presence.

Draft projection: Fifth- to sixth-round pick.

Scout's take: "I didn't like him. He' short. I didn't see him as more than a run-and-chase guy. You'd like to see more step and fill."

LOLB DERRELL JOHNSON, #56

EAST CAROLINA　　▶ GRADE: 5.24

Ht: 6-1 3/4 | Wt: 254 | Sp: 4.60e | Arm: 30 | Hand: 9

History: First name is pronounced "durr-ELL." Prepped in Baltimore before spending a year at Wyoming Seminary Prep (PA). Played 12 games in 2010, starting the final 11 as a 4-3 defensive end, and recorded 40 tackles, 4 1/2 for loss and a sack. Played defensive end in a 3-4 in '11 when he started all 12 games and notched 39-5 1/2-3 with two forced fumbles. Shifted to a rush linebacker role in '12, posting 62-11-7 in 13 starts. Was the Pirates' leading tackler in '13 when he started all 13 games and compiled 80-14-8 with three batted passes, an interception and a forced fumble.

Strengths: Experienced, four-year starter. Flashes shock and violence in his punch. Jars tight ends and slot receivers off their routes. Displays old-man strength to dig a ditch and set the edge. Swats big blockers and plays with tenacity. Can convert speed to power and uproot blockers. Extremely tough and durable.

Weaknesses: Has noticeably short flappers and gets caught on the line and too often velcroed to blocks. Is very tightly wound with minimal coverage range. Lacks hip flexibility to come to balance in space vs. quick backs (misses tackles). Will be a 24-year-old rookie.

Future: A strong, stocky, compactly built, leverage-power rusher who operates mostly out of crouched, 2-point stance and brings a bulldog tenacity to the field. Would be most ideally suited for an aggressive, one-gapping 3-4 front such as the Colts, Ravens or Steelers in a similar mold as Cowboys 2008 sixth-round pick Erik Walden. Was not invited to the Combine, but possesses make it qualities and could prove to be a surprise.

Draft projection: Priority free agent.

Scout's take: "He's just a guy. It's going to be hard to overcome those short arms."

ROLB-SLB CHRISTIAN JONES, #7

FLORIDA STATE　　▶ GRADE: 5.40

Ht: 6-3 1/8 | Wt: 240 | Sp: 4.74 | Arm: 33 1/2 | Hand: 9 5/8

History: Father and brother also played for the Seminoles. Highly recruited Florida native. Was a reserve/special-teams player in 2010 when he was credited with 18 tackles, three for loss and three sacks with a pass breakup in

14 games. Started all 13 games at strong-side linebacker in '13, producing 56-6-3 with two pass breakups and two forced fumbles. Was FSU's leading tackler in '12 — started all 14 games at weak-side linebacker and racked up 95-7-0 with three pass breakups and a fumble return touchdown. In '13, started 12-of-13 games played —first two at middle linebacker, final 10 at SLB — and totaled 56-8-2 with an interception. Was suspended for the Bethune-Cookman contest and did not start against Boston College.

Strengths: Looks the part. Physical tackler. Highly athletic. Fast and rangy — flows laterally and chases sideline to sideline. Willing to take on lead blocks. Drops easily into zone and gets depth. Able to match with tight ends in coverage. Versatile — has played Will, Sam and defensive end. Looked more explosive off the edge as a senior. Uses his arms and hands to press, tug and rip free. Good flexibility and agility to flatten and shows closing burst to the quarterback. Four-down utility and core special-teams potential. Tough, durable, three-year starter. Loves football and works at it.

Weaknesses: Is a bit high-waisted. Average instincts slow his play speed — still developing diagnostic skills. Hesitates to read and react. Can be more physical at the point of attack. Tends to slip or run around blocks. Needs to improve hand use. Does not jolt blockers and too often gets stuck. Short initial steps as a rush end. Could stand to improve pass-rush arsenal. Power element is missing. Average production — does not leave his imprint on enough games.

Future: Chiseled, height-weight-speed see-and-go reactor with intriguing athleticism, versatility and upside who shows in flashes, but leaves evaluators wanting more. Is likely to boost his stock during the pre-draft process, and could warrant consideration from 4-3 teams as a Sam or Will, or from 3-4 teams as a rush linebacker. Play will reach another level if/when his processor speed catches up to his physical talent.

Draft projection: Second- to third-round pick.

Scout's take: "I put him at the top of four because of mental concerns. That's what really bothers me. When he's at linebacker, he has speed and can run and chase. I don't deny that at all. Every time he is forced to read his keys, he is always trailing because he does not locate the ball quickly. If you put him at end with his hand in the dirt, he can use his speed to turn the corner. I don't think he shows up the way you want him to show up. I gave him a late three on size and speed."

ROLB-DRE HOWARD JONES, #7

SHEPHERD   ▶ GRADE: 5.25

Ht: 6-2 1/4 | Wt: 235 | Sp: 4.61 | Arm: 34 1/8 | Hand: 9 1/2

History: Prepped in Virginia. Was a non-qualifier coming out of high school. Did not play in 2008-09. Was recruited as a 187-pound receiver then tried at outside linebacker before settling at defensive end. Started 48 games over four seasons — totaled 39 tackles, 18 for loss and six sacks with two batted passes, two forced fumbles and two blocked kicks in '10 (14 games); 31-23 1/2-12 with an interception, three forced fumbles, two blocked kicks in '11 (11 games); 34-15 1/2-9 in '12 (11 games); and 35-21 1/2-8 with a batted pass and two forced fumbles in '13 (12 games). Owns Shepherd's career sacks record (35).

Strengths: Muscular build with long arms. Intriguing athleticism. Outstanding straight-line speed and leaping ability. Explosive edge burst. Displays good balance, body control and agility as a rusher. Dips inside suddenly. Closes fast and shows striking ability. Flashes power potential. Has special-teams experience. Durable four-year starter.

Weaknesses: Is undersized and vulnerable at the point of attack. Does not set a hard edge. Hand use and pass-rush technique need to be coached up. Tight hips exposed in space — struggles to change direction efficiently or break down to secure 1-on-1 tackles (inconsistent in this area). Tight hips. Green eyes and instincts — does not exhibit a feel for blocking schemes and struggles to locate the ball. Football intelligence is lacking — will require simple assignments.

Future: Lean, explosive, highly athletic rush linebacker prospect who overwhelmed inferior tackles at the Division II level and has clear developmental value and upside potential. Best deployed with pinned ears and see-ball, get-ball instructions, Jones is raw, but has enticing speed and crude pass-rush ability for a patient, positional coach to mold.

Draft projection: Fourth- to fifth-round pick.

ROLB-DRE DEVON KENNARD, #42

USC   ▶ GRADE: 5.10

Ht: 6-3 | Wt: 249 | Sp: 4.69 | Arm: 33 3/8 | Hand: 9 3/8

History: Father, Derek, was an 11-year NFL offensive lineman with the Cardinals, Saints and Cowboys (1986-96). Devon Was a USA Today All-American as an Arizona prep. Tore his right ACL and meniscus as a senior in 2008. Played his first year under then-head coach Pete Carroll and defensive coordinator Rocky Seto — played all 13 games as a true freshman in '09, starting the final four at strong-side linebacker, and recorded 34 tackles, two for loss and zero sacks with three pass breakups and a forced fumble. Had his left thumb surgically repaired prior to '10 spring practice. Played in defensive coordinator Monte Kiffin's scheme in the next three seasons. Played all 13 games in '10, starting the first eight at middle linebacker (lost the job to Chris Galippo), and totaled 72-7-2 with a pass breakup and an interception. Had arthroscopic surgery to repair torn hip cartilage after the season. Moved to defensive end in '11 and split snaps with Wes Horton — started 5-of-12 games and tallied 29-4-2 with a safety. Tore a pectoral muscle during the summer and was sidelined for the '12 season. Deployed as an outside linebacker in defensive coordinator Clancy Pendergast's 3-4 scheme in '13 when he started all 14 games and collected 60-13 1/2-9 with four pass breakups. Team captain had the top GPA on the team, and was honored as USC's Most Inspirational Player and Co-Lifter of the Year.

Strengths: Well-proportioned, muscular build. Generally plays on his feet. Can drop into short zones. Good tackler. Has played outside linebacker, middle linebacker and defensive end. Smart and tough. Team captain with outstanding intangibles, including leadership traits and a professional approach.

Weaknesses: Lacks ideal body length and has small hands. Average athletic ability. Dull get-off. Limited explosion and power. Needs to cultivate pass-rush moves. Does not provide enough resistance against the run. Still developing instincts. Non-explosive athlete with pedestrian agility, as evidenced by poor 30-inch vertical and 7.25-second 3-cone marks.

Future: A well-put-together standup linebacker with NFL bloodlines, Kennard's intangibles outdistance his physical traits, as he lacks the juice to consistently heat up the edge in the pros.

Draft projection: Sixth- to seventh-round pick.

Scout's take: "He's a tweener. He was a part-time starter most of his career. He does not play fast."

WLB CHRISTIAN KIRKSEY, #20

IOWA   ▶ GRADE: 5.20
Ht: 6-1 3/4 | Wt: 233 | Sp: 4.70e | Arm: 32 3/8 | Hand: 9 3/8

History: Linebacker-fullback who won state titles in football and track as a Missouri prep. Saw limited action in 11 games in 2010, scratching six tackles, zero for loss and zero sacks. Did not play against Penn State (concussion) or Missouri in the Insight Bowl (right ankle). Stepped into the lineup in '11, starting all 13 games (first seven at weak-side linebacker, final six at "Leo") — produced 110 tackles, five for loss and a sack with two pass breakups and a forced fumble. Started all

12 at the "Leo" (played the weak side against Michigan) and totaled 95-3 1/2-2 with two pass breakups, two interception touchdowns and a forced fumble. Started all 13 games at "Leo" in '13 and recorded 104-5-2 1/2 with a pass breakup, an interception, two forced fumbles and a fumble return TD. Team captain. Did not run the 40, shuttles or 3-cone drill at the Combine (right hamstring).

Strengths: Agile and athletic. Flows to the ball when he has a clear path. Experience in space and over the slot. Has terrific personal and football character, including leadership traits. Two-time captain. Was a 21-year-old senior.

Weaknesses: Undersized — lacks ideal length and bulk. Looks like a safety at first glance. Outmuscled at the point of attack — gets stuck on blocks and covered up. Average eyes and instincts. Needs to be schemed free as a blitzer. Not a playmaker — just 3.5 sacks and 9.5 TFL in three seasons. Put up 225 pounds just 16 times, second-fewest among linebackers at the Combine.

Future: Small-framed, athletic, finesse, run-around Will linebacker who will have to stand out on special teams to earn a reserve spot.

Draft projection: Fourth- to fifth-round pick.

Scout's take: "I'm not a big fan of his actually. He doesn't run well. He's not very smart. He covers a lot of air. He's mostly a rush guy. He does not drop a lot. He plays in short area. He's a run-and-chase guy."

ROLB-DRE DEMARCUS LAWRENCE, #8 (JUNIOR)

BOISE STATE   ▶ GRADE: 6.10
Ht: 6-2 7/8 | Wt: 251 | Sp: 4.79 | Arm: 33 3/4 | Hand: 11

History: Played defensive end, tight end and offensive tackle as a South Carolina prep. Attended Butler Community College (KS), where he redshirted in 2010 and racked up 66 tackles, 27 for loss and 10 sacks in '11. Committed to Boise State and then-head coach Chris Peterson over offers from South Carolina, Oklahoma, Clemson and Tennessee, among others. Started all 11 games played at defensive end in '12, recording 48-13 1/2-9 1/2 with an interception, four forced fumbles, a blocked kick and a fumble return touchdown. Was suspended against UNLV and Washington (Maaco Bowl). Started all 12 games played at defensive end in '13, amassing 72-20 1/2-10 1/2 with a batted pass, three forced fumbles and two blocked kicks. Was suspended against Tennessee-Martin.

Strengths: Highly athletic. Fluid, flexible and rangy. Has long arms and meat hooks for hands. Terrific balance and body control. Has quick, coordinated hands and feet to slingshot off blocks. Has natural pass-rush ability — shows burst, bend and closing speed to hunt down quarterbacks. Dips inside suddenly. Terrific knee and ankle flexion — flattens efficiently and redirects and accelerates smoothly. Explosive tackler. Made an instant impact at BSU and was productive behind the line of scrimmage — 34 TFL and 20 sacks from 2012-13. Carries a swagger and plays with attitude.

Weaknesses: Could stand to get stronger and play with more pop and power in his hands. Lacks ideal bulk to play with his hand in the dirt. Gets knocked around when he exposes his frame. Doesn't control tight ends. Is weak at the point of attack and gets wiped out by double teams. Can be overaggressive and lose contain or fly by tackles. Can do a better job protecting his legs. Lacks experience playing in reverse. Character and stability need to be looked into.

Future: A loose, explosive, long-limbed athlete, Lawrence consistently pressurizes the edge and harasses quarterbacks. His pass-rushing ability rates among the best in this year's class, and he holds mass appeal. Lacks ideal stoutness at the point of attack, but could thrive as a 4-3 right end or 3-4 rush linebacker, and should contribute readily on passing downs.

Draft projection: Second-round pick.

Scout's take: "Lawrence has flex and bend, but I thought he would run better at the Combine. It could push him to the second (round). ... He looks like one of those old-school Raiders' linebackers. He can dip and rip off the edge. He's one of the best rush guys I have seen."

WLB BOSEKO LOKOMBO, #25

OREGON ▶ GRADE: 5.10

Ht: 6-2 1/8 | Wt: 225 | Sp: 4.66 | Arm: 33 3/8 | Hand: 9 7/8

History: Born in the Congo, moved to Montreal in 1996 and grew up in Abbotsford, British Columbia (Canadian citizen). Redshirted in 2009. Was a reserve/special-teams player his first two seasons. In '10, recorded 36 tackles, two for loss and zero sacks with three pass breakups and a fumble recovery touchdown in 13 games. In '11, tallied 33-3 1/2-2 with three pass breakups, two interception touchdowns and a forced fumble in 14 games. Started all 13 games at strong-side linebacker in '12, producing 39-4 1/2-2 with four pass breakups, two interceptions and a forced fumble. Started 11-of-13 games at SLB in '13, posting 63-7-3 with a pass breakup, an interception and a forced fumble. Was benched against Washington State and UCLA in favor of sophomore Tyson Coleman. Did not bench press or do the vertical jump at the Combine because of a torn left labrum (medical exclusion). Was drafted by the BC Lions in the third round of the '13 CFL draft after he was rated the No. 1 overall prospect according to the CFL Scouting Bureau.

Strengths: Flexible, loose-hipped athlete with

fluid movement skills. Good closing speed. Is agile and athletic enough to match up with tight ends, backs and even some slot receivers. Can buzz the flat and deter throws with closing speed. Shows good zone awareness moving forward and will deliver some jarring hits to intimidate crossers. Solid press-cover skills. Times the blitz well. Has all the athletic tools to become a solid special-teams contributor.

Weaknesses: Just a two-year starter and instincts are still developing — does not trigger quickly to what he sees and could take some time to assimilate a complex playbook. Lacks throwback linebacker toughness and functional playing strength. Often gets locked down once blockers get their hands on him. Can do a better job shedding blocks. Plays a bit recklessly and could do a better job wrapping up as a tackler. Was not an impactful special-teams performer.

Future: A run-and-chase, strong-side linebacker with speed that could easily be utilized on the weak side or allow him to develop as a nickel-cover linebacker. Does not possess ideal toughness or instincts for special teams. Canadian-born prospect could be most highly coveted by the CFL.

Draft projection: Late draftable pick.

Scout's take: "If he were tough, he absolutely gets drafted. He's just not a football player. (The coaches) have been trying to get it out of him his whole career. It's hit or miss and there is no way to measure it. Sometimes the pebbles drop, but the arrow is not pointing that way. He is smart. He's a good kid. I just don't know if it's in him. You have to be mentally tough to play in our league."

ROLB-DRE-ILB KHALIL MACK, #46

BUFFALO ▶ GRADE: 7.20

Ht: 6-2 5/8 | Wt: 251 | Sp: 4.64 | Arm: 33 1/4 | Hand: 10 1/4

History: Prepped in Florida, where he was primarily a basketball player until his senior year — Buffalo was only FBS offer. Tore his patellar tendon as an underclassman. Redshirted in 2009. Played outside linebacker in a 3-4 for the Bulls, and started all 48 games he played. In '10, played 12 games and recorded 68 tackles, 14 1/2 for loss and 4 1/2 sacks with 10 pass breakups and two forced fumbles. Tallied 65-20 1/2-5 1/2 with two pass breakups, an interception and five forced fumbles. Was suspended for the '12 season opener against Georgia after he got into a fight with a teammate. On the season, totaled 94-21-8 with two pass breakups and four forced fumbles in 12 games. Was a Butkus Award finalist in '13 when he led the Bulls in tackling for the second year in a row in '13 — registered 100-19-10 1/2 with seven pass breakups, three interceptions (two touchdowns) and five forced fumbles in 13 games. Team captain. Three-time first-team all Mid-American Conference.

Strengths: Disruptive first-step quickness — immediately re-creates the line of scrimmage and plays in the backfield (record tackle-for-loss production). Outstanding instincts — locates the ball quickly and is around the ball a lot. Very good body control, bend and balance — plays on his feet and is seldom on the ground. Developed pass-rush moves (rip, dip and inside counter). Very explosive — broad jumped 10 feet, 8 inches and boasts a rare 40-inch vertical.. Excellent pursuit — tracks down ball carriers from behind. Sacrifices his body and sells out around piles. Strikes with authority — hits on the rise, violently jars ball carriers backward on impact and has a knack for dislodging the ball. Highly motivated. Played big vs. better competition (see Ohio State). Can zone drop and buzz to the flat with ease. Highly competitive and energetic. Regularly was the focus of defensive game plans and still produced despite facing multiple blockers and extra protection consistently rolled his way.

Weaknesses: Produced nondescript performance with a MAC title game berth on the line vs. Bowling Green and regularly faced inferior MAC competition. Plays a bit too recklessly and out of control. Can learn to run the arc with better lean.

Future: A havoc-wreaking rush linebacker with the burst and acceleration to excel as a right defensive end in a "40" front, Mack has demonstrated the instincts, toughness, athletic ability and explosive power to line up at any linebacker position in an even or odd front and factor readily. Is a four-year starter who made an immediate impact upon his arrival and is well primed for the NFL game. Looks every bit the part, comes from a humble, grounded family and offers the full package to become an impact performer in the pros.

Draft projection: Top-10 pick.

Scout's take: "Khalil Mack is a beast. He plays like King Kong. He sets the edge and locks out. He has the L.T. (Lawrence Taylor) cut. He is L.T. ... Even if he's facing lesser competition, he was a dominant player this year. I've never seen a guy more accounted for every play at the college level. They do everything to block that guy. There are times when he has three guys assigned to him and he's still making plays."

LOLB-DLE CASSIUS MARSH, #99

UCLA   ▶ GRADE: 5.37

Ht: 6-4 | Wt: 252 | Sp: 4.89 | Arm: 32 3/4 | Hand: 9 1/2

History: Father, Curtis Sr., was a receiver who played 15 games with the Jaguars and Steelers (1995-97), and brother, Curtis, is a cornerback with the Eagles. Raised by single mother and prepped at Westlake Village (CA) Oaks Christian. Originally committed to LSU, but switched to UCLA to remain close to home. As a true freshman in 2010 (wore jersey No. 71), played 12 games, starting four at defensive tackle, and recorded 23 tackles, one-half for loss and zero sacks with a batted pass. Started 8-of-12 games in '11 (wore jersey No. 3), tallying 22-4-2. Was suspended against California and Arizona State for his role in an on-field brawl against Arizona. Was deployed as a 3-4 five-technique his final two seasons. Started all 14 games in '12 and totaled 50-10 1/2-8 with two batted passes, two forced fumbles and two blocked kicks. Also caught a touchdown pass as a tight end. Was benched against Stanford after he was ejected from the Cal contest — was called for offside penalties on consecutive plays, then threw a punch (mid-play) in response to a Cal blocker extending a high, two-handed punch to Marsh's head off the snap. Pulled out of the East-West Shrine Game after hurting his wrist in practice. Was nearly 300 pounds as a freshman, but played in the 260s as an upperclassman.

Strengths: Outstanding effort and field energy. Good pursuit production — flattens and chases. Plays past the whistle and keeps working to come free. Sacrifices his body around piles. Flushes production to teammates. Flashes strength and power on the edge. Uses his hands well to control and shed blockers. Emotional leader — plays with intensity. Tough and durable. Has NFL pedigree (father and brother). Versatile — lines up inside and outside. Has contributed as a tight end.

Weaknesses: Lacks ideal foot speed to outquick left tackles. Could stand to improve weight-room strength and functional core strength. Is tightly wound and will rise out of his stance and play tall. Can be overly emotional, lose focus and play undisciplined (too many errors). Managed just 14 bench-press reps, fewest among defensive lineman and linebackers at the Combine. Will require a strong positional coach.

Future: Very active, high-motor, steady, consistent producer. Lacks ideal bulk for the inside and speed to work the edges, but can set the edge and bring value to an odd front in a LOLB role or as a Sam linebacker. Is most natural moving forward piercing gaps. Will need to be managed, needs to cut down on errors and must learn to play within the structure of the defense.

Draft projection: Fourth- to fifth-round pick.

Scout's take: "I didn't like the way he left the Shrine game. He said he hurt his wrist, but he never got treatment. He has all the tats and is not a well-structured guy. There's little definition in his body. I was disappointed in person after liking some things he did on tape."

MLB JAMES MORRIS, #44

IOWA ▶ GRADE: 5.20

Ht: 6-0 7/8 | Wt: 241 | Sp: 4.79 | Arm: 30 3/4 | Hand: 9 1/8

History: High school linebacker-running back who won three state titles and was Iowa's Gatorade Player of the Year twice. Played all 13 games as a true freshman in 2010, starting the final six at middle linebacker, and recorded 70 tackles, 2 1/2 for loss and a sack with four pass breakups. Started all 12 games in '11 — six at MLB, six at weak-side linebacker — and led Hawkeye tacklers by posting 110-3 1/2-0 with a pass breakup and an interception. Did not play against Northwestern (left ankle). Played through a pre-season groin injury in '12 when he started 11-of-12 games played at MLB. Hurt his right elbow against Purdue and did not start against Michigan. Started all 13 games at MLB in '13, registering 106-17-7 with three pass breakups, four interceptions and two forced fumbles. Two-time captain.

Strengths: Good eyes, instincts and motor — is around the ball a lot. Plays with a good base and does not cross his feet. Understands run fits. Clings to receivers passing through his zone. Urgent buzzing to the flat. Very tough and durable — will play through pain. Experienced, three-and-a-half-year starter. Very strong personal and football character. Accountable. Team leader. Extremely competitive. Outstanding weight-room explosion — can power-clean nearly 400 pounds.

Weaknesses: Very stiff-hipped and short-armed. Has short arms and pedestrian strength (18 bench-press reps). Tends to play tall, get caught up in traffic and engulfed at the point of attack. Much of production comes moving laterally down the field. Does not drive his legs through contact and tackles low. Average functional strength and explosion. Marginal playing range. Tends to overrun the ball. Limited closing speed. Gives up separation in man coverage and struggles carrying crossers or keeping stride with backs and tight ends. Late to arrive on blitz assignments and gets knocked off path. Does not play on special teams.

Future: A disciplined, football-smart, 4-3 Mike linebacker with the toughness, discipline and determination desired in a core special-teams player. Athletic limitations could force him to earn his way as a backup.

Draft projection: Late draftable pick.

Scout's take: "I love his production. What you see is what you get. He'll show guys the way. ... He could be a teamer for a long time."

ILB C.J. MOSLEY, #32

ALABAMA ▶ GRADE: 6.40

Ht: 6-2 | Wt: 234 | Sp: 4.66| Arm: 33 3/8 | Hand: 10 3/4

History: Alabama native amassed over 500 tackles in his high school career, garnering Parade All-American honors as a senior. Started all 13 games as a true freshman, starting three at "Mike" (strong inside) linebacker, and recorded 69 tackles, 1 1/2-1/2 with 10 pass breakups and two interception touchdowns. Started 6-of-11 games played at weak inside linebacker in '11 and tallied 37-4 1/2-2 with two pass breakups and an interception. Dislocated his right elbow against Arkansas and sat out against Florida and Vanderbilt. Played all 14 games in '12, starting nine as the Tide's "Will" 'backer in sub-packages, and produced 107-8-4 with two pass breakups, two interceptions and a forced fumble. Suffered a dislocated hip in the BCS Championship against LSU, then had off-season shoulder surgery to repair a torn right labrum. Won the Butkus Award (nation's top linebacker) and was the Southeastern Conference Defensive Player of the Year (coaches) in '13 — started all 13 games at weak inside linebacker and was Alabama's leading tackler for the second consecutive season, racking up 108-9-0 with five pass breakups and a forced fumble. Also was a finalist for the Lombardi and Nagurski awards. Team captain won a pair of national championships. Did not bench press or run the 40-yard dash at the Combine because of a right shoulder injury.

Strengths: Exceptional instincts — triggers fast downhill. Outstanding urgency. Plays with very good knee bend, balance and base. Secure, drive-through tackler. Hits with explosion and jars ball carriers on impact. Excellent lateral agility — flows fast and ranges to the sideline. Exceptional weight-room worker with good functional play strength — plays bigger than his size. Outstanding eyes and anticipation vs. the run. Very good coverage awareness with the ball in front of him — clings to tight ends passing through zones and blankets speed backs in man coverage. Respected leadership presence — lines up his teammates and directs traffic. Film junkie. Excellent attitude, effort, field intensity and overall energy. Exceptional football and personal character. Highly competitive. Humble, selfless team player. Outstanding football IQ. Scheme-diverse and versatile. Strong special-teams coverage performer.

Weaknesses: Has a narrow build. Has been slowed by elbow, hip and shoulder injuries throughout his career and long-term durability will require thorough inspection by medical examiners. Gets hung up on the blitz (shoulder stiffness) and must learn how to use more finesse picking a side instead of relying on bull power and striking blockers down the middle. Can learn to do a better job shooting his hands to shock defenders and disengage from blocks. Could be challenged matching up down the field with his back to the ball vs. flex TEs in the slot (man coverage). Could stand to become a more vocal leader.

Future: Smart, instinctive, fast-flowing, every-down linebacker capable of manning any position in a "40" front or steering a defense from the weak side in a "30" front, where he starred for a national-championship defense as a junior and carried the Tide as a senior. Has the football temperament, desire and work habits to emerge as a tackling machine in the pros. Has Pro Bowl potential.

Draft projection: First-round pick.

Scout's take: "He's very easy on the eyes. He is all over the field. ...I'm not sure he has quite the foot speed or snap I was expecting. He's not the most physical guy either. He needs to be protected. He reminds me a lot of DeMeco Ryans, who was not an elite athlete either."

ROLB-DLE TRENT MURPHY, #93

STANFORD   ▶ GRADE: 5.65

Ht: 6-5 3/8 | Wt: 250 | Sp: 4.86 | Arm: 33 7/8 | Hand: 11 1/8

History: High school defensive end-tight end who also played basketball and ran track as a prep in Arizona, where he won a state championship. Redshirted in 2009. Appeared in two games in '10 and scratched two tackles, one for loss and one sack before a broken foot sidelined him. In '11, started all 13 games at outside linebacker in the Cardinal's 3-4, tallying 40-10-6 1/2 with a pass breakup. Started all 14 games at OLB in '12 and totaled 56-18-10 with four pass breakups, an interception and a forced fumble. Led the nation in sacks in '13 when he started all 14 games at OLB and registered 62-23 1/2-15 with six pass breakups, an interception touchdown, two forced fumbles and a blocked kick. Also was used with his hand in the dirt in nickel. Team captain.

Strengths: Naturally big-boned with a good frame to add bulk if desired. Very good instincts. Above-average athlete — bends fairly well. Massive mitts (11-plus) measured bigger than any other player at the Combine. Good hand use — can jolt blockers with his punch. Controls the line of scrimmage and consistently outleverages tight ends. Very physical re-routing tight ends at the line. Outstanding motor and sack production — led the country in sacks (15) as a senior. Tough, smart and hardworking with a throwback personality. Leader vocally and by example. Will hold teammates accountable and represent the program with class.

Weaknesses: Very average weight-room strength. Underdeveloped upper body. Can be folded and neutralized by down blocks against more physical blockers (see Notre Dame). Cannot square up and play honest vs. top power. Has coverage limitations — is tight and late to transition. More natural moving forward than in reverse. Coverage limitations show up vs. backs. Can be stressed vs. speed in the open

field.

Future: As a base end in an even front or a LOLB in an odd front, Murphy's instincts, motor and toughness are what define his success and could allow him to eventually become a double-digit sack producer in the pros. Will require a few years to adapt to the speed of the NFL game.

Draft projection: Second- to third-round pick.

Scout's take: "He is solid. He is a fourth-rounder to me. You know who he is. He is a poor man's Jared Allen. They both had about the same sack production coming out. Jared Allen ran a 4.75. Murphy ran a little worse — he's not as fast. Both are not superstrong but have a knack for rushing the passer. Jared only had 13 reps on the bench. This kid had 22, and is a little naturally bigger and stronger. They are very similar. Both are very productive, understand angles and can come underneath blocks. Someone might take Murphy higher as a 3-4 rush guy, a Pittsburgh or Baltimore. I am not sure he can be that guy. I think he's going to be best as a base defensive end."

ROLB-DRE JONATHAN NEWSOME, #11

BALL STATE   ▶ GRADE: 5.17

Ht: 6-2 5/8 | Wt: 247 | Sp: 4.73 | Arm: 33 1/4 | Hand: 9 5/8

History: Prepped at Glenville High in Ohio, where he played for Ted Ginn Sr. Began his college career at Ohio State, where he played five games as a true freshman in 2009 (wore jersey No. 55) and recorded five tackles, zero for loss and zero sacks. Appeared in all 13 games in '10 (one start as an injury replacement) and was credited with 15-0-0 with a blocked kick. Did not keep up academically (sat out '11 spring practice) or climb the depth chart at OSU. Transferred and sat out '11 per NCAA rules. Was arrested twice in August '12 — for shoplifting male enhancement pills and for marijuana possession. Served a two-game suspension before starting all 11 games played at right defensive end and notching 52-12 1/2-8 1/2 with a batted pass. Started 11-of-12 games played in '13, tallying 64-11 1/2-8 with a batted pass, an interception and two forced fumbles. Did not play against Army or start against North Texas (ankle).

Strengths: Very good edge burst. Has a long second step and attacks the edges with speed and leverage. Flattens down the line — good lateral pursuit. Can get depth in coverage and spot drop. Flashes explosive striking ability as a tackler.

Weaknesses: Strength-deficient and gets hammered in the box. Thin-legged and narrow-based. Too light to set the edge. Limited cover skills — is tight in the hips and not natural moving in reverse or coming out of breaks.

Immature early in college career.

Future: A 4-3 open-side speed rusher ideally suited for an elephant end or 3-4 Jack linebacker role. Is at his best rushing the passer and has shown improved maturity since departing Ohio State before the 2011 season.

Draft projection: Fifth- to sixth-round pick.

WLB-SS KEVIN PIERRE-LOUIS, #24

BOSTON COLLEGE ▶ GRADE: 5.10
Ht: 6-0 | Wt: 232 | Sp: 4.51 | Arm: 32 1/4 | Hand: 10 1/8

History: Was Connecticut's Gatorade Player of the Year. Also played basketball and lacrosse. Played the weak side his first three seasons. As a true freshman in 2010, started all 13 games and produced 93 tackles, 2 1/2 for loss and zero sacks with three pass breakups. Started all nine games played in '11 and notched 74-6-0 with four pass breakups and a forced fumble. Missed three games while nursing a high right ankle sprain. Started all nine games played in '12 and collected 85-4-2 with three pass breakups. Missed three games after pulling his right quad. Moved to the strong side in '13 when he started all 13 games and registered 108-10.5-6 with an interception.

Strengths: Tight-skinned, muscular build. Big hands. Athletic knee-bender. Flows well laterally. Protects his legs and slips blocks. Motivated and hardworking. Productive four-year starter. Combine all-star put on a show in Indianapolis — ran in the low 4.5s, pumped 28 bench-press reps, posted a 39-inch vertical, recorded a 10-foot, 8-inch broad jump, finished the short shuttle in 4.02 seconds and ran a 6.92-second 3-cone drill.

Weaknesses: Needs to improve functional strength. Average eyes and diagnostic skills. Loses sight of the ball, gets sucked in by playaction and takes false steps. Gets knocked out of the hole at the point of attack. Stays wired to blocks. Has man-cover limitations. Has tweener traits — lacks ideal bulk for linebacker and speed for safety.

Future: Small-framed, experienced, productive, finesse weak-side linebacker who has bulked up 15-20 pounds in the last year. Helped himself with an outstanding Combine performance, and is best-suited in a fast-flow scheme in which he can utilize his athleticism to run and hit. Has traits to be used on special teams and develop as a nickel linebacker.

Draft projection: Late draftable pick.

ROLB-DRE RONALD POWELL, #7 (JUNIOR)

FLORIDA ▶ GRADE: 5.35
Ht: 6-3 1/8 | Wt: 237 | Sp: 4.66 | Arm: 32 1/2 | Hand: 9 3/8

History: Consensus No. 1 defensive end recruit in the nation coming out of California. Played all 13 games as a true freshman in 2010 (one start at strong-side linebacker) and tallied 26 tackles, three for loss and a sack with two pass breakups. Started 12 games at the "Buck" (hybrid defensive end/linebacker) in '11 and totaled 32-9-6 with a forced fumble. Suffered an upper-body injury against LSU and sat out against Auburn. Sat out the '12 season when he tore his left ACL twice. Started 8-of-11 games played in '13 — six at the "Buck," two at "Sam" — and managed 26-7-4. Did not start against Tennessee, then sprained his ankle against LSU, which kept him out of the Missouri contest and kept him out of the starting lineup against Georgia and Vanderbilt. Strained his left hamstring running the 40-yard dash at the Combine and did not participate in drills or run shuttles and the 3-cone drill.

Strengths: Looks the part — well-proportioned, athletic, muscular build. Natural bender. Terrific agility. Can stunt and loop. Closes fast. Flashes strong hands and power potential. Loose hips to zone drop. Was deployed as a stand-up linebacker and hand-in-the-dirt rush end. Has untapped potential.

Weaknesses: Inconsistent get-off. Average eyes and instincts — has to see it before he triggers. Shoddy edge setter. Plays short-armed, gets locked up and allows linemen to capture his outside shoulder. Aimless, unrefined pass rusher. Intensity and urgency leave something to be desired. Has coasted on natural talent. Had his tires pumped since high school — entitlement was an issue as a young player and his personality could rub some people the wrong way. Injury history.

Future: Powell is a physically gifted, inconsistent, college "Buck" (hybrid defensive end/outside linebacker) with crude strength and athleticism. Has developmental value as a stand-up rush linebacker, but must dedicate himself to the craft and realize he's no longer the big man on campus.

Draft projection: Third- to fourth-round pick.

Scout's take: "I just finished him. I put him in the fifth (round). He's intriguing because he plays some linebacker. He's coming off double-knee surgeries. He's not truly explosive but he has some power, which is what I liked. He's athletic enough to drop, but his value is moving forward."

SLB-DRE TREVOR REILLY, #9

UTAH ▶ GRADE: 5.35
Ht: 6-4 3/4 | Wt: 245 | Sp: 4.65e | Arm: 32 1/4 | Hand: 9 1/2

History: Married with two daughters — youngest, Shayn, was diagnosed with kidney cancer just prior to the 2013 season. Trevor was a high school linebacker-tight end who also played basketball and volleyball as a prep. Served a two-year LDS mission in Sweden before joining the Utes and redshirting in 2009. Appeared in 11 games in '10, tallying

19 tackles, 5 1/2 for loss and two sacks with a pass breakup. Sat out two games while nursing a high right ankle sprain. Started 7-of-13 games in '11 — five at the "Stud" linebacker, two at left end — and recorded 47-9-5 with two pass breakups and four forced fumbles. Played the '12 season on a torn right ACL and meniscus — started all 12 games (eight at "Stud," four at right end) and contributed 69-6 1/2-4 1/2 with three pass breakups, an interception and three forced fumbles. Was the Utes' leading tackler in '13 when he started all 12 games — eight at RDE, two at "Stud," one at Rover, one at middle linebacker — and notched 100-16-8 1/2 with a pass breakup, an interception and a forced fumble. Team captain. Was a medical exclusion at the Combine (right knee).

Strengths: Very solidly built frame. Good functional playing strength to beat blocks and defend the run. Locates the ball quickly and is around it a lot. Crashes the line hard and plays with energy. Flashes shock in his punch. Fine arm-under move to come underneath blockers and work the edges. Can control and disrupt tight ends. Takes good angles. Solid tackler. Ultra-tough, mentally and physically (played through ACL injury as a junior). Extremely competitive. Very good football intelligence — can line up a defense. Versatile — has played every LB position and can interchange with ease. Respected tone-setter. Outstanding work ethic. Identifies with the game. Ultra-competitive.

Weaknesses: Average athletic ability and lateral agility. Can be stymied by power. Stiff-hipped and robotic moving in reverse. Has limitations in man coverage and can be mismatched by athletic tight ends. Wore a brace on his right knee and plant strength did not appear at full strength. Had arthroscopic surgery on the knee following the season and will require closer medical evaluation. Overaged — will be a 26-year-old rookie.

Future: A country-strong, throwback, wrangler cowboy with the toughness desired to set the edge and the motor, intensity and competitiveness to produce effort sacks. Can factor as a 3-4 rush linebacker in an odd front or match up with tight ends as a strong-side linebacker in an even front. Could contribute readily as a situational rusher and, with continued strength gains, emerge as a DE prospect. Versatility is a plus.

Draft projection: Fourth- to fifth-round pick.

Scout's take: "He played more end this year. You have to go back to last year to see him at linebacker more. I love his motor."

ROLB-DRE MICHAEL SAM, #52
MISSOURI   ▶ GRADE: 5.09
Ht: 6-2 | Wt: 261 | Sp: 4.91 | Arm: 33 3/8 | Hand: 9 3/8

History: Also lettered in track and powerlifting as a Texas prep. Redshirted in 2009. Played all 13 games in '10 (one start) and tallied 24 tackles, seven for loss and 3 1/2 for sacks with an interception and a forced fumble. Played all 13 games in '11 (one start) and collected 29-3-1-1 1/2 with an interception. Started 9-of-12 games in '12 and was credited with 22-7-4 1/2 with two forced fumbles. Did not start against Central Florida, Vanderbilt and Alabama. Was the Southeastern Conference Defensive Player of the Year (AP) in '13 when he started all 14 games and registered 48-19-11 1/2 with two batted passes and two forced fumbles. Would be the first openly gay active player in NFL history — came out to his teammates in August, then announced his sexuality publicly prior to the Combine.

Strengths: Good arm length. Anticipates the snap and has a very good initial first step. Plays hard — gives great effort and competes every down. Good on-field intensity and demeanor. Attacks the edges aggressively and motor runs hot. Outstanding weight-room strength — can squat a small house. Very durable.

Weaknesses: Lacks burst and acceleration off the edge to get a step on blockers and finish. Sack production results from effort and production flushed to him and is not creatively produced with savvy pass-rush moves, speed, power or bend. Average hip flexibility and snap — struggles clearing his hips at the top of his rush and trimming the corner. Adequate anchor vs. the run. Is late to disengage from blocks. Does not strike with authority. Inconsistent tackler. Late bloomer who could require time to adapt to the pro game. Poor Combine showing — bench-pressed 225 pounds just 17 times, recorded a 7.8-second 3-cone drill and posted an abysmal 25 1/2-inch vertical jump.

Future: A productive, 4-3 weakside rusher who came on as a senior and it made his last season his best. Could fit most ideally as a 3-4 outside linebacker in a zone-blitzing scheme like the Steelers or Ravens.

Draft projection: Priority free agent.

Scout's take: "I didn't like that undersized defensive end, No. 52. He is just a guy. All his production comes against inferior opponents. He can't anchor or get off blocks. He's stiff and needs reps. He's a straight-line edge guy. He can't set the edge. You'd like to see him do more vs. meaty competition."

WLB RYAN SHAZIER, #2 (JUNIOR)
OHIO STATE   ▶ GRADE: 6.27
Ht: 6-1 1/8 | Wt: 237 | Sp: 4.38 | Arm: 32 3/8 | Hand: 10

History: Prepped in Florida. Originally committed to play for Urban Meyer at Florida, but Meyer resigned. Shazier then signed to play for Jim Tressel at Ohio State, but Tressel resigned five months later. Wound up playing for Luke Fickell for a season, then reunited with Meyer his final two seasons in Columbus. Played all 13 games in 2011, starting the final two at weak-side linebacker, and recorded 57 tackles, five for loss and three sacks with two forced tackles and a blocked kick. Started all 12 games played at WLB in '12, registering 115-17-5 with 11 pass breakups, an interception touchdown and three forced fumbles. Was a Butkus Award finalist in '13 after he led the Big Ten in tackles and tackles for loss — started all 13 games at WLB and racked up 134-22 1/2-6 with four pass breakups and four forced fumbles. Team captain joined James Laurinaitis, A.J. Hawk, Chris Spielman and Pepper Johnson as Buckeye linebackers to lead the team in tackles two consecutive seasons. Did not run or work out at the Combine (left hamstring).

Strengths: Highly productive, disruptive playmaker vs. the run and pass. Shoots gaps and plays behind the line of scrimmage (compiled 39.5 TFL the last two seasons). Agile to slip blocks. Quick, strong hands to shed. Knifes gaps and flows very well laterally. Striking tackler — uncoils on contact. Excellent speed and range — opens up his stride in space and really covers ground. Bends naturally. Changes direction and accelerates with ease. Explosive first step as a pass rusher — shows the ability to dip, bend and run the arc low to the ground. Ample athleticism and flexibility to mark backs and tight ends. Led all players at the Combine with a 42-inch vertical jump and blazed a sub-4.4 40 time at his pro day. Four-down utility. Arrow is pointing up.

Weaknesses: Lacks ideal size and bulk. Still developing eyes and instincts — will diagnose and trigger more quickly down the road. Gets caught in traffic or engulfed by larger blockers when he hesitates to step downhill. Prone to overaggressiveness — occasionally overruns plays or loses cutback contain. Could stand to improve his eyes, awareness, anticipation and reactions as a zone defender. Took some time to acclimate before making an impact.

Future: The Big Ten's leading tackler, Shazier flies around the field and his unique athletic ability stands out. Offers a tremendous combination of speed, tackling and coverage skills to become a playmaker as a run-and-hit 4-3 Will or perhaps a 3-4 weakside 'backer if protected by a block-occupying nose tackle. Value is increased by the fact that he will not have to come off the field.

Draft projection: First-round pick.

Scout's take: "He can fly. Everyone was enamored with (Alec) Ogletree's speed last year. Shazier is as advertised."

ROLB PRINCE SHEMBO, #55

NOTRE DAME ▶ GRADE: 5.32

Ht: 6-1 3/8 | Wt: 253 | Sp: 4.71 | Arm: 33 1/8 | Hand: 10 1/2

History: Father immigrated to the United States from the Congo in 1986. Prince also played basketball and ran track as a North Carolina prep. Ankle injury limited him to five games his senior season. Appeared in all 13 games as a true freshman in 2010 and collected 15 tackles, five for loss and 4 1/2 sacks with a forced fumble. Started 8-of-12 games played in '11 (seven at 3-4 outside linebacker, one at defensive end) and tallied 31-3 1/2-2. Missed the Michigan State game after his father, who was in town for the game, suffered a brain aneurysm. Left turf toe injury required surgery, sidelining him during '12 spring practice. In the fall, started all 13 games at OLB and produced 51-10 1/2-7 1/2 with a pass breakup. Started all 13 games at OLB and totaled 48-5 1/2-5 1/2. Acknowledged at the Combine that he was the player linked to an alleged sexual assault in a dorm room made by a former Saint Mary's College student who committed suicide 10 days later. Shembo was never charged in connection with the incident.

Strengths: Large hands. Good balance and knee bend. Strong and physical — can stuff tight ends and is surprisingly robust at the point of attack. Outstanding leaping ability — boasts a 38 1/2-inch vertical. Flows laterally and pursues to the boundary. Strong tackler. Flashes power-leverage potential. Effective stunting and looping. Operated from 2- and 3-point stance and played on special teams.

Weaknesses: Lacks ideal body length, elite flexibility and closing speed. Average eyes and instincts (see-and-go reactor). Can improve hand use. Hip tightness shows in space and when required to drop into coverage.

Future: Thickly built, high-motor, highly competitive edge defender who projects best as a left outside linebacker in a 3-4 scheme. Lacks desirable dimensions, flexibility and finishing speed, but has more than enough play strength, tenacity and toughness to compensate.

Draft projection: Fourth- to fifth-round pick.

MLB SHAYNE SKOV, #11

STANFORD ▶ GRADE: 5.40

Ht: 6-2 1/4 | Wt: 245 | Sp: 4.95e | Arm: 30 5/8 | Hand: 10

History: Highly recruited out of New York, where he also lettered in basketball and track and field. Played all 13 games as a true freshman in 2009, starting the final seven at Will linebacker, and recorded 62 tackles, three for loss and zero sacks with a pass breakup. In '10, moved to inside linebacker in the Cardinal's 3-4 scheme and was the leading tackler — posted 84-10 1/2-7 1/2 with five pass breakups and two forced fumbles. Missed the first two games of the season while nursing a bursa sac injury. In '11, managed 19-5-1 1/2 with a pass breakup in three starts before tearing his ACL and MCL and breaking the tibia in his left leg (required three surgeries). Was arrested for DUI in February '12 and was suspended for the season opener against San Jose State. On the season, started all 13 games at ILB and totaled 81-9-2 1/2 with a pass breakup. Was a Butkus Award finalist and the Cardinals' leading tackler for the third time in '13 when he started all 14 games and registered 109-13-5 1/2 with four pass breakups and three forced fumbles. Team captain. Was medically excluded at the Combine (left calf).

Strengths: Outstanding instincts and recognition — plays much faster than he clocks on a stopwatch. Goes full throttle and plays very hard. Times up the blitz extremely well. Explosive tackler. Alert in coverage. Intense emotional leader. Vocal leader. Has a love for the game and it shows. Ideal special-teams temperament. Fluent in Spanish.

Weaknesses: Marginal foot speed — limited twitch and agility to adjust to movement in coverage and could be exposed by NFL backs and tight ends (though still does not look fully recovered from ACL injury). Has very short arms. Can play with too much abandon and recklessly miss some tackles flying to the ball (out of control). Long-term durability is a concern — has already had multiple knee surgeries.

Future: A ballhawking, two-down Mike linebacker with a natural feel for the game, Skov has still not returned to pre-injury form and does not have full plant strength in his knee.

Draft projection: Third- to fourth-round pick.

Scout's take: "I'm not a Skov fan. He can't run. He can't take on or get off blocks. He's a scheme guy. I think his impact at our level will be minimal at best. There are not a lot of 5-flat linebackers playing in the league right now."

MLB YAWIN SMALLWOOD, #33

CONNECTICUT ▶ GRADE: 5.22

Ht: 6-2 1/4 | Wt: 246 | Sp: 5.01 | Arm: 31 3/4 | Hand: 9 1/2

History: Strong safety-option quarterback who also played basketball as a Massachusetts prep. Redshirted in 2010. Started all 36 games of his career at middle linebacker, pacing UCONN tacklers his final two seasons — totaled 94 tackles, 2 1/2 for loss and 1 1/2 sacks with three pass breakups, an interception, a forced fumble and a fumble return touchdown in '11; 120-15-4 with four pass breakups and two forced fumbles in '12; and 118-9 1/2-4 with nine pass breakups, an interception TD and two forced fumbles in '13. Team captain. Strained his left hamstring running the 40-yard dash at the Combine.

Strengths: Good size, acceleration and straight-line speed. Plays on his feet and sidesteps blocks. Gets depth in his zone drops and keeps pace with backs in coverage. Highly productive three-year starter. Respected, coachable team captain. Very good leaping ability (36 1/2-inch vertical).

Weaknesses: Average eyes and instincts. Does not use his hands violently to take on and discard blocks. Shows some lower-body stiffness. Dull lateral agility. Does not play downhill and can be a step late to the perimeter. Inconsistent run fits and tackling — too often fails to wrap and drive through ball carriers.

Future: Productive college middle linebacker at his best when he's kept clean or has a clear path. Projects best in a 4-3, where he has enough athleticism and functionality in coverage to play in the middle. Has starter-caliber potential, but might be the type you look to replace.

Draft projection: Late draftable pick.

Scout's take: "He's overrated."

WLB TELVIN SMITH, #22

FLORIDA STATE ▶ GRADE: 5.38

Ht: 6-3 | Wt: 218 | Sp: 4.52 | Arm: 32 1/2 | Hand: 10 1/4

History: Prepped in Georgia, where he won a state championship. Appeared in all 14 games as a true freshman in 2010, recording 18 tackles, three for loss and three sacks with a pass breakup. Played 13 games in '11, starting one at weakside linebacker as an injury replacement, and tallied 42-8 1/2-3 with three pass breakups, an interception and a forced fumble. Served a one-game suspension against Charleston Southern (undisclosed). Did not crack the starting lineup in '12, but split time with middle linebacker Vince Williams and contributed 64-9 1/2-1 with three pass breakups and a forced fumble in 14 games. Was the Seminoles' leading tackler in '13 when he started all 14 games at WLB and registered 9-9 1/2-2 with four pass breakups and three interceptions (two touchdowns) for the national champs. Did not bench press at the Combine (right shoulder).

Strengths: Fiery on-field emotional leader. Plays with passion and it shows — beelines to the ball and brings energy to the defense. Very good eyes, anticipation and instincts — sniffs out screens, takes good cut-off angles and negotiates through traffic easily. Plays downhill and often arrives behind the line of scrimmage before ball carriers see him. Outstanding functional football-playing speed. Fluid mover. Outstanding closing speed to the ball. Reliable open-field tackler — runs through contact. Good coverage skill — shadows receivers and has a feel for zones. Very likeable, gregarious personality that can unite a locker room and command the LB group. Has been very durable (despite lack of thickness). Has learned what it means to work, and football comes easy to him.

Weaknesses: Despite contributing immediately in college, has been only a one-year full-time starter. Wiry and needs to add bulk to his narrow frame to withstand the rigors of NFL contact — is almost built like a free safety. Is not a strong, drive-through tackler — tends to go low. Average hand use and play strength. Could struggle matching up with bigger, more physical tight ends.

Future: A fast-flowing, instinctive, run-and-hit weakside linebacker capable of producing at a high level if he can bulk up and withstand the rigors of the NFL. Has all-pro potential in a scheme such as the Buccaneers or Cowboys.

Draft projection: Fourth- to fifth-round pick.

Scout's take: "My problem with him is that he's just light in the (butt). I don't know what you do with him. I like him as a football player. I put him in the fourth (round). Some will put him lower. I didn't hear of any having him earlier. He is tall, but he was playing games in the 212-217 range. That will turn a lot of people off."

SLB TYLER STARR, #11
SOUTH DAKOTA   ▶ GRADE: 5.00
Ht: 6-4 1/8 | Wt: 250 | Sp: 4.94 | Arm: 32 1/2 | Hand: 9 1/2

History: Engaged with a son. Prepped at a small school in Iowa, where he won a state basketball championship and went to three state title games in football. Redshirted in 2009 and did not play in '10 (academics). Started all 11 games at defensive end in '11, recording 51 tackles, 19 for loss and 14 sacks with a batted pass and seven forced fumbles. Played hurt in '12, but was a Buck Buchanan Award (FCS Outstanding Defensive Player) finalist — started 10-of-11 games as a rush linebacker and posted 74-7-4 with two pass breakups, two forced fumbles and a blocked kick. Did not start against Northern Iowa. Was the Missouri Valley Conference Defensive Player of the Year in '13 — started 11-of-12 games and registered 71-15-9 with four pass breakups, an interception and four forced fumbles. Was ejected for targeting against Missouri State and had to sit out the first half against Indiana State. Participated in the East-West Shrine Game.

Strengths: Good athletic ability and acceleration. Can run with tight ends in coverage. Good pursuit effort — chases hard and flattens down the line. Productive three-year starter.

Weaknesses: Small hands. Limited core strength and knockback power. Not stout. Unrefined hand use. Does not have a plan as a

pass rusher.

Future: Athletic, productive, raw rush linebacker prospect who could also be tried as a Sam linebacker. Needs to develop more core strength, improve technically and make his mark on special teams to warrant developmental consideration.

Draft projection: Priority free agent.

WLB JORDAN TRIPP, #37
MONTANA   ▶ GRADE: 5.10
Ht: 6-2 3/4 | Wt: 234 | Sp: 4.67 | Arm: 30 3/4 | Hand: 9 5/8

History: Montana native whose father and grandfather also played for the Grizzlies. Jordan also ran track in high school. Was primarily a special-teams player as a true freshman in 2009 (wore jersey No. 44), tallying 23 tackles, zero for loss and zero sacks in 15 games. In '10, started 9-of-11 games at strong-side linebacker and was credited with 99-9-3 1/2 with three pass breakups and an interception touchdown. In '11, managed 18-1 1/2-0 in three starts at SLB before suffering a season-ending torn right labrum injury. Moved to the weak side in '12 and started all 11 games, notching 95-13 1/2-5 1/2 with two pass breakups, an interception, four forced fumbles and a fumble recovery touchdown. Started all 13 games at WLB in '13, registering 100-5 1/2-2 with two pass breakups, three interceptions, a forced fumble, a blocked kick and a fumble recovery touchdown. Two-time team captain. Wore Montana's legacy jersey No. 37 his final two seasons. Participated in East-West Shrine Game and Senior Bowl.

Strengths: Triggers fast downhill vs. the run. Diagnoses quickly and is around the ball a lot. Outstanding motor, intensity and effort. Extremely competitive. Very tough. Outstanding weight-room work ethic. Sculpted with very minimal body fat. Elected team captain. Exceptional character. Emergency long snapper (started all four years). Has a special-teams temperament. Takes the game very seriously. Athleticism was on display at the Combine — paced linebackers with a 3.96-second short shuttle, recorded a 6.89-second 3-cone drill and vertical jumped 37 1/2 inches.

Weaknesses: Has short flappers and gets stuck on blocks. Can do a better job using his hands to stack and shed. Plays a bit too out of control. Tightness shows up in space trying to break down and secure open-field tackles (misses too many). Wound tight in coverage and not quick to redirect (allows separation).

Future: A tough, determined, competitive overachiever capable of earning a job as a backup linebacker and special-teams performer.

Draft projection: Late draftable pick.

LINEBACKERS

ILB DEVIN "UANI" UNGA, #41

BYU   ▶ GRADE: 5.10

Ht: 6-1 1/8 | Wt: 231 | Sp: 4.85e | Arm: 31 3/8 | Hand: 10

History: Married. Comes from a large Tongan football family, including several relatives who played Division I football and in the NFL. Born and raised in California before moving to Hawaii in high school — played tight end and starred on the hardwood, winning state titles in football and basketball. Began his college career at Oregon State — was part of the 2006 recruiting class, but served a two-year LDS mission in Guatemala. Joined OSU in '09 (wore jersey No. 41) — converted to linebacker and contributed on special teams, tallying 18 tackles, one-half for loss and zero sacks in 12 games. Appeared in all 12 games in '10 and collected 32-2-1. Dislocated his left elbow in the season finale against Oregon. Transferred to BYU, walked on and sat out '11 per NCAA rules. Was a backup inside linebacker in '12, recording 28-3-1 with one pass breakup, an interception and a forced fumble in 13 games. Stepped into the lineup in '13 and was the Cougars' leading tackler — started all 13 games at "Mike" in BYU's 3-4 scheme and racked up 143-7 1/2-0 with three pass breakups and two forced fumbles. Suffered a chest contusion against Virginia then reportedly played through a broken hand mid-season. Suffered a torn right ACL, MCL and meniscus in the fourth quarter of the Kraft Fight Hunger Bowl against Washington. Team captain. Was medically excluded at the Combine (knee)

Strengths: Good eyes to key and diagnose — football smart. Plays on his feet and bends well. Steps downhill and has good take-on strength to stack and shed blockers. Motor runs hot in pursuit. Solid tackler. Drops competently into zone and shows nice awareness and reactions. Experience in a 3-4 defense. Has a special-teams mentality. Well-respected, motivated, hardworking leader. Comes from a football family.

Weaknesses: Lacks ideal height and length. Has very small hands. Lacks ideal foot speed — can be a step late to the perimeter. Can be covered up and negated when he plays on his heels and exposes his frame to larger linemen. Needs to be schemed free as a blitzer. Relatively inexperienced. Is overaged with limited upside — will be a 26-year-old rookie.

Future: An overaged, competitive, physical linebacker of Tongan descent, Unga went from walk-on to captain at BYU, where he was a tackling machine in his lone season as a starter. Skill set and college responsibilities translate well to the pro game, and he's capable of serving as a core special-teams player and solid backup for a 3-4 team.

Draft projection: Late draftable pick.

ROLB-DRE KYLE VAN NOY, #3

BYU   ▶ GRADE: 5.43

Ht: 6-3 1/8 | Wt: 243 | Sp: 4.71 | Arm: 31 5/8 | Hand: 9 5/8

History: Engaged. Raised by adoptive parents. Linebacker-receiver who won a football state championship, ran track and played basketball and baseball as a Nevada prep. Days before 2009 National Signing Day, was arrested for DUI, jeopardizing his scholarship to BYU. When given the opportunity to be released of his commitment and sign elsewhere, he reaffirmed his commitment to BYU and accepted the terms of delayed enrollment, including a full year abiding by the school's honor code and endorsement from an ecclesiastical leader. Also wrote a letter to head coach Bronco Mendenhall, expressing remorse and promising to earn back his trust. A month later, was cited for eluding police — got caught with alcohol, ran from police and was Tasered. Charges were eventually dropped and the incident was not publicized, but Van Noy flew to Provo in order to confess to Mendenhall in person, at which time he admitted needing help to straighten out his life. Mendenhall vouched for Van Noy, and the school honored his scholarship the following year. Prior to the '10 season, got sick and lost 30 pounds. Played all 13 games in the fall (wore jersey No. 45), starting two at strong outside linebacker in BYU's 3-4 scheme, and was credited with 35 tackles, 7 1/2 for loss and two sacks with two pass breakups and two forced fumbles. Moved to the weak side permanently in '11 when he started 8-of-13 games and produced 68-15-7 with three pass breakups, three interceptions, three forced fumbles and a blocked kick. Sat out '12 spring practice while recovering from surgery to repair a torn right labrum. Started all 26 games the next two seasons — totaled 53-22-13 with five pass breakups, two interceptions (one touchdown), six forced fumbles and two blocked kicks in '12; and 70-17 1/2-4 with seven pass breakups, two interceptions and a safety in '13.

Strengths: Has a muscular, well-proportioned build. Quick get-off. Knifes gaps. Good pass-rush ability — can push the pocket or pressure the edge. Keeps working to the quarterback and has deceptive closing speed. Eyes the quarterback and tries to get his hands in the passing lane. Athletic with good movement skills in all directions — equipped to keep pace with backs and tight ends in coverage. Is rangy and can open up his stride and run vertical. Glides on the field. Scheme versatile. Football smart.

Weaknesses: Has short arms. Lacks elite length and flexibility to bend and flatten. Average instincts and diagnose. Still developing eye discipline. Needs to cultivate a more sophisticated arsenal of pass-rush moves. Leaves some production on the field. Leaves his feet to tackle and slips off the ball carrier. Hit-or-miss run defender. Could stand to improve his upper-body strength and stack-and-shed ability. Average motor — could pursue with more urgency.

Future: Good-sized, athletic, smooth-moving stand-up player who projects best as a 3-4 right outside linebacker, but could also warrant consideration from 4-3 teams as a Will or Sam. Is not without flaws, but has unique ability to play up the field, laterally or in reverse.

Draft projection: Third-round pick.

Scout's take: "(Van Noy) has a knack to rush the passer. I see him being more of a nickel, rotational rusher than a full-time starter."

ILB AVERY WILLIAMSON, #40

KENTUCKY   ▶ GRADE: 5.20

Ht: 6-1 | Wt: 246 | Sp: 4.66 | Arm: 32 3/4 | Hand: 9 1/2

History: Prepped in Tennessee, where he played in two state championship games and was honored as the Outstanding Senior of his graduating class, recognizing academics, character and athletics. Played 12 games in 2010 and was credited with 10 tackles, zero for loss and zero sacks with a pass breakup. Appeared in 12 games in '11 and collected 49-1.5-0 with an interception and forced fumble. Started at 24 games at middle linebacker and led the Wildcats in tackles his final two seasons — totaled 135-4.5-3 with four pass breakups, an interception and two forced fumbles in '12; and 102-4-1 in '13. Team captain.

Strengths: Good size. Plays with a good, wide base. Very productive tackler. Outstanding personal and football character — works hard, is accountable and commands respect. Smart, understands the game and can make all the calls and on-field adjustments.

Weaknesses: Average athletic ability and foot quickness — is a step late to the perimeter. Struggles to disengage from blockers once he is locked up. Limited cover range and reactions — is late to recognize and gets sucked up by playaction. Average functional strength. Is not a take-on thumper. His 30 1/2-inch vertical was worst among middle linebackers at the Combine.

Future: A functional, between-the-tackles run stopper with a chance to make it on the inside of a 3-4 defense where he can patrol the middle. Can be targeted in coverage and will need to make a mark on special teams to stick.

Draft projection: Late draftable pick.

ILB-SLB JORDAN ZUMWALT, #35

UCLA   ▶ GRADE: 5.23

Ht: 6-4 | Wt: 235 | Sp: 4.76 | Arm: 31 1/4 | Hand: 8 3/4

History: Highly recruited inside linebacker who also played basketball as a California prep. Verballed to Stanford, but signed with UCLA. Played 11 games as a true freshman in 2010 — injuries thrust him into the starting lineup at middle linebacker the final four games and he produced 32 tackles, three for loss and three sacks. Played all 13 games in '11, starting four (three at weak-side linebacker, one at MLB), and notched 60-6-0 with a pass breakup and an interception. Playing in a 3-4 in '12 — started 9-of-13 games (five at left inside linebacker, four at left outside linebacker) and totaled 71-8-2 with a pass breakup, two forced fumbles and a blocked kick. Did not play against Colorado after a scooter accident required stitches, leaving him unable to wear a helmet. Started all 13 games in '13 (12 at LILB, one at LOLB) and registered 93-5 1/2-0 with two interceptions and three forced fumbles. Did not bench press at the Combine (left shoulder).

Strengths: Very competitive with a fiery, on-field temperament. Explosive hitter. Throws his body around recklessly and times up the blitz well (disruptive presence). Is around the ball a lot. Very good football intelligence — lines up teammates and makes adjustments. Versatile and has played all linebacker positions and contributed as a fullback in short-yardage situations. Defensive tone-setter — has a love for the game and it shows. Plays big on big stages — capped his career with co-MVP effort in the Sun Bowl vs. Virginia Tech, when he knocked Logan Thomas unconscious and returned an interception 43 yards.

Weaknesses: Does not play strong. Mechanical mover. Tight-hipped with average change of direction. Gets outflanked to the corner vs. speed. Average knockback body power — does not strike with thump to drive back ball carriers. Catches too much. Struggles to disengage from blocks when he is locked up. Limited coverage range. Has small hands and a relatively short wing span given his height.

Future: High-energy overachiever with a special-teams temperament. Stands out most for his competitiveness, effort, versatility and swagger. Brings the feisty type of attitude desired on a Jeff Fisher or Jim Schwartz defense. Will factor immediately on special teams and could work his way into a starting lineup.

Draft projection: Fourth- to fifth-round pick.

Scout's take: "Zumwalt has no pop, can't run and can't get off blocks. When you see him in person, his body type is so skinny-looking. It's not inspiring in any way."

DEFENSIVE BACKS

OKLAHOMA STATE CB

JUSTIN GILBERT

NAWROCKI'S TOP 10

10	ANTONE EXUM
9	RASHAAD REYNOLDS
8	MARQUESTON HUFF
7	JASON VERRETT
6	KYLE FULLER
5	BRADLEY ROBY
4	HA HA CLINTON-DIX
3	DARQUEZE DENNARD
2	CALVIN PRYOR
1	

SS MO ALEXANDER, #14

UTAH STATE ▶ GRADE: 5.24

Ht: 6-1 1/4 | Wt: 220 | Sp: 4.54 | Arm: 32 5/8 | Hand: 8 7/8

History: Birth name is Maurice. St. Louis native who also earned all-state recognition in wrestling and track as a prep. Began his college career at Arizona Western College in 2009, playing in 10 games and recording 81 tackles and two interceptions with 17 1/2 tackles for loss, seven sacks and two forced fumbles. Appeared in 12 games in '10 and had 98 tackles, four pass breakups and one interception with 19 tackles for loss (for 116 yards), eight sacks and one forced fumble. The 19 tackles for loss ranked second in the NJCAA, while the yards lost total ranked first. Moved on to Utah State in '11 and played outside linebacker, appearing in 12 games (eight starts) with 45 tackles, seven tackles for loss, three sacks and one pass breakup. During the off-season, he punched a teammate in the face after a party (the teammate subsequently underwent emergency surgery) and charges were filed. He was originally facing a second-degree felony, but he pleaded guilty to a misdemeanor reduced charge of aggravated assault resulting in bodily injury. After initially being ordered to serve a year in jail, the judge suspended all but 45 days of the jail sentence. He was kicked off the team for the '12 season but was given a second chance, returning in '13. He started 13 games at free safety, registering 80 tackles, six pass breakups and one interception with nine tackles for loss, 3 1/2 sacks and two forced fumbles. Missed the San Diego County Credit Union Poinsettia Bowl after undergoing wrist surgery, which also prevented him from bench pressing at the Combine (medical exclusion).

Strengths: Very good size and movement skills. Covers ground. Has a 38-inch vertical jump. Drops into the box and fits in the run game. Physical tackler. Effective blitzer. Aggressive and energetic. Has special-teams experience.

Weaknesses: Miscast in deep coverage. Has man-coverage limitations. Lacks foot speed to keep pace with receivers. Inconsistent ball reactions — in position to make plays, but doesn't. Can be overaggressive and take poor angles. Has tweener traits.

Future: Big, physical, athletic, converted linebacker who will have to carve a niche as a box defender and special-teams contributor to hold down a roster spot as a reserve safety. Size and aggressiveness will earn him a look in a league increasingly desirous of such traits in the secondary.

Draft projection: Fourth- to fifth-round pick.

Scout's take: "He's a converted linebacker who strikes with some thump. He has some intriguing traits. He wouldn't start for us. He's a backup, but he has the traits to ascend if he stays (out of trouble)."

RCB RICARDO ALLEN, #21

PURDUE ▶ GRADE: 5.05

Ht: 5-9 1/8 | Wt: 187 | Sp: 4.61 | Arm: 30 | Hand: 9 1/4

History: Also participated in soccer and track as a Florida prep. Started all 12 games at left cornerback as a true freshman for Purdue in 2010, recording 73 tackles, four pass breakups and three interceptions with 3 1/2 tackles for loss and one sack. Led the team in picks and returned a pair for touchdowns, scampering 94 yards vs. Michigan and 35 yards at Michigan State. Made 13 starts at left cornerback in '11 and posted 79-4-3 with three tackles for loss and one forced fumble. Scored on 37-yard interception return against Minnesota. Blocked a field goal attempt on the final play of the game in the season opener against Middle Tennessee. Returned one punt for seven yards. Tallied 45-4-1 in 13 games (11 starts) in '12 with four tackles for loss and one sack. Returned an interception 39 yards for a touchdown against Marshall. Had one punt return for 25 yards. Started 10 games at left cornerback and two games at nickelback in '13 and tallied 53-3-6 with four tackles for loss, one sack and one forced fumble. Team captain. Saw action in all 50 possible games during his Purdue career, finishing with 13 interceptions — the second-highest total in school history.

Strengths: Athletic with fluid movement skills. Plants and drives with urgency and shows good closing burst. Showed a knack for making plays — returned four of 13 career INTs for TDs). Active and energetic. Durable four-year starter. Solid personal and football character.

Weaknesses: Undersized — at a physical disadvantage vs. bigger receivers. Limited functional strength — is not equipped to press and or tackle forcefully. Inconsistent run support. Below-average timed speed. Eyes get stuck in the backfield — vulnerable to quarterback manipulation and double moves.

Average transitional quickness. Allows too big of a cushion.

Future: Short, lean-framed, battle-tested corner who lacks exceptional athletic traits and will always have physical limitations, but has enough competitiveness and ball sills to compete for a spot as a reserve.

Draft projection: Priority free agent.

SS DION BAILEY, #18 (JUNIOR)

USC ▶ GRADE: 5.20

Ht: 5-11 3/4 | Wt: 201 | Sp: 4.66 | Arm: 32 | Hand: 9 1/2

History: California native. Redshirted in 2010. During '11 spring practice, he moved from safety to linebacker, and started 11 games on the strong side — tied for the team lead with 81 tackles and had eight tackles for loss and two sacks with two pass breakups, two interceptions and one forced fumble. Missed one game with a concussion. Was named the Pac-12 Freshman Defensive Player of the Year. In '12, tallied 80-8-1 with five pass breakups, four interceptions and one forced fumble in 13 starts at SLB. In '13, he missed spring practice while recuperating from off-season shoulder surgery. He also dropped 10 pounds in order to move back to the safety position. Mainly lined up in the nickel position, appearing in 14 games (11 starts) and recording 61 tackles, six pass breakups and five interceptions with 6 1/2 tackles for loss, 1/2 sack and one forced fumble.

Strengths: Good hands to intercept. Was an impact defender as a redshirt freshman despite playing out of place as an undersized linebacker.

Weaknesses: Durability is a concern. Has pedestrian speed — struggles to match with slot receivers. Lacks experience in deep coverage. Still developing positional instincts and feel for route combinations. Takes some inaccurate angles. Goes low and misses tackles. Has tweener traits.

Future: Classic linebacker-safety tweener whose best shot to carve a niche in the pros could come as a nickel linebacker, where he could utilize his ball skills and be used as a blitzer. Will have to make his mark on special teams.

Draft projection: Fifth- to sixth-round pick.

Scout's take: "I'm not really sure what to do with him. He's like a nickel linebacker / safety. He has pretty good ball skills. He doesn't even start. He starts three-quarters of the time. Against Stanford, he had a pick in the end zone. He's not a full-time player. I have a hard time comparing him to anyone."

RCB-KR DEION BELUE, #13

ALABAMA   ▶ GRADE: 5.09

Ht: 5-11 | Wt: 182 | Sp: 4.60e | Arm: 31 1/2| Hand: 8 1/8

History: His last name is pronounced "BLUE." Alabama native who played defensive back, running back and kick returner in high school. Was a non-qualifier and went to Northeast Mississippi Community College — appeared in eight games in 2010, recording 20 tackles, four pass breakups and zero interceptions with one forced fumble. Had 11 combined kick returns for 223 yards (20.3 average) and one touchdown. Appeared in 10 games in '11 and posted 24-8-1 with one tackle for loss and one sack. Returned his interception for a 58-yard touchdown. Also returned kickoffs and punts, combining for 33-693-2 (21.0). Finally arrived on the Alabama campus in '12 and started all 14 games at cornerback for the national champions, recording 40-7-2 with 6 1/2 tackles for loss and one forced fumble. Scored on a 57-yard fumble return against Western Carolina. Was hampered most of '13 by a turf toe injury he suffered prior to the season, which forced him to miss two games. Started 11 contests at cornerback and totaled 20-3-1 with one tackle for loss. Did not work out at the Combine (right turf toe).

Strengths: Moves fluidly and pedals smoothly. Has short-area quickness to mirror off the line. Good read-and-react skills. Aware in zone. Has special-teams experience as a jammer. Dependable character. Has a professional approach to the game. Competitive and tough — plays hurt and does not shy from a challenge.

Weaknesses: Has been dinged up and durability is an issue. Size is just adequate — could stand to bulk up and improve functional strength. Has short arms and very small hands. Disadvantaged vs. bigger, stronger receivers. Not explosive. Gives ground at the break point. Loses phase. Minimal ball production. Inconsistent downfield ball reactions. Weak, shoddy tackler.

Future: Lean, high-cut, press-bail corner with enough field speed, range and competitiveness to compete for a sub-package role. Played hurt as a senior and has desirable intangibles, though he must shore up his tackling and show effectiveness on special teams to give himself a chance.

Draft projection: Priority free agent.

RCB BENE BENWIKERE, #21

SAN JOSE STATE   ▶ GRADE: 5.18

Ht: 5-10 3/4 | Wt: 195 | Sp: 4.63 | Arm: 30 | Hand: 9 1/8

History: His name is pronounced "Ben-ay Ben-WICK-urr-rhee." His cousin, Chris Owens, has played cornerback in the NFL with Atlanta, Cleveland and Miami. Prepped in California, where he won a state championship, played basketball and ran track. Had arthroscopic surgery in high school to repair his right MCL. Played safety in his freshman year at San Jose State in '10, appearing in 13 games (nine starts) and recording 74 tackles, four pass breakups and one interception with 1 1/2 tackles for loss and two forced fumbles. Saw most of his action at cornerback in '11 and appeared in 10 games (two starts), posting 18-3-1 with one-half tackle for loss. Also caught one pass for 11 yards. Played the second half of the campaign with an injured right wrist and underwent arthroscopic surgery after the season. In '12, played in 13 games (eight starts) and recorded 67-4-7 with 7 1/2 tackles for loss and one forced fumble. Began the year seeing action in nickel coverages before starting the last seven games of the season. Tied a school record with a three-interception performance against Louisiana Tech. Scored touchdowns on a 37-yard fumble recovery against New Mexico State and a 47-yard interception return against Idaho. In '13, totaled 55-11-5 with two tackles for loss and one sack in 11 starts. Missed one game with a concussion. Concluded his career with a school-record 14 interceptions.

Strengths: Good size. Outstanding leaping ability — posted a 40 1/2-inch vertical jump at the Combine. Excellent ball skills — plays the ball in the air like a receiver. Competes in the air, can highpoint the ball and snag INTs with his hands. Quick to read run and pass. Has special-teams experience, including as a gunner and jammer. Good football intelligence. Demonstrated secondary versatility — has played corner, safety and nickel back.

Weaknesses: Needs to spend more time in the weight room — pushed 225 pounds just 10 times at the Combine. Could stand to improve his tackling. Below-average timed speed — struggled matching with the explosive vertical speed of Stanford WR Ty Montgomery. Production inflated by lesser competition.

Future: Smoother-than-fast, ballhawking nickel corner who is more effective as a pass defender than run supporter. Benwikere's game lacks physicality, yet his zone cover skills could allow him to carve a role in the slot and on special teams. Would benefit from a demanding position coach.

Draft projection: Fifth- to sixth-round pick.

Scout's take: "He's not as strong as you'd like because the wrist injury set him back in the weight room. He's going to struggle in man coverage. If you confine him to short areas, he has a chance. He is an athlete with good hands, and he makes plays on the ball. You see him jump routes and play the ball aggressively in the air."

SS NAT BERHE, #20

SAN DIEGO STATE ▶ GRADE: 5.14

Ht: 5-10 1/2 | Wt: 193 | Sp: 4.71 | Arm: 30 5/8 | Hand: 8 1/2

History: His last name is pronounced "burr-HEY." Lettered in football and track as a California prep. Redshirted in 2009. Played in 12 games in '10, including two starts out of the warrior spot, and recorded 39 tackles, four pass breakups and one interception with one tackle for loss. Missed one game with a concussion. Started all 13 games in '11, with the first six at the "Warrior" and the final seven at "Aztec" (hybrid safety-linebacker positions) — had 67-4-2 with 3 1/2 tackles for loss and one forced fumble. Led SDSU in total tackles in '12 and had 94-5-2 with two tackles for loss in 13 starts out of the "Aztec." Led the team in tackles in '13, starting 13 times at "Aztec" and recording 99-6-0 with 5 1/2 tackles for loss and one sack. Team captain.

Strengths: Instinctive defender with a nose for the ball. Secondary leader. Reads and reacts quickly. Active and energetic — terrific pursuit effort. Motor runs hot. Plays fast. Good balance and body control. Smooth pedal. Good ball reactions. Disguises coverages. Sells blitzes and baits quarterbacks (see vs. Fresno State's David Carr). Tough, confident and competitive. Aggressive tackler. Plays with abandon. Flashes explosive striking ability. Lives and breathes football. Experienced, four-year starter with desirable makeup. Very likeable personality.

Weaknesses: Cornerback size with short arms and small hands. Has a light frame with limited weight potential and could stand to get stronger. Pedestrian timed speed. Plays a bit out of control and will miss some tackles in the open-field. Takes some bad angles. Leaks yards when he comes in high and has to grab and drag instead of driving through the ball carrier. Average production on the ball. Limited special-teams experience.

Future: Compactly built, highly competitive strong safety who flies around the field, though he lacks ideal speed. Has the look of a solid backup and core special-teams player with potential to compete for a more prominent role down the line.

Draft projection: Late draftable pick.

Scout's take: "He's a safety trapped in a cornerback's body. Nothing on paper looks exciting. He is a good, hard-nosed football player though. I wouldn't be surprised if he found a way to make a roster. Coaches will love him. I graded him as a (priority free agent)."

SS-RCB TRE BOSTON, #10

NORTH CAROLINA ▶ GRADE: 5.10

Ht: 5-11 5/8 | Wt: 204 | Sp: 4.59 | Arm: 31 3/8 | Hand: 9 3/4

History: Full name is Jayestin Tre'von Boston. Played both defensive back and running back as a Florida prep. Played in 10 games as a true freshman in 2010, making three starts at right cornerback and one at left corner and recording 32 tackles, four pass breakups and one interception with one tackle for loss and two forced fumbles. Missed three games with a sprained ankle. In '11, started 11-of-13 games (four at LCB, four at nickel and three at free safety) and had 70-2-3 with 1 1/2 tackles for loss and one forced fumble. Led the team in tackles in '12, starting 12 games (nine at FS, three at SS) and totaling 86-6-4 with one tackle for loss. Had a 36-yard interception return for a touchdown at Virginia. Made 13 starts at free safety in '13, registering 94-8-5 with 4 1/2 tackles for loss. Led the team in tackles.

Strengths: Can secure tackles in the box when he has a clear path. Drops downhill quickly and can slip into short hole. Vocal leader of secondary. Three-year starter with experience at safety and corner.

Weaknesses: Average instincts — could stand to improve diagnostic ability and anticipation. Choppy pedal and stiff transition. Limited range — does not explode off the hash or cover enough ground with the ball in the air. Takes some inaccurate angles and struggles to break down in space. Selective hitter and inconsistent tackler in general. Personality could clash with some people.

Future: Converted cornerback and free/strong safety tweener whose inconsistent play and questionable physicality will turn teams off. Will have to turn heads on special teams to have longevity as a backup.

Draft projection: Late draftable pick.

Scout's take: "He freelances too much. You see him come up and make a big play, but he is not supposed to be there. When he is supposed to be there, he blows it and gives up a big play. He's good in run support and filling the alley, and he's a solid competitive tackler. He's loose in coverage — I didn't see the range. He's effective controlling between the tackles in the middle of the field. I didn't see outside ability. I thought he was more of a strong safety type. I put him in the sixth (round). He was immature early. How that's viewed could affect his standing."

RCB BASHAUD BREELAND, #17 (JUNIOR)

CLEMSON　　▶ GRADE: 5.41

Ht: 5-11 3/8 | Wt: 197 | Sp: 4.62 | Arm: 31 3/4 | Hand: 9

History: Has an infant daughter. Played quarterback and defensive back as a South Carolina prep. Also lettered in basketball and track, winning state titles in the 400-meter hurdles as both a sophomore and junior. Redshirted in 2010. Saw his first collegiate action in '11 and played in 14 games (seven starts) at cornerback, recording 53 tackles, four pass breakups and two interceptions with one tackle for loss. Was limited during an injury-plagued '12 season, registering 32-3-0 with 2 1/2 tackles for loss and one sack in 10 games (five starts). Suffered an abdominal strain early in the year and eventually underwent groin surgery in December, missing the final three games of the year. Had a breakout '13 campaign, appearing in 13 games (12 starts) and totaling 74-13-4 with five tackles for loss, two sacks and two forced fumbles. Was suspended for the first half of the Maryland contest after he was ejected for targeting against Florida State.

Strengths: Fluid athlete. Quick-footed and loose-hipped. Can shadow, mirror and stay in phase. Plays with a sense of urgency and is aggressive supporting the run. Gives effort to pursue from the back side.

Weaknesses: Needs to bulk up and get functionally stronger. Gets wired on blocks. Lacks ideal speed. Average explosion and leaping ability. Plays into the boundary. Tends to play out of control and his tackling technique needs work — misses too many. Exposed vs. Florida State's Rashad Greene.

Future: Lean, rangy cover corner who sticks his nose in run support and competes against bigger receivers. Is relatively raw, but has an appealing temperament and moldable tools.

Draft projection: Third-round pick.

Scout's take: "He looked really good in drill work, but he runs 4.6 all day. I was a little disappointed at the Combine. He didn't look as smooth opening his hips and breaking on balls. I thought he would have been better after watching him on tape. I wanted to see a guy with a little more fight in him. He shorted his pedal sometimes."

FS TERRENCE BROOKS, #31

FLORIDA STATE　　▶ GRADE: 5.29

Ht: 5-10 7/8 | Wt: 198 | Sp: 4.42 | Arm: 31 | Hand: 9

History: Was a two-way player as a Florida prep, playing cornerback, wide receiver and running back. Appeared in 10 games as a true freshman 2010, recording two tackles, one pass breakup and zero interceptions as a backup cornerback and special-teams player. Did not play in four games (coach's decision). Served as FSU's dime defender in '11, recording 17-5-1 with one-half tackle for loss in 11 games. Recorded his first career interception against Notre Dame, picking off a pass in the end zone to clinch the Champs Sports Bowl. Missed two contests (coach's decision). After spending two years in a reserve role, he started all 14 games at free safety in '12 and had 51-4-2 with one tackle for loss and one forced fumble. Started 13 games for the '13 national champions (five at free safety, eight at strong safety), registering 56-5-2 with eight tackles for loss, one sack and two forced fumbles. Missed the Wake Forest game because of a concussion and left the Miami game at halftime for the same reason.

Strengths: Fluid and flexible. Pedals and transitions smoothly. Has cornerback speed — plays fast and covers ground. Has a 38-inch vertical jump. Patrols zones with awareness and anticipation to react to threats. Keys quickly, trusts his eyes and does not hesitate. Aggressive in run support — swoops down with urgency, runs the alley and plays with abandon. Dependable makeup — solid character. Tough and durable. Has ability and mentality to contribute on special teams.

Weaknesses: Could stand to bulk up and get stronger. Inconsistent tackler — arrives out of control, does not always see what he hits and will miss some tackles seeking the knockout blow. Is built like a cornerback, sustained a concussion as a senior and durability could be an issue given his aggressive playing style. Minimal production on the ball — was not a playmaker. Has average hands and leaves some INTs on the field. Poor short-shuttle time (7.35 seconds) at the Combine.

Future: Lean, athletic, confident, competitive hybrid safety who should be a solid backup and core special-teams player at a minimum given his combination of fluidity, range and physicality. Has starter-caliber ability if he can improve his ball skills, and offers versatility as a "robber" or box defender.

Draft projection: Third- to fourth-round pick.

Scout's take: "He is a little safety. He had a concussion and shoulder issues. He doesn't play that fast. He has little production. Everyone makes mistakes evaluating these guys in shorts. He has the height-weight-speed. He's built like a corner. It's a big man's game. Receivers are getting bigger. Tight ends can run. If anything, he is a nickel safety. He's not a ballhawk."

SS DEONE BUCANNON, #20

WASHINGTON STATE   ▶ GRADE: 5.42
Ht: 6-1 | Wt: 211 | Sp: 4.49 | Arm: 32 3/8 | Hand: 9 3/4

History: His name is pronounced "DAY-own byew-CAN-nin)." Defensive back-receiver who also golfed as a California prep. Fractured his left collarbone in his final high school game. Played in 12 games (eight starts at strong safety) as a true freshman in 2010 and had 84 tackles, five pass breakups and two interceptions with four tackles for loss and two forced fumbles. Started 11-of-12 games in '11 and registered 80-4-3 with two tackles for loss, one forced fumble and one blocked field goal. Appeared in 12 games (11 starts) in '12 and had 106-4-4 with three tackles for loss, one sack and one forced fumble. Led the team in tackles. Was suspended for the first half of the UNLV contest as punishment for a hit to the head on a defenseless receiver. In '13, started all 13 games and totaled 114-1-6 with 4 1/2 tackles for loss and three forced fumbles. Led the Pac-12 in tackles and tied for the lead in interceptions. Also played on the kickoff and punt coverage teams and tied for the team-lead with seven special-teams tackles. Three-time captain concluded his college career ranking among the WSU all-time leaders in tackles (384) and interceptions (15).

Strengths: Good length and overall size. Reads run and drops downhill quickly. Has an old-school mentality — likes contact and is a physical tackler (seeks to punish the ball carrier). Shows pop on contact. Covers kicks and has an ideal mentality for special teams. Productive four-year starter.

Weaknesses: Struggles to recover from missteps and will not track anyone down from behind. Some tightness in his hips. Takes some inaccurate angles. Man-coverage limitations (struggles to mirror slot receivers). Can be overaggressive and miss tackles. Does not always arrive under control in space — can be shook in the hole. Lacks discipline on the field and makes too many mental mistakes.

Future: Good-sized, athletic, physical safety who stands out as a straight-line striker on tape and sets the tone. Has coverage limitations, but brings aggressiveness and intensity to carve a niche as a downhill box defender and core special-teams player. Must learn to become more assignment sound to maximize his potential. Has some similarities to Tampa Bay FS Dashon Goldson.

Draft projection: Second- to third-round pick.

Scout's take: "A lot of people are enamored with the kid because he is big and a pretty big hitter and has 15 interceptions. Watch him get juked by (Marcus) Mariota and give up a 60-yard TD or earholed because he does not have a feel and never sees the crackback coming. He gets shook out of his jock because he is too stiff to redirect."

LCB-PR TRAVIS CARRIE, #18

OHIO   ▶ GRADE: 5.36
Ht: 5-11 5/8 | Wt: 206 | Sp: 4.49 | Arm: 31 7/8 | Hand: 9 3/4

History: The California prep lettered for two years despite undergoing open heart surgery as a sophomore. As a true freshman in 2008, played in 11 games (one start) and recorded 35 tackles, one pass breakup and one interception. Returned five punts for 57 yards (11.4-yard average). Missed the '09 season, as he needed surgery to repair a torn labrum in his left hip. Also ran into trouble when he bought a computer that had been stolen from the school; he pleaded guilty to receiving stolen property and was sentenced to 48 hours in jail. Returned to the field in '10 and made 12 starts at cornerback, tallying 39-5-0 with 5 1/2 tackles for loss, two sacks and two forced fumbles. Was 19-197-0 (10.4) as a punt returner. Missed one game with a concussion. Played in 14 games (13 starts) in '11 and totaled 49-13-4 with 1 1/2 tackles for loss. As a punt returner, he was 11-138-1 (12.5) with a 65-yard touchdown against New Mexico State. Sat out the '12 season as a medical redshirt — fractured his right shoulder during the first week of camp, requiring surgery. Appeared in all 13 games (12 starts) in '13 and had 42-8-4 with 1 1/2 tackles for loss and one sack with 21-267 (12.7) as a punt returner. Returned a pair of interceptions for scores against Massachusetts (66 yards and 30 yards). Team captain. Did not work out at the Combine because of a right knee (lateral meniscus) injury.

Strengths: Outstanding size — looks the part of an NFL defensive back with a sculpted physique and nice length. Equipped to jam. Has speed to carry receivers vertically. Good zone awareness and ball reactions. Good hands to intercept. Sets the edge in run support. Smart and instinctive. Confident and competitive. Was a productive punt returner and has worked as a gunner.

Weaknesses: Tweener traits. Pedals tight. Shows some stiffness in his pedal and transition. Footwork needs to be coached up. Does not explode out of transition or display burst to recover. Average pop on contact. Will be a 24-year-old rookie — missed two full seasons because of hip and shoulder injuries.

Future: Smoother-than-explosive, height-weight-speed prospect who will draw the attention of Cover-2 teams given his physicality, ball skills and tackling. Special-teams ability adds to value.

Draft projection: Fourth- to fifth-round pick.

Scout's take: "He's a big press corner with a lot of tools. He's coming off the knee injury. He missed a year. ... He's a smooth, fluid, athletic type player with adequate straight-line speed. He is a lot better in tight, physical man coverage. He struggles to open up, flip and turn. He's a good hitter in run support."

FS HA HA CLINTON-DIX, #6 (JUNIOR)

ALABAMA   ▶ GRADE: 6.10

Ht: 6-1 3/8 | Wt: 208 | Sp: 4.58 | Arm: 32 3/8 | Hand: 9

History: His full name is Ha'Sean Clinton-Dix. Elite recruit out of Florida, where he doubled as a running back and kick returner. Played in 13 games for Alabama as a true freshman in '11 and recorded 11 tackles and two pass breakups. Was a key performer for the national champions in '12, appearing in all 14 games (10 starts) at safety. Had 37 tackles, four pass breakups and five interceptions with one-half tackle for loss and one forced fumble. Tied for the SEC lead in interceptions, including picks in the SEC Championship win over Georgia and the BCS National Championship win over Notre Dame. In '13, he played in 11 games (nine starts at free safety) and totaled 51-4-2 with 3 1/2 tackles for loss. Received a suspension for accepting a short-term loan of less than $500 from an assistant coach, missing two games. Injured his knee against Auburn November 30, necessitating surgery on the meniscus tear, but returned to the field for the Allstate Sugar Bowl.

Strengths: Good size and wing span. Quick to read and react. Enough speed and fluidity to keep pace with slot receivers or tight ends. Ranges off the hash. Good hands to intercept. Takes direct angles to the ball. Drops downhill urgently, runs the alley and does not shy from contact — wipes out ballcarries. Secure tackler. Can break down and tackle in space. Has special-teams experience. Well-coached in a pro-style defense.

Weaknesses: Has a narrow build and lacks ideal bulk — could stand to get stronger. Not an elite athlete — ordinary speed and leaping ability. Occasionally gets stuck on blocks. Could stand to iron out his pedal. Does not always play with abandon — plays conservatively at times and can be late fitting in the run game or getting off the hash. Average ball production

and playmaking ability. Not as natural in the box. Was not an exceptional ballhawk or an intimidating eraser.

Future: Hype exceeded his performance in Tuscaloosa, but Clinton-Dix offers starter-caliber instincts, range, coverage skills and tackling ability as a free safety. Should be a Day One starter.

Draft projection: First-round pick.

Scout's take: "When I sat down and watched him, I was a little disappointed. I didn't think he was as good of an athlete as I thought he was going to be. Some other (scouts) were trying to compare him to Mark Barron and LaRon Landry and all the guys that went high. This guy is not the same. I didn't see the cover skills that everyone seems to be raving about. I thought he was lacking some of that."

NCB ROSS COCKRELL, #6

DUKE   ▶ GRADE: 5.34

Ht: 6-0 | Wt: 191 | Sp: 4.56 | Arm: 29 7/8 | Hand: 9

History: High school cornerback-receiver who also played basketball and ran track as a North Carolina prep. After redshirting in 2009, he made his collegiate debut in '10 and started 12 games at cornerback, recording 60 tackles, seven pass breakups and a team-high three interceptions. Made 11 starts in '11, recording 56-9-1 with one tackle for loss. Missed one game with a leg injury. Tallied 71-13-5 with four tackles for loss, one sack and one forced fumble in '12 (13 starts). Had a school-record 75-yard blocked field goal return for a touchdown against Florida International and had a 32-yard interception return for a score against North Carolina Central. In '13, made 13 starts and recorded 46-12-3 with two tackles for loss, one sack and one forced fumble. Missed one game with an ankle injury. Team captain. Concluded his career as Duke's all-time leader in interceptions (12) and passes broken up (41).

Strengths: Plays smart and has a good feel for the game — eyes, anticipation and awareness. Plays with discipline and takes a consistent approach. Good route recognition. Lines up in the slot and is quick and agile enough to handle dynamic receivers. Sorts through route combinations and maintains positioning. Good leaping ability — competes for the ball in the air. Has jammer experience on special teams.

Weaknesses: Has small hands, short arms and a thin frame, especially in the lower body. Limited press strength to match up against bigger receivers. Often plays to the boundary. Has some tightness in his hips that shows re-directing — allows separation at the break point. Does not step up and take on blocks and overall game lacks physicality.

Future: Good-sized, smart, ballhawking zone corner who plays fast and could bring immediate value as a nickel back and contribute on special teams.

Draft projection: Fourth- to fifth-round pick.

Scout's take: "I gave him a sixth-round grade. He has length, but he is not a physical type. He is more of a man-off type. He will do well in zone to sit and read because he is a smart kid. He is not a step-up, take-on guy. I didn't see him play press well. He's built decent up top, but he's a stick in the lower (body) and not fluid. I don't see the quick twitch. He often gets beat off the break. I was expected to see a third-rounder, and I wound up putting a six on him."

RCB AARON COLVIN, #14

OKLAHOMA ▶ GRADE: 5.27

Ht: 5-11 3/8 | Wt: 177 | Sp: 4.55e | Arm: 31 | Hand: 9 1/4

History: His last name is pronounced "COLE-vin." Oklahoma native. Arrived on campus in 2010 and played in 14 games (one start at cornerback) as a true freshman, totaling 34-3-0 with three tackles for loss and one forced fumble. Was moved to strong safety in '11 and had 84-6-0 with 4 1/2 tackles for loss and one-half sack in 12 total starts (including one at cornerback). Missed one game because of a concussion. Following the season, he underwent shoulder surgery and was not on the field during spring drills. Returned to cornerback for the '12 season and registered 61-11-4 with 2 1/2 tackles for loss and two sacks in 13 starts. Despite missing time in '13 with turf toe and shoulder injuries, he recorded 55-3-1 with five tackles for loss and one sack in 11 games (10 starts). Returned a blocked extra-point 98 yards for two points against Kansas. Missed two games to concussions (West Virginia. In January '14, he tore his right ACL during Senior Bowl practice, necessitating surgery (Dr. James Andrews), and was medically excluded from the Combine.

Strengths: Looks the part — good size, body length and athletic ability. Fine technician. Smart and instinctive — can sort out combo routes. Matches up well with taller receivers and can carry them vertically downfield. Functional tackler. Hardworking, respected team leader who will hold teammates accountable. Experienced, three-year starter.

Weaknesses: Average bend, feet and twitch, which negates his transitional quickness and allows receivers to create separation out of breaks. Does not play fast. Lacks striking power. Gets hung up on blocks. Has a concussion

history.

Future: Long, smart, tough, zone corner whose body is not built to withstand heavy contact or the aggression with which he likes to play. Will grow on evaluators the more they watch him and has the instincts to eventually compete for a starting job, though teams could always be looking to upgrade his lack of speed and athletic ability. Torn ACL injury suffered at the Senior Bowl will affect his readiness for the season and could drop his draft status by a round or two.

Draft projection: Fourth- to fifth-round pick.

Scout's take: "I like his size and the way he looks physically. He is tough. He is not a good athlete."

NCB-SS ALDEN DARBY, #4

ARIZONA STATE ▶ GRADE: 5.20

Ht: 5-10 1/8 | Wt: 194 | Sp: 4.66 | Arm: 30 | Hand: 8 1/2

History: Grew up poor in a dangerous part of Long Beach, Calif. Biological parents were in and out of jail, and Alden did not have a place to call home — often had to seek out family members and teammates' families for a bed to sleep in. Was raised by his step-father, who steered him to Millikan High instead of powerhouse Cal Poly so Alden could earn his keep and make his own name. Played quarterback, receiver, defensive back and kick returner, but was lightly recruited before qualifying academically and landing a scholarship at ASU. As a true freshman in 2010, played 11 games and was credited with 14 tackles, zero pass breakups and zero interceptions. Played all 13 games in '11, starting the final two as a nickel back, and collected 51-3-3 (one touchdown) and a tackle for loss. Started all 27 games the next two seasons at boundary safety — totaled 80-7-3 (one TD) with 5 1/2 tackles for loss, two sacks a forced fumble in '12 (13 games) and 72-9-4 with two tackles for loss and two forced fumbles in '13 (14 games). Team captain was the first ASU player given the Pat Tillman Practice Jersey, which head coach Todd Graham gives to those who embody the positive characteristics of the football program and the university. Did not bench press at his pro day (shoulder).

Strengths: Versatile and has played every position in the secondary — safety, corner and nickelback. Football smart — makes the secondary calls and checks. Good strength and pop on contact. Highly respected team leader with a team-first attitude. Outstanding football character. Valuable special teams contributor with gunner experience. Displayed playmaking ability vs. USC the last two years.

Weaknesses: Is tall in his pedal (rises). Has man coverage limitations (average speed and agility to keep phase vertically). Can become a more consistent, secure tackler — plays a bit out of control. Does not show range to get deep over the top and leverage the field from the deep middle (late to arrive). Not a natural hands catcher.

Future: A true tweener, Darby is built like a cornerback but lacks the foot speed to match up one-on-one with receivers and does not have ideal bulk for the safety position. Has overcome a lot of adversity in his life and has make-it intangibles that could resonate with a coaching staff and inspire a locker room. Is worth trying as a zone corner, could add depth to a secondary and compete on special teams.

Draft projection: Late draftable pick.

Scout's take: "He's an undersized safety. He's smart with really good strength and pop. He's a cross between a safety and corner. He's lean, ripped up and chiseled, but he does not have the speed of a corner or the bulk of a safety. I like him as a leader and all that. I wish he were a better tackler. He's limited for what we want."

RCB-RS CHRIS DAVIS, #11

AUBURN ▶ GRADE: 5.12

Ht: 5-9 7/8 | Wt: 202 | Sp: 4.56 | Arm: 31 | Hand: 9 1/4

History: Has a son. Also played basketball as an Alabama prep. Played in all 14 games for Auburn as a true freshman in 2010 and had 19 tackles, three pass breakups and zero interceptions. Was injured on the opening kickoff of the BCS National Championship Game against Oregon, rolling his right ankle and missing the rest of the contest. Started 11 games at cornerback in '11 and had 60-4-0 with a forced fumble. Missed two games because of a high ankle sprain. Saw action in nine games in '12 (six starts) and totaled 41-3-0 with 1 1/2 tackles for loss. Missed three games after suffering a concussion. Had a memorable senior season in '13, starting 12 games and tallying 74-15-0 with 2 1/2 tackles for loss and one forced fumble. On November 30 against previously No. 1 Alabama, he returned a missed 57-yard field goal 109 yards with no time remaining on the clock for a game-winning touchdown. Saw his first collegiate action returning punts and finished third in the nation in punt return average, returning 17 for 318 yards (18.7-yard average) and an 85-yard score against Tennessee. Missed two games with an ankle injury. Did not work out at the Combine because of a right knee injury (medical exclusion).

Strengths: Physical supporting the run — fills quickly and likes to hit. Tough pound-for-pound. Takes on bigger receivers with aggression and sets a hard edge. Plays off blocks well. Good open-field tackler. Good press strength to re-route receivers at the line. Alert in zones. Has big-play return ability (recorded most memorable play of the 2013 season returning field goal 109 yards for TD vs. Alabama). Can factor as a punt returner with a low center of gravity and good run strength. Emotional, energetic field presence. Respected team leader.

Weaknesses: Is short, short-armed and very stiff-hipped. Straight-linish and tight transitioning — allows separation at break points. Marginal ball skills and hands (zero career interceptions). Gets caught playing flat-footed and peeking. Can do a better job carrying receivers in short zones. Mismatched vs. bigger receivers and struggles contending in the red zone.

Future: A compact, physical zone corner with intriguing return skill, Davis will be more challenged by his lack of height and tight hips in the pros. His intangibles, toughness against the run and ability to factor as a punt returner will allow him to carve out a role.

Draft projection: Fifth- to sixth-round pick.

Scout's take: "I heard a great one today. One of the younger scouts said — 'Davis plays really well vs. big guys.' I asked him, 'How'd that work out against Florida State.' Maybe he can check the cover of *Sports Illustrated* where (Kelvin) Benjamin is catching the game-winner on him in the national championship game. I heard some (scouts) putting Davis in the second round in the fall, getting caught up in his size and comparing him to the kid who Kansas City (Javier Arenas) took in the second round a few years ago. How did that work out for them. He's on the street now. Guys can try to manufacture players all they want. I know he got some notoriety from the big field goal return (to beat Alabama). As a corner, he's a free agent. He will get stretched and beat over the top."

BCB DARQUEZE DENNARD, #31

MICHIGAN STATE ▶ GRADE: 6.10

Ht: 5-10 7/8 | Wt: 199 | Sp: 4.51 | Arm: 30 1/4 | Hand: 9

History: His name is pronounced "DAR-kwez duh-NARD." His cousin, Alfonzo Dennard, is a cornerback with the Patriots. Two-way standout as a Georgia prep. As a senior in 2009, he caught 11 touchdown passes, returned two of his nine interceptions for scores and ran back two punts for touchdowns. Also lettered in basketball and track. Saw action in six games (two starts at boundary corner) as a true freshman in 2010, recording 11 tackles, zero pass breakups and zero interceptions with two tackles for loss, one sack and one forced fumble. Did not see action in two early season games (coach's decision) and missed the final five games with a knee injury. Made 11 starts at boundary corner in '11 and totaled 42-3-3 with one tackle for loss. Tied a Spartans bowl-game record with two interceptions in an Outback Bowl victory over Georgia, including a 38-yard touchdown return. Missed three games with an ankle injury. Started 13 games at field corner in '12, tallying 52-7-3 with 3 1/2 tackles for loss. After the season, he underwent double hernia surgery and was limited in spring drills. Was the Jim Thorpe Award winner as the nation's best defensive back in '13, starting 14 times at boundary corner and recording 62-10-4 with 3 1/2 tackles for loss and two forced fumbles. Became the first Spartans cornerback to earn unanimous first-team all-America honors and also was selected as the Big Ten's Defensive Back of the Year. Team captain. Did not do drills at the Combine because of a left hamstring injury.

Strengths: Looks the part — well-proportioned, muscular physique with strong calves and thin ankles. Good press strength. Controlled, efficient pedal. Field-fast with competitive play speed. Transitions cleanly in man-off coverage. Has very good eyes and anticipation and reacts quickly to what he sees. Good pattern recognition — sorts out what he sees quickly. Stays in the hip pocket downfield. Swift speed turn. Likeable personality. Accountable with leadership traits.

Weaknesses: Has been slowed by injuries and durability needs to be examined closely (double hernia surgery). Showed some hip stiffness in Combine drills. Was not asked to play a lot of zone coverage. Could stand to get functionally stronger and work to disengage from blocks. Could show more consistent willingness to support the run and set a hard edge. Selective physicality.

Future: Solidly built, athletic, instinctive, press-man cover man who took his game to another level as a senior. Brings intensity, confidence and competitiveness to the corner. Offers size to lock horns with bigger receivers, and has a ceiling as a No. 2 cover man.

Draft projection: First-round pick.

Scout's take: "I put him in the third early in the year. He'll go higher with all the pub on him now. Some of the short-area stuff he is not very good at. Our (scouts) had grades on him from the first through the third round. He'll probably go in the second. Maybe he gets into the late first."

LCB-KR PIERRE DESIR, #3

LINDENWOOD   ▶ GRADE: 5.42

Ht: 6-1 | Wt: 198 | Sp: 4.59 | Arm: 33 | Hand: 9 5/8

History: Married with two daughters. A native of Port Au Prince, Haiti, he emigrated to the St. Louis area with his parents when he was four years old. In January 2010, his grandfather and an eight-month-old cousin were among those killed in the earthquakes that devastated Haiti. Had two surgeries in 2004 to repair a chipped bone in the growth plate of his left knee. Began his college career at Division II Washburn University in Kansas, redshirting in 2008. In '09, he played 11 games at cornerback and recorded 33 tackles, six pass breakups and four seven interceptions to go with two forced fumbles. Had 10 kickoff returns for 294 yards (29.4-yard average). Appeared in 12 games in '10 and had 33-4-5 with 5 1/2 tackles for loss, two sacks and one forced fumble while returning kickoffs 17-333 (19.6). Sat out in '11, moving his family back home to Missouri and transferring to Division II Lindenwood University. In '12, tallied 60-9-9 with 2 1/2 tackles for loss and one sack in 12 starts. His school-record nine interceptions ranked second among all NCAA levels. Was the '13 winner of the Cliff Harris Award, given to the nation's top small college defensive back, after recording 33-8-4 with one tackle for loss and one forced fumble. Earned invitations to the East-West Shrine Game and the Senior Bowl.

Strengths: Outstanding body and arm length — looks the part. Explosive athlete — 11-foot, 1-inch broad jump was second-best at the Combine. Has loose hips and a fluid pedal. Superb two-year production on the ball. Natural interceptor — attacks the ball in the air like a receiver and tracks it very well. Plays big in critical situations. Very confident demeanor. Outstanding zone instincts — sees patterns developing and jumps routes. Solid tackler. Mature and accountable. Experienced, four-year starter. Demonstrated toughness to play hurt.

Weaknesses: Average timed speed. Loses a half-step in transition and will struggle to carry NFL receivers vertically. Does not consistently play to his size as a run defender. Could stand to do a better job wrapping as a tackler and filling faster — does not always play to his size in the run game. Production was inflated by marginal competition.

Future: Overaged, exceptional-sized, zone cover man who was a big fish in a Division II small pond, though he did not look out of place when he was introduced to Division I all-stars after the season. Size, ball skills and anticipation will appeal to teams such as the Seahawks, Jaguars and Buccaneers.

Draft projection: Fourth- to fifth-round pick.

Scout's take: "Someone will get caught up in his size and give him a chance. We have him in the fifth right now on our board."

SS AHMAD DIXON, #6

BAYLOR   ▶ GRADE: 5.22
Ht: 6-0 | Wt: 212 | Sp: 4.64 | Arm: 32 1/4 | Hand: 9 7/8

History: Highly recruited Texas prep who also lettered in track, advancing to the state meet as part of the 4x400-meter relay team as a sophomore. Appeared in 11 games as a true freshman in 2010, seeing action as a backup safety and on special teams. Recorded 16 tackles and one forced fumble. Missed two games with an undisclosed injury. Moved into a starting role in '11, starting 13 times at the hybrid nickelback position and registering 89 tackles, three pass breakups and one interception with 5 1/2 tackles for loss. Made the switch from safety to nickelback during spring drills. Returned his first career interception 55 yards for a touchdown against Rice. In '12, he started all 13 games at the nickel position and had 102-3-2 with 5 1/2 tackles for loss and one

sack. In '13, tallied 81-6-1 with two tackles for loss in 13 games (12 starts). Had 11 starts at safety and one at nickelback. His one missed start was a result of a targeting penalty against TCU, forcing him to the sideline for the first half of the ensuing Texas affair. Was arrested on misdemeanor assault charges in September, but was subsequently cleared by a grand jury.

Strengths: Very good size. Is aggressive stepping downhill and supporting the run. Closes fast to the ball. Secure, wrap tackler. Takes efficient angles and is a reliable last line of defense. Good backside chase pursuit. Solid special-teams potential.

Weaknesses: Very tight in the hips — straight-linish. Pedals tall and is late transitioning. Average recovery speed. Limited cover skills and awareness. Marginal ball skills and small, shaky hands (four career INTs in three seasons as a starter). Very average football IQ — takes an extra tick to sort out routes and digest what he sees. Narrow vision. Limited agility and change of direction in man coverage. See-and-go reactor (not instant or anticipatory diagnosing). Not a forceful tackler or explosive hitter. Posted worst vertical jump (32 inches), broad jump (9 feet, 2 inches) and 3-cone drill (7.55 seconds) among defensive backs at the Combine. Cleared of charges, but September assault incident requires closer scrutiny.

Future: Box safety possessing the physical talent to compete in the NFL and even earn a starting job eventually if he can stay focused, commit to a playbook and hone his eyes. Should be able to factor readily on special teams. Coverage limitations will leave him vulnerable and would be best in a very simple scheme.

Draft projection: Fifth- to sixth-round pick.

Scout's take: "I just left Baylor. I put Dixon in the sixth (round). He can't sort it out. He had bad ball skills. He has to play in the box. He is a straight-line, tight-hipped striker, and you can't ask him to handle a lot."

LCB BRANDON DIXON, #1

NORTHWEST MISSOURI STATE ▶ GRADE: 5.29
Ht: 5-11 1/2 | Wt: 203 | Sp: 4.41 | Arm: 32 1/2 | Hand: 9

History: Prepped in Florida. Began his college career at Joliet Junior College in Illinois in 2010, appearing in 10 games and recording 21 tackles, four pass breakups and three interceptions with 2 1/2 tackles for loss and one sack. In '11, tallied 37-7-2 in seven games with one-half tackle for loss. Moved on to Division II Northwest Missouri State in '12, lining up opposite his brother at the cornerback spots. In 13 starts, he totaled 38-5-5 with one tackle for loss. Had two interceptions in his Bearcat debut against East Central, including a 38-yard touchdown return. Also had two punt returns for

27 yards. Registered 36-11-1 with one tackle for loss and a fumble return for a touchdown in '13 (14 starts). Helped lead his school to the NCAA Division II football championship.

Strengths: Excellent size, musculature and body length. Nice balance and body control. Quick-footed to mirror off the line. Can flip his hips and run vertically. Good plant-and-drive quickness. Willing to step up and throw his weight around in run support. Has special-teams experience. Tough and durable. Competitive and motivated.

Weaknesses: Has small hands. Lacks elite explosion and top-end speed. Ordinary leaping ability and ball skills to contend with taller high fliers. Faulty diagnostic skills — processes slowly and reacts more than he anticipates. Gets caught squatting and peeking. Inconsistent tackler. Poor football aptitude — requires extra reps to grasp complicated assignments.

Future: Big, athletic, Division II standout and JUCO product whose size, length and physicality will appeal to teams in search of a developmental press corner. Could also be viewed as a potential safety conversion, but does not exhibit requisite instincts and dependability as a tackler.

Draft projection: Late draftable pick.

Scout's take: "I interviewed him and his brother. All they do is man cover. You ask them about zone coverage, and they couldn't tell you the first thing about it. Someone will see their size and like their ability to press. If you keep it simple for them, there could be some value. I could see Seattle being interested."

FS-LCB JONATHAN DOWLING, #1 (JUNIOR)

WESTERN KENTUCKY   ▶ GRADE: 5.29
Ht: 6-2 3/4 | Wt: 190 | Sp: 4.52 | Arm: 33 1/8 | Hand: 9 1/4

History: Was rated as one of the top safeties in the country as a Florida prep. During his senior season, he had 14 interceptions (returning two for touchdowns) and three blocked punts. Also lettered in track. Began his college career at Florida, seeing action in two games as a true freshman in 2010. In November, though, he was kicked off the team in-season by coach Urban Meyer for reportedly not complying with staff and coaches as well as skipping class. Sat out in '11, transferring to Western Kentucky. Returned to the field in '12 and immediately made his presence felt, recording 68 tackles, seven pass breakups and six interceptions with 2 1/2 tackles for loss and two forced fumbles in 12 games (11 starts) at free safety. Scored on a 39-yard interception return against North Texas. Was suspended one game for a hit classified as "flagrant and dangerous" which had earned him an ejection. Started 12 games and tallied 67-7-3

with one tackle for loss and an NCAA-leading six forced fumbles in '13. Returned a blocked field goal 70 yards for a touchdown against Morgan State.

Strengths: Has a rangy frame with room for added bulk. Excellent height and long arms to contend in the air and play the pocket. Good hands to snatch interceptions. Nice linear fluidity. Covers ground with long strides — rangy off the hash to get over the top. Flashes striking ability when his shoulder blows connect. Playmaking ability — 9 INTs and 8 FFs in last two seasons. Has special-teams experience covering kicks.

Weaknesses: High-cut and lanky for a safety — durability could be an issue and he needs to add body armor. Repped 225 pounds just eight times at the Combine. Gets bullied in the box. Average eyes and instincts. Takes some inaccurate angles. Shoddy tackler with poor fundamentals — hits too high, ankle-bites low or launches himself and whiffs. Talks too much and shows off-putting body language. Questionable mental toughness. Thinks he's better than he is. Character, maturity and coachability should be looked into.

Future: Lean, long-levered, smooth-muscled, finesse free safety with speed and range, though he's more interested in hitting than securing tackles — he does not provide dependability desired on the back end.

Draft projection: Fourth- to fifth-round pick.

RCB-FS ANTONE EXUM, #1

VIRGINIA TECH   ▶ GRADE: 5.45
Ht: 5-11 5/8 | Wt: 213 | Sp: 4.59 | Arm: 31 5/8 | Hand: 9 5/8

History: His first name is pronounced "AN-tone." High school defensive back-quarterback who also returned kicks as a Virginia prep. Redshirted in 2009. Saw his first collegiate action in '10 and played in 14 games, including four starts at free safety and one start at the WHIP linebacker position — had 45 tackles, a team-high nine pass breakups and zero interceptions with 1 1/2 tackles for loss and one forced fumble. Was suspended for the first quarter of the Orange Bowl for missing a team curfew. Started all 14 games in '11 (11 FS, three at rover) and had 89-10-1 with five tackles for loss, 1 1/2 sacks and two forced fumbles. During spring drills in '12, he was moved to cornerback and had a breakout year, totaling 48-16-5 with 1 1/2 tackles for loss and two forced fumbles in 13 starts. Was named the MVP of the Russell Athletic Bowl, returning an interception 32 yards in the Hokies' victory over Rutgers. Suffered a torn ACL and lateral meniscus of his right knee in a pickup basketball game in January '13, necessitating surgery (Dr. James Andrews). Was unable to participate in off-season workouts and spring drills. After sitting out the first seven weeks of the season, he returned to the field in October and started three games, tallying 4-1-0. Early in his third start against Miami, he sprained his left ankle and missed the rest of the year.

Strengths: Thickly built with defined muscle, a nice wing span and thin ankles. Very good body control and ball skills — adjusts well in the air. Fluid pedal and movement skill for his size. Very good press strength to hem receivers at the line. Has extensive experience at safety and was used as a gunner and jammer on special teams. Very smart and well-spoken.

Weaknesses: Average short-area quickness and leaping ability. Technique needs to be coached up. Not natural commanding the back end and making coverage adjustments vs. complex schemes. — Likes to do things his own way — confidence borders on arrogance and could rub some people the wrong way

Future: Big, strong cornerback with appealing size, field speed and press-coverage ability. Must prove that he can recover from offseason knee surgery and return to being the player he was as a junior.

Draft projection: Third- to fourth-round pick.

Scout's take: "He is a good athlete. He can man cover. If you put him in a zone system where he has to make a lot of adjustments, he will struggle. He has played safety and corner. I don't think he is a safety. He is a corner in the league. That's where his value will be. You have to go back to his junior year to appreciate what he can do."

LCB KYLE FULLER, #17

VIRGINIA TECH   ▶ GRADE: 5.90

Ht: 5-11 3/4 | Wt: 190 | Sp: 4.49 | Arm: 32 7/8 | Hand: 9 3/8

History: Is part of a quartet of Fuller brothers to play for Virginia Tech. His oldest brother, Vincent, lettered for the Hokies from 2001-2004 and played parts of seven years in the NFL with Tennessee and Detroit. Was teammates with brother Corey (who is now with the Lions) in 2012. Played alongside his youngest brother Kendall in the Tech secondary in 2013. His cousin, Damien Russell, started the family tradition when he played for the Hokies from 1988-1991. In high school, the Baltimore native missed most of his senior year with a finger injury. Arrived in '10 and saw action in 12 games as a true freshman, starting six games (two at boundary corner, one at field corner, three at the whip linebacker position) — recorded 32 tackles, six pass breakups and zero interceptions with four tackles for loss and one forced fumble. Made all 14 starts in '11 (seven at CB, seven at the nickelback/whip) and had 65-7-2 with a team-high 14 1/2

tackles for loss, 4 1/2 sacks and one forced fumble. Recovered a blocked punt in the end zone against Appalachian State. Started all 13 games at cornerback in '12 and had 52-5-2 with three tackles for loss and one forced fumble. Was limited to nine games (eight starts) in '13 with a sports hernia, undergoing surgery in late November (Dr. William Meyers). Missed four games with the injury. Had 24-10-2 with two tackles for loss, one forced fumble and his first career blocked punt. Team captain.

Strengths: Good size, arm length and balance. Plays faster than he times thanks to keen instincts, anticipation and route recognition. Zone aware with good eyes, ball reactions and hands to intercept. Outstanding leaping ability — has a 38 1/2-inch vertical jump and broad jumped 10 feet, 8 inches at the Combine. Willing run supporter. Has special-teams experience, including as a gunner and jammer. Tough and durable — logged 41 career starts. Team captain who understands what it means to be a pro. Was a 21-year-old senior.

Weaknesses: Could stand to get stronger — managed just 12 benchpress reps at the Combine. Man-cover limitations. Lacks twitch for the position. Has a choppy pedal and some tightness in transition. Gives up separation at the break point. Average production on the ball. Shows some stiffness when required to break down and tackle in space. Slips off some tackles. . Squats on routes and is susceptible to double moves.

Future: Narrow-framed, confident, competitive off-man/zone corner with nice length, field speed and awareness. Is capable of contributing early on special teams and in sub packages.

Draft projection: Second- to third-round pick.

Scout's take: "(Fuller) is a physical player. He's a man cover guy. He's not an off cover guy. He has to be in a system where he's playing man."

RCB E.J. GAINES, #31

MISSOURI   ▶ GRADE: 5.27

Ht: 5-9 5/8 | Wt: 190 | Sp: 4.51 | Arm: 30 3/8 | Hand: 9 3/8

History: Cornerback-running back who also played basketball and ran track as a Missouri prep. Played in 13 games as a true freshman in 2010 and recorded 26 tackles, one pass breakup and zero interceptions as a special-teams player and reserve defensive back. Took over as a starting cornerback in '11 and tallied 69-16-2 with three tackles for loss and one forced fumble. The combined 18 passes defended set a Mizzou record and ranked fourth in the NCAA. Returned nine punts for 98 yards (10.9-yard average) and one touchdown, a 44-

scamper against Western Illinois. In '12, he totaled 74-11-1 with seven tackles for loss and two forced fumbles. Scored on a 13-yard fumble recovery against Kentucky. In '13, recorded 75-3-5 with four tackles for loss. In the SEC Championship game against Auburn, he had an 11-yard fumble recovery for a TD. Missed two games with a quad strain. Team captain. Bench pressed at the Combine, but was medically excluded otherwise (pelvis).

Strengths: Good muscularity and thin ankles. Fills aggressively and supports the run. Likes to hit. Plays with confidence and carries a swagger. Good attitude and football demeanor. Competes hard and brings energy to the field. Good eyes and route recognition. Has experience matching up with slot receivers in nickel coverage and has returned punts. Very good career production on the ball. Proven special teams coverage defender.

Weaknesses: Is short and short-armed. Plays a lot into the boundary. Shows some tightness in his hips. Average transitional quickness — lacks ideal burst and acceleration to recover and close ground. Can do a better job disengaging from blocks. Most of interception production stemmed from tips and overthrown balls (not created). Average hands.

Future: Strong, physical zone corner with the toughness, awareness and football IQ to function highly in short spaces. A solid tackler, Gaines plays bigger than his size and takes a professional approach. Can make an immediate impact on special teams and work his way into a lineup.

Draft projection: Fourth- to fifth-round pick.

RCB PHILLIP GAINES, #15

RICE ▶ GRADE: 5.33

Ht: 6-0 3/8 | Wt: 193 | Sp: 4.38 | Arm: 31 7/8 | Hand: 9 5/8

History: Also lettered in track as a Texas prep. Played in nine games as a true freshman 2009 (starting four times at field corner and twice at boundary corner) and had 31 tackles, three pass breakups and zero interceptions with one tackle for loss. Missed the final three games because of a broken right wrist. Saw action in 12 games (10 starts at boundary corner) in '10 and had 64-6-0 with two tackles for loss, one sack and one forced fumble. Had a blocked PAT against Tulsa. In April '11, he was arrested on a misdemeanor possession of two ounces or less of marijuana. He posted a $500 bail and was sentenced to one year of probation. In the fall, he started the first four games at left cornerback, but sustained a foot injury in the Southern Miss game. Missed the remainder of the year and was granted a medical hardship by the NCAA. Totaled 11-2-0 with two tackles for loss and one sack. Returned healthy in '12

and started all 13 games at right cornerback, tallying 33-18-0 with two tackles for loss. Ranked second nationally with his 18 pass breakups. Returned a fumble 12 yards for a touchdown against Memphis. In '13, started 13 times at RCB and recorded 36-9-4 with four tackles for loss. Was suspended for the season opener for an undisclosed violation of team rules. Set a school record with his 38 career pass breakups.

Strengths: Nice length. Terrific timed speed — blazed sub-4.4 times at the Combine. Can be deployed in zone coverage. Plays the pocket. Good production on the ball — 35 passes defended the last two seasons. Tough and competitive. Is hardworking and well respected by coaches and teammates. Recorded second-quickest 3-cone drill among cornerbacks at the Combine (6.62 seconds).

Weaknesses: Durability is a concern (has been dinged up). Underdeveloped and underpowered. Does not play to timed speed. Not equipped to handle man-to-man responsibility. Poor run supporter and tackler. Does not project as a core special-teams player. Tweener traits.

Future: Lean, active zone corner whose ball skills will have to carry him. Could earn a roster spot on pure measurables, but lacks lacks desirable functional speed, twitch and physicality.

Draft projection: Fourth- to fifth-round pick.

LCB-RS JUSTIN GILBERT, #4

OKLAHOMA STATE ▶ GRADE: 6.45

Ht: 6-0 1/8 | Wt: 202 | Sp: 4.37 | Arm: 33 1/8 | Hand: 8 5/8

History: Played quarterback and defensive back as a Texas prep, also competing in basketball and track. Burst on the scene as a true freshman in 2010, returning 26 kickoffs for 698 yards (26.8-yard average) and two touchdowns while returning eight punts for 55 yards (6.9) in 12 games. As a reserve defensive back and special teams player, he had 18 tackles, one pass breakup and zero interceptions with one forced fumble. Missed one game with an undisclosed injury. Started 13 games at cornerback in '11 and had 59-10-5 with one tackle for loss. As a kickoff returner, he went 26-703-2 (27.0) with a pair of scores. Had interceptions against a trio of quarterbacks who became NFL Top 10 picks — Stanford's Andrew Luck, Baylor's Robert Griffin III and Texas A&M's Ryan Tannehill. In 13 starts in '12, he tallied 63-9-0 with 2 1/2 tackles for loss and one forced fumble. As a kickoff returner, he was 32-827-1 (25.8) with a 96-yard scoring romp against West Virginia. Was a Jim Thorpe Award finalist in '13 after registering 42-7-7 in 13 games (10 starts) with 18-453-1 (25.2) as a kickoff returner. Had interception returns for touchdowns of 31 yards at Iowa State and 43 yards at Texas. Did not start against Kansas State, sitting out the first half after being ejected the week before against West Virginia. Did not start and was limited against Baylor with an injured left shoulder. Concluded his college career with eight non-offensive touchdowns, including six on kickoff returns — one shy of the NCAA record.

Strengths: Outstanding size-speed ratio and athletic ability — pumped 20 benchpress reps and was the fastest cornerback at the Combine. Long arms. Fluid movement skills — makes it look easy flipping his hips and reacting to the thrown ball. Very good transitional quickness and recovery speed. Superb feet and agility to pop out of his breaks and close on the ball — explosively quick. Natural interceptor with very good hand-eye coordination, leaping ability and overall ball skills. Very good vision and traffic burst as a returner (6 career kickoff-return TDs).

Weaknesses: Is a bit soft-tempered — not as aggressive or physical in run support as you would expect for his size. Can do a better job shedding blockers. Too often lets teammates arrive first at the scene. Spent time in the doghouse as a young player. Has some growing up to do — maintains a lockdown corner's ego, at times coasts on his natural talent and is not immune to mental errors.

Future: The most talented cover corner in this year's draft class, Gilbert has size, speed and flexibility to blanket receivers at the next level. Also brings impact ability as a kick returner. Is capable of stepping into the starting lineup from Day One and playing at a high level if he adheres to a professional approach to the craft. Could stand to improve in run support.

Draft projection: Top-10 pick.

Scout's take: "(Gilbert) struggled as a junior. I don't think he is a bad kid. He may be naive and a little soft. But where do you find corners that are big, fast and athletic. From what I have seen, he is top 15 easy. I go across the country, and I haven't seen one better yet. ...Watch him vs. West Virginia last year and he and Steadman Bailey went at it and got the best of each other. I'm not sure how overall tough he is in the run game. He has a medium build with a really tight waist. Ball skills is what he has — he can turn it over."

RCB DEMETRI "MEECH" GOODSON, #3

BAYLOR ▶ GRADE: 5.05
Ht: 5-11 | Wt: 194 | Sp: 4.52 | Arm: 31 3/4 | Hand: 9 1/4

History: His brother, Mike, is a running back for the Jets. Demetri began his college career as a basketball player at Gonzaga, averaging 5.1 points per game in 103 contests over three seasons. In 2011, he decided to give football another try and transferred to Baylor. Saw

action in four games as a defensive reserve and on special teams, recording one tackle and returning three kickoffs for 100 yards and zero touchdowns (33.3-yard average). Tore ligaments in his right ankle on a kickoff October 8, missing the rest of the season. Earned a starting cornerback job in '12 and started the first three games of the season. Did not start the fourth game, but fractured his right forearm in two spots in the first quarter against West Virginia and missed the remainder of the year. Had 16 tackles, two pass breakups and one interception with two tackles for loss. Also was 2-49-0 (24.5) returning kickoffs. He was granted a medical-hardship waiver to play in '13 and saw his most extensive gridiron action, appearing in 11 games (10 starts) and tallying 26-13-3. Led the team in interceptions, including a pick against Central Florida's Blake Bortles in the Tostitos Fiesta Bowl. Missed the first two games of the season with a bone bruise after reinjuring his right arm in one of the final fall scrimmages.

Strengths: Excellent size. Good athletic ability, hand-eye coordination and ball production. Can turn and run vertical. Nice plant-and-drive — breaks on throws. Has a 37-inch vertical. Has some upside. Comes from an athletic family and has NFL bloodlines.

Weaknesses: Has been unable to stay in one piece and durability is a major concern. Has short arms and small hands. Needs to get stronger. Relatively inexperienced with green instincts. Press technique needs to be coached up. Loses separation at the break point. Limited tackle production — gets stuck on blocks and doesn't set a hard edge. Will be a 25-year-old rookie.

Future: Overaged, injury-prone, height-weight-speed prospect with a basketball background. Shows in flashes when he's able to rely on his reactionary skills and natural athleticism to break up throws, but he is raw and will have to prove he offers developmental value.

Draft projection: Priority free agent.

LCB ANDRE HAL, #23

VANDERBILT ▶ GRADE: 5.23
Ht: 5-10 3/8 | Wt: 188 | Sp: 4.51 | Arm: 30 1/2 | Hand: 8 5/8

History: His last name is pronounced "HAL." The Baton Rouge-area prep was a four-year starter at defensive back. Also lettered in basketball and track, and was a member of a state champion 4x200-meter relay team. Played in 12 games (two starts at cornerback) as a true freshman in 2010, recording 15 tackles, one pass breakup and zero interceptions. Returned 11 kickoffs for 260 yards (23.6-yard average) and zero touchdowns. Appeared in all 13 games in '11 as a reserve defensive back, tallying 21-1-1. As a kickoff returner, he was 31-738-1 (23.8) with a 96-yard touchdown against Georgia. Moved into the starting lineup in '12 and made 13 starts at cornerback, registering 48-14-2 with two tackles for loss. Was 12-275-0 (22.9) returning kickoffs. In '13, he tallied 49-15-3 with 6 1/2 tackles for loss in 12 games (11 starts). His overall 18 passes defended led the SEC. Missed one game with an injury. Team captain.

Strengths: Has man-cover skills — good balance and flexibility to mirror receivers off the line. Enough speed to run with receivers. Good zone awareness, read-and-react and plant-and-drive. Confident and competitive. Has kickoff-return experience. Solid intangibles.

Weaknesses: Lacks ideal length — has short arms and small hands. Disadvantaged vs. bigger, physical receivers. Limited functional strength to pry himself off blocks. Could stand to refine his technique. Tends to clutch and grab when he's beat, which happens too frequently. Gets out of phase and does not demonstrate a feel for routes. Average leaping ability.

Future: Adequate-sized, pesky corner lacking desirable length and physicality to survive outside. Has competitive makeup for the position to vie for a No. 4 or No. 5 corner spot.

Draft projection: Fifth- to sixth-round pick.

Scout's take: "I thought he was decent coming downhill and supporting. He really struggled in coverage — wide receivers were able to turn him around and beat him out of breaks and over the top. He always loses route awareness and route leverage. Others liked him more than I did. I thought I would see a solid mid-round guy. I beat him up pretty good. I've heard as high as the fourth or fifth. I did not give him a good grade personally."

RCB-SS VICTOR HAMPTON, #27 (JUNIOR)
SOUTH CAROLINA ▶ GRADE: 5.24
Ht: 5-9 | Wt: 197 | Sp: 4.59 | Arm: 31 1/4 | Hand: 9 1/4

History: Had a checkered prep career, getting kicked off three high school teams before moving to Darlington (SC) High in 2009 — earned all-state honors despite playing only six games due to eligibility issues following a transfer. Originally committed to Florida, but the Gators backed off after his dismissal from his football team in Charlotte. Signed with South Carolina in February 2010, and was arrested for underage drinking two days later. Redshirted in '10. The following June, he was kicked off the team for breaking unspecified team rules; he was reinstated the following week and hit with a three-game suspension. Finally saw his first Gamecocks action in the fall of '11 as a reserve cornerback and kick returner,

recording 14 tackles, three pass breakups and one interception. As a starting cornerback in '12, he tallied 40-6-1 with three tackles for loss and one sack. Made 12 starts; in the non-start against Florida, the first defensive play was a goal-line situation. In that game, he returned a blocked extra point for a two-point conversion. Played in all 13 games in '13, and was in the starting lineup 10 times. Did not start against Georgia or in the Capital One Bowl against Wisconsin after unspecified violations of team rules. Recorded 51-9-3 with five tackles for loss and one forced fumble. Had 10 career kickoff returns for 242 yards (24.2-yard average) and 11 punt returns for 25 yards (2.3).

Strengths: Well put together. Good movement skill. Plays with attitude and brings a swagger. Supports the run aggressively and is a physical tackler. Reads the quarterback and jumps routes. Good transitional quickness for his size. Drives hard on the ball. Good anticipation and ball skills. Offers safety-cornerback versatility.

Weaknesses: Character will require careful evaluation — has been troubled by a number of off-field issues dating back to high school, when he attended four different schools. Has had issues with anger management, emotional outbursts and team suspensions. Could be susceptible to unsportsmanlike conduct penalties given tendency to talk and taunt. Lacks ideal height. Below-average timed speed and leaping ability for a corner. Can do a better job using his hands to reroute receivers in press coverage. Weight has ballooned as high as 215.

Future: Thick-bodied defensive back with cornerback and safety traits whose size and speed likely dictate his future at safety in the NFL. Character concerns will cloud his draft status and have already knocked him off some draft boards, and bust potential might outweigh his upside.

Draft projection: Fifth- to sixth-round pick.

Scout's take: "They call him Pacman. He has a lot of pent-up anger. Structure would be very good for him. He's had a lot of issues and is going to be high-maintenance. ... He has some talent though — he really does. He gets in trouble grabbing too much, but he does a good job in man coverage."

FS-LCB MARQUESTON HUFF, #2
WYOMING ▶ GRADE: 5.57
Ht: 5-11 1/8 | Wt: 196 | Sp: 4.49 | Arm: 31 3/8 | Hand: 9

History: The Texas prep lettered in football and track and field. Arrived at Wyoming in 2010 and appeared in all 12 games as a true freshman, recording 18 tackles, one pass breakup and one interception. Saw action as a nickel back and on special teams. Moved into the lineup in '11 and started 13 games at cornerback, registering 47-

2-3 with 2 1/2 tackles for loss and three fumble recoveries. Accounted for both of Wyoming's defensive scores, scooping up fumbles for TD runs of eight yards at Bowling Green and 48 yards at Air Force. Played in 12 games (10 starts) at cornerback in '12 and had 57-7-0 with 1 1/2 tackles for loss, two forced fumbles and one blocked extra-point attempt. Production blossomed after taking over the free safety role in '13, tallying 127-6-2 with three tackles for loss, one forced fumble and one blocked field goal attempt. Team captain.

Strengths: Lean, athletic build. Fluid and sudden with terrific balance. Outstanding speed — carries receivers vertically and flies around the field. Sudden plant and drive. Can elevate to contend in the air and make athletic interceptions. Does not hesitate to support the run. Scheme versatile. Sharp mentally. Three-year starter. Rose to the occasion against better competition and produced big against Nebraska.

Weaknesses: Has very small hands. Gets lax with his technique. Inconsistent, subpar tackler as a safety. Average ball production. Performance is up and down — tapered off as the season wound down.

Future: Fast, rangy, tough, loquacious defensive back who was pushed to play safety to fill a need in his senior season, and offers intriguing versatility on the back end. Projects ideally as a cornerback in the pros, where his explosiveness and physicality will appeal to a wide range of teams. Should contribute readily on special teams and has eventual starter potential.

Draft projection: Third-round pick.

Scout's take: "I really liked him on my school call at the beginning of the fall. His speed is legit, and he plays it. He had a killer game against Nebraska, and I peeked at him later in the year and he wasn't doing much. He kind of shut it down. That was his M.O. — he was an underachiever his whole career. Maybe an agent got in his ear. Who knows — the team was not very good. He is tough and fast. I think he has to be a corner. He was playing safety this year. He's an interesting guy."

RCB BENNETT JACKSON, #2

NOTRE DAME   ▶ GRADE: 5.20
Ht: 5-11 7/8 | Wt: 195 | Sp: 4.51 | Arm: 31 3/8 | Hand: 9 1/4

History: Receiver-defensive back who also competed in sprints and hurdles as a New Jersey prep. Arrived at Notre Dame as a wide receiver in '10 and saw action in 13 games as a true freshman — returned 29 kickoffs for 645 yards (22.2-yard average). Also recorded 10 special-teams tackles. Was primarily used on special teams in '11 as he made the conversion from wide receiver to cornerback, appearing in

13 games — had 18 tackles, including seven on special teams, and was 3-32 (10.7) on kickoff returns. Ran the 60-meter high hurdles for the Notre Dame track team during the '12 indoor season. In the fall, he moved into a full-time role in the secondary, starting 13 games at cornerback and tallying 65 tackles, four pass breakups and four interceptions with 1 1/2 tackles for loss. Played all year with a torn right labrum, which required off-season surgery. Started all 13 games in '13 and registered 64-3-2 with five tackles for loss and one forced fumble. Scored his first Irish touchdown on a 34-yard interception return against Purdue. Team captain.

Strengths: Intriguing height and athleticism. Good hands to intercept (former WR). Demonstrated explosion and lateral agility at the Combine — recorded impressive marks in the vertical jump (38 inches), broad jump (10 feet, 8 inches) and 20-yard shuttle (4.00 seconds). Tough and durable. Has special-teams experience. Team captain with leadership traits and solid football and personal character.

Weaknesses: Could stand to bulk up and get stronger — weak jam to hem and reroute. Still honing technique as instincts as a cornerback. Tends to react instead of anticipate. Choppy transition. Allows too much separation too often. Leaky tackler. Ordinary production on the ball.

Future: Looks the part and has developmental value given his athleticism and desirable makeup, but did not take a significant step forward as a senior. Has traits to contribute initially on special teams while he works on becoming a more well-rounded cornerback.

Draft projection: Fourth- to fifth-round pick.

RCB KENDALL JAMES, #5

MAINE   ▶ GRADE: 5.26
Ht: 5-10 1/4 | Wt: 180 | Sp: 4.44 | Arm: 29 1/2 | Hand: 8

History: Defensive back-receiver who also played basketball and was a member of a state-champion track squad as a New Jersey prep. Redshirted in 2009. Played in 11 games in '10 and made 16 tackles with zero pass breakups and zero interceptions as a reserve defensive back and special-teams player. Started 13 games at right cornerback in '11 and had 50-4-3 with one forced fumble. In '12, he registered 46-12-3 with two forced fumbles in 11 starts at RCB. Scored his lone collegiate touchdown on a 100-yard interception return at Bryant. In '13, recorded 36-9-2 with 2 1/2 tackles for loss in 13 starts at RCB. Also had a blocked field goal against New Hampshire. Did not broad jump at the Combine (hamstring).

Strengths: Outstanding timed speed and leaping ability (39-inch vertical). Terrific balance, body control and agility. Fluid and flexible with loose hips and ankles to transition and change direction smoothly. Mirrors in man coverage. Aware in zone. Plants and drives quickly. Shows burst to close and recover. Good ball skills. Will come up and stick his nose in run support. Has special-teams experience as a gunner. Three-year starter.

Weaknesses: Does not look the part — is skinny with extremely short arms and his hands measured the smallest of all players at the Combine. Must bulk up and get functionally stronger — gets wired to blocks. Benchpressed 225 pounds just nine times at the Combine, one of the lowest totals among DBs. Does not have strength to press — will be outmuscled by larger receivers outside the numbers. Tackles low and needs help from the cavalry when he cannot chop down ball carriers with momentum. Lacks experience playing inside.

Future: Undersized, extremely short-armed, feisty corner with potential to contribute as a sub-package defender. Offers appealing fluidity, twitch, speed and ball skills, though he will always face size and strength limitations.

Draft projection: Fourth- to fifth-round pick.

RCB STANLEY JEAN-BAPTISTE, #16
NEBRASKA   ▶ GRADE: 5.29
Ht: 6-2 5/8 | Wt: 218 | Sp: 4.61 | Arm: 32 3/8 | Hand: 8 5/8

History: Was a wide receiver/safety as a Miami prep. Following high school, he spent one year at North Carolina Tech Preparatory Christian Academy, catching 36 passes for 580 yards. He attended Fort Scott (Kansas) Community College for one year, but did not see any football action. Redshirted as a receiver with Nebraska in 2010. Began the '11 season as a wide receiver before being converted to cornerback early in the campaign. Went on to play in nine games (including one start at right cornerback) and had nine tackles, one pass breakup and one interception. Saw action in 14 games in '12 (five starts at left cornerback) and registered 24-9-2. Had a 48-yard interception return for a score against Minnesota. Was Nebraska's top cover cornerback in '13, starting all 13 games and registering 41-12-4 with three tackles for loss and one sack. Had an interception in each of his first four games, including a 43-yard score against Southern Miss.

Strengths: Physically impressive on the hoof — looks every bit the part with outstanding size and length to mix it up with bigger receivers. Good balance and body control. Jumps routes. Has good hands to intercept and can highpoint throws. Flashes functional strength to reroute receivers, discard blocks and tackle ball carriers. Very productive on the ball in limited time as a starter — 22 pass PBUs and seven INTs in 19 starts at Nebraska. Works to get better and made strides as a senior. Explosion was on display at the Combine, where he posted a 41 1/2-inch vertical jump (best among defensive backs) and 10-foot, 8-inch broad jump.

Weaknesses: Has relatively small hands. Not especially strong for his size. Stiff hips. Is not a quick-twitch athlete and struggles to mirror sudden receivers. Lacks elite top-end speed (long-strider). Green positional instincts. Picks and chooses his spots to be physical — inconsistent run defender. Has tweener traits. Football aptitude is lacking — could struggle to grasp and execute complex assignments. Will be a 24-year-old rookie.

Future: A converted receiver, Jean-Baptiste possesses intriguing ball skills, rare leaping ability and clear upside, though he lacks ideal speed and flexibility, is smoother than he is sudden and does not consistently play to his size. Warrants developmental consideration from teams employing press or Cover-2, and will be in demand given the league's trend towards bigger defensive backs.

Draft projection: Fourth- to fifth-round pick.

Scout's take: "I didn't care for his tape. He is not very aware. He'll go in the third round on his size alone, but he plays small."

LCB-FS DONTAE JOHNSON, #25
NORTH CAROLINA STATE   ▶ GRADE: 5.32
Ht: 6-2 1/8 | Wt: 200 | Sp: 4.46 | Arm: 31 1/2 | Hand: 8 5/8

History: His first name is pronounced "DAHN-tay." Safety-receiver who also played basketball as a New Jersey prep. Played in 13 games (one start) as a true freshman for North Carolina State in 2010 and had 22 tackles, one pass breakup and zero interceptions. His first career start came at free safety against Boston College. Also returned three kickoffs for 40 yards (13.3-yard average). Played primarily as a nickel defender in '11, appearing in 13 games (two starts) and tallying 27-4-0 with three tackles for loss and three sacks. Moved to the boundary cornerback starting slot in '12 and recorded 70-8-0 with six tackles for loss, one sack and one forced fumble. Teamed with Redskins '13 second-rounder David Amerson to make up the tallest pair of starting cornerbacks in the country. Opened '13 at cornerback before switching back to free safety midway through the year. In 12 games (five starts at cornerback, seven at safety), he totaled 82-5-3.

Strengths: Good height, balance and athleticism. Can run with tight ends in coverage. Zone aware. Efficient plant-and-drive. Has a 38 1/2-inch vertical jump. Sets a hard edge in run support — works to get off blocks, throws his weight around and tackles aggressively. Has played safety, cornerback, nickel and special teams. Smart and hardworking.

Weaknesses: Is lean and needs to bulk up and get stronger. Has short arms and small hands. Lacks elite top-end speed (struggled mightily to contain Clemson WR Sammy Watkins). Hesitates to diagnose from depth and takes some inaccurate angles. Shows tightness in transition. Struggles to break down and tackle in space. Ordinary ball production.

Future: Wiry, narrow-framed, high-cut, athletic defensive back who would be best in a predominantly zone scheme where he would have value as a versatile backup.

Draft projection: Fifth- to sixth-round pick.

Scout's take: "I liked him a little bit. He's a decent tackler with size and range ability. I put him in the middle of four. He's playing safety now, but if you want him at corner, it might push him up."

RCB-NS LAMARCUS JOYNER, #20

FLORIDA STATE   ▶ GRADE: 5.24
Ht: 5-8 | Wt: 184 | Sp: 4.56 | Arm: 31 1/2 | Hand: 9 1/2

History: Elite defensive back recruit out of Florida prep powerhouse St. Thomas Aquinas, where he played cornerback and piled up 1,090 all-purpose yards on just 79 touches en route to being named USA Today's National Defensive Player of the Year. Arrived at Florida State in 2010 and played in all 14 games as a true freshman, recording 23 tackles, three pass breakups and one interception. Returned 16 kickoffs for 329 yards (20.6-yard average). Started all 13 games at free safety in '11 and tallied 54-3-4 with two tackles for loss and one sack. Was 13-397-0 (30.5) returning kickoffs. Moved into the strong safety role in '12, starting 14 games and totaling 51-5-1 with 1 1/2 tackles for loss. Was 18-424-0 (23.6) as a kickoff returner. Was a Jim Thorpe Award finalist in '13, starting six times at cornerback and eight times in a nickel position for the national champions — posted 69-4-2 with seven tackles for loss, 5 1/2 sacks and three forced fumbles. Also went 5-110-0 (22.0) returning kickoffs. His sack total ranked first among NCAA defensive backs. Did not miss a game in his four years at Florida State, concluding his time there with 41 consecutive starts.

Strengths: Instinctive and anticipatory. Advanced understanding from the back end — makes subtle, pre-snap adjustments and diagnoses plays. Steps downhill quickly. Outstanding overall production in all facets. Good competitive playing speed — runs as fast as he needs to. Very good football-playing demeanor — confident and opportunistic. Showed up in big games and made clutch plays (see Clemson). Times up the blitz very well and

plays bigger than his size. Has contributed as a gunner and displayed good short-area burst in the return game. Exceptional work ethic and leadership traits. Respected, vocal team leader with an infectious attitude that can unite a locker room. Has been extremely durable, especially given his size and playing style.

Weaknesses: Average athlete. Tight-hipped and rounds off breaks — not sudden. Lacks foot speed to carry receivers vertically from the slot and is seldom placed in situations where he can be distressed in downfield coverage. Lacks size and stature for press coverage. Can be out-quicked by shifty slot receivers. Marginal recovery speed and catch-up burst when he gets caught peeking. Struggles to match up with size and speed in man coverage. Very average 3-cone drill (7.26 seconds) and short shuttle (4.40) for his size. Makes mental mistakes too much in banjo coverage and struggles to sort out bunch sets. Does not have a body ideally built to withstand a 16-game season.

Future: A terrific college football player and galvanizing leader for a national champion, Joyner is a tweener lacking unique physical traits for the pro game, and his dimensions leave him vulnerable to mismatches. However, he possesses special intangibles which could enable him to make his mark on special teams and compete for a sub-package role as a short-hole plugger where he can make plays on the ball in front of him.

Draft projection: Fourth- to fifth-round pick.

Scout's take: "I like him. He is just small. He is best as a nickel safety. He has pretty good cover skills. He is a little tight-hipped so he can get beat off hard breaks. He is not sudden so he will give up separation to a (Julian) Edelman. That is where he gives up catches in games. When he can play off and react to (routes) underneath, he does a really good job. At corner, he is the same way — his size and stature work against him. He doesn't have elite speed to be a corner, but he's a helluva little football player. I put him in the fourth (round)."

FS KENNY LADLER, #1

VANDERBILT   ▶ GRADE: 4.95
Ht: 6-0 1/8 | Wt: 207 | Sp: 4.69 | Arm: 31 5/8 | Hand: 9 5/8

History: Stone Mountain, Ga. product who also ran track in high school. As a true freshman in 2010, played all 12 games at strong safety (nine starts) — had 57 tackles, two pass breakups and one interception with 5 1/2 tackles for loss and one forced fumble. Appeared in 13 games in '11, making six starts at free safety, and recorded 53-3-1 with one tackle for loss. Made 12 starts at FS in '12 and totaled 90-1-2 with 3 1/2 tackles for loss, one sack and one forced fumble. Missed one game with an undisclosed injury. In '13, he saw action in 13 games at FS (12 starts) and registered 91-4-5 with one tackle for loss and a school-record five forced fumbles (tied for the most in the NCAA). Led the team in tackles and interceptions, while his 65 solo tackles ranked second in the SEC. Did not start the Wake Forest game after being ejected the previous week for a targeting infraction. Did not run shuttles or participate in drills at the Combine (right hamstring).

Strengths: Good size, movement and flexibility. Efficient plant and drive on throws in front of him. Shows the ability to swoop downhill and support the run. Tries for the strip (forced five fumbles as a senior). Asset in the building — terrific character. Durable and experienced. Was a 21-year-old senior. Benchpressed 225 pounds 24 times at the Combine, second most among DBs.

Weaknesses: Pedestrian timed speed. Average instincts and anticipation — can be a tick late to read and react. Poor center fielder. Manipulated by QBs. Unreliable last line of defense. Inconsistent open-field tackler. Average tackle strength — catches contact. Strong safety only.

Future: Lean, athletic, finesse free safety with the chops to hold down a backup job in a system where he could react to plays in front of him, though he will have to demonstrate utility on special teams to stick.

Draft projection: Priority free agent.

Scout's take: "(Ladler) was the guy that I thought had the best chance of all the DB's there. He is a sixth-round type. He's good in run support. He struggles when he has to flip his hips and adjust on the move. He had to gather a lot, and I didn't see the closing burst, but he was the one guy of their secondary group who I thought had a chance, mainly because of his size."

RCB NEVIN LAWSON, #5

UTAH STATE ▶ GRADE: 4.80

Ht: 5-9 1/2 | Wt: 190 | Sp: 4.48 | Arm: 31 1/2 | Hand: 9

History: The Kingston, Jamaica native was a starter at cornerback and running back as a Florida prep. Also lettered as a sprinter in track. Appeared in nine games (two starts) for Utah State as a true freshman in 2010 and had 12 tackles, two pass breakups and one interception with one-half tackle for loss. Won a starting cornerback spot in '11 and recorded 73-11-1 with one forced fumble. Started all 13 games in '12 and recorded 63-10-0 with four tackles for loss and two sacks. In '13, totaled 57-13-4 in 14 games (13 starts). Had his first career two-interception game against Boise State, returning one for a 65-yard score.

Strengths: Muscular build with nice arm length. Plays with his eyes. Reads and reacts quickly. Has skills to man up receivers. Soft-footed with flexible hips to pedal easily and transition smoothly. Good zone awareness and reactions. Productive on the ball. Effective blitzer. Has special-teams experience as a gunner and jammer. Durable three-year starter. Has matured and taken a more professional approach as an upperclassman.

Weaknesses: Press technique needs refinement. Too often allows free release. Clutching, grabbing and incurring flags have been issues in the past. Ball skills are a work in progress. Leaves some production on the field. Inconsistent run supporter. Struggled to contain USC WR Marqise Lee.

Future: Adequate-sized, talented, inconsistent cornerback with moldable tools and scheme versatility, though he requires polish and patience.

Draft projection: Priority free agent.

SS ISAIAH LEWIS, #9

MICHIGAN STATE ▶ GRADE: 5.18

Ht: 5-9 7/8 | Wt: 211 | Sp: 4.61 | Arm: 31 1/2 | Hand: 9 5/8

History: Also played basketball as an Indianapolis prep. Appeared in all 13 games as a true freshman in 2010, recording 15 tackles and one pass breakup with zero interceptions. Started the season opener at free safety vs. Western Michigan, then was primarily used on special teams the rest of the year. Won the starting strong safety job in '11 and had 74-3-4 (two touchdowns) in 14 games with 2 1/2 tackles for loss. Made 13 starts at SS in '12 and registered 80-6-2 with 1 1/2 tackles for loss. In '13, recorded 58-8-2 with one tackle for loss in 13 games (12 starts). Underwent arthroscopic knee surgery following the second week of the season, missing the Youngstown State game and snapping his consecutive-starts streak at 29. Came back the following week, seeing limited time against Notre Dame, then was back in the starting lineup the rest of the season.

Strengths: Terrific motor — supports the run aggressively and gives consistent effort in pursuit. Plays bigger than his size and throws his weight around — pounces on ball carriers. Good zone awareness. Makes plays on the ball and has good hands to make athletic interceptions. Physical and competitive. Made secondary calls and is football smart. Has special-teams experience. Tough, durable three-year starter.

Weaknesses: Lacks ideal size and needs to get stronger. Can be a tick late to diagnose and lacks burst to recover. Average explosiveness, speed and range. Has man-coverage limitations — struggles to keep up with speedy slot receivers. Can be overaggressive and arrive out of control. Misses tackles when he goes for the kill shot.

Future: Physical, aggressive strong safety at his best playing downhill and filling in run defense, though you wish he had more juice athletically. Special teams will have to be his ticket.

Draft projection: Fifth- to sixth-round pick.

ss CRAIG LOSTON, #6

LSU　　　　　　　　　　　　　　▶ GRADE: 5.31

Ht: 6-0 5/8 | Wt: 217 | Sp: 4.64 | Arm: 30 3/4 | Hand: 9 3/4

History: His cousin, Russell Shepard, is a wide receiver with the Buccaneers; the two were teammates at LSU. Another cousin, Brodney Pool, spent seven seasons in the NFL with the Browns and Jets (2005-11). Loston is a Houston native who garnered Parade All-American honors. Signed with LSU in 2009, but did not make it past the NCAA clearinghouse for his initial college eligibility until late in camp. Suffered a hand injury that required surgery, causing him to redshirt. Returned to the field in '10 and played in 13 games (two starts), recording 22 tackles, two pass breakups and one interception with one tackle for loss. Was utilized as a reserve safety and special-teams player in '11, appearing in 11 games and tallying 14-1-0 with one forced fumble. Missed three games with injuries (concussion, hyperextended right leg). Moved into the starting lineup in '12, playing in 12 games at strong safety and recording 55-1-3 with three tackles for loss. Had a 100-yard interception return for a score against Mississippi State. Missed one game with a toe injury. In '13, he registered 57-3-3 with four tackles for loss and one sack in 10 starts. Missed three games with leg and groin injuries.

Strengths: Solidly built and well-proportioned. Good eyes and anticipation. Reacts aggressively to plays in front of him and buzzes the flat. Good route recognition. Can carry receivers deep and match up with tight ends in man coverage. Steps downhill and can secure open-field tackles. Is tough, sacrifices his body and will deliver some jarring hits. Helps line up the defense and make adjustments. Is noticeably the vocal leader of the secondary (very animated communicator). Gunner and jammer on special teams. Has NFL pedigree. Football smart, smart, hardworking and accountable.

Weaknesses: Has short arms. Shows some hip tightness that restricts transitional quickness. Tends to rise in his pedal. Gives up separation in man coverage vs. receivers. Limited leaping ability. Can be overaggressive — overruns some plays and misses tackles he should secure. Can do a better job of driving through contact instead of leaving his feet. Durability is an issue

— has struggled to remain healthy (despite recovering relatively quickly).

Future: A big, physical strong safety with enough hybrid traits to offer interchangeable versatility. Looked better as a junior in the shadow of Eric Reid, but is a vocal secondary leader with starter-caliber ability as a box defender.

Draft projection: Fourth- to fifth-round pick.

Scout's take: "He doesn't really do anything for me. He might go in the fourth (round). I had a solid backup grade on him. I was not fired up. I think he is an okay player."

rcb DEXTER McDOUGLE, #25

MARYLAND　　　　　　　　　　　▶ GRADE: 5.12

Ht: 5-10 1/4 | Wt: 196 | Sp: 4.49 | Arm: 30 5/8 | Hand: 9 5/8

History: Virginia prep missed most of his junior season, breaking two of his knuckles in a freak practice injury. Redshirted in 2009. Saw his first game action in '10, appearing in 11 games and recording 22 tackles, three pass breakups and zero interceptions. Returned five kickoffs for 71 yards (14.2-yard average). His season was cut short in early December when he was involved in a scooter accident, requiring surgery to repair a broken collarbone. Was elevated to starting cornerback in '11 and had 44-6-3 with 2 1/2 tackles for loss and one forced fumble in 12 games. Scored on a 66-yard fumble return against North Carolina State. Started all 12 games at cornerback in '12 and recorded 71-5-0 with three tackles for loss. Made three starts in '13, tallying 14-2-3, before suffering a season-ending injury September 14. Late that afternoon against Connecticut, in a game in which he already had two interceptions (including a 49-yard touchdown return), he dove low for a tackle and severely jammed his shoulder, necessitating surgery. Spent the rest of his college season traveling to every away game, attending every practice and sitting through every meeting. As a result, coach Randy Edsall presented him with the inaugural Dexter McDougle Ultimate Team Player Award at Maryland's end-of-year banquet. Shoulder injury prevented him from working out at the Combine (medical exclusion).

Strengths: Excellent speed to keep pace vertically. Reads and reacts quickly. Mirrors off the line. Good balance, agility and change of direction. Zone aware. Plants and drives efficiently. Has short-area quickness and stop-and-start acceleration. Covers ground with the ball in the air and shows burst to close. Solid tackler. Fits in multiple schemes. Good teammate.

Weaknesses: Lacks ideal height. Short on length and strength to jam and re-route receivers — too often yields uncontested release off the line. Occasionally gets caught trying to read the quarterback's mail — squats on routes, bites on fakes and gets beat. Durability could be an issue.

Future: Short, compactly built, athletic cornerback who was playing well before his season ended prematurely. Has the speed, quickness, competitiveness and toughness to compete for a role as a sub-package slot defender.

Draft projection: Late draftable pick.

RCB-FS KEITH McGILL, #1

UTAH   ▶ GRADE: 5.42
Ht: 6-3 3/8 | Wt: 211 | Sp: 4.51 | Arm: 33 1/4 | Hand: 10 1/4

History: Has a daughter. The California prep earned letters in football, basketball and track, graduating high school in 2007. After not playing in 2008, he enrolled at Cerritos (CA) College in '09 and played in 11 games at free safety, recording 24 tackles, three pass breakups and four interceptions with one-half tackle for loss and one forced fumble. Earned Southern California Football Association Northern Conference Defensive Player of the Year honors in '10, tallying 37-5-7 with one forced fumble, two blocked kicks and a fumble recovery for a touchdown. Blocked a field goal attempt by Bakersfield College on the last play of the game, finishing the play by receiving a lateral at the 35-yard line and scoring the game-winning touchdown. Arrived at Utah in '11 and saw action in the season's first five games (including a start at free safety against USC), recording 12-1-0. Sustained a season-ending shoulder injury in the Arizona State game. Missed the entire '12 season due to extensive rehab of the shoulder, which required surgery. Was healthy in '13 and started all 12 games at cornerback, totaling 37-12-1 with one-half tackle for loss. Returned an interception 19 yards for a touchdown against UCLA.

Strengths: Rare size with extremely long arms and large hands — looks every bit the part. Very good athletic ability. Explosive — recorded 39-inch vertical jump and 10-foot, 9-inch broad jump. Versatile and can play safety or corner.

Weaknesses: Lacks the physicality and toughness desired at safety. Does not support the run aggressively or play to his size. Average transitional quickness. Still has some junior-college habits. Footwork needs refinement. Record the worst 3-cone time (7.29 seconds) among cornerbacks at the Combine. Will be a 25-year-old rookie. Still has some junior-college work habits and needs to learn what it means to be a pro.

Future: Big, athletic, press-man corner with intriguing dimensions and movement skills. However, he does not consistently play to his size, needs to adopt a professional approach to the game and will have to be micromanaged. Would ideally fit in Seattle or Jacksonville.

Draft projection: Third-round pick.

Scout's take: "He is a big corner. You see him on tape and you think he's a camp body. You see him at practice and you think, he is a 5(th rounder). He's the type of guy that will generate a buzz at the Senior Bowl and be a hot riser because of the way he looks. His arms look like they are 36 inches. Sometimes it looks like a guy is just an average athlete on tape, but he's a good athlete when you see him in person. He'll go in the second- or third-round to Pete Carroll."

RCB TERRANCE MITCHELL, #27 (JUNIOR)

OREGON   ▶ GRADE: 5.37
Ht: 5-11 1/8 | Wt: 192 | Sp: 4.61 | Arm: 30 1/8 | Hand: 8 1/2

History: Cornerback-running back who also lettered in basketball as a California prep. Redshirted in 2010. Won the starting left cornerback job in '11 and had 45 tackles, 10 pass breakups and two interceptions with three tackles for loss and three forced fumbles in 14 games (12 starts). Started all 13 games at LCB in '12 and recorded 40-8-0. Made '13 starts at LCB in '13 and tallied 59-7-5 (one TD) with one forced fumble. Was ejected in the first quarter of the season opener against Nicholls for a targeting infraction. Did not bench press at the Combine (pectoral).

Strengths: Good size and length with a well-proportioned body. Quick-footed pedal. Shows read-and-react skills and nice anticipation to break on throws. Good hand-eye coordination. Gambler's mentality that enables him to make plays. High school skill-position traits show after he intercepts. Aggressive and competitive. Three-year starter. Recorded the best 3-cone drill (6.57 seconds) and 20-yard shuttle (tie, 4.00) among cornerbacks at the Combine.

Weaknesses: Has short arms and small hands. Is lean and functionally weak — lacks press strength to impede receivers off the line. Tight-hipped. Gets wired on blocks outside. Needs to clean up his pedal. Inefficient plant-and-drive — average balance and body control through transition. Falls out of the hip pocket and loses phase downfield. Lacks elite top-end speed and recovery burst — needs help on explosive receivers. Average physicality and tackling ability. Tends to clutch and grab and draw flags.

Future: Wiry, smoother-than-sudden, off-man/cover-3 corner who upped his visibility as a junior by showing improved playmaking ability, which prompted a premature leap to the NFL. Could compete for a job as a No. 4, but lack of ideal explosiveness, top-end speed and bump-and-run ability limits his ceiling.

Draft projection: Third- to fourth-round pick.

Scout's take: "His size is what's appealing about him, but he's not an elite athlete. I didn't like his closing speed and was not a big fan overall, but I think he'll get pushed up because of his size."

LCB JABARI PRICE, #4

NORTH CAROLINA   ▶ GRADE: 5.17

Ht: 5-10 5/8 | Wt: 200 | Sp: 4.46 | Arm: 31 5/8 | Hand: 9 1/8

History: Played cornerback and safety as a Florida prep. Was selected as an All-American Scholar by the United States Achievement Academy. Enrolled at North Carolina in 2010 and played in all 13 games as a true freshman, recording 20 tackles, five pass breakups and one interception. Started the final four games of the season at left cornerback and saw significant action on special teams. During fall practice prior to the '11 campaign, he tore a tendon in his left hand during a blocking drill (which necessitated surgery) and missed the first five games. In eight contests after his return (two starts), he had 16-2-0 with one tackle for loss. Made 11 starts in '12 and registered 76-9-1 with four tackles for loss, one sack and one forced fumble. Missed the season finale with a shoulder injury. Was healthy all season in '13, tallying 80-9-0 with 4 1/2 tackles for loss and one forced fumble in 13 starts.

Strengths: Good speed and acceleration — can turn and run deep. Competes in the air. Aggressive, productive tackler — doesn't hesitate to support the run. Has worked as a gunner on special teams.

Weaknesses: Adequate size. Limited instincts and anticipation. Loses separation at the break point. Loses phase when his eyes get stuck in the backfield. Tends to clutch and grab. Dull plant-and-drive. Was not a playmaker — recorded just two career INTs. Still has some maturing to do.

Future: Fairly nondescript cornerback who does not excel in man or zone coverage. Speed and tackling ability play well on special teams, where he will have to stand out to have a chance.

Draft projection: Late draftable pick.

FS CALVIN PRYOR, #25 (JUNIOR)

LOUSVILLE   ▶ GRADE: 6.15

Ht: 5-11 1/8 | Wt: 207 | Sp: 4.58 | Arm: 31 3/8 | Hand: 9 1/8

History: Played safety and running back as a Florida prep. Arrived at Louisville in 2011 and appeared in all 13 games as a true freshman — starting the final seven contests at free safety. Immediately made his presence felt, recording 43 tackles five pass breakups and two interceptions with three tackles for loss, one sack and two forced fumbles. Finished second on the team in tackles in '12, starting 13 times and recording 100-5-2 with 2 1/2 tackles for loss, one sack and a team-best five forced fumbles. In '13, totaled 75-5-3 with 5 1/2 tackles for loss and two forced fumbles in 12 games. Had a three-game stretch of knocking opposing players out of a contest. Missed the only game of his collegiate career November 23 vs. Memphis, as he was suspended for a violation of an unspecified team rule. Did not run shuttles or 3-cone drill at the Combine (right toe).

Strengths: Carries a swagger and plays with confidence. Runs the alley and throws his weight around. Physical, lights-out hitter (see second defensive snap of UCF game). Made a highlight-reel, one-handed INT in the same game. Instinctive and aggressive. Defensive tempo-setter. Good pre-snap recognition — makes adjustments. Can leverage the field off the hash and cover ground. Good zone recognition. Rangy enough to play center field.

Weaknesses: Plays with too much reckless abandon and lacks discipline playing the cutback. Takes some bad angles and can be outflanked to the perimeter. Average production on the ball. Is not asked to play a lot of man coverage. Average leaping ability.

Future: Perhaps the most explosive hitter in this year's crop of safeties, Pryor is a big, physical hammer in the run game, bringing the ability to intimidate and erase. Factor in his instincts and range and Pryor has the ability to start as a rookie.

Draft projection: First-round pick.

Scout's take: "(Pryor) is a hammer. He plays lights out. I'm not concerned about how he ran. Rodney Harrison ran a 4.6, and he was that type of hammer."

RCB LOUCHEIZ PURIFOY, #15 (JUNIOR)

FLORIDA   ▶ GRADE: 5.31

Ht: 5-11 1/2 | Wt: 190 | Sp: 4.61 | Arm: 32 3/4 | Hand: 8 1/2

History: His name is pronounced "lou-CHEZ PURE-uh-foye." Florida native. Appeared in 13 games as a true freshman in 2011, playing primarily on special teams. Recorded 27 tackles (team-best 22 on special teams), zero pass breakups and zero interceptions with a forced fumble. Played in 13 games (12 starts) in '12 and recorded 51-5-0 with one tackle for loss and three forced fumbles (all on special teams, along with a blocked punt and a blocked field goal). Returned seven kickoffs for 167 yards (23.9-yard average). In

February '13, he was arrested and charged with misdemeanor possession of marijuana; the case was subsequently dismissed. Was one of five Gators suspended for the season opener for an unspecified violation of team rules. Went on to appear in 11 games (seven starts), tallying 24-7-2 with 3 1/2 tackles for loss, two sacks, one forced fumble and one blocked punt. Recorded his first career interception against Arkansas, returning the pick 42 yards for a touchdown. Was 4-82-0 (20.5) returning kickoffs and 3-35-0 (11.7) returning punts.

Strengths: Good size, arm length and athleticism. Fluid and light on his feet. Transitions smoothly. Can flip his hips and carry receivers deep. Flashes playmaking ability. Good hands to intercept. Tries to strip the ball out. Has special-teams experience returning and covering kicks — was productive as a gunner earlier in his career. Conditioned, confident and competitive. Has upside.

Weaknesses: Shared reps as a junior. Needs to get functionally stronger to jam/re-route and shed blocks. Produced only six reps on the 225-pound benchpress test, lowest among all defensive backs. Did not run well at the Combine, recording below-average times in the 4.6s. Gives up separation at the break point and gets outmuscled at the catch point. Inconsistent, leaky, underpowered tackler. Instincts and anticipation are lacking. Technique needs to be coached up — opens the gate and gets beat off the snap. Leaves production on the field — in position, but doesn't make the play. Questionable tackle and ball production. Marginal run strength as a returner.

Future: Lean, fluid, finesse cover man with better raw, physical ability than his inconsistent performance indicates. Has starter-caliber athleticism, but poor instincts, tackling and tape are reasons for pause.

Draft projection: Third- to fourth-round pick.

Scout's take: "I'm not a fan. We interviewed him. He didn't come across as dependable. His play was up and down. They rotated him a lot. He's been suspended for issues. Someone might reach and take him in the third (round). He's off our board."

RCB KEVIN REASER, #3

FLORIDA ATLANTIC　▶ GRADE: 5.14

Ht: 5-10 3/4 | Wt: 189 | Sp:4.55e | Arm: 30 3/4 | Hand: 9 1/2

History: Was a two-spot athlete as a Miami prep, lettering in football and track. Enrolled at Florida Atlantic in 2009 and redshirted as a freshman. Played in 10 games (including three starts) at cornerback in 2010 and had 26 tackles,

zero pass breakups and one interception with one tackle for loss. Started all 12 games in '11 and had 61-7-2 with 2 1/2 tackles for loss. Returned four kickoffs for 82 yards (20.5-yard average). In '12, he made 12 starts and registered 45-3-2 with 1 1/2 tackles for loss. Recovered a fumble at Western Kentucky and scooped it up for a nine-yard score. Started FAU's first six games of '13 before tearing his left ACL in an October contest against UAB. Registered 25-4-0 with two tackles for loss. Underwent four months of rehab after undergoing surgery on his left knee and was invited to the '14 NFL Combine. After meeting with doctors in Indianapolis who were concerned about his MRI, he flew to Pensacola to see Dr. James Andrews, who explained that his body was rejecting the graft used from a cadaver in repairing his ACL. Subsequently underwent a second surgery February 27 in which a graft was used from his own patellar tendon.

Strengths: Has a solid build and demonstrated strength at the Combine, benchpressing 225 pounds 22 times. Demonstrates nice balance and body control in his pedal — turns his feet over rapidly and is comfortable in reverse. Confident in off-man coverage — maintains good cushion and keeps receivers in front of him. Nice shadow and mirror in man coverage. Smooth-hipped. Good football intelligence. Understands run fits. Respected team leader.

Weaknesses: Average agility and long speed. Lacks strength in run support and could stand to be more aggressive filling. Tackles low. Not explosive. Nonchalant football-playing demeanor. Does not play with confidence or trigger quickly to what he sees. Average ball skills.

Future: Good-sized, smooth-moving, man-cover corner who showed the ability to mirror before a knee injury cut short his senior season. Mental toughness and determination will be put to the test, as he faces rehabilitation for a second surgery and an uphill battle to earn an NFL job.

Draft projection: Priority free agent.

Scout's take: "I was concerned about his speed before the knee injury. I don't think he'll get drafted after it."

FS ED REYNOLDS, #29 (JUNIOR)

STANFORD　▶ GRADE: 5.10

Ht: 6-1 | Wt: 207 | Sp: 4.57 | Arm: 30 3/4 | Hand: 8 1/2

History: His father, Ed, played 135 games at linebacker for the Patriots and Giants from 1983-1992 and went on to work in the NFL central office for 12 years. The Virginia prep also lettered in track, setting a school indoor triple jump record (44-3.3). Enrolled at Stanford in 2010 and appeared in five games as a freshman, recording six tackles. Was slated to be a candidate to start in '11, but was injured in spring drills when a wide receiver went airborne and landed on his knee. Had surgery for a torn ACL and missed the campaign. Returned in '12 and won the starting free safety job, starting all 14 games and recording 47 tackles, five pass breakups and six interceptions. His team-high interception total was the highest by a Stanford player since 1973. Returned a school-record three of those picks for scores (25 yards against Washington State, 52 yards at Colorado and 71 against Duke). His combined 301 yards on interception returns was the second-highest total in NCAA history (USC's Charles Phillips, 302 in 1974). Appeared in 14 games in '13 (13 starts) and tallied 87-4-1 with one tackle for loss. Was third on the team in tackles. Did not start against Washington State after being ejected the previous week for a targeting infraction. Elected not to run the shuttles or 3-cone drill at the Combine.

Strengths: Good size to contend with tight ends. Reads the quarterback and displays good instincts and anticipation. Showed ballhawking skills as a junior. Functional range off the hash. Wrap tackler. Has NFL bloodlines.

Weaknesses: Small hands. Very average play speed, twitch and flexibility. Unsudden change of direction. Lacks burst to close suddenly or recover when beat. Occasionally loses field leverage and takes some inaccurate angles. Leaks yards after contact. Misses too many tackles in the open field and can be run over (see Utah). Can be manipulated by quarterbacks. Limited experience in man coverage. Poor leaping ability.

Future: Big, assignment-sound, Cover-2 safety who brings a dependability factor, but lacks ideal athletic ability and physicality. Is the type you look to replace as a starter, but could have longevity as a backup.

Draft projection: Fifth- to sixth-round pick.

Scout's take: "I gave him a free-agent grade. Watch the Utah game and you'll turn it off it off before halftime. He must have missed eight tackles. He is stiff, stiff, stiff. There is a lot of hype and buzz around all of his picks (six) last year, but he had a lot of pressure coming upfront, kind of like Seattle makes all their big, slow corners look better than they are."

he was primarily used as a special teams player in '10 and had 14 tackles in 12 games. In '11, reported to fall camp listed as third on the depth chart, but moved into the starting lineup because of injuries and never looked back. Started all 12 games at right cornerback and registered 68 tackles, eight pass breakups and one interception with one tackle for loss. Started 13 games in '12 and recorded 75-13-3 with 1 1/2 tackles for loss and one forced fumble. Was limited in the '13 spring after undergoing off-season knee surgery (cyst removal) before participating for OSU in track (60 meters). During the fall, he tied for the conference lead in interceptions, starting 13 games and tallying 61-4-6 with 3 1/2 tackles for loss, one sack and two forced fumbles. Set a school single-game mark with two fumbles returned for touchdowns in the Sheraton Hawai'i Bowl against Boise State, earning game MVP honors. Had six punt returns for 31 yards (5.2-yard average). Team captain.

Strengths: Instinctive with good eyes, anticipation and awareness. Very athletic — tied for the quickest short shuttle among cornerbacks at the Combine (4.00 seconds), and was one of the top performers in the bench press (20 reps) and 3-cone drill (6.72 seconds).. Transitions easily with loose hips and clean footwork. Quick, agile and light on his feet. Aggressive in run support. Solid tackler. Plays with discipline. Good leaping ability. Has a special-teams temperament and excels as a gunner. Extremely intelligent and football smart. Outstanding intangibles, including leadership traits. Durable and experienced.

Weaknesses: Thinly built and lacks ideal strength. Can be knocked back in a pile and could stand to strike with more pop and explosion. Recovery speed is only average.

Future: Athletic, sticky coverman whose position-specific traits and consistent performance inspire confidence he has what it takes to contribute readily in the pros. Has starter-caliber physical ability, a natural feel for the game and sterling intangibles. Underrated, low-risk prospect.

Draft projection: Third- to fourth-round pick.

Scout's take: "He is probably going to rise from what I have seen so far. He is just not very strong. He's a good athlete with good feet. I liked him. Size is what's going to hurt him. He's got an average body. I stamped a pretty big grade on him."

RCB RASHAAD REYNOLDS, #16

OREGON STATE   ▶ GRADE: 5.45

Ht: 5-9 7/8 | Wt: 189 | Sp: 4.51 | Arm: 31 5/8 | Hand: 9 3/4

History: Defensive back-quarterback who also played basketball, wrestled and ran track as a California prep. After redshirting in 2009,

LCB MARCUS ROBERSON, #5 (JUNIOR)

FLORIDA   ▶ GRADE: 5.40

Ht: 6-0 1/4 | Wt: 191 | Sp: 4.61 | Arm: 31 | Hand: 9 1/4

History: Was rated as one of the top cornerback prospects in the country as a Ft. Lauderdale prep, helping lead his St. Thomas

Aquinas squad to a state championship and the No. 3 national ranking. Enrolled at Florida in 2011 and immediately moved into the lineup at cornerback, starting 10 games and recording 22 tackles, two pass breakups and one interception with one-half tackle for loss. In September, he was arrested by university police for underage drinking. Suffered a season-ending neck injury in November against South Carolina, which required surgery. Missed most of spring practice in '12 because of the injury, but returned to the field in the fall and played in all 13 games (four starts) — tallying 23-12-2 with one tackle for loss, one sack and one forced fumble. Also returned two punts for 81 yards (40.5-yard average). Battled injuries in '13, seeing action in just seven games (four starts) and recording 11-3-0. Went 14-129-0 (9.2) on punt returns and 1-16-0 returning kickoffs. Strained the PCL in his left knee in the season's second game, forcing him to the sidelines for the next three contests. Aggravated the injury in his third game back, forcing him back off the field. In addition, he was suspended for the South Carolina game for an unspecified violation of team rules. Made it back for the season finale, seeing limited action against Florida State.

Strengths: Very good size and body length. Transitions efficiently and shows nice plant-and-drive quickness. Flashes ball skills to break up plays. Has punt-return experience — can elude the first tackler and gain what's blocked.

Weaknesses: Needs to bulk up and get functionally stronger (managed just eight benchpress reps at the Combine). Struggles with bigger, stronger receivers. Lacks elite top-end speed to keep pace with burners. Anticipation and route recognition are lacking. Susceptible to double moves. Tends to clutch and grab when he's beat. Inconsistent ball reactions. Poor tackler. Recorded just 34 tackles the last two seasons. Relatively inexperienced. Durability has been an issue.

Future: Lean, athletic, finesse cornerback who is best deployed in off-man or zone coverage, and has potential to develop into a No. 2 or No. 3 corner if he regains his sophomore form. However, he lacks desirable instincts and tackling ability, and did not elevate his game in 2013 when injuries, suspension and inconsistency marred his junior season.

Draft projection: Second- to third-round pick.

Scout's take: "He is a big, press corner with length. I think he needs to (mature). He's got a long ways to go. But I like him a lot better than the other corner (at Florida)."

LCB BRADLEY ROBY, #1 (JUNIOR)

OHIO STATE ▶ GRADE: 6.00

Ht: 5-11 1/4 | Wt: 194 | Sp: 4.39 | Arm: 31 1/2 | Hand: 10 1/4

History: Played receiver and defensive back as a Georgia prep. Redshirted in 2010 before starting all 13 games at cornerback in '11, recording 47 tackles, six pass breakups and tied for the team lead with three interceptions with 3 1/2 tackles for loss. Tied the OSU school record for pass breakups after posting 63-17-2 with two tackles for loss, one sack and a blocked kick in 11 starts in '12. Missed the UAB game with a shoulder injury. Was the only defensive player in the country to score three different ways — recovered a fumbled punt in the end zone vs. Miami, blocked a punt in the end zone against Indiana and a 41-yard interception return against Nebraska. Was arrested in July ' 13 after an altercation with a bouncer in a Bloomington, Ind. bar. Was originally charged with a Class A misdemeanor battery which was lowered to Class B disorderly conduct and was ultimately dismissed after video tape evidence was discovered. Was still suspended for the '13 season opener vs. Buffalo by coach Urban Meyer. Started 11 of 12 games played and logged 70-13-3 with two tackles for loss. Scored two touchdowns on a blocked punt against Northwestern and a 63-yard interception return vs. Illinois. Did not play in the Orange Bowl against Clemson with a bone bruise in his knee.

Strengths: Good size. Has thin ankles and large hands. Quick-twitch athlete with prototypical speed. Can mirror off the line and shadow slot receivers. Has 38 1/2-inch vertical. Terrific balance. Loose-hipped, quick-footed and agile (4.04-second 3-cone drill). Smooth transition and change of direction. Flips his hips and has ample speed to carry receivers downfield. Plants and drives in a blink. Quick-handed to play the pocket. Excellent ball production. Shows recovery speed. Physical and aggressive. Feisty, willing tackler — does not hesitate to sacrifice his body. Displays good zone awareness and has experience in off-man. Dangerous as a blitzer and kick-block rusher. Worked as a gunner.

Weaknesses: Inconsistent performance as a junior. Can be boxed out by tall receivers and outmuscled for "50-50" balls. Could stand to improve jam strength in order to hem/re-route receivers bigger receivers. Gets wired to blocks. Durability could be an issue given his physical playing style. Could stand to iron out his pedal. Gets caught peeking — lets receivers behind him and is vulnerable to double moves. Misses some 1-on-1 tackles in space. Character should be looked into.

Future: Urgent, confident, competitive athlete with an intriguing combination of speed, suddenness, ball skills and tackling ability. Has broad appeal given his scheme versatility, and should be able to contribute readily as nickel slot defender and special-teams contributor. Has a ceiling as a No. 2.

Draft projection: Top-40 pick.

Scout's take: "He didn't have a good year. Smaller corners typically don't do great. He doesn't play like Antoine Winfield."

FS DANIEL SORENSEN, #9

BYU   ▶ GRADE: 5.05

Ht: 6-1 3/8 | Wt: 205 | Sp: 4.67 | Arm: 31 | Hand: 8 1/2

History: Married. Four of his brothers have played college football, including Brad (QB) who was a 2013 seventh-rounder by the Chargers. Prepped in California, where was a two-way standout who also punted. As a true freshman in 2010, played in 13 contest and managed 17 tackles, zero pass breakups and one interception with 3 1/2 tackles for loss and one sack as an outside linebacker. Missed the Air Force game with bone spurs in his left ankle. Missed the '09 and '10 seasons while doing his LDS mission in Costa Rica. Moved to the KAT (strong) safety position on his return in '11 and logged 61-6-2 with two tackles for loss and scored on a 30-yard interception return against Idaho State in 13 starts. In '12posted 68-5-3 with two tackles for loss and two forced fumbles in 13 starts at KAT safety. Team leader in pass breakups in '13 from his safety position with 65-12-2 with four tackles for loss and a blocked field goal against Utah State in 13 starts. Had a concussion against Wisconsin. Team captain.

Strengths: Good size. Produced the best 3-cone time (6.47 seconds) of any participant at the Combine and recorded the best 20-yard shuttle (3.95) and 60-yard shuttle time (10.80) of any defensive back. Is tough and willing to sacrifice his body. Dependable tackler. Jumps routes and has functional range. Makes the secondary calls and checks and understands coverages like a coach. Passionate about the game and works at the craft — has a professional approach. Displayed very natural hands in Combine drills. Reliable special teams contributor. High school punter capable of handling punts in emergency situations.

Weaknesses: Has small hands. Is stiff in the hips and plays a bit flat-footed. Challenged by elite speed. Is not a blow-up hitter. Does not possess the top-end speed to range to the sideline and make plays on the ball — not a true

center fielder. Average career production on the ball. Poor leaper. Will be a 24-year-old rookie.

Future: Durable, experienced overachiever with enough range to survive on the back end and enough toughness to drop into the box. Size, linear field speed and football smarts could enable him to make a living as a backup and special-teams contributor

Draft projection: Priority free agent.

Scout's take: "He's more smart than instinctive. He's not a big hitter. He's stiff in the hips. He might get drafted late — not for us."

FS DEZMEN SOUTHWARD, #12

WISCONSIN   ▶ GRADE: 5.39

Ht: 6-0 1/4 | Wt: 211 | Sp: 4.41 | Arm: 30 5/8 | Hand: 10

History: His stepfather, Eli Rasheed, played football at Indiana and is currently the defensive line coach at Toledo. Didn't start playing football until his senior year, when he started at defensive back for national champion St. Thomas Aquinas in Florida. Also lettered in basketball and track. Redshirted in 2009 before playing in all 13 games as a reserve in '10, making eight tackles, zero passbreakups and zero interceptions. Saw action in 13 games (three starts at strong safety) in '11 and logged 35-2-0 with two forced fumbles. Did not play against Illinois (coach's decision). Moved into the starting lineup at free safety in '12 and produced 69-4-1 with eight tackles for loss and one forced fumble in 14 games. Had a career-high 12 tackles in the Big Ten Championship game vs. Nebraska. Filled in on the track team in the spring of '13 after some sprinters were injured, running the 100 meters and the 4x100 relay. Moved to strong safety for the '13 campaign and recorded 40-5-1 with 3 1/2 tackles for loss and one forced fumble in 13 starts. Was medically excluded at the Combine because wrist and spine injuries.

Strengths: Excellent size and large hands. Good straight-line speed. Bends his knees and pedals softly. Reacts well to plays in front of him. Played a hybrid safety role at UW, including defending slot receivers (even played CB in a pinch against BYU). Special-teams experience. Recorded a 4.38-second 40-time, a 42-inch vertical jump and 6.50-second 3-cone time at his pro day workout.

Weaknesses: Short arms. Average flexibility and range. Still developing positional instincts and diagnostic skills. Man-coverage limitations — dull transitional quickness and closing burst. Ordinary production on the ball — not a playmaker. Does not punish or intimidate. Reliability should be looked into.

Future: Southward, who played only one year of high school football, is a size-speed prospect still learning positional nuances. Could get his foot in the door on special teams and buy some time to develop as a reserve. Eye-popping pro day performance after being snubbed from the Combine could elevate his draft standing and invite a team to gamble on his immense upside.

Draft projection: Third- to fourth-round pick.

Scout's take: "He has so much upside. He'll be a fast-riser this spring."

FS VINNIE SUNSERI, #3 (JUNIOR)

ALABAMA   ▶ GRADE: 5.14

Ht: 5-11 1/8 | Wt: 210 | Sp: 4.55e | Arm: 30 | Hand: 10

History: His father, Sal Sunseri, is the defensive ends coach at Florida State. As a junior linebacker, he was named the 2009 Bronco Nagurski Defensive Player of the Year in North Carolina after 107 tackles and 15 tackles for loss. Moved to Tuscaloosa for his senior season after his dad became the outside linebackers coach at Alabama. Named the 6A Defensive Player of the Year in Alabama in 2010. Enrolled in January 2011 and participated in spring practice. Played in all 13 games as a true freshman, serving as a backup safety and special teams player while making 31 tackles, one pass breakup and zero interceptions with one forced fumble. Was the Tide's starting Dime back in '12, making eight starts in 14 games. Logged 54-3-2 with six tackles for loss and 1 1/2 sacks. Began the '13 season with a bang by scoring the first two touchdowns of his career on interception returns — a 38-yard return in the season opener against Virginia Tech and a 73-yard return vs. Texas A&M the following week. Started the first seven games at safety before suffering a torn ACL on the opening kickoff against Arkansas on October 19 and finishing the year with 20-4-2 with one tackle for loss. Was medically excluded from the Combine (knee).

Strengths: Good size and big hands. Reads and reacts quickly. Assignment-sound and well-coached. Drops downhill to support the run and has experience in deep-zone coverage. Dependable wrap tackler. Good production. Vocal leader who commanded the secondary and made all the calls. Stood out on special teams as a younger player and has the makeup to be a special-teams captain in the pros.

Weaknesses: Short arms. Lacks elite top-end speed. Not a quick-twitch athlete. Does not explode off the hash and closing burst is just average — late getting over the top. Has man-coverage limitations — struggles to matchup

with slot receivers. Occasionally fails to break down or overruns ball carriers in space. Dull pop on contact — not an explosive, blow-up tackler. Started just 15 games.

Future: A coach's son, Sunseri has requisite athletic ability for the pro game, but his head for the game rates among his best traits. Has the size, tackling ability and dependability to make a living as a backup and core special-teams player. Draft stock could be impacted by season-ending torn ACL.

Draft projection: Fifth- to sixth-round pick.

NCB-SS JEMEA THOMAS, #14

GEORGIA TECH   ▶ GRADE: 5.14

Ht: 5-9 1/4 | Wt: 192 | Sp: 4.54 | Arm: 30 5/8 | Hand: 10

History: Name pronounced "ja-ME-a." Prepped in Georgia, where he was the Class AA Defensive Player of the Year. Also ran track. Began 2009 fall camp as a running back before switching to defensive back and recording 10 tackles, zero pass breakups and zero interceptions while playing in all 14 games. Redshirted in '10 due to poor grades. Appeared in all 13 games with two starts (Clemson, Utah) in '11 and managed 50-6-3 with four tackles for loss, two sacks and one forced fumble. Took over the punt returner job for the last five contests, returning three punts for 31 yards (10.3-yard average). Led the team in interceptions in '12, logging 86-6-4 with three tackles for loss while making all 14 starts — the first five games at CB and the last nine at safety. Team leader in tackles and pass breakups in '13 with 88-8-2 with 6 1/2 tackles for loss, three sacks and two forced fumbles in 13 starts. Played in 54 career games to tie the GT record and saw action at every position in the secondary. Had nine career kickoff returns for 204 yards (22.7-yard average). Strained a back muscle bench pressing at the Combine and did not do drills.

Strengths: Has large hands and is strong for his size. Sacrifices his body and supports the run willingly — likes contact. Takes good angles and understands run-game fits. Quietly confident. Mentally and physically tough. Good short-area zone awareness — reacting to throws is front of him is a strength. Tough and durable to play hurt. Highly respected. Hardworking and accountable. Experienced, four-year starter.

Weaknesses: Lacks ideal height and has short arms. Frame is nearly maxed out. Stiff hips. Gives up some ground and allows separation in man coverage vs. quickness. Easily mismatched by size vs. tight ends. Average range — lacks desirable length and fluidity to patrol the back end. Hands are iffy.

Future: Strong, tough, durable, downhill box safety whose hip tightness is limiting, but he brings desirable grit, physicality and competitiveness and could latch on as a situational nickel-safety and special-teams player.

Draft projection: Late draftable pick.

Scout's take: "He is a tough little player. He is just small. He's a tweener. He has played some corner and safety. He's probably a better fit as a safety. He has some hip stiffness. He will struggle matching up in press (coverage) at corner. He reminded me a little bit of (Lamarcus) Joyner from Florida State, but he's not as athletic. They both play nickel. I put (Thomas) in the sixth (round)."

FS-NCB BROCK VEREEN, #21

MINNESOTA   ▶ GRADE: 5.37

Ht: 5-11 5/8 | Wt: 199 | Sp: 4.47 | Arm: 30 | Hand: 8 1/4

History: His father, Henry, was drafted by Tampa Bay before going to the Canadian Football League, and his brother, Shane, is a running back for the New England Patriots. Brock was a defensive back-running back who also ran track as a California prep. Saw action in nine games as a true freshman in 2010, making four starts at cornerback, and managed 10 tackles, zero pass breakups and zero interceptions. Started all 12 games at CB in '11 and posted 67-7-1 with 3 1/2 tackles for loss and one forced fumble. Was limited during '12 spring practice with a torn meniscus and was converted to a safety. Began the '12 season as a backup safety before starting seven of the final eight contests, registered 64-9-2 with 1 1/2 tackles for loss and one-half sack in 13 games. Logged 59-6-1 with 2 1/2 tackles for loss and one forced fumble. Started all 13 games — the first six games at safety and the last seven at cornerback.

Strengths: Very good athlete with fluid movement skills and good range. Competes hard. Runs the alley and can negotiate traffic. Good zone awareness and route recognition. Understands angles and leverage. Can carry receivers in man coverage with little wasted movement in transition on speed turns. Good leaping ability. Very smart, motivated, team player with a passion for the game. Can line up the defense. Outstanding work ethic. Contributes as a gunner on special teams. Has NFL pedigree. Pumped 25 benchpress reps, most among DBs at the Combine, and recorded a 4.07-second short shuttle, second among safeties.

Weaknesses: Has tiny hands, short arms and lacks overall bulk. Does not have ideal length to match up with NFL tight ends in coverage. Not an explosive hitter or forceful tackler. Hands are suspect — smothers the ball and has just four career interceptions. Long-term durability could be a concern.

Future: Intelligent, athletic, rangy free safety with desirable strength and cover skills to go along with football bloodlines. Needs to improve against the run, but is instinctive and brings terrific intangibles that could propel him into a role as a starter and defensive leader.

Draft projection: Third- to fourth-round pick.

Scout's take: "He is a nickel corner, not a safety in my opinion. He might have a chance as a free safety. I could see him landing in the fourth (round). He's really smart."

RCB JASON VERRETT, #2

TCU   ▶ GRADE: 5.75

Ht: 5-9 1/2 | Wt: 189 | Sp: 4.38 | Arm: 30 5/8 | Hand: 9 1/4

History: Last name is pronounced "VER-rett." Played defensive back and running back as a California prep. Attended Santa Rosa (Calif.) JC, where he grayshirted in 2009 while learning to play defensive back. Returned to the field for the '10 season, playing in seven games and missing three contests with a hamstring injury and was ranked the sixth-best junior college DB. Transferred to TCU in '11 and played in all 13 games (10 starts), logging 58 tackles, four pass breakups and one interception with 1 1/2 tackles for loss. Had arthroscopic surgery on his left knee during '12 spring practice. Led the Big 12 in interceptions in the fall after posting 63-16-6 with five tackles for loss and a blocked field in 13 starts. Suffered a torn meniscus in his right knee against Texas but played in final two games before having surgery in January '13. Named co-Big 12 Defensive Player of the Year after logging 39-14-2 with 3 1/2 tackles for loss, one sack and one forced fumble in 11 starts. Played most of the season with a torn labrum originally injured in the third game against Texas Tech and re-injured in November. Had the shoulder surgically repaired in March.

Strengths: Quick, twitchy and explosive popping out of his pedal. Good eyes, anticipation and footwork. Very feisty and athletic. Outstanding instincts. Superb reactive quickness and recovery speed. Very good ball skills — consistently makes plays on the ball. Very willing in run support and plays bigger than his size. Athleticism was on display at the Combine — 40-yard dash, 3-cone drill (6.69

seconds), short shuttle (4.00) vertical jump (39 inches) and broad jump (10 feet, 8 inches) ranked among the best of the cornerbacks.

Weaknesses: Does not look the part — is short and short-armed with a small, thin-waisted, thin-boned body. Durability is an issue — struggles to stay healthy and is not built to endure the physical toll of the NFL, particularly as a starter. Low-dive tackler (misses some). Can be overwhelmed by bigger blockers and struggles to shed blocks. Average play strength. Had a bout with lost confidence as a younger player when he nearly quit after being embarrassed by Robert Griffin III and a high-powered Baylor offense.

Future: Feisty, aggressive, undersized nickel corner with potential to ascend to a No. 2 if he can stay in one piece. Is not the physical prototype for the position, but compensates with outstanding athleticism, blazing speed and a tenacious temperament. Is a terrific football player who boasts toughness and competitiveness reminiscent of Cortland Finnegan.

Draft projection: Second-round pick.

Scout's take: "He is fun to watch. You watch him on tape and you get excited. I saw him in person in the fall, and he didn't look like he was 175 pounds soaking wet. He's skinny. That's my biggest concern. He is quick, explosive and athletic. He is a pesty pain in the (butt) to shake. ...I love him. I think he is a very good player. He is just small. Worst case, he'll be a starting nickel. He's tough enough to start out wide, but his body will get banged up as a full-time starter. I'm not sure if he will hold up. He reminds me a little bit of Alphonso Smith, who went in the second round (37th overall) to Denver (in 2009)."

FS JIMMIE WARD, #15

NORTHERN ILLINOIS   ▶ GRADE: 5.36
Ht: 5-10 3/4 | Wt: 197 | Sp: 4.48 | Arm: 31 | Hand: 9 3/8

History: Has a child. Prepped in Alabama. As a true freshman in 2010, he logged 21 tackles, one pass breakup and zero interceptions with one forced fumble and a school-record three blocked punts. Returned a blocked punt 15 yards for a touchdown. Played in all 14 games, seeing extensive action as a backup free safety and on special teams. Registered 100-4-1 with 2 1/2 tackles for loss, one sack, one forced fumble and one blocked punt against Army in 14 games (12 starts at cornerback) in '11. Led the Huskies in tackles in '12 after posting 104-11-3 with one tackle for loss and one forced fumble in 13 starts at free safety. Missed the UMASS game with sprained A/C joint in his

right shoulder. In '13, logged 95-10-7 with 2 1/2 tackles for loss, one sack and one forced fumble in 14 starts. Had a 62-yard touchdown return for a score against Purdue. Did not work out at the Combine because of a foot injury (medical exclusion).

Strengths: Intense, active and energetic. Zooms around the field and stands out on tape. Aggressive run supporter — triggers quickly, flies downhill and chops down ball carriers. Breaks on throws and shows short-area burst to close. Has quick hands to snatch interceptions. Confident and energetic. Experienced and productive. Has a 38-inch vertical jump.

Weaknesses: Size is just adequate — lacks ideal bulk and is built more like a cornerback than a safety. Benchpressed 225 pounds just nine times at the Combine, second fewest among DBs. Gets snagged on blocks and struggles to disengage. Can be a tick late diagnosing pass, gaining depth and digesting route combos. Lacks elite top-end speed. Has man-coverage limitations. Inconsistent downfield ball reactions with his back to the throw. Shows lower-body stiffness in space. Could rub some people the wrong way. Has some maturing to do and needs to learn what it means to prepare like a pro.

Future: Wiry, active, aggressive defensive back at his best playing downhill and reacting to plays in front him. Lacks ideal size, instincts, range and cover skills, but could carve a niche as a nickel safety and special-teams contributor.

Draft projection: Fourth- to fifth-round pick.

Scout's take: "He's a nickel safety. That's what he is. You can find those guys in the fourth round. If they are really good, you might start looking in the third. (Ward) doesn't start for us as a safety or in nickel. I put him in the fifth (round) for us."

RCB TODD WASHINGTON, #1

SOUTHEASTERN LOUISIANA   ▶ GRADE: 5.15
Ht: 5-11 3/8 | Wt: 196 | Sp: 4.55e | Arm: 31 1/8 | Hand: 8 3/4

History: Prepped in Louisiana. Began his college career at Memphis in 2010 and played in nine contests (six starts), recording nine tackles, one pass breakup and two interceptions with one tackle for loss. Missed two games with a hip pointer. Decided to transfer to Southeastern Louisiana for the '11 season to be closer to his family. Logged 15-2-1 in eight games (seven starts) and missed three games with an ankle injury. Made 11-of-12 starts (all but Sam Houston) in '12 and managed 27-9-1 with two tackles for loss. Had an injury-plagued '13, missing the final six games with turf toe, and logged 15-8-0 in eight starts. Did not work out at the Combine (foot).

Strengths: Good size. Experienced in press and off-man coverage and has slot experience. Good route recognition to shadow and mirror and ride the hip pocket. Secure open-field tackler. Nice football intelligence. Serves as a jammer on special teams.

Weaknesses: Has short arms and small hands. Average athlete. Limited weight-room strength. Can do a better job fending off blocks. Can be overaggressive jumping routes in front of him. Could stand to improve eye discipline — too easily manipulated and could improve positioning. Inconsistent technique. Does not carry a lot of swagger and is not a ballhawk.

Future: Good-sized, press-man corner with developing instincts and enough cover skill to warrant a chance to develop.

Draft projection: Late draftable pick.

LCB JAYLEN WATKINS, #14
FLORIDA   ▶ GRADE: 5.15
Ht: 5-11 1/2 | Wt: 194 | Sp: 4.41 | Arm: 30 5/8 | Hand: 9 5/8

History: Brother, Sammy, was a star receiver at Clemson and projects as a top-10 pick. Jaylen was a highly recruited Florida native who also ran track in addition to playing cornerback and quarterback. Had surgery on his left quadriceps in April 2010. Appeared in 10 games as a true freshman in the fall, mostly as a gunner on punt returns, and recorded eight tackles, one pass breakup and zero interceptions. Missed spring practice in '11 after hernia surgery before posting 34-5-0 with one tackle for loss in 13 games (eight starts, including the last six) during the fall. Started 11-of-13 games at CB in '12 and tallied 39-8-3 with one tackle for loss. Returned his first career interception 26 yards for a score against Kentucky. In '13, registered 52-7-0 with two tackles for loss in 12 games — made six starts at safety and three at CB. Hurt his right Achilles at the Senior Bowl, and did not do positional drills at the Combine (medical exclusion).

Strengths: Nice size and strength for a cornerback (22 benchpress reps at the Combine). Excellent speed. Good fluidity and movement skills. Alert in zones. Flashes some playmaking ability. Versatile — lined up as a corner, safety and nickel defender and played on all special teams.

Weaknesses: Thin-framed, small-boned and short-armed with minimal muscular development. Lacks ideal size and strength for a safety and quickness and burst for a corner. Average press strength to re-route receivers. Allows separation at break points — late to transition out of his pedal. Too grabby. Selective hitter -- shows up in spurts. Not a physical tackler. Tends to propel his shoulder into ball carriers and needs to do a better job securing tackles.

Future: A fluid, loose-hipped, versatile cover man who projects to a No. 3 or No. 4 corner in the pros, Watkins could most ideally fit in the slot, with enough physicality to defend the run and fine short-area cover skills to match up with shifty receivers.

Draft projection: Fourth- to fifth-round pick.

RCB LAVELLE WESTBROOKS, #18
GEORGIA SOUTHERN   ▶ GRADE: 5.27
Ht: 5-11 1/2 | Wt: 186 | Sp: 4.63 | Arm: 32 3/8 | Hand: 9 3/4

History: Also competed in long-jump and triple-jump as a Georgia prep. Appeared in 13 games with seven starts as a true freshman in 2010, posting 32 tackles, three pass breakups and two interceptions with three tackles for loss and one sack. Totaled 60-3-1 with one tackle of loss in 13 games with 12 starts at safety in '11. Did not play in the season opener vs. Samford. Started 12 of his 13 games played at cornerback in '12 and tied for the team in lead in pass breakups after posting 43-7-2. Scored his first career touchdown with a 72-yard interception return against Samford. Made 10 starts in '13 and logged 32-7-2 with one tackle for loss and one sack and didn't play in season finale win at Florida (undisclosed injury).

Strengths: Nice arm length and press strength. Efficient pedal. Good plant and drive. Aggressive jumping routes when he sees it. Functional in run support — leverages the field and takes good angles. Good closing speed. Solid, face-up tackler.

Weaknesses: Size is just adequate. Not an explosive athlete. Short-area quickness is lacking. Green instincts. Loses phase in transition. Average production on the ball. Faced marginal competition and could struggle adjusting to the speed of the pro game.

Future: Adequate-sized, shuffle-and-bail corner who shed weight to convert from safety to cornerback. Has length and moldable tools, but will require patience.

Draft projection: Fifth to sixth-round pick.

Scout's take: "I put him late in the fifth. One of his negatives is the long speed. He has length and is decent in run support. You see acceleration and close down hill. He has decent hips. I would like to see him a little bit more balanced and under control and a better tackler in space. Others have put him a lot higher. I've heard as high as the third (round) on him (in the fall)."

SPECIALISTS

PK CHRIS BOSWELL, #9

RICE ▶ GRADE: 5.09

Ht: 6-2 1/4 | Wt: 185 | Sp: 5.10e | Arm: 31 1/4 | Hand: 8 5/8

History: The Texas prep kicked in the U.S. Army Bowl and was perfect on all 172 extra point attempts in high school. Also lettered in baseball and soccer. Redshirted in 2009 before taking over placekicking duties, connecting 11-of-17 field-goal attempts, with a long of 50, and 41-of-44 point-after tries in '10. Handled six kickoffs for a 54.0 average and one touchback. Led the team in scoring with 82 points in '11 after hitting on 17-of-21 FG attempts, with a long of 54, and 31-of-32 PATs with 59-63.1-14 on kickoffs. Connected on 23-of-29 FGs, tying the school-record with a 57 yarder, and 45-of-47 PATs with 80-63.8-49 on kickoffs in '12. Hit 5-of-6 FGs against SMU, including three over 50 yards. Set school records for field goals made and total points (114) while leading the nation with six made field goals over 50 yards. In '13, he connected on 14-of-21 FGs, with a long of 56, and 47-of-49 PATs while kicking off 79-64.2-57. Finished career with 359 points, two shy of the school record. Had four blocked field goals in his career (three in '10 and one in '13).

Strengths: Very good leg strength to convert consistently beyond 50 yards, with 13 career 50-yard-plus field goals. Consistently drives the ball through the end zone on kickoffs. Has proven he can handle pressure. Works at his craft. Confident approach. Outstanding career production — Rice career record-holder in many categories. Four-year starter.

Weaknesses: Marginal rise, lift and hang-time on kickoffs. Tends to line the ball with a low trajectory. Could stand to hasten his approach (8 career missed extra-point attempts). Has a quirky follow-through.

Summary: Tall, right-footed, 3-by-2 kicker with NFL starter-caliber leg strength and kickoff potential.

Draft projection: Late draftable pick.

P STEVEN CLARK, #30

AUBURN ▶ GRADE: 4.85

Ht: 6-5 | Wt: 231 | Sp: 5.15e | Arm: 31 3/4 | Hand: 9

History: The Missouri prep was an all-state punter, who also played tight end and defensive end. As a freshman in 2010, booted nine punts for 34.9-yard average with a long of 42 and two dropped inside the 20-yard line. Was a finalist for the Ray Guy Award in '11 and led the SEC with 33 punts inside the 20 after totaling 72-40.8-L58-33. Recorded 70-39.8-L54-15 in '12. Graduated in May and played the '13 season as a graduate student, booming

56-42.6-L58-26. During the year, he began using more of an Aussie punt, which travels end over end and bounces back toward the punter. Had only 22 of 207 career punts returned (10.6 percent) and didn't have a punt blocked.

Strengths: Outstanding size. Very good ball control, accuracy and placement. Good hang time. Fields the ball cleanly and adjusts well to off-target snaps. Works hard and studies his craft. Handles pressure well. Very durable — has never missed a game.

Weaknesses: Ball does not explode off his foot. Does not drive the ball for distance. Can improve touch-to-toe times and speed up get-off (three-step punter). Has short arms. Average athlete. Limited in coverage.

Summary: Big-bodied boomer who is most effective on a short field where he can kick with accuracy, control and generate great hang time.

Draft projection: Priority free agent.

PK-P ANTHONY FERA, #4

TEXAS ▶ GRADE: 4.95

Ht: 6-1 | Wt: 211 | Sp: 5.10e | Arm: 31 | Hand: 9 1/8

History: The Texas prep was an Under Armor All-American before redshirting at Penn State in 2009. Punted 46 times for a 41.4-yard average with a long of 74 (career high) and 13 dropped inside the 20-yard line and partially handled kickoff duty with 34 kicks for a 68.2-yard average and 15 touchbacks in '10. Was arrested in June '11 and pleaded guilty to charges of purchasing alcohol for a minor and disorderly conduct. Led the Nittany Lions with 82 points in the fall after connecting on 14-of-17 field goals with a long of 46 and all 20 PATs, while handling kickoffs (45-65.2-10) and punts 64-42.0-L69-18. Following the Jerry Sandusky scandal, he was granted immediate eligibility for '12 by the NCAA to transfer to Texas without being forced to sit out a season and wanted to be closer to his mother who has MS. Had a very difficult first season at Texas, connecting on 2-of-4 FGs with a long of 42 and 23-of-25 PATs in only six contest. Missed the first four games after suffering a groin injury during fall camp, the Kansas State game with a hip injury and didn't play against TCU and Oregon State. Had a great bounce back campaign in '13 as he was a consensus All-America selection and a finalist for the Lou Groza Award after booming punts 75-40.7-32 and connecting on 20-of-22 FGs with a long of 50 and 45-of-46 PATs.

Strengths: Fine accuracy, placement and hang-time as a punter. Consistently accurate field-goal range inside 40 (did not miss as a senior) and shows range beyond 50. Has experience on big stages. Versatile.

Weaknesses: Average lift and rise as a kicker. Lacks ideal leg strength as a kickoff specialist.

Summary: Jack-of-all-trades, master of none. Showed significantly improved accuracy as a senior and can compete for a job in a camp.

Draft projection: Free agent.

PK ZACH HOCKER, #18

ARKANSAS   ▶ GRADE: 4.60

Ht: 6-0 | Wt: 189 | Sp: 5.00e | Arm: 30 1/8 | Hand: 8 5/8

History: Also punted as an Arkansas prep. Connected on 16-of-19 field-goal attempts with a long of 51 and all 56 extra point tries for a team-leading 104 points in 2010. Broke the school record for points by a kicker in '11 with 118 after making 21-of-27 FGs with a long of 50 and 55-of-57 PATs. Also kicked off 93 times for a 67.8-yard average with 40 touchdowns. Made 11-of-18 FGs with a long of 46 and all 32 PATs while also kicking off (58-64.7-39) in '12. Hit on 13-of-15 FGs with a career long of 54 and all 28 PATs in addition to kicking off (50-63.2-34) in '13. Also punted seven times for a 45.7-yard average with a long of 77 and one inside the 20-yard line. Led the Razorbacks in scoring each season and holds school records for points by a kicker (354), FG percentage (77.2), PATs made (171), PAT attempted (173) and field goals (61).

Strengths: Good leg speed. Consistently converted beyond 50 (3-4 as a senior) and has enough velocity to hang the ball on kickoffs. Well-grounded and humble.

Weaknesses: Thinly built and undersized. Does not possess a powerful leg. The ball does not explode off his foot (rise). Struggled to handle pressure early in his career.

Summary: Soccer-style kicker whose leg strength and accuracy seemed to be weakening heading into his senior season, with diminished accuracy and range. Rebounded to make his senior season his best. Could warrant consideration in a camp.

Draft projection: Free agent.

LS MARCUS HEIT, #63

KANSAS   ▶ GRADE: 5.10

Ht: 6-3 | Wt: 258 | Sp: 4.91 | Arm: 31 3/8 | Hand: 9 7/8

History: Redshirted in 2009. Played in 12-of-13 games in 2011; and all 12 in each of '12 and '13. Was perfect on all 363 snaps during his college career.

Strengths: Good size. Functional ball velocity. Very good accuracy and ball placement. Is tough and will play through pain. Works at his craft.

Weaknesses: Has very short arms. Marginal weight-room strength. Average athlete. Limited coverage speed and body control to break down in the open field and secure tackles. Marginal tackle production. No position versatility.

Summary: Functional college long-snapper capable of competing for a job. Lacks any standout traits and limited coverage skill and overall athletic ability could reduce his chances.

Draft projection: Priority free agent.

P TOM HORNSEY, #43

MEMPHIS   ▶ GRADE: 5.00

Ht: 6-3 | Wt: 221 | Sp: 5.05e | Arm: 31 | Hand: 9 1/8

History: The native of Australia played tennis and Australian Rules Football as a prep. Spent the 2009-2010 year attending ProKick Australia learning the fundamentals of punting before coming to the States. Booted 80 punts for a 42.7-yard average with a long of 63 and 24 inside the 20-yard line during his first taste of American football in '10. Led the nation and set the school record for number of punts in '11 after booming 95-42-L66-23. In '12, produced 60-43.4-L63-25 and had right knee surgery (torn meniscus) in May. Won the Ray Guy Award in '13 after recording 62-45.2-L79-29 and was the American Athletic Conference's Co-Special Teams Player of the Year. Was a threat during his career on fake punts, converting all four of his attempts with three rushes for 62 yards and completed a 61-yard pass. Is 25-years-old.

Strengths: Very good leg strength. Catches cleanly and approach is very consistent. Drives the ball for distance and is capable of flipping the field. Very good hang time. Handles pressure and the elements well. Works at his craft. Experienced, four-year starter. Serves as the holder on FGs and PATs.

Weaknesses: Very short arms and small hands. Could stand to hasten his delivery and generate better rise — the ball does not explode off his foot. Accuracy and placement leave room for improvement. Overaged and will be a 25-year-old rookie. Very limited tackler.

Summary: A right-footed, two-step, strong-legged Aussie punter who is still learning how to apply his craft, Hornsey showed consistent improvement throughout his career and made his senior season his best. Has upside to earn a job.

Draft projection: Priority free agent.

P RICHIE LEONE, #15

HOUSTON   ▶ GRADE: 4.95

Ht: 6-3 | Wt: 211 | Sp: 5.05e | Arm: 31 3/4 | Hand: 8 7/8

History: The Georgia prep was an all-state selection. As a true freshman in 2010, punted 35 times for a 41.4-yard average with a long of 63 and 12 inside the 20-yard line while also kicking off 59 times for 64.5-yard average and seven touchbacks. Booted 51-41.1-L63-15 and kicked off 35-63.5-5 in '11. Led Conference USA in punting average in '12 after booming 60-45.5-L77-18 and kicking off (71-62.7-25). In '13, recorded 73-43.2-L65-34 punting and 78-63.5-37 on kickoffs. Was the place kicker for the first seven games, connecting on 11-of-17 field-goal attempts with a long of 40 and all 32 extra point attempts.

Strengths: Outstanding leg strength — drives the ball. Works at his craft. Experienced, four-year starter. Outstanding production. Can handle kickoffs.

Weaknesses: Small hands and short arms.

Tightly wound, limited athlete. Could speed up delivery and get-off times — too methodical and long in his approach. Nonfactor in coverage.

Summary: Big, strong-legged, powerful punter capable of booming the ball with good hang, distance and accuracy. Has the tools to earn a starting job and serve as an emergency kickoff specialist.

Draft projection: Free agent.

P CODY MANDELL, #29

ALABAMA   ▶ GRADE: 5.09

Ht: 6-2 | Wt: 216 | Sp: 4.84 | Arm: 31 1/8 | Hand: 9 3/4

History: The Louisiana prep originally accepted an offer from Tulane but was not academically eligible and the scholarship was pulled. Enrolled at Alabama as a preferred walk-on in 2010 and became the starter, booting 41 punts for a 39.2-yard average with 13 inside the 20-yard line to earn Freshman All-SEC honors. Totaled 39-39.3-L52-11 in '11. Boomed 50-44.3-L61-19 as a junior in '12 and 39-47.1-L63-15 in '13. Graduated.

Strengths: Very good size. Good hands — adjusts well to the ball. Efficient touch-to-toe times. Works at his craft. Demonstrated ability to handle the elements. Solid coverage safety outlet — has enough athletic ability to tackle. Experienced, four-year starter in the SEC — has played on the biggest of stages and shown he can handle pressure.

Weaknesses: Inconsistent follow-through and drive. Ball does not explode off his foot. Does not consistently drive the ball.

Summary: Hardworking former walk-on has shown improvement every season and has the leg strength, focus and precision to become a field-flipping weapon in the pros.

Draft projection: Late draftable pick.

P PAT O'DONNELL, #16

MIAMI (FLA.)   ▶ GRADE: 4.95

Ht: 6-4 | Wt: 220 | Sp: 4.90e | Arm: 32 1/2 | Hand: 9 3/4

History: Was a three-year letterwinner in track and football as a Florida prep. Began his collegiate career at Cincinnati and punted in three games in 2009, recording seven punts for a 37.9-yard average with a long of 50 and two punts inside the 20-yard line, before redshirting with an undisclosed injury. Booted 52.41.9-L61-16 in '10. Was a first-team All-Big East selection in '11 after logging 63-43.8-L76-26 punting and 61 kickoffs for a 64.2-yard average and seven touchbacks. In '12, booted 59-41.8-L65-23 and 75-63.4-36 on kickoffs. Graduated from Cincinnati and transferred to Miami (Fla.) for his final season in '13. Set the Canes single-season record with a 47.1 yard per punt average after recording 53-47.1-71-19 and 79-63.1-37 on kickoffs. Was also the holder on field goals and extra point attempts. Did 23 repetitions of 225 pounds on the bench press at the Combine — more than six tight ends, 19 running backs, 21 defensive linemen and all 37 wide receivers.

Strengths: Very good leg strength to drive the ball. Experienced four-year starter. Handles kickoffs and served as the holder on PATs. Dedicated to his craft and the game is important to him.

Weaknesses: Inconsistent hang time. Can improve placement and accuracy. Average athlete. Overly analytical and outthinks the game. Could stand to hone his mental toughness and learn to handle pressure.

Summary: Outstanding-sized, right-footed, two-step punter transferred from Cincinnati upon graduation to be closer to home and hone his own technique. Has the leg strength to compete for a job, but must continue to hone his control and improve his directional punting.

Draft projection: Priority free agent.

PK CAIRO SANTOS, #19

TULANE   ▶ GRADE: 5.10

Ht: 5-8 | Wt: 164 | Sp: 5.25e | Arm: 28 1/2 | Hand: 8 7/8

History: Name is pronounced "KY-ro." Born in Brazil. Came to the United States as a foreign exchange student in Florida. Was a three-year letterman who played wide receiver in addition to kicking. Led the team in scoring as a true freshman in 2010 after connecting on 13-of-16 field goals with a long of 39 and 32-of-33 extra point attempts. Also had 57 kickoffs for a 59.1-yard average and one touchback. In '11, logged 11-of-18 FGs for a career 59 yards and 33-of-34 PATs while also kicking off 16-62.6-0. Punted 15 times for a 41.0-yard average with a long of 54 and eight kicks inside the 20-yard line. Won the Lou Groza Award as the nation's best kicker in '12 after a near-perfect 21-of-21 on FG attempts and 26-of-27 PATs. Handled kickoffs 55-64.1-31. Was a first-team All-Conference USA selection in '13 after making 16-of-23 FGs with a long of 56 and all 38 PATs while kicking off (62-64.4-47). Tragedy struck in September as his father was killed while performing an airplane stunt in Brazil.

Strengths: Takes a consistent approach and is consistently accurate from inside 50 with range to 60 yards. Good leg speed. Has shown he can handle pressure and come through in the clutch — converted game-winning kicks vs. North Texas and East Carolina in back-to-back weeks. Good work ethic. Four-year starter. Can serve as an emergency punter.

Weaknesses: Tiny-framed. Average rise and lift. Marginal follow-through. Lacks power to drive the ball on kickoffs. Could stand to speed up his approach. Placement and hang-time on kickoffs has room for improvement. Benefited from kicking indoors.

Summary: Brazilian-born, right-footed, 3-by-2, soccer-style kicker captured the Lou Groza award after converting all 21 field goals as a junior and has gradually improved his leg strength.

Draft projection: Late draftable pick.

PLAYER RANKINGS

QUARTERBACKS

RK. NAME	SCHOOL	GRADE	ALERTS
1. Blake Bortles	Central Florida	6.32	Jr.
2. Teddy Bridgewater	Louisville	6.24	Jr.
3. Derek Carr	Fresno State	6.10	
4. Johnny Manziel	Texas A&M	5.90	Soph.-3
5. Jimmy Garoppolo	Eastern Illinois	5.75	
6. A.J. McCarron	Alabama	5.65	
7. Logan Thomas	Virginia Tech	5.42	
8. Zach Mettenberger	LSU	5.27	X
9. Tajh Boyd	Clemson	5.22	
10. Tom Savage	Pittsburgh	5.21	
11. Stephen Morris	Miami (Fla.)	5.20	
12. Jeff Matthews	Cornell	5.20	
13. David Fales	San Jose State	5.18	
14. Aaron Murray	Georgia	5.17	X
15. Bryn Renner	North Carolina	5.10	
16. Connor Shaw	South Carolina	5.10	
17. Jordan Lynch	Northern Illinois	5.05	RB, SS
18. Keith Wenning	Ball State	5.00	
19. Dustin Vaughan	West Texas A&M	4.85	
20. Smith Brett	Wyoming	4.80	Jr.
21. Casey Pachall	TCU	4.50	X, Ch.
22. Joe Clancy	Merrimack	4.50	
23. Keith Price	Washington	4.50	
24. Tommy Rees	Notre Dame	4.50	
25. Chase Rettig	Boston College	4.50	
26. Garrett Gilbert	SMU	4.50	
27. Brendon Kay	Cincinnati	4.50	
28. Brock Jensen	North Dakota State	4.50	
29. Denarius McGhee	Montana State	4.50	
30. Adam Kennedy	Arkansas State	4.50	
31. Kenneth Guiton	Ohio State	4.50	
32. Corey Robinson	Troy	4.50	
33. Kory Faulkner	Southern Illinois	4.50	
34. James Franklin	Missouri	4.50	
35. Kolton Browning	Louisiana-Monroe	4.50	X
36. Sean Schroeder	Hawaii	4.50	
37. Nathan Scheelhase	Illinois	4.50	
38. Jamal Londry-Jackson	Appalachian State	4.50	

FULLBACKS

RK. NAME	SCHOOL	GRADE	ALERTS
1. Trey Millard	Oklahoma	5.12	RB
2. Jay Prosch	Auburn	5.10	
3. JC Copeland	LSU	5.09	
4. Ryan Hewitt	Stanford	5.05	
5. Ray Agnew	Southern Illinois	5.00	
6. Kiero Small	Arkansas	4.90	
7. Chad Young	San Diego State	4.80	
8. Maurice Hagens	Miami (Fla.)	4.70	
9. Chad Abram	Florida State	4.50	
10. Nikita Whitlock	Wake Forest	4.50	

RUNNING BACKS

RK. NAME	SCHOOL	GRADE	ALERTS
1. Carlos Hyde	Ohio State	6.25	
2. Tre Mason	Auburn	5.80	Jr.
3. Jeremy Hill	LSU	5.65	Jr.
4. Andre Williams	Boston College	5.62	
5. Devonta Freeman	Florida State	5.57	Jr.
6. Bishop Sankey	Washington	5.55	Jr.
7. Ka'Deem Carey	Arizona	5.42	Jr.
8. Terrrance West	Towson	5.37	Jr.

GRADE SCALE FOR NFL PROSPECTS

9.0 — A once-in-a-generation player (e.g. Bo Jackson, Deion Sanders).

8.00-8.99 — Perennial All-Pro (e.g. Anthony Munoz).

7.00-7.99 — Eventual All-Pro.

6.50-6.99 — Sure-fire first-rounder should make immediate impact.

6.00-6.49 — Likely first-rounder capable of starting readily.

5.60-5.99 — Likely second-rounder with immediate starter potential.

5.40-5.59 — Likely third-rounder minimally with sub-starter potential.

5.21-5.39 — Should make a roster and contribute on special teams.

5.11-5.20 — Potential late-rounder with fair chance to earn a roster spot.

4.75-5.10 — Late draftable or priority free agent capable of battling for a roster spot.

4.00-4.75 — Solid free agent capable of being invited to an NFL training camp.

KEY TO SYMBOLS IN PLAYER RANKINGS

Jr. — Player is a junior.

Soph-3 — Player is a third-year sophomore.

QB — Can also play quarterback or the position that is listed, such as RS for return specialist.

Ch. — Character (i.e. history of arrests, team suspensions or off-field problems) can affect draft status.

X — Has a current injury situation that could affect camp status.

XX — Past or present durability concerns could affect draft status.

XXX — Serious injury concern.

Players are ranked according to their grades, not necessarily in the order they will be drafted. Factors such as a drafting team's needs and the abundance or scarcity of available talent at a given position can cause a player to be drafted higher or lower than his grade would indicate. All grades take into account workouts up to and including the Indianapolis Scouting Combine. Post-Combine workouts were not factored.

RK. NAME	SCHOOL	GRADE	ALERTS
9. Jerick McKinnon	Georgia Southern	5.37	CB, RS
10. De'Anthony Thomas	Oregon	5.36	Jr., RS
11. Charles Sims	West Virginia	5.35	
12. Storm Johnson	Central Florida	5.34	Jr.
13. Lache Seastrunk	Baylor	5.28	Jr.
14. Alfred Blue	LSU	5.25	Jr.
15. LaDarius Perkins	Mississippi State	5.23	
16. Tyler Gaffney	Stanford	5.23	Jr., BB
17. David Fluellen	Toledo	5.22	
18. Antonio Andrews	Western Kentucky	5.20	
19. Lorenzo Taliaferro	Coastal Carolina	5.18	
20. Marion Grice	Arizona State	5.14	
21. James Wilder	Florida State	5.12	Jr., FB
22. George Atkinson	Notre Dame	5.11	Jr.
23. Isaiah Crowell	Alabama State	5.10	
24. Adam Muema	San Diego State	5.09	Jr.
25. Henry Josey	Missouri	5.08	Jr.
26. Jerome Smith	Syracuse	5.05	FB
27. Silas Redd	USC	5.05	
28. Kapri Bibbs	Colorado State	5.05	
29. Damien Williams	Oklahoma	5.05	
30. Tim Cornett	UNLV	5.02	
31. James White	Wisconsin	5.01	
32. Rajion Neal	Tennessee	5.00	Jr.
33. Zach Bauman	Northern Arizona	5.00	
34. Timothy Flanders	Sam Houston State	4.85	
35. Ben Malena	Texas A&M	4.50	
36. Brennan Clay	Oklahoma	4.50	
37. Anthony LaCoste	Air Force	4.50	
38. Brendan Bigelow	California	4.50	
39. Jason Simpson	San Jose State	4.50	
40. Waymon James	TCU	4.50	
41. David Sims	Georgia Tech	4.50	
42. Zurlon Tipton	Central Michigan	4.50	
43. D'Wayne Adams	Portland State	4.50	
44. David Oku	Arkansas State	4.50	
45. Roderick McDowell	Clemson	4.50	
46. Marcus Shaw	South Florida	4.50	
47. Darrin Reaves	UAB	4.50	Jr.
48. Roy Finch	Oklahoma	4.50	
49. Raymond Sanders	Kentucky	4.50	
50. Jeff Scott	Mississippi	4.50	
51. Jordan Hall	Ohio State	4.50	
52. John Spooney	Brown	4.50	
53. Trey Watts	Tulsa	4.50	

WIDE RECEIVERS

RK. NAME	SCHOOL	GRADE	ALERTS
1. Sammy Watkins	Clemson	7.25	Jr., RS
2. Mike Evans	Texas A&M	6.35	Jr.
3. Kelvin Benjamin	Florida State	6.30	Jr.
4. Marqise Lee	USC	6.23	Jr.
5. Odell Beckham	LSU	6.00	Jr.
6. Davante Adams	Fresno State	5.96	Jr.
7. Donte Moncrief	Mississippi	5.85	Jr.
8. Brandin Cooks	Oregon State	5.85	Jr.
9. Jordan Matthews	Vanderbilt	5.80	
10. Allen Robinson	Penn State	5.70	Jr.
11. Jarvis Landry	LSU	5.60	Jr.
12. Dri Archer	Kent State	5.45	RB, RS
13. Brandon Coleman	Rutgers	5.42	Jr.
14. Shaq Evans	UCLA	5.42	
15. Bruce Ellington	South Carolina	5.39	Jr., RS
16. T.J. Jones	Notre Dame	5.35	
17. Martavis Bryant	Clemson	5.34	Jr.
18. Jeff Janis	Saginaw Valley State	5.34	
19. Kevin Norwood	Alabama	5.34	
20. Kain Colter	Northwestern	5.28	X
21. Josh Huff	Oregon	5.28	
22. Paul Richardson	Colorado	5.27	Jr.
23. Jared Abbrederis	Wisconsin	5.27	
24. Cody Latimer	Indiana	5.24	Jr.
25. Mike Davis	Texas	5.24	
26. Jeremy Gallon	Michigan	5.24	
27. John Brown	Pittsburgh State	5.24	
28. Devin Street	Pittsburgh	5.23	
29. Jalen Saunders	Oklahoma	5.22	PR
30. L'Damian Washington	Missouri	5.20	
31. Robert Herron	Wyoming	5.20	
32. Isaiah Burse	Fresno State	5.20	RS
33. Tevin Reese	Baylor	5.17	RS
34. Mike Hazel	Coastal Carolina	5.17	
35. Willie Snead	Ball State	5.16	
36. Chris Boyd	Vanderbilt	5.15	
37. Josh Stewart	Oklahoma State	5.14	
38. Ryan Grant	Tulane	5.12	
39. Solomon Patton	Florida	5.10	KR
40. Allen Hurns	Miami (Fla.)	5.10	
41. Erik Lora	Eastern Illinois	5.10	
42. Marcus Lucas	Missouri	5.10	
43. Austin Franklin	New Mexico State	5.10	
44. Damian Copleand	Louisville	5.10	
45. Mike Campanaro	Wake Forest	5.09	
46. Chandler Jones	San Jose State	5.09	
47. Cody Hoffman	BYU	5.07	KR
48. Bennie Fowler	Michigan State	5.03	
49. Philly Brown	Ohio State	5.00	
50. Walter Powell	Murray State	4.90	
51. Tracy Moore	Oklahoma State	4.85	
52. Quincy Enunwa	Nebraska	4.80	
53. Anthony Denham	Utah	4.80	
54. Albert Wilson	Georgia State	4.75	
55. Bernard Reedy	Toledo	4.50	RS
56. Ja'Mes Logan	Mississippi State	4.50	
57. Seantavius Jones	Valdosta State	4.50	

58. A.J. Marshall	Wake Forest	4.50
59. Patrick Laird	Army	4.50
60. Albert Huntley	Cumberland (Ky.)	4.50
61. Jarrod West	Syracuse	4.50
62. Alex Amidon	Boston College	4.50
63. Eric Ward	Texas Tech	4.50
64. Eric Thomas	Troy	4.50
65. D.J. Coles	Virginia Tech	4.50
66. Julian Horton	Arkansas	4.50
67. Lacoltan Bester	Oklahoma	4.50
68. Kevin Smith	Washington	4.50
69. Kenny Shaw	Florida State	4.50
70. Jaz Reynolds	Oklahoma	4.50
71. Vince Mayle	Washington State	4.50
72. Mike Williams	California (Pa.)	4.50
73. Alex Neutz	Buffalo	4.50
74. Sentavious Jones	Valdosta State	4.50
75. Tyshon Goode	Kent State	4.50
76. Noel Grigsby	San Jose State	4.50
77. Derel Walker	Texas A&M	4.50
78. Mike Milburn	Delaware	4.50
79. Darryl Surgent	Louisiana-Lafayette	4.50
80. Eric Ward	Texas Tech	4.50
81. Eric Thomas	Troy	4.50
82. Gerald Ford	Valdosta State	4.50
83. Chris Gant	Hawaii	4.50
84. Greg Hardin	North Dakota	4.50
85. Caleb Herring	UNLV	4.50
86. Terrence Miller	Arizona	4.50
87. Diontae Spencer	McNeese State	4.50
88. Corey Washington	Newberry	4.50
89. Michael Washington	Appalachian State	4.50
90. Geraldo Boldewijn	Boise State	4.50
91. Alex Amidon	Boston College	4.50
92. Taylor Gabriel	Abilene Christian	4.50
93. Keenan Holman	SMU	4.50
94. Jonathan Krause	Vanderbilt	4.50
95. Zachary Pendleton	Jackson State	4.50
96. Nathan Slaughter	West Texas A&M	4.50
97. Jeremy Butler	Tennessee-Martin	4.50
98. Javonte Herndon	Arkansas	4.50
99. Ronrei Lloyd	Central Missouri State	4.50
100. Colin Lockett	San Diego State	4.50
101. Quintin Payton	North Carolina State	4.50
102. Ryan Culbreath	Furman	4.50
103. Devon Smith	Marshall	4.50
104. Brandon Wimberly	Nevada	4.50
105. Tony Washington	Appalachian State	4.50

TIGHT ENDS

RK. NAME	SCHOOL	GRADE	ALERTS
1. Eric Ebron	North Carolina	6.40	Jr.
2. Troy Niklas	Notre Dame	5.65	Jr.

3. Jace Amaro	Texas Tech	5.55	Jr.
4. Austin Seferian-Jenkins	Washington	5.50	Jr., Ch.
5. CJ Fiedorowicz	Iowa	5.48	
6. Colt Lyerla	Oregon	5.33	Jr., H-B, Ch.
7. Marcel Jensen	Frenso State	5.26	
8. AC Leonard	Tennessee State	5.22	
9. Richard Rodgers	California	5.20	Jr.
10. Trey Burton	Florida	5.20	H-B, WR
11. Reggie Jordan	Missouri Western State	5.18	
12. Crockett Gillmore	Colorado State	5.12	
13. Rob Blanchflower	Massachusetts	5.11	
14. Jacob Pedersen	Wisconsin	5.10	
15. Xavier Grimble	USC	5.10	Jr.
16. Arthur Lynch	Georgia	5.10	
17. Jake Murphy	Utah	5.10	Jr.
18. Joe Dun Duncan	Dixie State	5.05	X
19. Alex Bayer	Bowling Green	5.00	
20. Nic Jacobs	McNeese State	5.00	Jr.
21. Jordan Najvar	Baylor	4.85	
22. Donald Tialavea	Utah State	4.80	
23. Ted Bolser	Indiana	4.60	
24. Brian Wozniak	Wisconsin	4.50	
25. Kaneakua Friel	Brigham Young	4.60	
26. Blake Jackson	Oklahoma State	4.50	
27. Ryan Hubbell	Louisville	4.50	
28. Craig Wenrick	UTEP	4.50	
29. Asante-Jabari Cleveland	Miami (Fla.)	4.50	
30. Asa Watson	North Carolina State	4.50	
31. Gabe Holmes	Purdue	4.50	
32. Cody Booth	Temple	4.50	
33. Jake Long	Nebraska	4.50	
34. Jacob Maxwell	Louisiana-Lafayette	4.50	
35. Scott Simonson	Assumption	4.50	
36. Jonathan Thompson	Louisiana-Lafayette	4.50	
37. Nehemiah Hicks	Texas A&M	4.50	
38. Blake Annen	Cincinnati	4.50	
39. Michael Flacco	New Haven	4.50	
40. Justin Jones	East Carolina	4.50	
41. Justin Perillo	Maine	4.50	
42. Gabe Linehan	Boise State	4.50	
43. Eric Waters	Missouri	4.50	
44. Jerod Monk	Baylor	4.50	
45. Evan Wilson	Illinois	4.50	

CENTERS

RK. NAME	SCHOOL	GRADE	ALERTS
1. Marcus Martin	USC	5.60	Jr., OG
2. Travis Swanson	Arkansas	5.50	
3. Weston Richburg	Colorado State	5.32	
4. Russell Bodine	North Carolina	5.32	OG
5. Jonotthan Harrison-Nelson	Florida	5.24	
6. Gabe Ikard	Oklahoma	5.23	
7. Tyler Larsen	Utah State	5.20	

RK. NAME	SCHOOL	GRADE	ALERTS
8. Corey Linsley	Ohio State	5.18	
9. Bryan Stork	Florida State	5.15	OG
10. Matt Armstrong	Grand Valley State	5.14	
11. James Stone	Tennessee	5.10	
12. Matthew Paradis	Boise State	5.02	
13. Zac Kerin	Toledo	5.00	
14. Dillon Farrell	New Mexico	5.01	
15. Josh Allen	Louisiana-Monroe	4.75	
16. Khalil Wilkes	Stanford	4.50	
17. Luke Bowanko	Virginia	4.50	
18. Sean Conway	Western Kentucky	4.50	
19. Vyncent Jones	Utah	4.50	
20. Jared Wheeler	Miami (Fla.)	4.50	
21. Cole Pensick	Nebraska	4.50	
22. Pat Eger	West Virginia	4.50	
23. Gus Handler	Colorado	4.50	
24. Macky MacPherson	Syracuse	4.50	
25. Ashton Miller	Eastern Washington	4.50	
26. Jay Finch	Georgia Tech	4.50	
27. Kamran Joyer	Louisville	4.50	
28. Dan Sprague	Cincinnati	4.50	
29. Nate Richards	Rice	4.50	
30. Koby Koebensky	Arizona State	4.50	

OFFENSIVE GUARDS

RK. NAME	SCHOOL	GRADE	ALERTS
1. Zack Martin	Notre Dame	6.18	OT, C
2. Gabe Jackson	Mississippi	5.85	
3. Joel Bitonio	Nevada	5.75	OT, C
4. Xavier Su'a-Filo	UCLA	5.70	Jr.
5. Trai Turner	LSU	5.52	
6. David Yankey	Stanford	5.50	Jr., OT
7. Cyril Richardson	Baylor	5.40	
8. Chris Watt	Notre Dame	5.40	X
9. Dakota Dozier	Furman	5.36	
10. John Urschel	Penn State	5.27	C
11. Zach Fulton	Tennessee	5.27	
12. Brandon Linder	Miami (Fla.)	5.26	
13. Spencer Long	Nebraska	5.26	X
14. Ryan Groy	Wisconsin	5.25	
15. Anthony Steen	Alabama	5.24	
16. Kadeem Edwards	Tennessee State	5.24	
17. Jon Halapio	Florida	4.95	
18. Matt Feiler	Bloomsburg	4.90	
19. Conor Boffeli	Iowa	4.80	
20. Garrett Scott	Marshall	4.85	
21. Austin Wentworth	Fresno State	4.80	
22. Chris Burnette	Georgia	4.80	
23. Antwan Lowery	Rutgers	4.75	
24. Chris Elkins	Youngstown State	4.50	
25. Parker Graham	Oklahoma State	4.50	
26. Jordan McGray	UCF	4.50	
27. Andrew Norwell	Ohio State	4.50	

RK. NAME	SCHOOL	GRADE
28. Dallas Lee	Georgia	4.50
29. D.J. Morrell	Old Dominion	4.50
30. Will Simmons	East Carolina	4.50
31. Karim Barton	Morgan State	4.50
32. Brian Clark	Bloomsburg	4.50
33. Kevin Danser	Stanford	4.50
34. Trey Hopkins	Texas	4.50
35. Ronald Patrick	South Carolina	4.50
36. Jasen Carlson	Buffalo	4.50
37. Kevin Friend	Connecticut	4.50
38. Grant Enger	Oregon State	4.50
39. Alex Bullard	Tennessee	4.50
40. Justin McCray	Central Florida	4.50
41. Keenan Taylor	Kansas State	4.50
42. Stefan Huber	Baylor	4.50
43. John Fullington	Washington State	4.50
44. Jacob Fahrenkrug	Florida State	4.50

OFFENSIVE TACKLES

RK. NAME	SCHOOL	GRADE	ALERTS
1. Greg Robinson	Auburn	7.60	Soph.-3
2. Jake Matthews	Texas A&M	7.20	
3. Taylor Lewan	Michigan	6.18	
4. Cyrus Kouandjio	Alabama	5.75	Jr.
5. Ja'Wuan James	Tennessee	5.70	
6. Seantrel Henderson	Miami (Fla.)	5.62	
7. Antonio Richardson	Tennessee	5.58	Jr.
8. Jack Mewhort	Ohio State	5.55	
9. Brandon Thomas	Clemson	5.45	OG
10. James Hurst	North Carolina	5.39	X
11. Michael Schofield	Michigan	5.37	
12. Laurent Duvernay-Tardif	McGill University (Can.)	5.33	
13. Morgan Moses	Virginia	5.30	
14. Wesley Johnson	Vanderbilt	5.28	
15. Charles Leno	Boise State	5.25	
16. Billy Turner	North Dakota State	5.24	
17. Cameron Fleming	Stanford	5.22	Jr.
18. Justin Britt	Missouri	5.18	
19. Matt Patchan	Boston College	5.18	
20. Luke Lucas	Kansas State	5.16	
21. Matt Hall	Bellhaven	4.50	
22. Kevin Graf	USC	4.50	
23. Jeremiah Sirles	Nebraska	4.50	
24. Danny Kistler	Montana	4.50	
25. Kyle Bryant	Youngstown State	4.50	
26. Evan Finkenberg	Arizona State	4.50	
27. Matt Feiler	Bloomsburg	4.50	
28. Donald Hawkins	Texas	4.50	
29. Bryce Quigley	San Diego State	4.50	
30. Austin Wentworth	Fresno State	4.50	
31. Hunter Steward	Liberty	4.50	
32. Charles Goodwin	North Carolina Central	4.50	
33. Michael Amdall	UTEP	4.50	

34. Robert Crisp	North Carolina State	4.50
35. Curtis Feigt	West Virginia	4.50
36. Marshall Biard	Colorado State	4.50
37. Kenarious Gates	Georgia	4.50
38. Josh Wells	James Madison	4.50
39. Jared Wheeler	Miami (Fla.)	4.50
40. Erle Ladson	Delaware	4.50
41. Ryan McGrath	Ohio	4.50
42. Brent Qvale	Nebraska	4.50
43. James Bennett	Connecticut	4.50
44. Trevor Foy	Purdue	4.50
45. Donald Hawkins	Texas	4.50
46. Kevin Pamphile	Purdue	4.50
47. Ryan Gradney-Riggins	Fort Valley State	4.50
48. David Hurd	Arkansas	4.50
49. Emmanuel McCray	Mississippi	4.50
50. Donald Hawkins	Texas	4.50
51. Kyle Koehne	Florida	4.50
52. Kevin Mitchell	Kentucky	4.50
53. William Simmons	East Carolina	4.50

DEFENSIVE ENDS

RK. NAME	SCHOOL	GRADE	ALERTS
1. Jadeveon Clowney	South Carolina	7.50	Jr., OLB
2. Stephon Tuitt	Notre Dame	6.35	Jr., DT
3. Kony Ealy	Missouri	5.75	Jr., DT
4. Ed Stinson	Alabama	5.65	
5. Kareem Martin	North Carolina	5.44	OLB
6. Scott Crichton	Oregon State	5.42	Jr.
7. Ronald Powell	Florida	5.35	Jr.
8. Larry Webster	Bloomsburg	5.35	OLB, TE
9. Chris Smith	Arkansas	5.31	OLB
10. Zach Moore	Concordia	5.24	DT
11. Ethan Westbrooks	West Texas A&M	5.23	OLB
12. Jeoffrey Pagan	Alabama	5.21	Jr., X
13. Will Clarke	West Virginia	5.20	
14. Aaron Lynch	South Florida	5.17	Jr., X
15. Jackson Jeffcoat	Texas	5.15	OLB
16. Eathyn Manumaleuna	Brigham Young	5.15	
17. Kasim Edebali	Boston College	5.10	DE
18. Devon Kennard	USC	5.10	
19. Josh Mauro	Stanford	5.09	
20. IK Enemkpali	Louisiana Tech	5.05	
21. George Uko	USC	5.05	
22. Tevin Mims	South Florida	4.90	
23. Garrison Smith	Georgia	4.85	
24. Chidera Uzo-Diribe	Colorado	4.50	
25. Denico Autry	Mississippi State	4.50	
26. Chaz Sutton	South Carolina	4.50	
27. Ben Gardner	Stanford	4.50	
28. Colton Underwood	Illinois State	4.50	
29. Rakim Cox	Wake Forest	4.50	
30. Bradley Daly	Montana State	4.50	

31. Jesse Joseph	Connecticut	4.50
32. Daniel Riley	Harding	4.50
33. Cody Bauer	Rice	4.50
34. Darryl Cato-Bishop	North Carolina State	4.50
35. Tim Jackson	North Carolina	4.50
36. Kris Redding	Wake Forest	4.50
37. Colby Way	Buffalo	4.50
38. Frances Mays	Florida A&M	4.50
39. Jacques Smith	Tennessee	4.50
40. Chris McAllister	Baylor	4.50

DEFENSIVE TACKLES

RK. NAME	SCHOOL	GRADE	ALERTS
1. Aaron Donald	Pittsburgh	6.32	DE
2. Ra'Shede Hageman	Minnesota	6.00	DE
3. Louis Nix	Notre Dame	5.90	Jr., NT
4. Timmy Jernigan	Florida State	5.70	Jr., NT
5. Daniel McCullers	Tennessee	5.65	NT
6. Anthony Johnson	LSU	5.55	Jr.
7. Ego Ferguson	LSU	5.44	Jr.
8. Shamar Stephen	Connecticut	5.42	NT
9. DaQuan Jones	Penn State	5.40	
10. Deandre Coleman	California	5.40	
11. Dominique Easley	Florida	5.40	XX
12. Caraun Reid	Princeton	5.35	X
13. Will Sutton	Arizona State	5.34	
14. Brent Urban	Virginia	5.32	X
15. Jason Bromley	Syracuse	5.32	
16. Tenny Palepoi	Utah	5.27	
17. Kelcy Quarles	South Carolina	5.22	Jr.
18. Taylor Hart	Oregon	5.22	
19. Chris Whaley	Texas	5.20	X
20. Ryan Carrethers	Arkansas State	5.15	NT
21. Khyri Thornton	Southern Mississippi	5.15	
22. Zachariah Kerr	Delaware	5.10	NT
23. Justin Ellis	Louisiana Tech	5.10	
24. Kaleb Ramsey	Boston College	5.00	DT, X
25. Mike Pennel	Colorado State-Pueblo	5.00	
26. Kerry Hyder	Texas Tech	4.90	
27. Kerry Wynn	Richmond	4.85	
28. Robert Thomas	Arkansas	4.75	X
29. Evan Gill	Manitoba (Can.)	4.75	
30. Bruce Gaston	Purdue	4.75	
31. Demonte McAllister	Florida State	4.50	
32. Beau Allen	Wisconsin	4.50	NT
33. Derrick Hopkins	Virginia Tech	4.50	
34. Mister Cobble	Kentucky	4.50	
35. Curtis Porter	Miami (Fla.)	4.50	
36. Justin Renfrow	Miami (Fla.)	4.50	
37. Isame Faciane	Florida International	4.50	
38. Chris Davenport	Tulane	4.50	
39. Johnnie Farms	Memphis	4.50	
40. Roosevelt Nix	Kent State	4.50	

41. Calvin Barnett	Oklahoma State	4.50	
42. Jamie Meder	Ashland	4.50	
43. Ken Bishop	Northern Illinois	4.50	
44. Lawrence Virgil	Valdosta State	4.50	
45. Ricky Tjong-A-Tjoe	Boise State	4.50	
46. Wade Keliikipi	Oregon	4.50	
47. Viliami Moala	California	4.50	Jr.

INSIDE LINEBACKERS

RK. NAME	SCHOOL	GRADE	ALERTS
1. C.J. Mosley	Alabama	6.40	OLB
2. Chris Borland	Wisconsin	5.55	
3. Preston Brown	Louisville	5.42	
4. Shayne Skov	Stanford	5.40	X
5. Max Bullough	Michigan State	5.25	
6. James Morris	Iowa	5.20	
7. Avery Williamson	Kentucky	5.20	
8. Jeremiah George	Iowa State	5.18	
9. Andrew Jackson	Western Kentucky	5.17	
10. Devin Unga	Brigham Young	5.10	
11. DeDe Lattimore	South Florida	5.00	
12. Glenn Carson	Penn State	5.00	
13. Caleb Lavey	Oklahoma State	4.75	
14. Chris Young	Arizona State	4.50	
15. Stephon Robertson	James Madison	4.50	
16. Greg Blair	Cincinnati	4.50	
17. Steele Vivitto	Boston College	4.50	
18. Keith Smith	San Jose State	4.50	
19. Justin Anderson	Louisiana-Lafayette	4.50	
20. Andrew Wilson	Missouri	4.50	
21. Nate Dreiling	Pittsburgh State	4.50	
22. Brock Coyle	Montana	4.50	

OUTSIDE LINEBACKERS

RK. NAME	SCHOOL	GRADE	ALERTS
1. Khalil Mack	Buffalo	7.20	DE, ILB
2. Anthony Barr	UCLA	6.60	DE
3. Ryan Shazier	Ohio State	6.27	Jr.
4. Demarcus Lawrence	Boise State	6.10	Jr., Ch.
5. Trent Murphy	Stanford	5.65	DE
6. Dee Ford	Auburn	5.57	DE, PRS
7. Jeremiah Attaochu	Georgia Tech	5.52	DE
8. Adrian Hubbard	Alabama	5.45	Jr.
9. Kyle Van Noy	Brigham Young	5.43	
10. Christian Jones	Florida State	5.40	DE
11. Marcus Smith	Louisville	5.39	PRS
12. Telvin Smith	Florida State	5.38	
13. Lamin Barrow	LSU	5.37	
14. Cassius Marsh	UCLA	5.37	DE
15. Trevor Reilly	Utah	5.35	DE
16. Prince Shembo	Notre Dame	5.32	
17. Carl Bradford	Arizona State	5.31	Jr., DE
18. James Gayle	Virginia Tech	5.31	
19. Howard Jones	Shepherd	5.25	DE

20. Khairi Fortt	California	5.25	Jr., X
21. Jordan Zumwalt	UCLA	5.23	
22. Yawin Smallwood	Connecticut	5.22	Jr.
23. Shaquil Barrett	Colorado State	5.20	
24. Christian Kirksey	Iowa	5.20	
25. Jonathan Brown	Illinois	5.20	
26. Newsome Jonathan	Ball State	5.17	DE
27. Jordan Tripp	Montana	5.10	
28. Boseko Lokombo	Oregon	5.10	
29. Kevin Pierre-Lewis	Boston College	5.10	
30. Michael Sam	Missouri	5.09	DE
31. Tyler Starr	South Dakota	5.00	
32. Anthony Hitchens	Iowa	4.95	
33. Derrell Johnson	East Carolina	4.75	
34. Xavius Boyd	Western Kentucky	4.75	ILB
35. Cody Peterson	Navy	4.50	
36. Nate Dreiling	Pittsburgh State	4.50	
37. Denicos Allen	Michigan State	4.50	
38. Eddie Lackey	Baylor	4.50	
39. Morgan Breslin	USC	4.50	
40. Jayrone Elliott	Toledo	4.50	
41. Spencer Hadley	BYU	4.50	
42. Deontae Skinner	Mississippi State	4.50	
43. Nate Askew	Texas A&M	4.50	
44. Marcus Whitfield	Maryland	4.50	
45. Corey Nelson	Oklahoma	4.50	
46. Will Smith	Texas Tech	4.50	
47. Marquis Flowers	Arizona	4.50	
48. Jamal Merrell	Rutgers	4.50	
49. Marquis Spruill	Syracuse	4.50	
50. Carlos Fields Jr.	Winston-Salem State	4.50	

CORNERBACKS

RK. NAME	SCHOOL	GRADE	ALERTS
1. Justin Gilbert	Oklahoma State	6.45	RS
2. Darqueze Dennard	Michigan State	6.10	
3. Bradley Roby	Ohio State	6.00	Jr., PR
4. Kyle Fuller	Virginia Tech	5.90	
5. Jason Verrett	TCU	5.75	
6. Marqueston Huff	Wyoming	5.57	FS
7. Rashaad Reynolds	Oregon State	5.45	
8. Antone Exum	Virginia Tech	5.45	
9. Keith McGill	Utah	5.42	FS
10. Pierre Desir	Lindenwood	5.42	
11. Bashaud Breeland	Clemson	5.41	Jr.
12. Marcus Roberson	Florida	5.40	Jr.
13. Terrance Mitchell	Oregon	5.37	Jr.
14. Travis Carrie	Ohio	5.36	RS
15. Ross Cockrell	Duke	5.34	
16. Phillip Gaines	Rice	5.33	
17. Dontae Johnson	North Carolina State	5.32	FS
18. Loucheiz Purifoy	Florida	5.31	Jr.
19. Stanley Jean-Baptiste	Nebraska	5.29	

RK. NAME	SCHOOL	GRADE	ALERTS
20. Jonathan Dowling	Western Kentucky	5.29	Jr., FS
21. Brandon Dixon	Northwest Missouri	5.29	
22. Aaron Colvin	Oklahoma	5.27	X
23. Lavelle Westbrooks	Georgia Southern	5.27	
24. E.J. Gaines	Missouri	5.27	
25. Kendall James	Maine	5.26	
26. Victor Hampton	South Carolina	5.24	Jr., PR, Ch.
27. Lamarcus Joyner	Florida State	5.24	
28. Andre Hal	Vanderbilt	5.23	
29. Bennett Jackson	Notre Dame	5.20	
30. Ben Benwikere	San Jose State	5.18	
31. Jabari Price	North Carolina	5.17	
32. Jaylen Watkins	Florida	5.15	
33. Todd Washington	Southeastern Louisiana	5.15	
34. Keith Reaser	Florida Atlantic	5.14	
35. Jemea Thomas	Georgia Tech	5.14	FS
36. Chris Davis	Auburn	5.12	RS
37. Dex McDougle	Maryland	5.12	
38. Deion Belue	Alabama	5.09	
39. Ricardo Allen	Purdue	5.05	
40. Demetri Goodson	Baylor	5.05	
41. Nevin Lawson	Utah State	4.80	
42. Walt Aikens	Libertty	4.80	
43. Marcus Williams	North Dakota State	4.80	
44. Carrington Byndom	Texas	4.80	
45. Shaquille Richardson	Arizona	4.80	
46. Mario Brown	Eastern Washington	4.50	
47. Najja Johnson	Buffalo	4.50	
48. Ciante Evans	Nebraska	4.50	
49. Osahon Irabor	Arizona State	4.50	
50. Zachary McMillen	Houston	4.50	
51. Anthony Goodwin	Montana	4.50	
52. Louis Young	Georgia Tech	4.50	
53. B.J. Lowery	Iowa	4.50	
54. Nick Addison	Bethune-Cookman	4.50	Jr.
55. Kenneth Acker	SMU	4.50	
56. Jordan Love	Towson	4.50	
57. Jimmy Legree	South Carolina	4.50	
58. Jeremy Brown	Florida	4.50	
59. Deron Wilson	Southern Mississippi	4.50	

STRONG SAFETIES

RK. NAME	SCHOOL	GRADE	ALERTS
1. Deone Bucannon	Washington State	5.42	
2. Jimmie Ward	Northern Illinois	5.36	
3. Maurice Alexander	Utah State	5.24	
4. Dion Bailey	USC	5.20	Jr.
5. Isaiah Lewis	Michigan State	5.18	
6. Nat Berhe	San Diego State	5.14	
7. Vinnie Sunseri	Alabama	5.14	
8. Tre Boston	North Carolina	5.10	
9. Sean Parker	Washington	5.05	
10. Stephen Obeng-Agyapong	Penn State	4.95	
11. Nickoe Whitley	Mississippi State	4.75	
12. Darwin Cook	West Virginia	4.50	
13. Brian Jackson	Oregon	4.50	

RK. NAME	SCHOOL	GRADE	ALERTS
14. Jerry Gates	Bowling Green State	4.50	
15. C.J. Barnett	Ohio State	4.50	
16. Deron Furr	Fort Valley State	4.50	

FREE SAFETIES

RK. NAME	SCHOOL	GRADE	ALERTS
1. Calvin Pryor	Louisville	6.15	Jr.
2. Ha Ha Clinton-Dix	Alabama	6.10	Jr.
3. Dez Southward	Wisconsin	5.39	
4. Brock Vereen	Minnesota	5.37	
5. Craig Loston	LSU	5.31	
6. Terrence Brooks	Florida State	5.27	
7. Ahmad Dixon	Baylor	5.22	
8. Alden Darby	Arizona State	5.20	
9. Ed Reynolds	Stanford	5.10	Jr.
10. Daniel Sorensen	Brigham Young	5.05	
11. Kenny Ladler	Vanderbilt	4.95	
12. Christian Bryant	Ohio State	4.95	
13. Daytawion Lowe	Oklahoma State	4.75	
14. Taylor Martinez	Nebraska	4.75	QB, WR
15. Hakeem Smith	Louisville	4.75	
16. Ty Zimmerman	Kansas State	4.50	
17. Ryan Bronson	McNeese State	4.50	
18. Pierre Warren	Jacksonville State	4.50	Jr.
19. Avery Patterson	Oregon	4.50	
20. Demetrius Wright	USC	4.50	
21. Damon Magazu	East Carolina	4.50	

PLACEKICKERS

RK. NAME	SCHOOL	GRADE	ALERTS
1. Cairo Santos	Tulane	5.10	
2. Chris Boswell	Rice	5.09	
3. Zach Hocker	Arkansas	4.60	
4. Anthony Fera	Texas	4.95	
5. Cody Parkey	Auburn	4.85	
6. Nate Freese	Boston College	4.50	
7. Jeff Budzien	Northwestern	4.50	
8. Cade Foster	Alabama	4.50	
9. Mike Meyer	Iowa	4.50	
10. Chandler Catanzaro	Clemson	4.50	

PUNTERS

RK. NAME	SCHOOL	GRADE	ALERTS
1. Cody Mandell	Alabama	5.09	
2. Tom Hornsey	Memphis	5.00	
3. Richie Leone	Houston	4.95	
4. Pat O'Donnell	Miami (Fla.)	4.95	
5. Steven Clark	Auburn	4.85	
6. Kirby Van Der Kamp	Iowa State	4.85	
7. Cody Webster	Purdue	4.50	
8. Tyler Campbell	Mississippi	4.50	
9. Matt Yoklic	Pittsburgh	4.50	
10. Baker Swederburg	Mississippi State	4.50	

LONG-SNAPPERS

RK. NAME	SCHOOL	GRADE	ALERTS
1. Marcus Heit	Kansas State	5.10	
2. Tyler Ott	Harvard	4.50	

BEST PLAYERS AVAILABLE BY GRADE

RK. POS, NAME, SCHOOL	GRADE	ALERTS
1. OT Greg Robinson, Auburn	7.60	Soph.-3
2. DE Jadeveon Clowney, South Carolina	7.50	Jr.
3. WR Sammy Watkins, Clemson	7.25	Jr.
4. OLB Khalil Mack, Buffalo	7.20	
5. OT Jake Matthews, Texas A&M	7.00	
6. OLB Anthony Barr, UCLA	6.60	
7. CB Justin Gilbert, Oklahoma State	6.45	RS
8. TE Eric Ebron, North Carolina	6.40	Jr.
9. ILB C.J. Mosley, Alabama	6.40	
10. DE Stephon Tuitt, Notre Dame	6.35	Jr.
11. WR Mike Evans, Texas A&M	6.35	Jr.
12. QB Blake Bortles, Central Florida	6.32	Jr.
13. DT Aaron Donald, Pittsburgh	6.32	
14. WR Kelvin Benjamin, Florida State	6.30	Jr.
15. OLB Ryan Shazier, Ohio State	6.27	Jr.
16. RB Carlos Hyde, Ohio State	6.25	
17. QB Teddy Bridgewater, Louisville	6.24	Jr.
18. WR Marqise Lee, USC	6.23	Jr.
19. OT Taylor Lewan, Michigan	6.18	
20. OG Zack Martin, Notre Dame	6.18	OT, C
21. FS Calvin Pryor, Louisville	6.15	Jr.
22. QB Derek Carr, Fresno State	6.10	
23. CB Darqueze Dennard, Michigan State	6.10	
24. OLB Demarcus Lawrence, Boise State	6.10	Jr., Ch.
25. FS Ha Ha Clinton-Dix, Alabama	6.10	Jr.
26. WR Odell Beckham, LSU	6.00	Jr., RS
27. CB Bradley Roby, Ohio State	6.00	PR
28. DT Ra'Shede Hageman, Minnesota	6.00	DE
29. WR Davante Adams, Fresno State	5.96	Jr.
30. DT Louis Nix, Notre Dame	5.90	Jr., NT
31. CB Kyle Fuller, Virginia Tech	5.90	
32. QB Johnny Manziel, Texas A&M	5.90	Soph.-3, Ch.
33. WR Donte Moncrief, Mississippi	5.85	Jr.
34. OG Gabe Jackson, Mississippi	5.85	
35. WR Brandin Cooks, Oregon State	5.85	Jr.
36. RB Tre Mason, Auburn	5.80	Jr.
37. WR Jordan Matthews, Vanderbilt	5.80	
38. OT Cyrus Kouandjio, Alabama	5.75	Jr.
39. QB Jimmy Garoppolo, Eastern Illinois	5.75	
40. DE Kony Ealy, Missouri	5.75	Jr.
41. OG Joel Bitonio, Nevada	5.75	OT, C
42. CB Jason Verrett, TCU	5.75	
43. DT Timmy Jernigan, Florida State	5.70	Jr.
44. WR Allen Robinson, Penn State	5.70	Jr.
45. OT Ja'Wuan James, Tennessee	5.70	
46. OG Xavier Su'a-Filo, UCLA	5.70	Jr.
47. QB AJ McCarron, Alabama	5.65	
48. TE Troy Niklas, Notre Dame	5.65	Jr.
49. RB Jeremy Hill, LSU	5.65	Jr.
50. DE Ed Stinson, Alabama	5.65	
51. OLB Trent Murphy, Stanford	5.65	DE
52. DT Daniel McCullers, Tennessee	5.65	NT
53. WR Andre Williams, Boston College	5.62	
54. OT Seantrel Henderson, Miami (Fla.)	5.62	Ch.
55. WR Jarvis Landry, LSU	5.60	Jr.
56. C Marcus Martin, USC	5.60	Jr., OG
57. OT Antonio Richardson, Tennessee	5.58	Jr.
58. OLB Dee Ford, Auburn	5.57	DE, PRS
59. RB Devonta Freeman, Florida State	5.57	Jr.
60. CB Marqueston Huff, Wyoming	5.57	FS
61. DT Anthony Johnson, LSU	5.55	Jr., NT
62. OT Jack Mewhort, Ohio State	5.55	
63. TE Jace Amaro, Texas Tech	5.55	Jr.
64. RB Bishop Sankey, Washington	5.55	Jr.
65. ILB Chris Borland, Wisconsin	5.55	
66. OLB Jeremiah Attaochu, Georgia Tech	5.52	DE
67. OG Trai Turner, LSU	5.52	Soph-3
68. C Travis Swanson, Arkansas	5.50	
69. OG David Yankey, Stanford	5.50	Jr., OT
70. TE Austin Seferian-Jenkins, Washington	5.50	Jr., Ch.
71. TE CJ Fiedorowicz, Iowa	5.48	
72. OLB Adrian Hubbard, Alabama	5.45	Jr.
73. OT Brandon Thomas, Clemson	5.45	OG
74. WR Dri Archer, Kent State	5.45	RB, RS
75. CB Rashaad Reynolds, Oregon State	5.45	
76. CB Antone Exum, Virginia Tech	5.45	
77. DT Ego Ferguson, LSU	5.44	
78. DE Kareem Martin, North Carolina	5.44	
79. OLB Kyle Van Noy, Brigham Young	5.43	Ch.
80. RB Ka'Deem Carey, Arizona	5.42	Jr., Ch.
81. NT Shamar Stephen, Connecticut	5.42	NT
82. CB Pierre Desir, Lindenwood	5.42	
83. ILB Preston Brown, Louisville	5.42	
84. DE Scott Crichton, Oregon State	5.42	
85. WR Brandon Coleman, Rutgers	5.42	Jr.
86. WR Shaq Evans, UCLA	5.42	
87. CB Keith McGill, Utah	5.42	FS
88. QB Logan Thomas, Virginia Tech	5.42	
89. SS Deone Bucannon, Washington State	5.42	
90. CB Bashaud Breeland, Clemson	5.41	
91. DT Deandre Coleman, California	5.40	
92. OG Chris Watt, Notre Dame	5.40	X
93. DT Dominique Easley, Florida	5.40	X
94. ILB Shayne Skov, Stanford	5.40	
95. CB Marcus Roberson, Florida	5.40	Jr.
96. OLB Christian Jones, Florida State	5.40	
97. OG Cyril Richardson, Baylor	5.40	
98. DT DaQuan Jones, Penn State	5.40	
99. OLB Marcus Smith, Louisville	5.39	DE
100. OT James Hurst, North Carolina	5.39	X
101. WR Bruce Ellington, South Carolina	5.39	Jr., RS
102. FS Dez Southward, Wisconsin	5.39	
103. OLB Telvin Smith, Florida State	5.38	
104. RB Jerick McKinnon, Georgia Southern	5.37	CB, RS
105. OLB Lamin Barrow, LSU	5.37	
106. OT Michael Schofield, Michigan	5.37	OG
107. FS Brock Vereen, Minnesota	5.37	
108. CB Terrance Mitchell, Oregon	5.37	
109. RB Terrrance West, Towson	5.37	Jr.
110. OLB Curtis Marsh, UCLA	5.37	DE
111. OG Dakota Dozier, Furman	5.36	
112. SS Jimmie Ward, Northern Illinois	5.36	
113. CB Travis Carrie, Ohio	5.36	RS
114. RB De'Anthony Thomas, Oregon	5.36	Jr., RS
115. DE Larry Webster, Bloomsburg	5.35	OLB, TE
116. DE Ronald Powell, Florida	5.35	
117. WR T.J. Jones, Notre Dame	5.35	
118. DT Caraun Reid, Princeton	5.35	
119. OLB Trevor Reilly, Utah	5.35	DE
120. RB Charles Sims, West Virginia	5.35	
121. WR Kevin Norwood, Alabama	5.34	
122. DT Will Sutton, Arizona State	5.34	
123. RB Storm Johnson, Central Florida	5.34	Jr.
124. WR Martavis Bryant, Clemson	5.34	Jr.
125. CB Ross Cockrell, Duke	5.34	
126. WR Jeff Janis, Saginaw Valley State	5.34	
127. OT Laurent Duvernay-Tardif, McGill (Can.)	5.33	
128. TE Colt Lyerla, Oregon	5.33	Jr., H-B, Ch.
129. DT Phillip Gaines, Rice	5.33	
130. C Weston Richburg, Colorado State	5.32	
131. C Russell Bodine, North Carolina	5.32	OG
132. CB Dontae Johnson, North Carolina State	5.32	FS
133. OLB Prince Shembo, Notre Dame	5.32	Ch.
134. DT Jason Bromley, Syracuse	5.32	"Jay"
135. DT Brent Urban, Virginia	5.32	X
136. OLB Carl Bradford, Arizona State	5.31	DE
137. DE Chris Smith, Arkansas	5.31	OLB
138. CB Loucheiz Purifoy, Florida	5.31	
139. FS Craig Loston, LSU	5.31	
140. OLB James Gayle, Virginia Tech	5.31	
141. OT Morgan Moses, Virginia	5.30	
142. CB Stanley Jean-Baptist, Nebraska	5.29	
143. CB Brandon Dixon, Northwest Missouri	5.29	
144. CB Jonathan Dowling, Western Kentucky	5.29	FS
145. WR Kain Colter, Northwestern	5.28	QB
146. RB Lache Seastrunk, Baylor	5.28	Jr.
147. WR Josh Huff, Oregon	5.28	
148. OT Wesley Johnson, Vanderbilt	5.28	C
149. WR Jared Abbrederis, Wisconsin	5.27	
150. QB Zach Mettenberger, LSU	5.27	X

PLAYER INDEX